God teaches through his Spirit
and through the letter that has been written
by the inspiration of his Spirit.

ULRICH ZWINGLI

Without the Scripture,
which has only Jesus Christ as its object,
we know nothing, and see only darkness
and confusion in the nature of God
and in nature herself.

BLAISE PASCAL

The gospel of God's historic act of grace
is the infallible power and authority
over both church and Bible.
It produced them both.

P. T. FORSYTH

When I am asked . . . which of these articles
of the Evangelical faith I am prepared to part with
at the instance of modern thought,
and in the interests of a re-constructed theology,
I answer, with fullest confidence:
None of them.

JAMES ORR

Orthodoxy is a knife-edge, a narrow path,
a *via media:* a position hard to maintain,
a path difficult to follow, a way easy to get wrong.

KENNETH LEECH

Christian Foundations

A THEOLOGY OF WORD & SPIRIT

HOLY SCRIPTURE

GOD THE ALMIGHTY

JESUS CHRIST

THE HOLY SPIRIT

THE CHURCH

THE LAST THINGS

CHRISTIAN
FOUNDATIONS

HOLY
SCRIPTURE

Revelation, Inspiration
& Interpretation

DONALD G. BLOESCH

IVP Academic

An imprint of InterVarsity Press
Downers Grove, Illinois

InterVarsity Press
P.O. Box 1400, Downers Grove, IL 60515-1426
World Wide Web: www.ivpress.com
E-mail: mail@ivpress.com

InterVarsity Press® *is the book-publishing division of InterVarsity Christian Fellowship/USA*®*, a student movement active on campus at hundreds of universities, colleges and schools of nursing in the United States of America, and a member movement of the International Fellowship of Evangelical Students. For information about local and regional activities, write Public Relations Dept., InterVarsity Christian Fellowship/USA, 6400 Schroeder Rd., P.O. Box 7895, Madison, WI 53707-7895, or visit the IVCF website at <www.intervarsity.org>.*

The Scripture quotations quoted herein are from the Revised Standard Version of the Bible, *copyright 1946, 1952, 1971 by the Division of Christian Education of the National Council of the Churches of Christ in the U.S.A. Used by permission. All rights reserved.*

Design: Cindy Kiple

Images: Guy Wolek

ISBN-10: 0-8308-2752-8
ISBN-13: 978-0-8308-2752-7

Printed in the United States of America ∞

Library of Congress Cataloging-in-Publication Data
Bloesch, Donald G., 1928-
  Holy Scripture: revelation, inspiration & interpretation / Donald G. Bloesch.
     p. cm.—(Christian foundations)
  Originally published: c1994.
  Includes bibliographical references and indexes.
  ISBN 0-8308-1412-4 (cloth: alk. paper)—ISBN 0-8308-2752-8 (pbk.: alk. paper)
     1. Bible—Hermeneutics. 2. Bible—Evidences, authority, etc. I. Title.
  BS476.B56 2006
  220.601—dc22

                                                                                    2005052140

P 20 19 18 17 16 15 14 13 12 11 10 9 8 7 6 5 4 3 2 1

Y 20 19 18 17 16 15 14 13 12 11 10 09 08 07 06 05

Dedicated to my mother,
Adele Bloesch,
and to the memory of my father,
Herbert Paul Bloesch

Acknowledgments

I am deeply grateful to the following persons without whose help this book could not have been completed: my wife, Brenda, for her painstaking work in checking references and editing; Debbie Lovett, for her expert typing of the final copy; Timothy Phillips of the Wheaton College Graduate School for the gift of his doctoral thesis on Francis Turretin, which helped me to see Protestant orthodoxy in a slightly different light; Joel Samuels, Mary Anne Knefel and Deb Pfab of the University of Dubuque Theological Seminary library, whose assistance and encouragement were greatly appreciated; Donald McKim and Jack Rogers, whose important book on biblical authority motivated me to articulate my own views; Ralph McInerny of the University of Notre Dame, who provided help with ecclesiastical Latin; and my grandfather, Ernst Bloesch, for his gift of the King James Version of the Bible on the day of my confirmation, through which I came to know the glorious mystery of Christ's work of redemption. Parts of these chapters were originally presented as lectures at a United Church of Canada renewal conference at the Old Dominion Church in Ottawa, Canada, on July 1–5, 1991.

Abbreviations for Biblical Translations

NRSV   New Revised Standard Version

NEB   New English Bible

REB   Revised English Bible

NASB   New American Standard Bible

KJV   King James Version

NKJ   New King James Version

NIV   New International Version

JB   Jerusalem Bible

NJB   New Jerusalem Bible

GNC   God's New Covenant

GNB   Good News Bible

(Note: Bible references not otherwise indicated are from the Revised Standard Version.)

Preface

One reason for writing this book is to give honor to Holy Scripture. I wish to defend the orthodox evangelical faith—from its friends as well as from its enemies. A biblicistic literalism that often borders on obscurantism can be as damaging as a biblical latitudinarianism that plays fast and loose with the biblical texts—accepting those texts, for example, that celebrate human dignity and freedom but dismissing those that are supposedly limited in scope and vision. I propose a third option—one that stands in continuity with the wisdom of the Christian past as well as remaining faithful to the deepest intentions of the biblical witness. I firmly believe that Scripture can be an authoritative and credible guide for faith and practice even in our day, when historical and literary criticism holds sway.

The Bible is not rightly understood when it is treated primarily as a collection of texts amenable to historical analysis and dissection. It is certainly a historical document, but it is much more than that. Its worthiness as a theological guide and norm does not become clear until it is acclaimed as the sword of the Spirit (Eph 6:17), the divinely chosen instrument by which the powers of sin and death are overthrown in the lives of those who believe.

We do not grasp the theological significance of the Bible until we see it in its paradoxical relationship to the Holy Spirit, who brings to us "the mind of Christ" (1 Cor 2:16) by which we can apprehend the revelational meaning of any particular biblical text. It is not simply what the Bible says historically that enables it to function as the supreme norm for the life of the church, but what it says existentially—that is, under the power of the Spirit. The illumination of the Spirit does not contradict the natural sense of the text but clarifies and fulfills this meaning when the text is seen in its wider context—the unfolding of sacred history culminating in the cross and resurrection of Jesus Christ.

My primary mentors in this volume are Martin Luther, John Calvin, Karl Barth, P. T. Forsyth and Emil Brunner. Other scholars who have had a signal influence on my thought in this area include Augustine, Pascal and Kierkegaard. I also acknowledge my indebtedness to some of the confessional statements of Protestant orthodoxy: the Augsburg Confession, Luther's Small Catechism, the Heidelberg Catechism, the Scots Confession and the Westminster Confession. I treat the creeds not as ruling norms but as norms ruled by the higher norm of the gospel attested in Holy Scripture.

It will become apparent that I draw on the insights not only of the Protestant Reformation but also of evangelical Pietism. One of my emphases is that truth in the salvific sense is not exhaustively rational but transformatively relational. We must avoid the Scylla of rationalism as well as the Charybdis of mysticism in affirming that the truth of the gospel is primarily a relationship of personal correspondence between the divine Revealer and the believer. This relationship entails rational understanding as well as the ecstasy of the experience of faith, but it cannot be reduced to either axioms of logic or states of human consciousness. We need to keep in mind that God himself is not simply an all-comprehending mind but dynamic will and energy, and an encounter with this God will therefore involve awe and wonder as well as insight and meaning.

In this book I hope to elucidate the paradoxical relationship between Holy Scripture and holy mother church. My thesis is that biblical and church authority are interdependent, but with church tradition subordinated to biblical revelation. The role of the church is to clarify and interpret what has already been decisively revealed in the person and work of Jesus Christ recorded in Holy Scripture. Just as Scripture was written under the inspiration of the Spirit, so the church is guided by the illumination of the Spirit as it seeks to bear witness to God's incomparable act of redemption in Jesus Christ. In the freedom of the Spirit the church may be permitted to define some mysteries of faith that are only hinted at in Scripture but nevertheless belong to the history of biblical revelation. An example is the mystery of the holy Trinity. Yet in its acts of definition the church must not claim to have stated the final word, for the final word will be spoken by Jesus Christ at his second advent when all things are consummated in his kingdom.

Like most theologians I do not relish being labeled, but I also recognize the inevitability of labels when writing theology. Some labels I readily accept, others I summarily reject. Those in the latter category include "Pelagian," "semi-Pelagian," "latitudinarian," "panentheist" and "fundamentalist." Among labels I accept, though always with qualification, are "evangelical," "catholic" and "Reformed." By "evangelical" I mean committed to the gospel and to the New Testament interpretation of the gospel. By "catholic" I have in mind fidelity to the historic tradition of the church, though this fidelity does not predicate blind submission to any stated interpretation in tradition. By "Reformed" I mean allegiance to the basic message of the Protestant Reformation, particularly as this message was enunciated by Calvin, Luther and Zwingli. I am willing to accept the designation "liberal" if it means a spirit of self-criticism, but I strongly disavow liberalism as an ism or ideology. Similarly I could be comfortable with the label "fundamental" but only when this notion includes the whole span of faith history. I reject the obscurantism and sectarianism that are often associated with the fundamentalist movement.

While not altogether happy with the designation "neo-orthodox," partly because of the vast array of positions that it represents, I much prefer it to Thomas Oden's "paleo-orthodox," which I see as a somewhat hasty return to the orthodoxy of the past. I believe in forging a new statement of orthodoxy that stands in continuity with the past but addresses issues and problems in the present.

It is fashionable in avant-garde circles today to champion a postmodern theology or a "postmodern orthodoxy" (Oden, Clark Pinnock). Postmodern theology has been born out of the collapse of modernity with its emphasis on the autonomy of reason and the inevitability of moral progress. Postmodern thinking betrays a reliance on imagination over discursive reason, a concern for the practicality of ideas rather than metaphysical truth, and a return to community and tradition. I do not associate myself with postmodern theology because of its avoidance of metaphysical questions, its seeming idealization of the past and its virtual reduction of the gospel to narrative. But I do believe that we are living in an age when Enlightenment modernity is indeed being challenged, and we need to speak to issues that are related to the new intellectual and cultural climate.

My policy is to retain the older vocabulary of the church as much as possible, but every phrase and definition must be interpreted anew in the light of the Word of God and the continuing guidance of the Holy Spirit. We must be cognizant of the fact that words change in their meaning as the historical-cultural matrix shifts, but it does not follow that the original words of the faith tradition must therefore be jettisoned in favor of an entirely new vocabulary informed by the latest philosophical trends. Even Paul Tillich, who introduced many new words into theological language, acknowledged that none of these can ever replace such original words as *sin, grace* and *love,* for these contain nuances of meaning that can only be appreciated by those who stand in the same context of faith commitment.

This book is designed to build bridges between various parties in the church but also to show where bridge building would be a venture in futility. We must not insist on total agreement on literary forms of Scripture or questions of authorship of biblical books as a basis for Christian fellowship. Some questions must be left open, but others are bottom-line and thus brook no compromise. The basic affirmations of the gospel must be embraced in toto, and the language of Scripture concerning God's revealing action in sacred history must be respected as the earthen vessel whereby we receive the hidden treasure of God's redeeming grace through the atoning sacrifice of Christ. We must be wary of a sectarianism that elevates peripherals into essentials, but we must also beware of falling into an eclecticism that draws on too many disparate sources of truth and does not adequately discriminate between truth and error.

I believe in one faith—the holy catholic faith, but this faith can never be exhaustively or definitively formulated by mortal human beings, though it can be truly confessed and proclaimed. Every interpretation is open to fresh articulation, though not all interpretations are reformable in the sense of being subject to revision. The apostolic interpretation of the meaning of the cross is absolutely normative and binding on the community of faith, though the church's understanding can be deepened through faithful reflection.

I believe in one church—the holy catholic and apostolic church, but this church must never be confined to any single historical institution. The holy catholic church is the invisible church of true believers that crosses all denominational lines and even includes some who may not be formal members of any ecclesiastical body. It excludes all, however, who are not truly committed to Jesus Christ as Savior and Lord, even if some of these might be active church participants. While not identical with any particular faith body, the holy catholic church is more manifest in some communions than others. It may indeed be only dimly reflected in churches that elevate their own programs over the gospel, that seek glory for themselves rather than glory to God alone *(soli Deo gloria)*. The holy catholic church is the kingdom of God, which is hidden in both church and world but is actively at work in history, seeking to bring all things to completion in Jesus Christ.

·ONE·

INTR<u>O</u>DUCTI<u>O</u>N

With deep roots and firm foundations, may you be strong to grasp,
with all God's people, what is the breadth and length and height
and depth of the love of Christ, and to know it,
though it is beyond knowledge.
EPHESIANS 3:18-19 NEB

Our senses are so feeble that we could never understand
a single word that God says to us, unless we are illumined by
his Holy Spirit, for carnal men cannot comprehend heavenly things.
JOHN CALVIN

Revelation did not come in a statement, but in a person. . . .
It has its truth, yet it is not a mere truth but a power;
its truth, its statement, its theology is part of it.
P. T. FORSYTH

Contemporary orthodoxy does very little to sustain
the classical dialogue on inspiration. The fountain of new ideas
has apparently run dry, for what was once a live issue
in the church has now ossified into a theological tradition.
EDWARD JOHN CARNELL

Scripture cannot be heard as a living Word spoken
to a contemporary community of faith on the suppositions of
contemporary biblical scholarship. Rather, it will inevitably
be presented as an anachronism, so inextricably related to political,
social, and economic factors of its time that
it has nothing to do with us today.
MARK ELLINGSEN

Behind the raging controversies today in both Protestantism and Roman Catholicism—including the politicizing of the church's mission, inclusive language for God and homosexual ordination—is an implacable cleft in the way people understand Holy Scripture. Does Scripture yield to the inquiring mind immutable, universal principles that can guide us in matters of faith and practice, or is Scripture itself the product of the age in which it was written and therefore devoid of any direct bearing on modern problems? Or is there yet another way of viewing scriptural authority that does justice to the mystery and hiddenness of God's self-condescension in Christ without jettisoning the conceptual element in revelation? Is our controlling norm an authoritative divine self-disclosure in a particular history and therefore mediated by a particular testimony, or is it the in-depth dimension of ordinary human experience, or simply an expanded human horizon?

As I see it, three options confront the church at this juncture of its history. First, an evangelical rationalism virtually equates Scripture with divine revelation and finds truth either by deducing conclusions from first principles set forth in Scripture or by deriving principles from the facts recorded in Scripture—the method of induction. A second option is a religioethical experientialism that makes human moral experience the supreme criterion in shaping theological understanding; the Bible is valued because it provides insights that elucidate the universal experience of transcendence. Finally, a biblical evangelicalism allows for the possibility of real knowledge of God, but always knowledge given anew by the Spirit of God in conjunction with the hearing and reading of the biblical message. In this view the Bible is the divinely prepared medium or channel of divine revelation rather than the revelation itself.

In its modern form experientialism (always a temptation for those who find orthodoxy too enervating or constricting) is most often associated with either an idealistic worldview that sees reality as basically mind or a naturalistic perspective that regards energy as the all-embracing reality. God becomes the transcendent ideal toward which nature moves or the creative force that animates nature. History is understood as the unfolding of spirit or the evolution of a primal consciousness.

Those who appeal to a special divine revelation in history might be considered supernatural creationists, since they hold that the world was created ex nihilo by a divine decree. All who stand in the tradition of the holy catholic faith are united in affirming the infinite transcendence of God over his creation. The difference between the biblical evangelical and the evangelical rationalist is that the latter regards the knowledge of God as a human possibility because of a universal divine revelation in nature and history. The biblical evangelical believes that real knowledge of God is not possible apart from faith, which is a gift of the Spirit of God. We do not mount up to the supernatural on a ladder of speculation (as in medieval scholasticism), but Christ descends to us, confronting us in our despair and need as the Savior of the world. Nature does not lead to grace; instead grace recasts and transforms nature.

The debate today revolves around conflicting understandings of truth. In modern parlance the true is the historically and scientifically demonstrable. In biblical perspective the true is the spiritually and redemptively transformative. For moderns the true is that which can be empirically verified. For the prophets of biblical history the true is that which authenticates itself through the power of the Spirit. The biblical conception of truth makes a place for the factual but insists that the factual neither exhausts the meaning of truth nor constitutes the essence of truth. The historical event can be a sign of the truth, an occasion for the revelation of the truth, but it is not the truth itself.

For biblical evangelicals, the truthfulness of the Bible cannot be determined by historical investigation, since this truth is inaccessible to human perception and conception (cf. Ps 139:6; Job 42:3; Dan 12:8; Rom 11:33-34; Phil 4:7).[1] The truth of the Bible is the revelational meaning of the events that are described, not the events in and of themselves. In traditional Protestant orthodoxy the Bible is the source of revealed truth, and the Spirit is the instrument by which this truth is known. It would perhaps be more biblical to contend that the source of revealed truth is the Spirit of God, and the instrument by which the Spirit makes this truth known is the Bible. The Bible can certainly be conceived as the mediate source of divine revelation. The ultimate source is then the living Christ, who speaks to us by his Spirit. Or the Bible can be said to be the historical source of revealed truth, and Christ in his unity with the Spirit the ultimate or eternal source and ground of truth.

Liberal theology anchors the authority of Scripture not in its message nor in the mode of its writing but in its power to evoke wonder and raise consciousness. Its credibility "derives not from its content but from its power to occasion new occurrences of revelation and new experiences of redemptive transformation when used in situations of proclamation, theological reflection, and personal self-understanding."[2] There is no doubt that Scripture does bring power and motivation to its hearers and readers, but surely its power lies in its message concerning God's act of reconciliation and redemption in Jesus Christ. The Word of God is indeed power and new life, but it is also wisdom and truth. The Spirit of God makes the words of Scripture come alive so that they speak truth to their hearers. The gospel is not simply an experience of divine power but a divine message that both illumines our mind and liberates our will so that we can make a meaningful commitment to our Savior.

Against the rationalists who reduce faith to intellectual assent to verbal truth and the experientialists and spiritualists who appeal to private illuminations over the written Word of God, I affirm the paradoxical unity of Word and Spirit so that the reception of the Word is both a rational apprehension and a redeeming experience. I have considerable difficulty with the view, so appealing to those of a rationalist bent, that the Bible is impregnated with universal, unchanging truths that are waiting to be discovered and formulated.[3] Instead, I hold that the Bible is filled with the Spirit of God, who brings new light to bear on ancient wisdom—light that leads us not only to renewed understanding but also to obedience.

As evangelical Christians we can and must speak of *foundations* of the faith. These are not, however, a priori principles or self-evident truths but the mighty deeds of God in the history of biblical Israel, the significance of which is veiled to us until our inner eyes are opened by the working of the Spirit. The ultimate foundation of our faith is the living God himself, who acts and moves in history but who is hidden from all sight and understanding, even from human imagination, until he makes himself known in his Word. Paul declares, "Scripture speaks of 'things beyond our seeing, things beyond our hearing, things beyond our imagining, all prepared by God for those who love him'; and these are what God has revealed to us through the Spirit" (1 Cor 2:9-10 REB). Natural reason cannot grasp the mystery of divine revelation, but human reasoning can be illumined by the Spirit so that we can know partly though not exhaustively, truly but not comprehensively (cf. 1 Cor 13:12; 2 Cor 5:7; Eph 3:4-5).

The Witness of Sacred Tradition

A perusal of the witness of the church fathers, the doctors of the medieval church, and the Reformers and their followers indicates an emerging consensus that the revelation of God is wider and deeper than the words of Holy Scripture. While all Christian traditions have had to cope with a rationalistic reductionism that turns revelation into a packaged formula, the great saints of the universal church have generally envisioned revelation as dynamic and personal. The Word of God is more than writing: it is wisdom and power.

For Augustine revelation is not simply the transmission of information but a communication that takes root in the depths of the human soul. "You had shot my heart through with the arrows of your love," he tells the Lord, "and I carried your words thrust deep into my inner being."[4] God speaks not merely to the outward ears of men and women but to the deep yearnings of the human spirit, and this truth is not assimilated unless it transforms human life.

In the Eastern church, Maximus the Confessor (d. 662) saw in Scripture a visible letter that is passing and "a hidden spirit underneath the letter" that never ceases to exist.[5]

> We say that the entire Holy Scripture is divided into flesh and spirit, as if it were a spiritual person. For the one who says that the text of Scripture is flesh and that its meaning is spirit or soul does not stray from the truth. The wise man is certainly the one who abandons the corruptible and belongs wholly to the incorruptible.[6]

To Bernard of Clairvaux, whom the Reformers held in high esteem, the Word of God is not primarily a book of general truths and principles but a transforming energy that brings light to the mind and power to the will. "The Word of God is not a sounding but a piercing Word, not pronounceable by the tongue but efficacious to the mind, not sensible to the ear but fascinating to the affection."[7]

In the theology of the Protestant Reformers the Word of God is a hidden wisdom "whose loftiness the weak human mind does not reach" (Calvin).[8] The light of God shines in the darkness of the fallen world, but the blind do not see this light until their eyes are opened by the Spirit of God. In Luther's view we do not acquire the wisdom of God by laws or by reason but only by simple faith, for what Scripture teaches is "incomprehensible and invisible."[9]

Calvin was adamant that the Word of God infinitely transcends the compass of human conception and imagination. "Our senses are so feeble that we could never understand a single word that God says to us, unless we are illumined by his Holy Spirit; for carnal men cannot comprehend heavenly things."[10] The Word of God is "a violent force" that urges us "to give obedience to it," the veritable "hand of God stretching itself out to act powerfully through the apostle in every way."[11] Knowledge of this Word "is not obtained in a natural way, or laid hold of by our mental power of comprehension, but it depends altogether on the revelation of the Spirit."[12]

According to Ulrich Zwingli, the renowned Reformer of Zurich, the Word of God cannot be judged by human logic, but through the work of the Spirit it creates an indelible impression on the human mind. Zwingli resolved to allow Scripture to interpret itself "by means of the Spirit of God" and not to rely on purely human interpretations.[13]

The left-wing Reformation (Anabaptists and Spiritualists) attached even more importance to the role of the Spirit in revealing the truth of God, though they sometimes failed to maintain the delicate balance between Word and Spirit.[14] They tended to see the Word of God as the wisdom of God, which is reflected in the Bible but not exhausted in the pages of a book or creed. Eberhard Arnold is typical of this general tradition: "The Word of God was living before the first pages of the Bible were written. It was living at the beginning of all things."[15]

Modern Errors

Through the centuries well-intentioned men and women have erred either by reducing revelation to rational information or by misunderstanding revelation as an ecstatic experience devoid of cognitive content. Modern fundamentalism illustrates the first error and existentialism the second. Karl Rahner can describe revelation as an altered state of consciousness rather than knowledge.[16] For Gregory Baum revelation "constitutes a new awareness in man through which he sees the world in a new light and commits himself to a new kind of action."[17] According to Rudolf Bultmann God makes himself known as absolute mystery and therefore can never be an object of human understanding.

While the Reformers were convinced that revelation transcends the parameters of human reason, they nevertheless insisted that we can really know because the Spirit of God descends into our reasoning, bringing light to those who dwell in darkness. We cannot know fully, but we can know in fact. The existentialist theologian Jacques Ellul goes too far when he concludes that "the content of faith" is "undefinable and ungraspable."[18] The content of faith can be defined because the message of the Bible is truly made known by the Holy Spirit. Yet this content cannot be defined exhaustively or definitively because mystery remains even in the act of revelation.

Another existentialist inclined to downplay if not deny the rational content of faith is John Macquarrie, who acknowledges his indebtedness to Martin Heidegger. Macquarrie maintains that revelation does not give us new items of knowledge but enables us to see things in a new way.[19] Revelation is not an I-Thou encounter but instead a state of being grasped by being. Meaning, it appears, has been overwhelmed by mystery.

Liberal Christianity has often made a distinction between the "kernel" of religion and its "husk" (Adolf von Harnack)[20] or "abiding experiences" and "changing categories" (Harry Emerson Fosdick).[21] Similarly Paul

Tillich, who drew from the well of liberal theology though not uncritically, clearly differentiated the symbols of faith from the reality to which they point. I too believe we must distinguish between the historical form and the transcendent content of divine revelation, but this content must not be confounded with general moral truths (as in Harnack) or with an all-pervasive mystical presence (as in Tillich). Instead, it is God's self-communication in Jesus Christ, which cannot be separated from its worldly form, the scriptural witness, and indeed is made known precisely in this form.

It has been fashionable in Protestant liberalism to subordinate the Bible to religious experience. William Newton Clarke insisted that "the Bible itself is an expression of experience. If this experience had not continued the Bible would have become only the record of an ancient and forgotten life, powerless to preserve Christianity in the world. This experience, on the contrary, would have preserved Christ's gift to man if there had been no Bible."[22] It would seem then that the church must look to its own life for its authority rather than to an extrinsic norm, viz., the gospel of God attested in Holy Scripture.

Although severely critical of the anthropocentric orientation of liberal theology and its utopian illusions, H. Richard Niebuhr nevertheless reflected the liberal legacy when he defined revelation as the moment in our interior history when we become aware of the transformative presence of the creative power that directs the universe and of the possibilities within the self to attain freedom and purpose in life.[23] For him revelation is not the impartation of the knowledge of God's will and purpose for a sinful world but the remolding of our religious and moral experience as we come to appreciate anew the memory of Jesus kept alive in the community of faith through the ages.[24] Among the seminal thinkers on whom Niebuhr drew were Immanuel Kant, Wilhelm Herrmann, Alfred North Whitehead,[25] Karl Barth and Ernst Troeltsch, the last perhaps having the major impact on his thought. I agree with Hendrikus Berkhof that Niebuhr was a transitional figure who anticipated neoliberalism,[26] in which the experience of being is more decisive than the scriptural witness to what God reveals and declares concerning himself and his plan for humanity.[27]

Another transitional theologian, Joseph Sittler, also underscored the critical role of experience:

> What do we mean when we refer to the Word of God? Primarily, we do not mean Scripture; there was a Word of God before there was any Bible. . . . The ultimate meaning of Word is not a document; but the documents were preserved by the ancient Hebrews and the early church because they testified, they bore witness, to the force of the Word. The people had experienced it, and they were transformed by it.[28]

Sittler did not make the mistake of viewing experience as an independent authority apart from the Word. Yet he indicated that what the prophets described was the force of the Word in their experience rather than the truth of God's revelation of his will and purpose to humanity. To be sure, this truth must be received in experience, but it nevertheless constitutes the criterion for judging and understanding our experiences.

What makes Christianity unique is not that it appeals to a hidden wisdom that cannot be fully encompassed in human understanding but that it insists that this wisdom became incarnate in history—in a particular individual and at a particular time and place. This means that the claims of faith are open to historical investigation, though they cannot be finally validated by such investigation, for it is not simply the events in sacred history but the action of God in these events that constitutes the supreme content of Christian faith.

Toward a Theology of Word and Spirit

Today theology needs to recover the paradoxical unity of Word and Spirit, for only on the basis of this unity can Scripture be made to come alive and be a transforming leaven in the life of the church. Scripture in itself is the *written* Word of God, comprising by virtue of its divine inspiration a reliable witness to the truth revealed by God in Jesus Christ. But it becomes the *living* Word when it actually communicates to us the truth and power of the cross of Christ through the illumination of the Spirit.

The word of the prophets and apostles in the Bible corresponds to the Word of God, the truth embodied in Jesus Christ, but it is not identical with it. Moreover, this correspondence is not obvious to reason and can be grasped only by the interior illumination of the Spirit. In the Bible we have an echo or reverberation of what God has declared in his redeeming word and act in Jesus Christ. The biblical word stands in continuity with the living Word, but only faith can discern the measure of this continuity.

The Word of God—the truth that proceeds out of the mouth of God—is living and dynamic. Too often in evangelical and conservative circles the Word is viewed as something static and frozen, waiting to be analyzed and dissected. But our ability to know the Word rests on the prior action of the Word. The Word himself must take the initiative and break through the barrier of human sin and finitude if we are to know the truth that regenerates and redeems. As the epistle to the Hebrews declares, "The word of God is living and powerful, and sharper than any two-edged sword, piercing even to the division of soul and spirit, and of joints and marrow, and is a discerner of the thoughts and intents of the heart" (4:12 NKJV).

I agree with Emil Brunner that the revelation of God "is not 'given' in a static manner; it is not a system of statements for man to take and use."[29] Rather it is a transforming reality that can be known only through searching the Scriptures in the context of the fellowship of faith. The Spirit of God does not simply enlighten the mind but motivates the will to demonstrate the truth of the gospel in daily obedience (cf. Deut 29:29).

The presence of the living Word in Holy Scripture is not an ontological necessity but a free decision of the God who acts and speaks. It is not something to take for granted but something to hope for on the basis of God's promises. To know God's Word is more than having an external knowledge of the words of Scripture. It is to be confronted with the reality of God in the interior depths of our being so that we know inwardly and not merely outwardly.[30] Those who know the Word of God are those who have his teaching in their hearts (Is 51:7 NRSV).

The certainty that the Christian finds is not rational certainty of metaphysical truth but confidence in the power of Christ to redeem from sin and death. It is "not intellectual certainty but evangelical, not scientific history but history impressive, creative, teleological. And that is why one turns away for a time, however gratefully, from the scholars to the theologians, from the critics' work upon the New Testament to the believers' work upon the Gospel."[31]

According to James Packer we must be able to say that the Bible is the Word of God not only instrumentally but also intrinsically.[32] I too can make this kind of affirmation because the Bible constitutes a reliable testimony to God's self-revelation in Christ by virtue of its divine inspiration. But it is not divine revelation intrinsically, for its revelatory status does not reside in its wording as such but in the Spirit of God, who fills the words with meaning and power. It is the written Word of God because its authors were inspired by God; it becomes the revealed Word of God when God himself speaks through the prophetic and apostolic witness, sealing the truth of this witness in our hearts.

One may also say that the Bible is intrinsically the Word of God in that it is encompassed by the "Word presence," the living reality of the Spirit of Christ. Because the sign participates in what it signifies, the Bible is included in the redemptive act of Christ as his Spirit works in the community of faith. The Bible in and of itself is not the Word of God—divine revelation—but it is translucent to this revelation by virtue of the Spirit of God working within it and within the mind of the reader and hearer.

I am not comfortable with the term *inerrancy* when applied to Scripture because it has been co-opted by a rationalistic, empiricistic mentality that reduces truth to facticity. Yet I wish to retain what is intended by this word—the abiding truthfulness and normativeness of the biblical witness. This truthfulness, however, is a property not of the human witness itself but of the Spirit who speaks in and through this witness.

It is a property of the object and goal of this witness—Jesus Christ.

What makes the Bible significant is not that it contains self-evident truth—truth that is universally recognizable—but that it conveys particular truth that is at the same time self-authenticating.[33] The Word of God is not an abstract principle but a personal address. From this address we can derive principles and guidelines for action, but the precepts drawn up by the church must never be confounded with the divine commandment and the divine promise, which constitute the content of the biblical revelation.

God's Word is absolute, but it comes to us in the form of the relative. Through the power of the Spirit we are nevertheless placed in a relationship with the absolute, and this means that our thoughts and activities have a sure anchor in eternity. We do not ascend to the absolute in faith, but the absolute descends to our level. He enters our personal history and speaks to us in our time-conditioned language. Without lifting us out of our cultural and historical milieu, he gives us a glimpse of eternity so that our confidence is no longer in the merely human and temporal but in the divine and transcendent. We must never identify our own formulation of God's truth with this truth itself, but we can claim that our formulations lead to this truth if they are indeed rooted in Scripture. We must oppose both the absolutizing of the relative (against some strands of orthodoxy) and the relativizing of the absolute (against the latest fashion in liberal theology). God's will and purpose are inviolable and irrevocable, but we know this will only through the lens of a historically and culturally conditioned human witness—Holy Scripture.

In order to maintain a theology of Word and Spirit, we need to combat the opposite errors of illuminism and rationalism. If we have the Spirit alone we are in the morass of illuminism and subjectivism. If we base our appeal on the Bible alone—apart from the work of the Spirit in the history of the people of God—we are in danger of reducing the message of faith to axioms of logic that can provide the basis for a rational system but are woefully inadequate for leading us into a personal relationship with the living Christ. The Bible is a sure and certain guide for the people of faith but only because it is the chosen vessel of the Spirit of God, who illuminates its pages, who enlightens and empowers its messengers, and who opens the eyes of the blind so that they may see and believe. The light of God's truth breaks through the darkness of the world's despair when people are confronted with the good news of what God has done for us in Jesus Christ, the good news contained in Holy Scripture and proclaimed in the church through the ages.

THE CRISIS IN BIBLICAL AUTHORITY

Behold, I will pour out my spirit unto you,
I will make known my words unto you.
P R O V E R B S   1 : 2 3   K J V

You had shot my heart through with the arrows of your love,
and I carried your words thrust deep into my inner being.
A U G U S T I N E

The external word is of no avail by itself unless animated
by the power of the Spirit. . . . All power of action, then,
resides in the Spirit himself, and thus all praise
ought to be entirely referred to God alone.
J O H N   C A L V I N

The Bible has done its great work, not as a document of history,
but as a means of grace, as a servant of the gospel,
lame, perhaps, and soiled, showing some signs of age, it may be,
but perfectly faithful, competent and effectual always.
P . T . F O R S Y T H

What is signally striking in theology in the past two decades is the collapse of the center and the growing polarization between liberals and evangelicals. Liberals have lost sight of the divinity of the Bible, and both camps have failed lamentably to uphold the divinity of the church. Unlike their mentors in the 1940s and 1950s, the new liberals have jettisoned the biblical guidelines on personal morality and have reduced ethics to the advocacy of social causes. Conservatives have maintained a strong posture in defense of traditional moral values, but they have been conspicuously silent concerning the morality of weapons of mass extermination.

Neo-orthodoxy, associated with the names of Karl Barth, Emil Brunner and the Niebuhr brothers, is not in total eclipse, but its particular emphases, including the theological unity of the Scriptures, have receded into the background. While calling for a recovery of biblical authority, it was unable to hold together the divine and the human sides of Scripture. It can be faulted for fostering a Nestorian approach to the Bible in which the divine word and the human word are only loosely associated and never function in an indissoluble unity. This is less true of Barth than of Brunner and the Niebuhrs.

The debilitating effects of historical criticism are still leaving their mark on both theology and biblical studies. The historicist theologian Ernst Troeltsch, whose influence on both Bultmann and H. Richard Niebuhr was considerable, maintained that "historical method, once . . . applied to biblical study, is a leaven that transforms everything, and finally shatters the whole framework of theological method as this has existed hitherto."[1] Edgar Krentz astutely observes, "The biblical books became historical documents to be studied and questioned like any other ancient sources. The Bible was no longer the criterion for the writing of history; rather history had become the criterion for understanding the Bible."[2]

In recent years the results of historical criticism have come under fire from within the discipline of biblical studies. Rolf Rendtorff of Heidelberg contends that the old methodological approach to the Old Testament is no longer dominant among younger scholars.

> The paradigm within which Old Testament scholarship has worked for more than a century, namely the old German *Literarkritik,* has lost its general acceptance. It is no longer possible to maintain that serious Old Testament scholarship has to be indispensably tied to this set of methodological principles . . . Old Testament scholarship now is in a stage of transition, and we cannot know whether there will be a new paradigm or if the near future will be characterized by a

plurality of approaches and methods.[3]

Rendtorff also questions the validity of the documentary hypothesis, which ascribes the formation of the Pentateuch to a redaction of four documents, commonly designated as JEDP. He suggests instead that "the Pentateuch developed not from continuous sources editorially combined but from a variety of traditions skillfully knit together over a considerable period of time."[4]

In contrast to the older critical approach, some scholars are finding an underlying unity in Isaiah. Carroll Stuhlmueller is convinced that an editor was responsible for the present form of the book, which was compiled from "the oral and written traditions" of three individuals and "the teaching of their disciples."[5] While commending *The New Jerome Biblical Commentary* as a superb scholarly achievement, C. S. Rodd faults it for accentuating "the division of 'Deutero-Isaiah and Trito-Isaiah' . . . from Isaiah 1—39, at a time when the essential unity of the book is being increasingly acknowledged."[6]

While a growing number of conservative evangelical scholars have tried to come to terms with historical and literary criticism of the Bible, many others have issued a blanket condemnation of this kind of methodology. Biblical inerrancy has become a slogan masking a not-so-hidden antipathy to the historical-critical approach to Scripture. There is a real question whether the retreat to an inerrantist position can safeguard the integrity of the biblical and catholic witness of the church. James Packer, for example, holds that the demand for inerrancy permits the interpretation of Adam and Eve as allegorical ciphers. In contrast, Francis Schaeffer regarded the factual historicity of Genesis 1—11 as the very cornerstone of biblical inerrancy.[7] Most evangelical scholars accept the historical facticity of the infancy narratives in Matthew and Luke, but Robert Gundry claims that in Matthew's version we have "creative midrash" in which historical events are embroidered by nonhistorical additions. After the appearance of his controversial commentary on Matthew, Gundry, though professing biblical inerrancy, was forced to withdraw from the Evangelical Theological Society (in December 1983).[8]

I believe the hope of theology rests on a genuine evangelical renaissance, but such a renaissance will not happen until evangelicals break out of their epistemic bondage to Enlightenment rationalism[9] and their cultural bondage to patriarchalism and capitalism. The answer does not lie, however, in aligning the faith with new ideologies (such as feminism and socialism) or with new philosophies (such as existentialism and process thought).

Many theologians (both liberal and conservative) are attracted to narrative theology, which approaches the text as an art form, concentrating on its literary qualities.[10] The historical setting of the text is regarded as secondary to its evocative power as story. For David Kelsey it is the literary patterns of Scripture rather than its transcendent content that make it authoritative.[11] This new movement can be seen as an attempt to evade both the question of the historicity of the events and miracles recorded in Scripture and the question of their metaphysical implications.

There is a corresponding crisis in Roman Catholicism today. Infallibility is being reinterpreted to mean indefectibility (perseverance in the truth) rather than incapacity to err (Hans Küng).[12] Scriptural miracles are increasingly explained in terms of the working of natural laws rather than divine intervention in nature. The historical basis of many of the scriptural stories is being called into question, and the consensus of tradition becomes the supreme criterion for faith and morals. Many of the younger Catholic theologians are attracted to the latest theological fashions—liberation theology, process theology, feminist theology and narrative theology. By contrast, the old guard is retreating to a papal authoritarianism that practically disallows any serious criticism of papal decrees and conciliar pronouncements.[13]

Inerrancy and Infallibility in Historical Perspective

Contrary to what is commonly believed in liberal and neo-orthodox circles, there is a long tradition in the church that represents the teaching of Scripture as being without error. References to the Scriptures as *inerrabilis* are to be found in Augustine, Aquinas and Duns Scotus. The adjective *infallibilis* was applied to Scripture by John Wycliffe and Jean de Gerson. Luther and Calvin described the Bible as being infallible and without error. Calvin referred to the Bible as "the unerring rule" for faith and practice. The word *inerrancy* first became current in English in the middle and later nineteenth century. It was first generally used by Roman Catholics and then by conservative Presbyterians.

The paramount question is whether the Bible itself teaches its own inerrancy. A second critical question is whether those who employ this terminology always mean the same thing. The truthfulness of Scripture is indeed espoused by the prophets and apostles, but it must be kept in mind that they were using "truth" and "truthfulness" in the Hebraic sense of faithfulness and veracity rather than precision and absolute factual accuracy, as in our modern empirical milieu.[14] The psalmist declares, "The sum of your word is truth" (Ps 119:160 NRSV). We are told in Ecclesiastes, "The Teacher searched to find just the right words, and what he wrote was upright and true" (12:10 NIV). Paul insists, "I am speaking the truth in Christ, I am not lying" (Rom 9:1). In the words of 3 John: "I testify to him . . . and you know my testimony is true" (v. 12).

It can be shown that all these references as well as many others that could be cited connote the fundamental trustworthiness and dependability of the messengers of God. We must not read into the biblical testimony a conception of truth that is tied to the epistemology of a naive realism in which the words directly present what they signify. A careful perusal of the Reformers indicates that their concern was the normativeness and veracity of the teaching and doctrine of Scripture. Calvin, who spoke of the accommodation of the Spirit to the language and culture of a particular people in history, was well aware of the limitations of the biblical writings in matters of science.[15]

The conception of the total inerrancy of the writing of Scripture developed out of the scholastic Reformed and Lutheran orthodoxy of the seventeenth and eighteenth centuries, though such a position can be inferred from various statements of the church fathers. The alliance of conservative Protestantism with the philosophy of Scottish Common Sense Realism gave impetus to the apologetics of evidentialism in which the case for biblical authority and inerrancy is made to rest on empirical validation.[16] It is sometimes alleged in these circles that the historical method alone can validate the claims of Scripture. John Warwick Montgomery goes so far as to insist that it is possible to prove the bodily resurrection of Jesus to the person outside the family of faith. For Montgomery, synthetic proofs based on empirical data do not give absolute certainty, but they can be sufficiently persuasive to induce a positive response to the claims of faith.[17]

As evangelical orthodoxy developed it tended more and more to identify the Bible with divine revelation, to regard the words of the Bible as the immediate or direct words of God. Early Protestant orthodoxy was careful to distinguish between the "inward" and "outward" form of Scripture, and only the former was in the strict sense the Word of God. In the spiritual movements of renewal after the Reformation—Pietism and Puritanism—a distinction was commonly made between the kernel and the shell of Scripture, between its content and its outward form.

The idea that the Word of God is to be equated with the autographs or original manuscripts is relatively modern,[18] though it can be found in the speculation of Protestant orthodox theologians not long after the Reformation. The truth in this point of view is that the original manuscripts do constitute the norm for testing the accuracy of the biblical wording, but the misconception is that textual criticism—the search for the earliest manuscripts—can yield the reality of the Word of God, which in the view of the Reformers is always transcendent and hidden from human sight and understanding.

Not all theologians who stood in the tradition of orthodoxy were ready to embrace an unqualified inerrancy. Already in 1894 James Orr concluded that it was a mistake to find the essence of the doctrine of inspiration in "a hard-and-fast inerrancy in minute matters of historical, geographical, chronological and scientific detail—for the most part indifferent to the substance of revelation."[19]

The contemporary evangelical Philip Edgcumbe Hughes roundly criticizes his conservative peers for risking the loss of the humanity of Scripture in a well-meaning but ill-fated attempt to safeguard its divinity:

> In the heat of the conflict there is a strong temptation, when insisting on the "divinity" of Scripture, to thrust aside its "humanity," and this can only be at the expense of upsetting the balance of the paradox and ignoring the mystery. There is then, inevitably, resort to rationalization, which in itself is a form of reductionism (even though this is the last thing that is intended) as the level is lowered to the capacity of human thought by putting the emphasis on one pole of the paradox. This tendency is sometimes displayed in the postulation that inerrancy belongs only to the original autographs, which (as far as we know) are no longer in existence. It is seen also in the deduction from this premise that we now possess only errant copies of these autographs. To be assured that these copies, though errant, are nonetheless infallible is far from helpful. The use of language in this confused and confusing manner is hardly conducive to sound reason and understanding. It creates, rather, the impression of verbal acrobatics.[20]

Need for Reinterpretation

As a theologian of the church universal interested in preserving traditional religious terminology as much as possible, I shall try to determine in what way words like *inerrancy* and *infallibility* can be maintained with the rise of higher criticism. I propose a theology of retrieval rather than a theology of revision.

Because the word *inerrancy* comes to us freighted with cultural and theological baggage that is questionable in the light of our expanded knowledge of the literature and history of the Bible, it is probably advisable to use other terms to convey what the fathers of the church generally meant when they referred to Scripture as without error. We must never say that the Bible teaches theological or historical error, but we need to recognize that not everything reported in the Bible may be in exact correspondence with historical and scientific fact as we know it today.[21]

We need to reaffirm Scripture as the unerring rule for faith and practice (Calvin), but we must avoid the hermeneutics of biblical literalism, which leads us into both scientific creationism with its young earth theory and dispensationalism—based on the literal fulfillment of all biblical prophecy. Inerrancy has too often been the cloak for biblical obscurantism, and thus other language may be preferable in explaining the divine authority and primacy of Scripture.

Another salient word used in church tradition to describe the divine quality of Scripture is *infallibility*. This term basically means that Scripture is incapable of deception or leading astray. More positively it suggests that Scripture unfailingly leads us into the truth that God reveals to us. Like the term *inerrancy,* however, infallibility when applied to Scripture cannot be affirmed without qualification. It is not simply the words of Scripture that make it infallible but the way in which these words are used by the Spirit of God.

Perhaps still more appropriate for describing biblical authority are terms like *veracity*—unflagging adherence to the truth—and *trustworthiness*—complete dependability in bearing witness to truth. Here again, however, we must insist that Scripture is veracious and trustworthy only because it is grounded in historical revelation and employed by the Holy Spirit to guide us into a knowledge of this revelation. Its words are true because they infallibly direct us to the One who alone is the perfect embodiment of truth, the "radiance of God's glory" (Heb 1:3 REB).

The truthfulness of the Bible resides in the divine author of Scripture who speaks in and through the words of human authors, who ipso facto reflect the limitations and ambiguities of their cultural and historical milieu. Appellations like infallibility, inerrancy, truthfulness and veracity are all relational. The biblical text is entirely truthful when it is seen in relation to its divine center, God's self-revelation in Jesus Christ. When separated from this center, the text is not perceived in its proper context and then becomes vulnerable to error and misunderstanding.

The Bible is divine in its ultimate origin and theological content but human in its mode of expression or literary form. There is something of the provisional and relative in the Bible, and to deny this feature is to lapse into a form of biblical docetism. But there is also something abiding, eternal, forever certain and forever true in Scripture. To deny this feature is to fall into an ebionitic type of heresy, which begins with the human imperfection of the Bible but never quite comes to terms with its divine perfection.

The truth of the Bible is available to us only when we strive to see the text in relation to the New Testament gospel. The apostolic writer declares, "The law contains but a shadow of the good things to come, not the true picture" (Heb 10:1 REB). The true or comprehensive picture of God's dealing with humanity is hidden from us until the text becomes for us a window to the light of the glory of God in Jesus Christ.

Reflecting the posture of a conservative Protestant orthodoxy, Wayne Grudem unabashedly concludes, "For the New Testament writers to say that God does not lie was to say that Scripture, which was to them God's words, never affirms anything that is contrary to fact."[22] In my judgment this is to confound the biblical understanding of truth with a modern empiricist understanding that conceives of Scripture as directly and immediately the words of God rather than the Word of God mediated through human words. Grudem can therefore make the astounding claim that Scripture in itself is "unchanging and eternal."[23] But even Jesus of Nazareth was mortal and temporal. Grudem ignores those passages that speak of the discontinuity between human speech and the Word of God (cf. Is 55:8-9; Ps 139:6; Job 42:3; Rom 11:33).

Neither do I feel comfortable with liberal scholars who call into question the divine unity of the Scriptures and speak of disparate theologies in the New Testament, even a plurality of kerygmas.[24] Within and behind the theological and cultural diversity in Scripture is an underlying unity of divine-revealing action and human response. The Bible constitutes a record and mirror of a sacred history that has a common source and unifying focus—the self-revelation of the living God in Jesus Christ.

The true humanity of Scripture involves a vulnerability to error and a limited cultural horizon because the writers lived in a particular time and place in history. Yet though the writers and the text bear the limitations imposed by cultural and historical contingency, the text by virtue of its inspiration and present illumination by the Holy Spirit opens to us a culturally transcendent horizon when seen in its relationship to Jesus Christ. This relationship constitutes the fullness of its meaning, its *sensus plenior.*

It is commonly said today that divine revelation is evocative rather than informative, ecstatic rather than cognitive. I maintain to the contrary that the Bible yields real knowledge about God and his plan of salvation as we see this in Jesus Christ. To understand the truth of faith we must be able to express it in propositions. But this knowledge remains purely intellectual unless it alters the direction of our lives. Salvific knowledge is knowledge that takes root in the interiority of our being and shapes human life and character.

The biblical writings are a powerful testimony not only of people's faith but also of God's truth. They reflect not only the belief of the authors but also the very mind of God. They not only serve to inspire faith in God but also are inspired by God so that our faith can be informed by divine revelation. My sentiments concur with Barth's: "We know what we say when we call the Bible the Word of God only when we recognize its human imperfection in face of its divine perfection, and its divine perfection in spite of its human imperfection."[25]

The object of our faith is not the church or the Scriptures, not even our experience of Jesus Christ. It is Jesus Christ himself, but Christ testified to in Scripture and proclaimed by the church. He is the One whom we meet concretely in the historical witness to his saving deeds. We commit ourselves not to the Jesus of history nor simply to the Christ of faith but to the Jesus Christ of eternity who entered into a particular history and is apprehended only in faith.

Models of Scriptural Authority

In my study of how theologians past and present have interpreted the Bible, I have come to the conclusion that at least three models of biblical authority are pertinent to the discussion today. They are related to different theological methodologies as well as to conflicting philosophical understandings of truth.

These models can be described as the sacramental, the scholastic and the liberal or modernist. The first sees the Bible as well as the church and the sacraments as an instrument or channel of divine activity. It envisages God as working through human and material instrumentality in relating himself to humanity. It does not deny the infinite qualitative difference between divinity and humanity but insists that the human is capable of bearing or conveying the divine. I find this model in Augustine, Calvin, Luther, Forsyth and Barth (at least in his middle period).

By the scholastic I mean that kind of theology that emphasizes the accessibility of the infinite to the finite and the possibility and indeed the desirability of systematizing the body of revealed knowledge given in Scripture. I detect this model especially in Protestant orthodoxy, though it is also partially present in such pillars of Catholic theology as Peter Lombard and Aquinas. It is particularly noticeable in the orthodoxy associated with the Princeton school of theology (Charles Hodge, A. A. Hodge and Benjamin Warfield) and today in the writings of evangelical theologians like Carl Henry, Millard Erickson, Ronald Nash and R. C. Sproul.

The third model is associated with the liberal theology that has its immediate source in the Enlightenment of the eighteenth and early nineteenth centuries, though it was anticipated in the spiritualists and mystics through the ages. It stresses the inseparability of the infinite and the finite and sees the infinite as residing in the finite as its ground and depth. Liberal theology focuses on God's immanence rather than his transcendence. Its goal is to bring Christian thought into dialogue with modernity, to mediate between Christ and culture in order to establish the credibility of Christian faith to its modern cultured despisers. Its orientation is anthropological and psychological rather than theological in that its primary concern is the effect of the divine on humanity rather than the nature of divinity as such. It is also inclined to see faith as standing in need of philosophical conceptualization and elucidation. Such renowned theologians of the nineteenth and early twentieth centuries as Friedrich Schleiermacher, Albrecht Ritschl, Wilhelm Herrmann and Ernst Troeltsch as well as Horace Bushnell, Shailer Mathews, Douglas Clyde Macintosh, Shirley Jackson Case and William Newton Clark in this country typify what I mean by liberal theology. This tradition resurfaces in Rudolf Bultmann, Paul Tillich, Langdon Gilkey, Henry Nelson Wieman, Harvey Cox, John Cobb, Peter Hodgson and Rosemary Ruether, though some of these would prefer the designation neoliberal or even postliberal.

These models are ideal types, in the sense used by Max Weber, Ernst Troeltsch and H. Richard Niebuhr. No one theologian or system of theology can be completely identified with any one model. Yet this kind of typology is helpful in clarifying the tensions that exist among different schools of theology on the subject of biblical authority.

The sacramental model sees the Bible as a divinely appointed medium or channel of revelation. The Bible is the earthen vessel in which we have a hidden treasure or the swaddling clothes in which the Christ child is laid (Luther). A distinction is often made between the sign (the letter of Scripture) and the thing signified (God's self-revelation in Christ). We do not have Christ apart from the sign, which, by the power of the Spirit, is effectual in communicating the mystery of Christ to us. The Bible is seen as both a human witness to divine truth and God's self-revelation through human authors. The relationship between the two sides—the human and the divine—is viewed in paradoxical fashion, a paradox analogous to the coexistence or coinherence of the divine and human natures in Jesus Christ. It is a paradox that can be apprehended only in faith. The Bible can therefore be spoken of as "the Word of God" and "the word of man" at the same time.

The scholastic model holds the Bible to be the written revelation of God, a revelation ascertainable by human reason, though efficacious only for faith. There is said to be a virtual or actual identity between the Bible and revelation. The Bible becomes a book of revealed utterances or divine oracles. Faith assents to what reason can already know. The truth can be procured by a scientific or historical investigation of the Scriptures, but it can have no saving effect in one's life apart from the gift of faith—an illumination by the Spirit.

In the liberal view the Bible is a record of the religious experience of a particular people in history. In the words of J. G. Herder: "Its language is human . . . its meaning, its whole purpose and use."[26] It is helpful to us because of the abiding values it transmits or the reproducible experiences it describes. Its conceptual categories may be archaic, but its ethical precepts or its principles for cultivating the spiritual life have an enduring quality.

The sacramental model understands revelation as God in action, God revealing the depth of his love and the mystery of his will to the eyes of faith. Revelation has a personal, a propositional and an experiential pole. What is revealed is a personal presence in conjunction with a spoken or written witness and received by a believing heart. This view also holds that God is hidden in his revelation, that the truth of God is not directly available to human perception or conception. God can be known only as he gives himself to be known (Barth). Or as Augustine said, the truth can be apprehended by the mind only if the will has been converted by the Spirit of God.

The scholastic understands the Bible as a book of revealed truths or revealed propositions. The knowledge given in revelation is suprarational, but it is held to stand in continuity with natural knowledge. Reason may not be able to fathom this truth, but it can understand or make sense of this truth.

For the liberal, revelation is self-discovery (Tillich) or a breakthrough into self-understanding (Bultmann). Or it is a reflection of God in human consciousness (Teilhard de Chardin), or an experience of the infinite depth and ground of all being (Tillich), or an awakening to God-consciousness (Schleiermacher) or an intuitive apprehension of the Eternal Now (Gerald Heard). The Bible is an aid in making contact with the deepest within the self, but it is not indispensable for this experience of oneness with God. What is given in revelation is not information concerning the nature of God or the plan of salvation but a new awareness of ourselves in relation to the divine and to fellow humanity.

Different understandings of faith are also evident in the three models. In the sacramental model faith is an existential commitment to the personal God revealed in Jesus Christ.[27] In scholastic theology faith is basically an intellectual assent to propositional truth. In the liberal approach faith is a venture of discovery that enables us to make contact with the creative power at work in nature and history. Or it is the stretching forth of the mind toward an insight not yet given. In the first model faith is included in the event of revelation. In the second, revelation is prior to faith. In the third, revelation tends to be subordinated to faith.

On the relation of humanity and divinity in Bible, church and sacrament, the sacramental approach sees the human as the instrumentality of the divine. The scholastic theologian views the human as an aspect of the divinity of the object in question. In the liberal or modernist model, humanity is a pointer to divinity, or the occasion by which we come to know divinity within us. Or, it is said, in order to find divinity, we must get beyond humanity.

On the infallibility of Scripture, the sacramental model teaches a derivative infallibility. The Bible does not have infallibility within itself, but through the power of the Spirit it carries the infallibility of the very truth of God. We may also speak of the Bible as having a functional infallibility in its role as the supreme rule of faith, conduct and worship. At the same time, it would not infallibly convey the truth of faith unless it had an infallible basis and goal. The Bible bears the stamp of infallibility through its unique inspiration and transmits infallible truth through the ongoing illumination of the Holy Spirit to people of faith. According to scholastic theology the Bible has absolute infallibility or total inerrancy. The authority of the Bible is now grounded in itself, in its mode of writing or its revelatory language rather than in God's self-communication through the historical events the Bible records. Liberal theology considers the Bible a fallible human record of experiences that can be reduplicated or reenacted in every age.

Not surprisingly there are substantial differences in the way theology itself is understood. In the sacramental view, theology is the systematic reflection on the mysteries of divine revelation for the purpose of presenting a viable and intelligible witness to this revelation in our time. In the scholastic model, theology consists in harmonizing the axioms of Scripture in order to arrive at a comprehensive life- and worldview. In the liberal-modernist approach, theology is an interpretation of our experiences of God in the light of the modern historical consciousness. It signifies basically a reconstruction of the biblical witness. For Herrmann, theology becomes thinking out our experience of God, not thinking out what God tells us about himself in Scripture. As Reinhold Niebuhr described it, theology is the elucidation of personal faith rather than an explication of God's self-communication in Scripture.[28]

One can see that the sacramental model has much more in common with the scholastic model than with the liberal one, for the first two are united in affirming the reality of an objective, absolute revelation of God in history. The important difference is that the sacramental model recognizes that this absolute Word of God is mediated through the relativity of human witness. We do not have the absolute except in the form of the relative. Yet this does not mean that the absolute remains apart from us; on the contrary, it makes contact with us through the work of the Spirit so that we can claim to have "the mind of Christ" (1 Cor 2:16). By attempting to make the mysteries of faith conducive to human understanding, scholastic theology virtually loses sight of the mystery and paradox in faith that the Bible indicates so abundantly must characterize the Christian walk in this life.

In its classical setting evangelical theology is sacramental, but in its varied expressions in history it has often taken the form of a rational-izing of divine revelation. I contend that evangelical theology will regain its vitality and relevance when it rediscovers the sacramental under-standing of truth, authority and revelation—an understanding found not only in the Bible itself but in the fathers of the church through the ages, particularly in the mainstream of the Protestant Reformation.

· THREE ·

THE MEANING
OF REVELATION

I became a minister according to the divine office which was
given to me for you, to make the word of God fully known,
the mystery hidden for ages and generations but now
made manifest to his saints.
COLOSSIANS 1:25-26

Our senses are so feeble that we could never understand a single
word that God says to us, unless we are illumined by his Holy Spirit;
for carnal men cannot comprehend heavenly things.
JOHN CALVIN

The Word of God is that which shows, impresses,
and brings the mind of God into our hearts.
PHILIPP SPENER

The mere letter in which the promise is put profiteth you nothing;
it is the spirit of the promise; it is the life of the Spirit
running through the veins of the promise that alone can profit you.
CHARLES H. SPURGEON

The Scriptures proceed not by conversion of God's word
into a literature but by taking up of a literature
to be a vehicle of God's word.
C. S. LEWIS

The babble of voices that constitutes modern theology is painfully
evident in the radically different ways people understand revelation. Much of the older Christian tradition interpreted revelation
as a higher form of knowledge that builds on and completes the natural
knowledge of God. In this perspective, which dominated both Catholic
and Protestant scholasticism, revelation is the divine disclosure of information concerning the nature of God and his will and purpose for the

world. It is both rational and propositional and thereby stands in direct continuity with ordinary knowledge. It exceeds the compass of human reason, but it does not contradict the canons of human rationality itself. In the older orthodoxy, which still attracts a considerable following, Scripture is the document of revelation, and its propositions constitute the content of revelation. Carl Henry puts it well: "The Holy Bible is a rational revelation of the nature of God and his will for fallen man."[1]

The concept of revelation has been decisively altered in both neo-Protestant and neo-Catholic theology.[2] In Schleiermacher's theology revelation becomes the communication of the Universe to the sensitive conscience. Elton Trueblood understands revelation as an immediate experience of the divine.[3] For Gregory Baum revelation constitutes a heightened human awareness that enables one to see the world in a new light.[4] Karl Rahner rejects the "purely extrinsic concept of revelation," which conceives it as a divine intervention in human history from the outside. Instead it is "the transcendental experience of the absolute and merciful closeness of God, even if this cannot be conceptually expressed . . . by everyone."[5] Revelation yields not new knowledge but a new consciousness. This mystical outlook is also shared by John Macquarrie, for whom the revelatory experience consists not in entering an I-Thou encounter but in being grasped by the power of being.[6]

In contradistinction to this mystical or experientialist understanding, another group of theologians associates revelation with history. For Wolfhart Pannenberg revelation is the light that is gleaned from the unfolding of universal history. G. Ernest Wright equates revelation with God's mighty deeds in sacred history.[7] Our knowledge of God in this perspective is indirect, for it is the result of faithful reflection on the movement of God in history.

In neo-orthodoxy revelation was interpreted as a divine-human encounter that takes place preeminently in the personal history of Jesus Christ and then in our personal histories insofar as we participate in the life, death and resurrection of Christ. It is not to be reduced to a body of propositions that are directly accessible to human reason; instead it is the action of God disclosing himself to the believing person in conjunction with the hearing of the gospel. The knowledge of revelation is one of personal acquaintance rather than propositional truth. According to Emil Brunner such knowledge is not on a par with general knowledge but "can only be heard and expressed in the form of an I-Thou communication."[8]

Although open to the insights of existentialist and neo-orthodox theologies, I have sought to retain the conceptual character of revelation even while subordinating it to personal self-disclosure. As I see it, revelation is God's self-communication through his selected instrumentality, especially the inspired witness of his prophets and apostles.[9] This act of self-communication entails not only the unveiling of his gracious and at the same time awesome presence but also the imparting of the knowledge of his will and purpose for humankind. This knowledge is conceptual as well as existential and can be formulated but never possessed or mastered in propositions.

I can agree with Thomas Finger when he describes revelation as "always moving, always personally challenging, always overflowing any event or formulation."[10] Even the propositions of the Bible are not yet revelation when they are only "comprehended as cognitive assertions."[11] Revelation is indeed cognitive, but it is much more than this. It is an act of communication by which God confronts the whole person with his redeeming mercy and glorious presence. It therefore involves not only the mind but also the will and affections.

The Word of God is not to be reduced to objective rational statements: it is God in action, God speaking and humans hearing. But this is an inward hearing that itself belongs to the miracle of revelation. As Luther phrased it, "I do not know it and do not understand it, but sounding from above and ringing in my ears I hear what is beyond the thought of man."[12]

My position stands in continuity with that of the Reformers as well as that of modern theologians like Barth and Brunner. It seeks to do justice to both the dynamic character of revelation and its intelligible character. For Calvin the Word of God was not essentially a propositional formula but "the hand of God stretching itself out to act powerfully through the apostle in every way,"[13] indeed a "violent force" that "urges us . . . to give obedience to it."[14] Revelation is being grasped by the power of the resurrected Christ and set in a completely new direction.

Revelation as Truth and Event

In the Scriptures revelation is truth and event at the same time. It is not static truth but truth that happens, truth that creates. In Second Isaiah we read: "Things now past I once revealed long ago, they went out from my mouth and I proclaimed them; then suddenly I acted and they happened" (Is 48:3 JB). In the Old Testament the word uttered by God (Hebrew *dabar*) can mean both word and act. It is a word filled with meaning and power: "He sends out His command to the earth; His word runs very swiftly" (Ps 147:15 NKJ; cf. Is 9:8).

Revelation is a "meeting" between God and the believer whereby God speaks and we hear. The "spoken word" is a metaphor containing two elements: personal encounter and the impartation of knowledge. The Hebrew word *galah* is used to refer both to God's self-manifestation and the communication of his message. In the New Testament revelation is both unveiling (Greek *apokalypsis*) and manifestation *(phaneroō, phanerōsis)*. It is also associated with *epiphaneia,* which denotes the appearance of divinity in earthly history. Revelation entails both divine presence and divine meaning.

God speaks directly and indirectly in the Bible. He speaks in pivotal events in history but occasionally directly to people in dreams and visions. He also speaks in the human conscience, and thus we find God within as well as without. I do not agree with Pannenberg, who denies a "direct self-revelation of God." What he upholds is "an indirect self-revelation in the mirror of his historical actions."[15]

History is the occasion, not the source of revelation. But history also furnishes the ingredients of revelation. The events of sacred history are not simply the medium of revelation but the material of revelation (Kenneth Hamilton). The content of what is revealed is not an ineffable experience of a transphenomenal reality but the divine significance of actual happenings in history.

The event of revelation has two poles: the historical and the experiential. Revelation is God speaking and the human being responding through the power of God's Spirit. God speaks not only in the Bible but also in the human heart. Revelation is the conjunction of divine revealing action and human response. The external knowledge of Scripture is united with the internal knowledge given by the Holy Spirit. When God pierces us with the arrows of his love, we carry his words thrust deep into our inner being.[16] Revelation occurs when the same Spirit who spoke by the mouth of the prophets and apostles finds entry into our hearts, convincing us that "they rendered faithfully what they had been told to say by God."[17]

Revelation happened in a final and definitive form in the apostolic encounter with Jesus Christ. But revelation happens again and again in the experience of the Spirit of Christ. We might say that "God's self-revelation is completed *in* the knowledge that we have of Him."[18]

Revelation focuses on Jesus Christ, but this decisive event was not isolated. It presupposes a revelatory history, which was a preparation for it and in which it was received. This is the "sacred history" that the Bible mirrors. It is possible therefore to speak of cumulative revelation and levels of revelation. The climax of revelation is the historical Jesus Christ, but some light concerning Christ was already given to the patriarchs and prophets of Israel.

Does revelation have a determinative or conceptual content? The fashion in modern theology is to empty revelation of its conceptual or rational element, to portray it as an absolute mystery that overwhelms rather than enlightens the believer. According to Schleiermacher, "Ideas and principles are all foreign to religion."[19] William Temple's aphorism, "Revelation is not in propositions, but in events," has become a cliché in much contemporary theology.[20] Revelation is sometimes reduced to an I-Thou encounter, which indicates a confrontation of wills rather than an impartation of knowledge. Martin Buber said: "Man receives, and he receives not a specific 'content' but a Presence, a Presence as power."[21] Otto Weber concludes that " 'truth' and 'revelation' are not to be understood so much noetically as factually and existentially."[22] For Bultmann the definitive point was that the Word of God is "an event in time—not that it conveys eternal truth."[23] Revelation, he claimed, is in the subjective understanding rather than in objective history. We are given a new self-understanding, not knowledge of the will and purpose of God.[24] Similarly, Tillich contended that "no definition of the contents of revelation is possible."[25] This same existentialist orientation is found in Ernst Fuchs, for whom revelation is a language event that involves not the communication of concepts but a call to action.[26]

Revelation is indeed an act, but is it not also a truth, *the* truth—about God and the world as well as about ourselves?[27] We are told that "grace and truth came through Jesus Christ" (Jn 1:17). Revelation certainly takes the form of encounter, but it includes knowledge of the significance of this encounter. It is the speech of God as well as the act of God. It is a *datum* (information) as well as a *dandum* (event). Calvin described Christ as being "clothed with his promises." In the words of the Westminster Confession: "It has pleased God to reveal Himself and to declare His will unto the Church" (1.1), this will being identified by the Reformers as the law and the gospel. What is revealed is not simply the radiance and power of the gospel but the *message* of the gospel.

I maintain that there is a built-in interpretation of the truth of faith within the Bible that is normative for us. This knowledge is not a comprehension of the totality of things, as in idealism, but a concrete understanding of a unique and definite occurrence.[28] The Bible describes it as a secret wisdom available only to people of faith, a wisdom or knowledge that has a particular content (1 Cor 2:6-7; Rom 11:33; Eph 1:17; Jas 3:17; 2 Pet 3:15). It is not simply the state of being grasped by the power of being (Tillich) but an illumination that enables the mind to discern specific truths revealed by God.

Yet the law and the gospel cannot be equated with objective propositions either in the creeds of the church or in Holy Scripture. They indicate the divinely given meaning of these propositions, a meaning that is never at the disposal of natural reason. To be sure, the divine promise and the divine command come to us through objective statements and words. But they always connote much more than a surface understanding of the text in question. These objective statements are not themselves revelation but the vehicle and outcome of revelation.

The propositions in the Bible are the result of revelation, the concrete embodiment of revelation. I agree with Bernard Ramm that the phrase *propositional revelation* is ambiguous, because revelation comes to us in a myriad of literary forms.[29] Yet I subscribe to the intent of this phrase—that revelation is intelligible and conceptual. It is more felicitous to say with Thomas F. Torrance that revelation is "dialogical," for this term combines the personal and the propositional.

The Word of God exists for us only when God is actually speaking and we are actually receiving his Word. Hans Urs von Balthasar puts it well: "What God says to us is his truth, not ours; it becomes ours only when he utters and gives it us, and we conform to it. For that reason it becomes a judgment on us in so far as we do not submit to God but rebel against him."[30]

God's revelation is his commandment and his promise, and these come to us in the form of written commandments and written testimonies. Yet they cannot be confined to what is objectively written, since their meaning-content includes their significance for those who hear God's Word in every new situation.

God's Word is absolute, but when it is appropriated and formulated by us it becomes relative. Our understanding and interpretation are only approximations of the Word of God. This is also true of the prophetic and apostolic interpretation in the Bible. Human beings even as people of faith can never claim to have the absolute or synoptic perspective, but they can claim to know the One who is himself the fount and ground of all meaning. This does not mean that we necessarily have a mistaken view of God's purposes—only that we have an incomplete view. We cannot hold the Word of God in our hands or in our minds, but God can enter our minds and unite his action with our action. He is not an objectified datum generally available to human understanding, but he can make himself an object for our understanding (Barth) so that we can really know and thereby truly believe, even though we cannot fully comprehend.

Interpretations of the Word of God can be handed down by the church from one generation to another, but none of us can actually know the Word of God until God personally reveals himself to us. When God speaks we will know it, for his word is "living and active, sharper than any two-edged sword" (Heb 4:12). The knowledge of God's Word is never merely conceptual knowledge but also existential knowledge. It is a knowledge more of the heart than of the head, more of the affection than of the intellect (Calvin).[31] It is a knowledge that causes men and women to tremble (cf. Is 66:2; Jer 23:9). It reduces the human being to nothingness but at the same time fills the person of faith with assurance and joy so that a new life is possible. It brings people freedom not to realize themselves along an ego-building trail of self-deception but to realize a holy vocation of being witnesses and ambassadors of our Lord Jesus Christ.

The knowledge of God given in revelation has many sides. It is conceptual because it enlightens our mind concerning the nature and purpose of God. It is existential because it affects the whole of human existence. It is personal because it involves a dialogue between two subjects. It is spiritual because it opens our inner eyes to a transcendent dimension of reality.

The knowledge of God is never ours until we are confronted by the creative, transforming power of God that seizes us and points us in a new direction. The psalmist graphically describes the encounter with divine reality: "Deep calls to deep at the sound of Thy waterfalls; All Thy breakers and Thy waves have rolled over me" (Ps 42:7 NASB). This knowledge is so wonderful that it is beyond our grasp; we can never reach it by our own power or exertion (Ps 139:6). Yet it can break into our lives from the beyond and become ours if only for a moment, but then we must seek for it again and again. Faith does not simply rest on understanding but strives for an ever greater understanding, even though acutely aware that the full picture of reality can never be ours on this side of death.

Existentialist theology can be appreciated for its critique of a rationalism that claims to know too much about God and the world. Yet existentialism leads directly into agnosticism and finally into atheism if it severs itself completely from essentialism, that is, from the hope of knowing reality in itself. Tillich maintained that "there cannot be a truth in human minds which is divine truth in itself."[32] For both Tillich and Bultmann God can never become an object for human knowledge and action, since this would make faith conceptual. They failed to see that God, though hidden from human perception, can nevertheless impress his truth on our minds. We cannot objectify God, but God can objectify himself and thereby make his truth available to us.

Revelation in history is only partial and fragmentary. People of faith look forward to the vision of God beyond history when we shall know even as we are known. Indeed, revelation in the biblical sense has an unmistakable eschatological thrust. The prophet is told: "Write down the revelation and make it plain on tablets so that a herald may run with it. For the revelation awaits an appointed time; it speaks of the end and will not prove false" (Hab 2:2-3 NIV; cf. Hos 2:19ff.; Jer 31:31ff.). Revelation refers to that future event when God fully discloses himself in judgment and salvation (cf. Rom 8:18-19; 1 Cor 3:13; 1 Pet 1:5).

Torrance powerfully enunciates the eschatological character of revelation:

> While God has made His Word audible and apprehensible with our human speech and thought, refusing to be limited by their inadequacy in making Himself known to us, He nevertheless refuses to be understood merely from within the conceptual framework of our natural thought and language but demands of that framework a logical reconstruction in accordance with His Word. Hence a theology faithful to what God has revealed and done in Jesus Christ must

involve a powerful element of apocalyptic, that is epistemologically speaking, an eschatological suspension of logical form in order to keep our thought ever open to what is radically new.[33]

Torrance goes on to contend that "the concrete universal cannot be netted by empirical means, any more than it can be caught through the analytical methods of formal logic."[34] Christ must break into our reasoning processes and remold them if we are ever to begin to know him as he knows us.

The full meaning and impact of the Word made flesh, of God becoming mortal in human history, is veiled not only to the natural understanding but also to the understanding of faith and awaits a new disclosure by God at the end of history. Now we walk by faith as pilgrims seeking a homeland. We have sufficient light to take us through this present darkness, but we will not know as we are known until the day of redemption, when the realities of the kingdom of God will be revealed to the whole world. This kingdom, which is now invisible, will become visible for all to see: faith will be taken up into sight, understanding will become knowledge, hope will be translated into joy.

Because revelation in its fullness lies at the very end of history, some theologians prefer to speak of *revealing* truths in the Bible rather than *revealed* truths (Gabriel Fackre). That is, light in its fullness eludes us, but the Bible can give us more light than we already possess. The truths of revelation are not the final truth, but they open us to the final truth, they give us a glimpse of the transcendent beyond history. I can empathize with this position, for I am acutely conscious of the relativity of all truth that has a historical and cultural matrix. Yet we must not surrender the claim of Christian faith that in the Bible we are presented with real truth, with truth that is absolute and unconditional because it is God's truth. Against evangelical rationalism, however, I maintain that we mortals can know this truth only conditionally and relatively. Theology is not "the crystallization of divine truth into systematic form,"[35] but a very human witness to divine truth, a witness that remains tentative and open-ended because historical understanding is not transcendent knowledge, faith is not sight. The truth in the Bible is revealed because it has a divine source, but it is at the same time partial and broken because it has a historical matrix. It throws light on the human situation, but light that is adequate only for our salvation and the living of a righteous life, not for comprehensive understanding. As biblical Christians we are neither gnostics (fully enlightened) nor agnostics but pilgrims who nevertheless have a compass (the Word of God) that can guide us to our destination.

Revelation and the Bible

The paramount question in discussions on divine revelation is, How is revelation related to the Bible? In my perspective the original reception of revelation is a component part of revelation. The biblical writers and their writings participated in the event of revelation. Yet revelation is not to be equated with the objective verbal representation of this reception. It is the difference between "thought-in-encounter" and "thinking-about-it" (Brunner).[36]

We need to acknowledge that the Holy Spirit guided the prophets in their reflection, but their articulation of this reflection is at least one step removed from the revelation itself. Their witness points to revelation, but it also mediates revelation, since the Spirit acts through the persons and words that he inspires.

The content of the Bible is indeed God's self-revelation in Jesus Christ, but this content comes to us in the form of a historical witness to this event or constellation of events. To know this content we need to get beyond "the right human thoughts about God" to "the right divine thoughts about men" (Barth).[37]

The biblical witness is binding because the prophets and apostles were ear- and eyewitnesses to what God did for us in the sacred history culminating in Jesus Christ. Moreover, these persons were guided by the Holy Spirit in their reflection and in their writing, and their writings now function as the vehicle of the Holy Spirit.

In our reading of the Bible and in our hearing of the biblical message, we become, through the miraculous action of the Holy Spirit, contemporaneous with the moment of revelation. We experience the power and impact of the gospel directly through the word that we hear. In another sense, however, our experience of Jesus Christ is indirect, since it is mediated through the outward means of preaching and hearing.

The Bible is not in and of itself the revelation of God but the divinely appointed means and channel of this revelation. It comprises the sacred writings that give us "the wisdom that leads to salvation through faith which is in Jesus Christ" (2 Tim 3:15 NASB). In Paul's epistle to the Romans, "the revelation of the mystery" of the gospel is clearly distinguished from "the prophetic Scriptures" through which this mystery is made known (Rom 16:25-26 NKJ). In Colossians the mystery that constitutes the Word of God is identified with "Christ in you, the hope of glory" (1:25-27). The distinction between the Word of God and the words of Scripture is also evident in Psalm 119:18 (GNB): "Open my eyes, so that I may see the wonderful truths in your law."

The Word of God transcends the human witness, and yet it comes to us only in the servant form of the human word. God's Word is not a spiritual idea or ideal of which the human word is only a sign. Maximus the Confessor betrayed a Platonic thrust when he distinguished between the "spirit" and the "flesh" of Scripture and then advocated abandoning what is corruptible and cleaving to that which is wholly incorruptible.[38]

There is indeed an inseparable connection between the revealed Word of God or the "mind of Christ" and the Bible. We can even speak of a unity or identity of witness and revelation, but it is an indirect identity, not a property of the witness but a matter of divine grace. I hold that the Word of God or the truth of revelation is embedded in Scripture because Scripture is encompassed by the presence of the Spirit of Christ. It is possible to argue that there is a direct identity between the substance or matter of the Bible and the transcendent Word and an indirect identity between the letter *(gramma)* and the Word. There is an inseparable relation but not an absolute identity between God's Word and the scriptural witness (cf. Ex 4:14-16; Ps 139:6; 1 Pet 1:10; 1 Cor 7:12, 25).

When the letter is separated from the Spirit who brings us life and salvation, it becomes a written code that kills (2 Cor 3:6).

Barth argued cogently that while there is not an *identity* or *coalescence* between the written Word of God and the revealed Word (as in a major strand of Protestant orthodoxy), there is nevertheless a *correspondence* by virtue of the inspiring work of the Spirit. Yet this correspondence is imperceptible to reason; it can be grasped only by faith. My own preference is to speak of a *conjunction* between the Word of God and sacred Scripture by the action of the Spirit. What we hear is not simply an echo or reverberation of the Word of God but the very Word of God who speaks in and with the biblical preacher—not by necessity but by an act of free grace.

The scriptural writings are not stenographic notes of God's audible voice. They constitute a human witness that becomes at the same time a divine witness through the revealing action of God on the writers, the writings and the readers. It is possible to read the Scriptures, even memorize them, and still fail to perceive the mystery of God's self-revelation in Jesus Christ (Jn 5:39).

If we make an absolute identity between the words of the Bible and the Word of God, then every command in Scripture becomes a universal or absolute command. We would then have divine sanction to put witches to death (cf. Ex 22:18). I cannot accept James Packer's view that "the biblical writers' thoughts" are, "strictly and precisely, the communicated thoughts of God."[39] Not every idea expressed in Scripture is the "mind of Christ," but every idea can become the vehicle of the mind of Christ.

The Bible is an instrumental norm for faith but not an absolute norm. Yet it is a real norm and not one that can be summarily dismissed. It communicates binding truth but truth that is not at our disposal. I reject the position of Auguste Sabatier: "As soon as the distinction is made in our consciousness between the word of God and the letter of holy Scripture, the first becomes independent of all human form and of all external guarantee."[40] This may be true for some theologians, but to hold to it in an absolute fashion manifestly contradicts the wisdom of the Reformers as well as the fathers of the church.

The proclamation of the church is likewise an instrumental norm and must be distinguished from the Word of God itself. Yet the sermonic witness, if it is grounded in Scripture, is inseparable from the Word of God. Paul rejoiced that when the Thessalonians received the Word of God, they accepted it "not as the word of men but as what it really is, the word of God, which is at work in you believers" (1 Thess 2:13). In 1 Peter 1:25 "the good news which was preached to you" is identified with the Word of God. The Second Helvetic Confession is unequivocal: "The preaching of the Word of God is the Word of God" (chap. 1).[41] The sermon is distinct from the Word but inseparably connected with it.

One might say that the Bible is the Word of God in a formal sense— as a light bulb is related to light. The light bulb is not itself the light but its medium. The light of God's truth is ordinarily shining in the Bible, but it is discerned only by the eyes of faith. Even Christians, however, do not see the light in its full splendor. It is refracted and obscured by the form of the Bible, but it nonetheless reaches us if we have faith.

Warfield gave the helpful illustration of light (the divine Word) filtering through a stained-glass window in a cathedral.[42] I wish to carry it further. I see the light of the sun illuminating the biblical figures or pictures on the window. But these pictures are also flawed by blemishes and shadows, reminding us of their participation in the real world of decay and death. It is up to the biblical exegete to distinguish between the overall picture or story and markings that are only incidental to this story.

Some conservatives (for example, John Warwick Montgomery), trying to show the inseparable unity of the Bible and revelation, have seized on Marshall McLuhan's dictum that the medium is the message. The medium is indeed part of the message, but it is an instrument, not the source, of the message. I hold that the message of revelation is explicit in some parts of the Bible and implicit in others. All parts bear witness to it, for there is nothing superfluous in the Bible, as even Schleiermacher acknowledged on rare occasions.

Yet our final authority is not what the Bible says but what God says in the Bible. To be sure, God says what his witnesses say, but he says much more. Indeed, some things that his witnesses say fall short of the full picture that God invites us to see (cf. 1 Pet 1:10-11).

This point is made poignantly clear by Gregory of Nyssa:

I have heard the Divinely inspired Scriptures disclose marvellous things about the transcendent Nature—yet what are they compared with that Nature Itself? For even if I were capable of grasping all that the Scripture says, yet that which is signified is more. . . . So it is also with the words said about God in Holy Scripture, which are expounded to us by men inspired by the Holy Spirit. If measured by our understanding, they are indeed exalted above all greatness; yet they do not reach the majesty of the truth.[43]

The qualitative transcendence of divine truth over the earthen vessels by which it is made known was an abiding theme of the magisterial Reformers. Calvin often described the Word of God as the heavenly doctrine of Scripture, and Scripture as the garment in which Christ comes to us. Indeed, "the highest proof of Scripture derives in general from the fact that God in person speaks in it."[44] Luther made a distinction between the inner and outer word: the latter is the Scripture and the former the revelation of Christ. Thus the Bible is the cradle wherein Christ is laid and the swaddling clothes in which Christ is wrapped. Or the Word of God is the water that comes to us through the pipes (the written witness). For Heinrich Bullinger it is the teaching of the apostles that "is the doctrine of God and the very true word of God."[45] Scripture, he said, is called the Word of God not because of the printed letter or the human voice that can be comprehended by the flesh but "because the meaning, which speaks through the human voice or is written with pen and ink on paper, is not originally from men, but is God's word, will and meaning."[46]

Many Anabaptists also drew this distinction between the Word of God and the Bible. Hans Denck wrote in 1528: "I hold Holy Scripture above all human treasures, but not so high as the Word of God, which is living, powerful and eternal; . . . for it is as God himself is, Spirit and not letter."[47] Eberhard Arnold, founder of the Bruderhof, depicted the Word of God as living before the Bible was even written.[48]

This critical demarcation between spirit and letter is also characteristic of the Puritans and Pietists. Richard Sibbes regarded "the word of God" as "ancienter than the Scripture," which is "but that *modus,* that manner of conveying the word of God."[49] According to John Goodwin, Christian faith is based not on any book or books but on the gracious counsels of God concerning the salvation of the world by Jesus Christ, "which indeed are represented and declared both in Translations and Originals, but are essentially distinct . . . from both."[50] For Philipp Spener, the luminary of German Pietism, the Bible contains an outer word (the printed page) and an inner Word (the understanding given by the Holy Spirit).[51] "The Word of God is that which shows, impresses, and brings the mind of Christ into our hearts."[52] Similarly, Charles Spurgeon cautioned that the mere letter in which the promise is put profits us nothing: "it is the spirit of the promise; it is the life of the Spirit running through the veins of the promise that alone can profit you."[53]

For Jonathan Edwards "God's Word is really *God's* Word when it is accompanied by the Spirit dwelling in the human heart; when unaccompanied by the Spirit it is simply another natural, human word."[54] In his view the human words of Scripture effect faith not by their own power but by a divine cause operative in them.

Accepting Scripture both as the Word of God and as the carrier and vehicle of the Word, Abraham Kuyper, nineteenth-century Dutch Calvinist evangelical, placed the accent on its instrumental character. His break with rationalism was decisive: "At no single point of the way is there place . . . for a support derived from demonstration or reasoning."[55] He spoke of the inspiration of the biblical writers and the content of their witness but disclaimed the magical rendition of sentences. He was critical of both subjectivistic Pietism and barren scholastic orthodoxy. The latter lost sight of the fact that "the inspiring motive for theology must always come from the subject."[56]

This same reluctance to identify Scripture and the Word of God was discernible in the evangelical Holiness preacher Joseph Smith. According to Delbert Rose,

> Smith cautiously distinguished between the Word of God and the Scriptures. The Word of God existed prior to and in some instances apart from the Scripture for centuries, and even Jesus' words . . . were not in written form at first. . . . Having the *body* of Scripture without the Spirit who inspired them is to be without the Word of God. To have the Word of God one must have both the letter of Scripture and the living Spirit illuminating that letter to the believing mind.[57]

One can see that Barth's typology of the three forms of the Word of God—the living Word, the written Word and the proclaimed Word—rests on solid Christian and evangelical tradition. This very distinction originated during the Reformation with Bullinger.[58] Barth insisted that only when the written or proclaimed word is united with the revealed Word does it become revelation. At the same time he affirmed something like a perichoresis between the forms of the Word of God, for the living Word, Jesus Christ, encompasses both Scripture and the sermon based on Scripture.[59] As I have indicated in a previous volume, this typology should be extended to include the inner word, the voice of conscience, for this too when united with Jesus Christ becomes an infallible criterion for faith and practice.[60]

With considerable acumen George Eldon Ladd defined revelation as an event plus the inspired interpretation.[61] My one criticism is that he left out the third necessary ingredient: inward illumination. Revelation has three facets: historical, propositional and experiential. The culmination of revelation, says Daniel Stevick, "is not a book but a believing person, not sentences but the new society in Christ."[62] Revelation reaches its goal in the life history of the reader and hearer. There is no revelation apart from the incarnate Word and the written Word. But likewise revelation does not exist unless the Holy Spirit brings the meaning and impact of this Word to bear on human beings, and this means the creation of a holy community—the fellowship of love.

The Bible is both the revelation and the means and bearer of revelation. It is revelation cast in written form and the original witness to revelation.[63] It is a component of revelation and a vehicle of revelation. It objectively contains revelation in the sense that its witness is based on revelation, but it becomes revelation for us only in the moment of decision, in the awakening to faith. Scripture is not simply a pointer to revelation (as Torrance sometimes describes it) but a carrier of revelation. Scripture is the mediate source of revelation, but only Jesus Christ is the original or eternal source.

Truth and Error in Protestant Orthodoxy

Protestant orthodoxy signified a valiant attempt to conserve the truths rediscovered in the Reformation by bringing philosophical resources to the aid of faith. Already in the sixteenth century Philipp Melanchthon tried to show that Aristotle could help the Christian articulate the formative principles of faith and ethics. In his *Apology of the Augsburg Confession* Melanchthon declared that "Aristotle wrote concerning civil morals so learnedly that nothing further concerning this need be demanded."[64] In sixteenth-century orthodoxy, reason was still for the most part subordinated to revelation. In the seventeenth century reason acquired growing importance as an instrument for interpreting scriptural truth. It was never the primary norm, but it now functioned as a secondary norm. In the eighteenth century it became an independent norm for many theologians.

While trying to remain true to *sola Scriptura,* Protestant orthodoxy could at the same time seek rational and empirical supports for faith. The Bible and human reason came to function as dual authorities for the Christian. The certainty of faith was transposed into an intellectual certainty. The witness of the Spirit in our hearts was not enough: evidence was garnered to show that the affirmations of Scripture corresponded to reality. Faith was presented in a manner calculated to appeal "to the mind's desire for symmetry, harmony, and comprehensiveness."[65] Method in theological thinking bore the unmistakable imprint of Descartes and Leibniz: certainty came to be contingent on clarity and precision.[66] The proofs for the existence of God, the plausibility of the biblical miracles and the trustworthiness of the biblical narratives were all elevated into prominence in theology.[67]

A rationalistic thrust had already appeared in Calvin, who saw miracles and prophecy as giving confirmation to the truth of the gospel. He also appealed to reason as well as to Scripture, even claiming that "the Lord has instituted nothing that is at variance with reason."[68] This did not prevent him from recognizing that reason in its fallen state is misdirected and cannot prepare the way for faith. Only when we exceed the capacity of our understanding and rise above ourselves can we apprehend the truth of faith.[69] "In regard to divine truth . . . human discernment is so defective and lost that the first step of advancement in the school of Christ is to renounce it."[70]

Luther could also appeal to natural wisdom, though his main emphasis was on revealed wisdom. Human beings in their fallen state can know something of the moral law of God, even have a sense of the power and holiness of God, but this knowledge only makes them ripe for idolatry. For both Reformers the natural knowledge of God renders us inexcusable before God; it does not prepare the way for faith.

On the whole, Protestant orthodoxy did not naively equate the Bible and revelation, though its language sometimes left this impression.[71] Some theologians distinguished between the external *forma* (the letter of Scripture) and the internal *forma* (the gospel).[72] Similarly, a distinction was drawn between the form and matter of the Bible, the first indicating the writing or *gramma* of Scripture and the second the saving message of Christ.[73] Due acknowledgment was often given to the ineradicable gulf between God's own wisdom *(theologia archetypa)* and the human or earthly reflection of this wisdom *(theologia ektypa)*.[74] Orthodox theologians also differentiated between the historical and normative authority of Scripture. Only that which Scripture commands and proclaims has normative authority. What is described as having happened in history has historical authority.

For the mainstream of Protestant orthodoxy the Bible is the *norma normans non normata*. It judges tradition but cannot be judged by tradition. Here the later theologians were entirely in conformity with the. Reformers. Yet they still tended to equate the Bible as a book with revelation. This view was less evident in the early stages of Reformed orthodoxy, which generally used "the Word of God" in a wider sense than simply the Scriptures to indicate, according to Heinrich Heppe, "all that God had spoken to the fathers in diverse ways and in latter times by his Son."[75] Later orthodoxy came to see the Bible as a transcript from God, thus detracting from the mystery of revelation.

Although a static concept of revelation gradually gained predominance over a dynamic concept, this was not true for all of orthodoxy. Matthias Flacius Illyricus (d. 1575) posited a *Sache* or content that constitutes the heart and center of Scripture and for the sake of which Scripture exists.[76] David Hollaz distinguished between what God has revealed (the absolute principle) and the scriptural witness to this (the relative principle).[77] Francis Turretin identified revelation with the divine wisdom to which Scripture directs us.[78] Peter Martyr entertained a similar view.[79]

The mainstream of Protestant orthodoxy from the sixteenth to the eighteenth century generally held to the correlation of Spirit and Word. At the same time, it was customary to see the Bible as the source of revealed truth and the Spirit as the instrument by which this truth is known. Calvin maintained that the Spirit of God is himself the source of revealed truth and the Bible the instrument by which the Spirit makes it known. Interestingly Charles Hodge contended in the first chapter of his *Systematic Theology* that the Holy Spirit's role is limited to the application of the rule of faith, not to the shaping of this rule.[80]

In the later orthodoxy (eighteenth-twentieth centuries), which fuses into modern fundamentalism, the rationalist note becomes still more evident. The spirit of Enlightenment rationalism was readily apparent in Jean-Alphonse Turretin (d. 1737), who never used the phrase *testi-*

monium Spiritus Sancti, insisting that any reasonable person could be convinced of the divine origin of Scripture by objective proofs.[81] Warfield described revelation as "the correlate of understanding" having "as its proximate end . . . the production of knowledge."[82] Gordon Clark does not hesitate to speak of "verbal revelation"; his adherence to innate ideas is incontestably closer to the Age of Reason than to the Reformation.[83] According to William Shedd, theology aims for a knowledge that is "free from contradictions."[84] In Bernard Ramm's judgment, the modern evangelical stress on propositional revelation is another version of Hegel's myth of pure language, which eliminates any distance between a concept in the mind and spoken words.[85]

This kind of rationalism stands in patent contradiction to Calvin's description of the relation of faith and reason:

> The Gospel towers over the insight of the human mind so that those who are considered intellectually of the first rank may look as high as they like, but they never reach its eminence. . . . The duller the human mind is for understanding the mysteries of God, and the greater its uncertainty, the surer is our faith, which is supported by the revelation of the Spirit of God.[86]

Barth gave this astute critique of later Protestant orthodoxy:

> The earnestness and zeal of the study now quite newly devoted to the Bible hardly needs stressing; it should, however, also be noted that it was not so much a case of man being open to the Bible as of the Bible having to be open to men at any price; man did not so much allow the Bible to be master as think that he should and could obtain quite definite instructions, powers and blessings from it.[87]

Against later orthodoxy and fundamentalism, I hold that the words of the Bible are revelatory but not revealed; they conform to the revelation and convey the revelation through the Spirit. The propositions in the Bible are the result of revelation, the concrete embodiment of revelation and the vehicle of revelation. I agree with Küng that propositions of faith are not directly God's word but "at best God's word attested and mediated by man's word: perceptible and transmissible by human propositions."[88] We do not hold to faith in propositions but to propositions of faith.

In fundamentalism "revelation is turned into a thing, an object, a thing-in-itself; it is packaged, externalized—'inscripturated.' "[89] A. W. Tozer was severely critical of those who teach that "if you learn the text you've got the truth."[90] They "see no beyond and no mystic depth, no mysterious heights, nothing supernatural or divine. . . . They have the text and the code and the creed, and to them that is the truth."[91]

Rationalistic orthodoxy fails to grasp the dynamic, inaccessible nature of revelation. God's Word cannot be frozen in the pages of Scripture just as it cannot be packaged or manipulated by the clerics of the church. Our final authority is not the Bible as a book or the Bible in and of itself but the Bible penetrated by the Spirit and discerned by Spirit-filled people.

Revelation does not consist of revealed truths that are objectively "there" in the Bible but rather in God's special act of condescension and the opening of our eyes to the significance of this act. Revelation is not exclusively objective but objective-subjective (cf. Is 53:1; 55:11; Eph 1:18; 2 Pet 1:19-21). Can there be a sound unless there is someone to hear it?

I heartily agree with Carl Henry that God reveals himself not only in acts but also in words. But does God reveal words and statements, and, if so, are they identical with the biblical words? Is there not a qualitative distance between the speech of God and the writing of humans? E. Stanley Jones reminds us that the Word became flesh, not printer's ink. Yet in a secondary sense the Word does also become printer's ink in that the word of truth must be inscribed before it is adequately received in human history. I affirm not only the Word incarnate but the Word inscribed.

We need to hold on to a double truth: the Bible is both God's testimony about himself and the human writers' inspired testimony about God (Sigmund Mowinckel).[92] God becomes incarnate in a person, Jesus Christ, not in words. The Bible is not the incarnate word of God, but it is the document of the revelation of God's word.

Like orthodox Protestants, Roman Catholics are accustomed to speaking of "revealed truths." Modern Protestants prefer to speak of "revelatory events" or of "revealing truths" (Fackre). My preference is to speak of "truths of revelation"—truths that rise out of revelation and therefore presuppose a conceptual content in revelation. If revealed truth, as traditionalists understand it, is equivalent to the meaning of the event, then we have common ground. I do not hold to revealed doctrines, but I can affirm truth that is revealed and that finds itself set in the form of doctrine. The event of the resurrection is virtually the same as the truth of the resurrection, for no event in the Bible is meaningful without an inspired interpretation.

It is important to affirm both the absolute character of God's self-revelation in Christ and the relative (but not necessarily erroneous) character of this revelation as it is articulated and documented in history. I agree with the judgment of Catholic theologian Karl Adam that "even God's supernatural revelation, even all those truths . . . taught us by divine revelation . . . do not enter our consciousness in their original nature . . . but are mediated through human conceptions and notions."[93]

Scripture is one step removed from revelation, and the sermon two steps removed. Yet through the action of the Spirit an analogical relation can be discerned between what the prophets say and what God says. The truth of revelation is objectively present in the Bible, but this truth is the invisible presence of the living Christ, which is veiled by the scriptural words as well as disclosed through them.

Brunner has given the helpful illustration of a phonograph record to make clear the paradoxical relation between the *Sache* or substance of Scripture and the outer form.[94] The voice on the record is the living Christ; the record is the biblical writing. We hear this voice only when we play the record in faith, but we also hear other sounds, background sounds, and we need to distinguish what is essential and what is marginal. Where his analogy breaks down is that the Spirit of God speaks to every person in a slightly different way. God's Word is always new, always specific and concrete.

A. W. Tozer distinguished between the voice of God "which is alive and free" and the written Word of God. It is only the present voice that makes the Bible a living witness to the truth. There must also be no confusion between the kernel of truth and the outward shell.

> The mind can grasp the shell but only the Spirit of God can lay hold of the internal essence. . . . We have forgotten that the essence of spiritual truth cannot come to the one who knows the external shell of truth unless there is first a miraculous operation of the Spirit within the heart.[95]

Later Protestant scholasticism not only veered in the direction of a monophysite doctrine of Scripture but also of a monophysite doctrine of Christ. The humanity of Christ was swallowed up in his divinity. There was a tendency to deny or to downplay the fact that Jesus experienced real temptations or that he was drastically limited in his knowledge of the world and history. The official confessions guarded against monophysitism and the major theologians were alert to this danger, but the danger was nevertheless real.

The Bible has a real humanity as do Jesus Christ and his church, the mystical body of Christ. We cannot posit within history a pure, distilled Word of God, free from all human traces. Ragnar Bring articulates Luther's general position: "Just as Christ was a man with an earthly mother, and lived in a specific time and place, in a concrete environment colored by its time, so also God gave his Word in the Bible in a specific language, in the milieu of a particular time."[96]

According to Bring we should think of the Word of God as being "in, through and under" the words of the Bible.[97] Neither the flesh of Jesus nor the pages of Scripture are to be identified with the very Word of God, but they both embody this Word. The Bible's participation in the truth of divine revelation is analogous to Jesus the man's participation in Christ as God.

The Bible is a truly human book, but it is also a divine book, a truth that has been widely disregarded in Protestant liberalism. Jesus gave the words of the Bible an authority tantamount to his own words: "If you believed Moses, you would believe me, for he wrote of me. But if you do not believe his writings, how will you believe my words?" (Jn 5:46–47).

The Bible participates in the transcendent Word of God—not directly but through the Spirit of God. Jesus participated in the Word of God directly and immediately. Jesus was completely transparent to God, though only to the eyes of faith. The Bible is translucent to God. Jesus was one with the Logos of God; the words of the Bible are one with the Word of God only indirectly. Jesus was and is the Word in and of himself. The biblical writing is the Word of revelation symbolically or indirectly— by the action of the Spirit. This is not to imply that the Bible does not really transmit revelation; on the contrary, it functions as an effectual sign of revelation, as a veritable means of grace, because it is encompassed by the Spirit, who brings the written record to life again and again in the event of the awakening to faith.

We can call the Bible the Word of God for several reasons. First, it brings us a message from God. Its words are the symbols and channels of the revelatory core of meaning that comes from God. Second, it is the inspired witness to revelation: it is the written Word of God. Third, it is the vehicle and carrier of revelation, the source of continuing revelation. Finally, it is the document of the final revelation and by the action of the Spirit participates in this revelation.[98] Form and content penetrate each other in Scripture and cannot be separated (Herman Bavinck). The Bible can be held to embody revelation, for the truth of revelation resides in the Bible.

We must avoid saying that the Bible is partly the Word of God and partly the word of human authors. It is both at the same time. God unites his word with the word of the text and so enables us to hear his very voice in the words of the text. I cannot say with Richard Prust that "man is the author of the words" of Scripture and God is the author of the doctrine.[99] The Bible is both a human witness to revelation and revelation itself through human words.

It is permissible to say that the Bible as the Word of God has two natures—the human and the divine. What is accessible to the natural person is only the human side. The divine side—the content and goal of Scripture—is made available to us through faith by the action of the Spirit. Critical scholarship by itself can do little more than cast light on the Bible as a historical document. Only the Spirit can plumb the depths of the mystery that constitutes the inner unity of the Bible—the mystery of Christ and his gospel.

That the Bible contains a palpably human and therefore culturally conditioned element does not make it any less the Word of God. It is precisely because its word is fully incarnate in history, concrete and specific, that it is the Word of God. The Word of God is not a timeless idea but a historical word with power. The revelational content of Scripture is ultimately derived from God, but it is relayed to us through human language and human interpretation. God has chosen to speak and act through human instrumentality so that his Word has a historical focus as well as an eternal ground.

Dietrich Bonhoeffer expressed well my own position:

> The norm for the Word of God in Scripture is the Word of God itself, and what we possess, reason, conscience, experience, are the materials to which this norm seeks to be applied. We too may say that the Word of God and the word of man are joined in Holy Scripture; but they are joined in such a way that God himself says where his Word is, and he says it through the *word of man*. The word of man does not cease to be a temporal, past word by becoming the Word of God; it is the Word of God precisely as such a historical temporal word.[100]

Yet the Word of God is not the text itself but the divinely intended meaning of the text. This meaning is hidden in the text or, better, in the context of wider Scripture. The Word of God is the eternal wisdom of God—not to be equated with human wisdom, which is also reflected in the Bible. The wisdom of God can only be spiritually discerned (1 Cor 2:14). The text is naturally discerned. Yet it is only in and through the text that we receive the spiritual wisdom from above.

For Luther the Word of God is both more broad and more narrow than the Bible. It is more broad because the voice of Christ cannot be restricted to the Bible. Moreover, we hear this voice better through preaching than reading. It is more narrow because not all parts of the Bible portray Christ. When Luther uses "the Word of God" in the broad sense to include the law, then the Bible becomes virtually equivalent to the Word.

The Bible is a revelation not only of God's person but of God's truth. Revelation is therefore both personal and propositional, or, better, dialogical—reminding us that we are dealing with an encounter of minds as well as of wills. The Word is both personal address and idea. It is not a timeless truth or an eternal idea in the Platonic sense but an incarnate idea, a word in history. It is both the action of God and the language of God. But the language of God is hidden and veiled as well as disclosed in the human language of the Bible.

We must not say with Protestant liberals that the human language of Scripture is "reformable" in the sense of being capable of correction. But we can say that it is "reformable" in the sense of being clarified or restated. Yet our efforts to expound and clarify must never be divorced from the biblical language. We must return again and again to the language of Canaan if our clarifications are to be consistent with the original meaning given in Scripture.

Protestant orthodoxy reduces the revelatory event to the biblical witness. Existentialist theology abstracts the event of revelation from the biblical witness. My criterion is not only the event but also the biblical interpretation of this event. Yet this interpretation is not immediately accessible to us in the pages of Scripture. What is perceptible to the eyes of the scholar is conflicting or diverging interpretations. The overall interpretation, which is there implicit in the Bible (explicit in parts of the Bible), is a gift of the Spirit. The key to the true interpretation is the Holy Spirit.

The fundamentalist error is to restrict the Word of God to the Bible. The neo-orthodox error is to imply that the Word of God has only an accidental relation to the Bible by virtue of the fact that God time and again speaks through it. The reconstituted, critical orthodoxy that I am expounding views the Word as inseparable from the Bible, as its ground and goal. The Bible is reconceived as the divinely appointed means by which God makes his Word known to the church in every age.

Revelation in Nature and History

Is there a revelation of God in nature? Yes, but only the one who believes perceives it as revelation. The natural person misunderstands it. Fallen humanity has a general awareness of God but not a true understanding. Such knowledge is sufficient to condemn but not to save. Such people know only the wrath of God, not the love of God. Natural theology is a blind alley because it is based on a knowledge that is deceptive and distorted. Yet a theology of creation is mandatory. Once we are enlightened by the Spirit of God, we can perceive the refracted light of the glory of God in his creation. Instead of a general revelation that can furnish the groundwork for special revelation, it is more biblical to speak of a universal reflection of God in nature that only those standing within the circle of faith can appreciate.

Modern evangelicalism betrays its indebtedness to the Enlightenment by positing a general revelation that frequently forms the basis for a natural theology. In this perspective, revelation is wholly objective and static rather than objective-subjective and dynamic. Millard Erickson illustrates this position: "God has given us an objective, valid, rational revelation of himself in nature, history, and human personality. It is there for anyone who wants to observe it. Regardless of whether anyone actually observes it, understands it, and believes it, it is nonetheless . . . objectively present."[101] Erickson is enough of a Calvinist, however, to be convinced that human sin prevents such a revelation from setting us on the road to salvation.[102] Nonetheless, his rationalism is apparent in his tacit endorsement of the view that even the resurrection of Jesus Christ "can be proved by reason, just as any other fact of history."[103]

In most of the twentieth century the emphasis has been on divine

revelation in history. This is true of neo-orthodox theologians like Reinhold Niebuhr and Oscar Cullmann, neoliberals like William Temple and
Wolfhart Pannenberg, and neofundamentalists like John Warwick Montgomery. Whereas biblical theologians like G. Ernest Wright referred to
the mighty deeds of God in history,[104] Pannenberg appeals to the revelation of God in universal history.[105]

While history is indeed the locus of God's revealing action, we must
be careful not to view history as the source of our knowledge of God.
History is not the basis of divine truth but the occasion or medium by
which this truth is known. Faith has its immediate roots in history, but
its ultimate roots are in eternity. We must not say with Pannenberg and
Gordon Kaufman that the ultimate arbiter of theological validity is the
movement of history itself.[106] This could mean that particular history
will be interpreted in the light of universal history. In my perspective all
of history can be adequately understood only from the vantage point of
eternity, which breaks into history at one particular point or series of
points—the events leading up to and culminating in Jesus Christ.

Historical knowledge of the human Jesus is not sufficient to yield the
revelational meaning of his life and work. When Peter confessed Jesus
as the Son of God, his Lord replied: "Flesh and blood has not revealed
this to you, but my Father who is in heaven" (Mt 16:17).

Christian faith is thoroughly historical, for the revelation of God takes
place in a particular history, but it is much more than historical. It
signifies the illumination of both history and nature from the vantage
point of eternity. I cannot agree with Pannenberg, who maintains that
history is the foundation of faith and not simply the condition for faith.
Barth had these cautionary words: "Whoever says history is not yet
saying revelation, nor Word of God as the Reformers called the Bible,
nor the subject to which man must submit himself with no possibility
of becoming its master."[107]

If faith is severed from history we could end in idealism or mysticism.
If faith is grounded in history we could end in relativism or naturalism.
Divine actuality and historical facticity need to be united in our contin-

uing inquiry concerning the fact of Jesus Christ (Thomas F. Torrance), but they must never be confused with one another.

Revelation and Reason

The enigmatic relationship between revelation and reason revolves around a number of questions. Is there a point of contact between revelation and reason, God and humanity? Is God the Wholly Other or the ground and depth of humanity? Does revelation fulfill or supplement human reason, or does it abrogate reason? Does grace fulfill or build on nature, or does it radically alter nature?

We are created in the image of God and therefore reflect his power and goodness. The image of God is not a participation in the divine essence but a relationship that must be cultivated and strengthened. Because the imago Dei has been defaced by sin, we are alienated from God even while being inescapably related to him.

The human race is separated from God not only by ontological fate but also by historical guilt. In order for God to be known, he must make himself known, and he has done this once for all times in the incarnation of his Son, Jesus Christ. But only those with eyes to see and ears to hear can discern the light that shines in Christ to the whole world.

Revelation is not esoteric (Ps 119:130; Is 45:19), but it is also not open to general reasonableness (Is 6:9-10; Jn 8:43, 47). God reveals himself only to those who turn to him in repentance and faith, and even then we know God only partially and brokenly, for the human mind is incapable of discerning the depths and heights of infinity.

In our empirical climate today it is easy to make perceptibility the criterion for truth. But what we perceive is the phenomenal world, not the noumenal, which transcends the reach of human perception and imagination. The truth of revelation is inaccessible to the empirical eye; only the eye of faith or an illuminated reason can discern it. The apostle's prayer for the Ephesians was "that the eyes of your heart may be enlightened in order that you may know the hope to which he has called you, the riches of his glorious inheritance in the saints, and his incomparably great power for us who believe" (Eph 1:18 NIV). In the words of Luke's Gospel: "He opened their understanding, that they might comprehend the Scriptures" (Lk 24:45 NKJ).

Reason can be enlisted in the service of revelation, but it cannot establish the truth of revelation. It can reflect on the meaning of revelation, but it cannot prepare the way for revelation. It can be seized by the Word of God and used for his glory, but it cannot of itself lay hold of God's Word or directly contribute to his glory.

Revelation contradicts not rationality but rationalism. It can bring reason into its service, but it strongly opposes autonomous or disobedient reason. Faithful reasoning is a sign that revelation has found its way into the inner recesses of our being. It does not presuppose that the sinner on the basis of his or her resources has discovered or gained possession of the treasure of God's grace and mercy.

Is there a point of contact *(Anknüpfungspunkt)* between fallen humanity and divine revelation? This was the question that divided Barth and Brunner in 1934, and I am closer to the former than the latter, who posited a capacity within the human person for revelation. One may readily acknowledge that outwardly there is a point of contact—with the interpreted message of revelation, the sermonic proclamation. One must be able to understand the words of the preacher before beginning to comprehend the meaning of the message. But this is a sociological, not a theological, point of contact. The meaning or truth of revelation can be discerned only through the power of the Spirit. We must be given new eyes to contemplate the heavenly mysteries that hitherto had dazzled us (Calvin).

There is a point of contact, but it is none other than God's Spirit, who implants faith within us, thereby enabling us to understand and believe. I do not affirm a "capacity for revelation" within humanity, as Brunner expressed it. There is a formal point of contact, which is best seen as sociological or psychological, not theological. But there is no material point of contact, that is, a power or light resident in humanity that enables us to apprehend the truth that God reveals to us. It is possible to speak of a point of contact between Christians and non-Christians, for we both share a common existential situation and in many cases a common language and culture. But there is no point of contact between the transcendent meaning of the Word of God and the gropings of the human imagination.

The truth of faith is intelligible but not comprehensible. It is knowable but incommensurable—resisting comparison with other truths. It is available through the power of the Spirit but impenetrable by the human mind. It can be received by reason but not possessed or mastered by it. It includes mystery, expressed in the form of paradox, that defies rational penetration; yet this truth can be acknowledged and acclaimed by reason. It cannot be fully assimilated into a rational system, for the love of Christ surpasses all human knowledge (Eph 3:19).

Revelation does not contradict the structure of reason, but it opposes the direction of human reasoning. It also transcends the horizon of reason: " 'Things beyond our seeing, things beyond our hearing, things beyond our imagining' . . . these it is that God has revealed to us through the Spirit" (1 Cor 2:9-10 NEB). Revelation not only expands our horizon but brings us a wholly new horizon, a radically new perspective on life and the world. Grace brings us the foundation for a new nature; it does not simply build on the nature that already exists. The old nature must not be cultivated or elevated but crucified (Rom 6:6; Gal 5:24).[108]

As an act of incomparable grace, God's revelation brings us a new purpose, a new direction, new desires, a new goal, a new heart. The psalmist implores, "Create in me a clean heart, O God, and put a new and right spirit within me" (Ps 51:10). Jeremiah deftly expresses the radical character of the new life: "I will give them a different heart and different behavior so that they will always fear me, for the good of themselves and their children after them" (Jer 32:39 JB). Barth reiterated this note: "If God's Law is written on his heart, if his heart is circumcised, if he acquires a new and different heart, this means that he himself, in so far as this has a decisive bearing on his whole being and act, becomes another man."[109] "When a man becomes a Christian, his natural origin in the procreative will of his human father is absolutely superseded and transcended."[110] Paul's conversion on the road to Damascus is a classic example—someone who was once a militant unbeliever becomes a zealous defender of the faith through being personally confronted by the risen Christ in the power of the Holy Spirit (cf. Acts 9:1-18; 22:1-16).[111]

Revelation by its very nature is salvific, for its goal is the conversion of the sinner. It is correlative not simply with knowledge but with the new being in Christ. This does not mean, however, that revelation necessarily eventuates in salvation—only that the human subject is introduced to salvation. Our eyes may be opened to the glory of God in Christ, but in the folly of sin we can close our eyes once again, we can sin against the Holy Spirit, and forfeit the salvation assured to us by virtue of divine election.

If the biblical text were itself revelation, then human reason could directly apprehend and even critique the Word of God. The Word of God is not, however, the surface meaning of the text but its revelational meaning—the text understood in the light of the clarification provided by the Holy Spirit, which brings home to us its christological and soteriological significance.

It should be readily apparent that my stand is in contradiction to a biblicism that bases the authority of the Bible on its divine perfection as a supernatural book. The authority of Scripture is then located in its form as an inspired book rather than in its content—the saving message of the cross and resurrection of Christ. In the biblicist view the divine inspiration and factual inerrancy of the Bible guarantee the truth of its message, and faith is directed first of all to the Bible as a sacred object rather than to Christ, the Lord and content of the Scriptures. With Luther and Calvin I affirm that the authority of Scripture is self-authenticating by virtue of its divine content—the heavenly gospel—and the object of faith is from first to last Christ himself.[112]

Appendix A: Conflict in Theological Method

My own position becomes more intelligible when seen against the background of the age-old debate on theological method. I shall here present a typology of theological method that shows where the great theologians have stood on this issue.

First, there are those who make the confession "I believe because it is absurd" *(credo quia absurdum est).* One believes not simply despite the evidence of reason but because reason finds the object of faith absurd or unintelligible. That the gospel is folly to the wise is a sign not of its falsity but of its truthfulness. The presumption of reason must be overcome before faith can begin to employ reason in its service. Faith is here understood as being against reason—yet this is always fallen or sinful reason. Once reason is humbled it can be used in the service of the glory of God. Yet even a faithful or enlightened reason will find the gospel paradoxical and absurd not because the gospel is irrational but because sin still resides in the Christian and will time and again bend reason to its own purposes. Faith is thus a venture in the darkness, a leap into the unknown. Theologians who could be called fideists in this sense include Tertullian, the early Luther, Kierkegaard, the early Barth and Jacques Ellul.

A second group of thinkers, mainly philosophers, adhere to the adage, "I will to believe in order to find meaning in life." Here faith is portrayed as an adventure into the future or a journey into the unknown. Its object is not the gospel but an inscrutable mystery or the transcendent reality of moral law. Faith is not a gift of God but a heroic act of the will, an act that must be renewed again and again. This is not fideism so much as psychologism in that faith is interpreted mainly in psychological, not theological, terms. It is a disposition of the psyche or soul rather than the grace of God at work in the situation of preaching and hearing, bringing new life to the sinner. The focus is on the psychic benefits of faith rather than on the alteration of one's status before God. Faith is held to be heterogeneous from reason: it concerns not the realm of knowledge but what cannot be known—at least theoretically or scientifically. Faith is an act of practical reason rather than theoretical reason. Thinkers who belong in this category are Immanuel Kant, William

James, Miguel de Unamuno and Hans Vaihinger.

The next category is "I believe in order to understand" *(credo ut intelligam)*. Here we venture forward in trust and commitment in the expectation that we will come to understand as new light is given to us. This position can be called a fideistic revelationalism. The object of faith is not the absurd or the absolute mystery but the wisdom of God incarnate in a particular person in history. Faith is not so much against reason as above reason. It concerns realities that transcend the compass of human reason but nevertheless have rational content. The object of faith is incomprehensible but not unintelligible. Faith seeks understanding *(fides quaerens intellectum)* as it moves forward in a darkness that is steadily being illumined and dispelled by light. Faith is certain of the truth of its object even in the midst of its uncertainty concerning itself. It is not so much a leap in the dark as a walking in the light, though the element of trust and venture is still there, since this light is invisible to the empirical eye. Theologians who can be associated with this position include Augustine, Anselm, Luther, Calvin, Barth and G. C. Berkouwer.

Radically different is the rationalist option—"I understand in order to believe" *(intelligo ut credam)*. This approach rests on the premise that faith is congruous with reason. A thoroughgoing rationalism is presupposed in *credo quia intelligo* (I believe because I understand). Neither of these stances necessarily rules out a decision of the will, but such a decision must be in accord with the light gained by reason and experience. Faith is conceived of as a rational commitment rather than a leap into the unknown. We should believe only what can be supported on rational grounds (Abelard). Or the path to true understanding lies in "the cooperation of divine grace and the power of reason" in the hearts of those who believe (John Scotus Erigena).[113] Indeed, "true authority is nothing other than the truth that has been discovered by the power of reason and committed to writing by the holy fathers."[114] Even when faith is seen as the beginning of the Christian pilgrimage, it is reason that brings certainty and meaning to the venture of faith. Truth cannot contradict truth, and thus truth discoverable by reason will reinforce rather than undercut the commitment of faith. Among theologians of a rationalist bent are Clement of Alexandria, John Scotus Erigena, Abelard, John Locke, Charles Hodge, Benjamin Warfield, Fernand van Steenberghen, Wolfhart Pannenberg, Carl Henry, Gordon Clark, Edward John Carnell[115] and Norman Geisler.

Theologians such as Augustine and Thomas Aquinas affirm both *credo ut intelligam* and *credo quia intelligo*. For Augustine we cannot properly believe unless we understand what is to be believed.[116] For Thomas reason can prepare the way for faith and also confirm the truthfulness of the affirmations of faith. We cannot induce faith by reason, but we can remove barriers to faith. Both Augustine and Thomas acknowledge that prefaith understanding does not dispose one to believe, but the latter more than the former would allow that such an understanding may facilitate faith if prevenient grace is at work in the inquirer.

The last category is "I obey in order to know." Here we find most of the great mystics of the church who emphasize that purgation must precede illumination. Faith is the result of obedience rather than of dialectical reasoning. Understanding too follows from obedience, praxis comes before logos. This position also resonates with the slogan of liberation theologians: "There can be no understanding of the gospel without the performance of the gospel." Doing the truth is prior to knowing the truth. Although this view certainly has some biblical support (Jn 3:21; 1 Jn 2:3), it overlooks the many other passages that point to the priority of being over action (Mt 7:16-20; Col 3:16-17; 1 Jn 3:9; 5:5).

Kierkegaard, a classic representative of fideism, could nevertheless make remarks that place him close to mysticism and ethicism: "The Christian thesis is not *intelligere ut credam*, nor is it *credere ut intelligam*. No, it is, Act according to the precepts and commandments of Christ, do the will of the Father—and you shall have faith."[117]

In his earlier writing Barth evidenced the influence of Kierkegaard, describing faith as a leap into the darkness of the unknown. As he progressed in his thought, however, Barth moved away from the Kierkegaardian stance toward Augustine and Anselm. He still affirmed faith as trust and venture, but this is only one element in faith and not the decisive one. The decisive element is the presence of God himself in our venture of faith, undergirding it and directing it. In the midst of the uncertainty that accompanies faith as a human act and venture, faith proceeds on the basis of a certainty that comes directly from God. "In the uncertainty which is characteristic of this human action as it is of all others, faith takes place, so far as its object is concerned, with the firmness which it is given by this object, with a certainty as hard as steel."[118] Psychologically considered, faith will always appear as a leap into the darkness of the unknown, but theologically faith is anchored in an illumination that pierces through this darkness. In his later years Barth was accustomed to speaking of faith as "acknowledgment" rather than "leap," though he never abandoned the existentialist thrust so conspicuous in his early writings.[119] At the same time, his criticisms of both Luther and Kierkegaard in this area show that his affinities are with an older tradition in the church—going back to Augustine and Anselm.

In a similar fashion to the mystics and Kierkegaard, Bonhoeffer acknowledged the priority of obedience over faith but regarded such obedience as a dead work of the law unless it eventuates in faith. Obedience may prepare the way for faith, but it cannot induce or generate faith. Bonhoeffer endeavored to hold the two in dialectical tension: "Only he who believes is obedient, and only he who is obedient believes."[120] He was acutely aware of the danger of works-righteousness that accompanies an emphasis on obedience before faith, but he also deplored the opposite peril—cheap grace. Yet when in a later period he affirmed that before a person "can know and find Christ he must first become righteous like those who strive and who suffer for the sake of justice, truth, and humanity,"[121] he seems to come dangerously close to making the Christian life of self-giving service the foundation and pivotal center of our salvation.

My own position gives priority to faith over understanding—yet faith not as an irrational leap but as a commitment involving reason as well as will. Faith is an awakening to the significance of what God in Christ has done for us, an awakening that eventuates in a commitment of the whole person to the living Christ. This commitment entails reason, will and feeling, but it is basically an act of the will. We believe against the presumption of our reason but not against the structure of our reason. We commit ourselves to that which is beyond the limits of human reason but not beyond the compass of reason itself (the *logos*). Once we have faith, we seek deeper insight into what we believe. I affirm both faith seeking understanding *(fides quaerens intellectum)* and an intellect seeking direction from faith *(intellectus quaerens fidem).*[122] Understanding must constantly return to faith just as faith constantly strives for deeper understanding. Faith is not mere opinion but a "steady and certain knowledge" (Calvin)—yet knowledge concerning realities beyond the compass of human reason. It is also only a partial knowledge that will finally be supplanted by a direct vision of God.

Faith is characterized by certainty of the promises of God, but uncertainty concerning itself. Faith excludes doubt, which is the intellectual form of sin, as well as the despair of life and of God, the very essence of sin.[123] Doubt and despair will invariably accompany faith because sin lives on even in the sanctified Christian, but faith opposes these instruments of death just as grace opposes sin. In faith we are lifted above our doubts and despair into the peace that passes understanding, the consolation that the storms of life cannot shake. We can go forward on our journey strengthened by the grace that undergirds our faith and makes our faith fruitful in works of service and sacrifice.

Faith is not a heroic will to believe but an obedient willing made possible by the working of the Spirit of God within us. It entails the submission as well as the illumination of reason. Faith is taking up the cross and following Christ, not embarking on a pilgrimage without a destination. Faith is not an unceasing search for God but a firm commitment to the will of God informed by an understanding of the Word of God. Faith is certain because it takes us out of ourselves, out of our despair and anguish, into a relationship to the living Christ that cannot be severed by the powers of sin, death and the devil. Faith is advancing toward a future that is assured to us by the promises of Jesus Christ in Holy Scripture.

FOUR

THE INSPIRATION OF SCRIPTURE

My spirit which rests on you and my words which I have
put into your mouth will never fail you.
ISAIAH 59:21 REB

We need not think that the Holy Spirit Himself or through an angel
had to speak words to the writers or to dictate them, but He gave
them divine truth through an inner enlightenment of the heart.
PHILIPP SPENER

Theologians are not infallible in the interpretation of Scripture.
It may ... happen in the future, as it has in the past, that interpretations
of the Bible, long confidently received, must be modified or abandoned. ...
This change of view as to the true meaning of the Bible may be
a painful trial to the Church.
CHARLES HODGE

The authority of the Scripture is not a matter to be defended,
so much as to be asserted. ... We need to remind ourselves frequently
that it is the preaching and exposition of the Bible that
really establishes its truth and authority.
D. MARTYN LLOYD-JONES

Finally, as regards the doctrine of inspiration,
it is not enough to believe in it; one must ask oneself:
Am I expecting it? Will God speak to me in this Scripture?
KARL BARTH

T he problem concerning the status of Scripture in the Christian community is how these sacred writings can be the product of both the infinite God and finite human beings. For believers the internal evidence within Scripture itself gives credence to the claim that Scripture bears the imprint of divine revelation.

Both Testaments amply testify to the divine origin of Scripture.

Phrases such as "God spoke," "Thus says the Lord," "The Word of the Lord came" abound, being used, according to one scholar, more than thirty-eight hundred times.[1] It is said that God will be with the mouth of Moses (Ex 4:14-16) and Moses will be as God to Pharaoh (7:1). The Decalogue is called "the writing of God" (32:16), having been produced by "the finger of God" (31:18). David declares, "The spirit of the Lord speaks through me; his message is on my lips" (2 Sam 23:2 GNB). In Jeremiah we read: "Behold, I have put my words in your mouth" (1:9).

In the New Testament the claim is made that "no prophecy ever came by the impulse of man, but men moved by the Holy Spirit spoke from God" (2 Pet 1:21). Even more forthright is 2 Timothy 3:16-17: "All scripture is inspired by God and is useful for teaching, for reproof, for correction, and for training in righteousness, so that everyone who belongs to God may be proficient, equipped for every good work" (NRSV).[2] Other New Testament passages that imply inspired writing include Hebrews 3:7, 9:8 and Revelation 1:1-3. We read that the Spirit of God "spoke by the mouth of his holy prophets from of old" (Lk 1:70; cf. Acts 1:16; 28:25) and that the apostles speak in words that the Holy Ghost teaches (1 Cor 2:13). The New Testament writers sometimes hypostatize the Old Testament writings as though they constituted a thinking, rational subject—an omniscient person. The Scriptures are said to speak (Rom 4:3; 9:17; 10:11; Jas 2:23); the Scriptures foresee (Gal 3:8); the Scriptures raise up Pharaoh (Rom 9:17). The Scriptures are called God's utterances or God's oracles (Rom 3:2).

It is not surprising that theologians through the ages have tended to speak of Scripture as a divine book or as revelation itself. Calvin concluded that "we owe to the Scripture the same reverence which we owe to God; because it has proceeded from him alone, and has nothing belonging to man mixed with it."[3] John Wesley declared that we must choose between God as the author and human authors. He also asserted that if we deny the reality of witchcraft we deny the Bible (cf. Ex 22:18). At the same time, he recognized the possibility of error in the genealogies (Notes on Mt 1:1).[4] According to the orthodox Lutheran theologian Quenstedt, "God alone" is to be called "the author of the Sacred Scriptures; the prophets and apostles cannot be called the authors, except by a kind of catachresis."[5] Dean Burgon of Christ Church Cathedral, Oxford, England, said in 1861: "The Bible is the very utterance of the Eternal: as much God's own word as if high heaven were open and we heard God speaking to us with human voice."[6]

With the rise of historical and literary criticism of Scripture, there has been a marked tendency to downplay if not deny the divine origin of Scripture and to emphasize its human qualities. Hans Küng argues that the Scriptures cannot properly be called the Word of God, for they are "merely the human testimonies of divine revelation in which the humanity, independence and historicity of the human authors always remain intact."[7] In the Presbyterian Confession of 1967 we read:

> The Scriptures, given under the guidance of the Holy Spirit, are nevertheless the words of men, conditioned by the language, thought forms, and literary fashions of the places and times at which they were written. They reflect views of life, history, and the cosmos which were then current.[8]

Yet this is a false dichotomy. The paradox is that Scripture is the Word of God as well as the words of mortals. It is both a human witness to God and God's witness to himself. The Scriptures have a dual authorship, which is reflected in 1 Peter 1:11: "They tried to find out what was the time, and what the circumstances, to which the spirit of Christ in them pointed" (NEB).

The traditional Roman Catholic position is that God is the primary author of Scripture and human beings the secondary authors. According to Augustine, "Since they wrote the things which He showed and uttered to them, it cannot be pretended that He is not the writer; for His members executed what their head dictated."[9] In this understanding, Scripture has a divine ground but a human form.

Yet there is a real question whether this position does not mirror a docetic view of Scripture. The human author is more than a passive instrument of the Spirit. The humanity of the Bible is not simply an instrument but the medium and matrix of the Word of God. The persons who wrote and compiled Scripture were real authors and editors. Scripture is not simply the Word of God or human words but the Word of God *in* human words.

Instead of speaking of Scripture as having a divine ground and human form, it is theologically more appropriate to contend that Scripture has a human content as well as a human form; at the same time, it also has a divine content and a divinely inspired form. The human form and content serve the divine meaning.

Protestant orthodoxy has taken the Greek word *theopneustos* (2 Tim 3:16) to signify the kind of verbal inspiration that entails divine dictation (with regard to the written form) and historical, scientific and theological inerrancy (with regard to the content). Benjamin Warfield held that it was not the mode of writing that was dictated but what was written. He interpreted *theopneustos* to mean that the Bible as a book or compendium of books was "breathed out by God, 'God-breathed,' the product of the creative breath of God."[10]

In my opinion Warfield was correct in his contention that inspiration means something more than "breathed into" in the sense of illumination (as liberals often describe it). Yet he sometimes spoke as if the Bible were directly divine, thereby failing to acknowledge its human, fallible character: "Though spoken through the instrumentality of men, it is, by virtue of the fact that these men spoke 'as borne by the Holy Spirit,' an immediately Divine word."[11] Scripture thus becomes transparent to its object, with the result that God's Word is readily accessible to human perception and conception.

In contrast, Protestant liberalism has been too quick to separate the inspired text and the revelation of Christ. Gordon Kaufman expresses a view now widespread in ecumenical circles: "Since it is Jesus Christ, and not the biblical words, that is God's revelation, it is misleading to refer to the text itself as 'inspired.' "[12]

The Reformation
The Protestant Reformers of the sixteenth century had a high view of

the Bible, but always the Bible united with the testimony of the Spirit. It was Luther's conviction that "Scripture is a book, to which there belongeth not only reading but also the right Expositor and Revealer, to wit, the Holy Spirit. Where He openeth not Scripture, it is not understood."[13] Calvin agreed: "The external word is of no avail by itself unless animated by the power of the Spirit. . . . All power of action, then, resides in the Spirit himself, and thus all praise ought to be entirely referred to God alone."[14] For the Reformers the Bible is the infallible rule for faith and practice; it contains all things necessary for salvation, but its saving truth can be perceived only by the illumination of the Holy Spirit.

In the writings of the mainline Reformers one can find statements affirming the divinity of Scripture together with statements acknowledging its frailty and humanity. At times they could speak of the words of the prophets and apostles as being the very words of God himself. They could say that the words of the Bible were "dictated by the Holy Spirit," but they often referred to the words of the preacher in the same way. Calvin called the Bible "the certain and unerring rule," but he meant the rule for faith. What distinguished the Reformers' concept of inspiration from the Catholic view was that their emphasis was more on the inspiration of the writings than of the writers.

While affirming that the Bible is the bearer of transcendent power and wisdom, the Reformers at the same time acknowledged a culturally conditioned element in the Bible.[15] Calvin observed that the preaching of the faithful in the Old Testament is "obscure, like something far off, and is embodied in types." They are therefore to be "classed as children."[16] He was frank to acknowledge that "no one then possessed discernment so clear as to be unaffected by the obscurity of the time."[17] Calvin accounted for the limitations in worldview evident in the Bible by the concept of accommodation, whereby the Holy Spirit entered into the thought world of that time rather than impose a heavenly metaphysic upon people who would not be able to absorb it. He recognized that the moon is represented as larger than Saturn when astronomy proves otherwise.[18] He suspected that Matthew, in describing the journey of the wise men, improperly labeled as a star what was probably a comet.[19] Before the advent of higher criticism, Calvin questioned the Petrine authorship of 2 Peter. Luther allowed for exaggerations in the Bible: "When one often reads that great numbers of people were slain—for example, eighty thousand—I believe that hardly one thousand were actually killed."[20] He could express doubt regarding the Mosaic authorship of the Pentateuch, the apostolic authorship of Jude and the redeeming value of such books as Revelation and James. He saw in the predictions of the prophets failure as well as success and considered the books of Kings more reliable than Chronicles. He acknowledged the book of Job to be real history but questioned whether everything happened exactly as recorded, holding that the author must have been endowed with both theological perspicacity and creative imagination.[21]

The Reformers definitely distinguished the mystery of the gospel from the literary and cultural form in which this mystery comes to us. At the same time, they were adamant that the whole Bible revolves around this mystery, that Jesus Christ is the center and apex of the biblical writings. They were also firm in their contention that natural reason is at a loss to perceive this mystery, which can be known only through the illuminating action of the Spirit of God.

Orthodoxy and Pietism

Protestant orthodoxy, which developed after the Reformation, was shaped not only by the polemic with Rome but also by conflicts within the various churches of the Reformation. It also had to deal with the rising spirit of secularism that became much more prominent in the eighteenth century. An attempt was made to ground the authority of Scripture in criteria shared with the outside world rather than in the living God who speaks within Scripture. The historical and scientific accuracy of Scripture was vigorously defended in the face of embarrassing questions raised by the great intellects of the age (such as Spinoza). "No error," said Abraham Calovius, "even in unimportant matters, no defect of memory, not to say untruth, can have any place in all the Holy

Scriptures."[22] It was asserted that Scripture not only does not err but cannot err. Lambert Daneau, who had studied under Calvin, was one who affirmed the total inerrancy of Scripture and employed Scripture as a credible source for natural science.[23] There was a concerted effort to ground faith in evidence that searching individuals could acknowledge. The Reformed theologian Moïse Amyraut held that the knowledge of faith and of science are of the same kind and that faith rests partly on rational demonstration.[24] For Amandus Polanus theology is the knowledge of propositions and conclusions derived from first principles.[25]

Attention was focused on the congruity rather than the discontinuity between the biblical vision of truth and philosophical and cultural understandings.[26] The Princeton theologian Archibald Alexander held that "the account which the Bible gives of the origin and character of man accords very exactly with reason and experience."[27] Charles Hodge believed Scripture to contain "nothing impossible, nothing absurd, nothing immoral, nothing inconsistent with any well-authenticated truth."[28]

The concern of the Reformers had been with the primacy and authority of Scripture, not its inerrancy. Protestant orthodoxy continued to pay lip service to biblical primacy, but the emphasis was now on its demonstrable infallibility. Reason was elevated as an authority alongside Scripture (though this view was more evident in later orthodoxy). The correlation between Spirit and Word was ultimately replaced by a subordination of Spirit to Word. The authority of the Bible was increasingly based on its mode of writing rather than on its capacity to direct us to Christ.

The extent of the divergence of Protestant orthodoxy from the Reformation continues to be a matter of scholarly debate.[29] Some theologians of orthodoxy stood remarkably close to the basic insights of the Reformers, but most of them lived in the same century as the Reformation. What distinguished the age of orthodoxy from the period of the Reformation was perhaps a different spirit more than a different content. This new spirit had its source in the supposed need to defend the faith, including the truth of the Bible, from the onslaughts of a rising rationalism.

In reaction to the hardening of orthodoxy into creedal formulas and ritual observances, movements of spiritual purification arose to reclaim the reality of the Spirit alongside the Word. The Puritans and Pietists were concerned with spiritual renewal even more than with right doctrine. Whereas orthodoxy had substituted the teaching authority of the scholars for the magisterium of the church, the Pietists maintained that the Bible interprets itself and is not dependent on learned scholarship for its credibility and authority. Furthermore, only regenerate persons can do theology, since the content of theology is spiritual reality, not axiomatic truth. By contrast, orthodoxy conceived of theology as a science in which an investigation of the data would yield uniform results.

The Pietists and Puritans generally made a careful distinction between letter and spirit, which was often obscured in orthodoxy. The letter is dead apart from the creative action of the Spirit upon both the text and the inner self of the believer. For August Hermann Francke Scripture is rightly interpreted "not by lexicons and dictionaries, but by doctrines revealed by God and by an inward teaching and unction of the Holy Ghost."[30] According to Jonathan Edwards spiritual understanding did "not consist in any new . . . doctrinal knowledge" but was a "supernatural understanding of divine things, that is peculiar to the saints, and which those who are not saints have nothing of."[31] "Take away the Spirit from the gospel," said John Owen, "and you render it 'a dead letter'; of no more use to Christians, than the Old Testament is of to the Jews."[32]

The emphasis of the Pietists was not on technical precision or the harmonizing of data but on the presence of the Spirit in the sacred writings. Because of their distinction between form and content, they were generally more open to the historical investigation of Scripture than the so-called orthodox party in the church. At the same time, by allowing the Spirit to preempt the rational element in faith, they were not able to muster the intellectual resources necessary to safeguard the integrity of the faith in a time of mounting rationalism. By elevating the Spirit over the Word, they failed to maintain the Reformation correlation of Spirit and Word. Calvin had claimed that the Bible is not only the instrument of the Spirit's witness but also the object of this witness. In radical Pietism dreams and private revelations also became authorities for faith. No longer an objective, universal criterion for truth, Scripture was reduced to an aid in understanding one's own experience of God and reality. Pietism joined with rationalism in paving the way for the triumph of autonomy over heteronomy. The University of Halle, founded as an institution for Pietism, became within one generation a bastion of rationalism.[33]

When authority is made to reside in the inner self, whether this be conscience or feeling, reason ineluctably regains its sovereignty because feeling and experience must finally be interpreted in order to give direction and meaning to life. Luther had said that our theology is certain because it takes us out of ourselves, out of our own experiences and deliberations into union with the living Christ of the Scriptures who never deceives. The Pietists and Puritans came to locate certainty in the quality of one's experiences or in the external marks of holiness in one's life. The focus became a journey inward, and the birth of the Son of God in the soul overshadowed the incarnation of the living God in human history. Here we see a linkup between radical Pietism and mysticism, although mainstream Pietism maintained a reserved attitude toward mysticism.

A consideration of the weaknesses of these movements should not blind us to their positive contributions. They completed the Reformation by stressing a reformation in life as well as in doctrine. While the Reformers had helped the theologians to discover the Bible, the Pietists introduced the Bible to the people. While the Reformers sought to safeguard the faith against doctrinal error, the Pietists carried the faith to foreign lands and demonstrated its power through social services to the poor and needy. It was out of the Pietist and evangelical awakenings that the social conscience of the nations was stirred so that finally action was taken against the slave trade, child labor, animal cruelty, gambling and a host of other evils.[34]

Fundamentalism

With the rise and triumph of the Enlightenment in the eighteenth and early nineteenth centuries, conservative Protestants donned a defensive posture and saw their mandate as defending the faith against growing worldliness and apostasy. Fundamentalism embraces a wide variety of movements and concerns, but basically it represents a biblicistic militancy intent on uprooting apostasy within the church and countering secularism without. By its concern for personal holiness it shows an affinity to Pietism, and by its apologetic concern it shows its continuity with Protestant orthodoxy. It seeks to defeat the unbelief of the age with the weapons of the culture. It appeals to the same criteria as the wider culture in order to bolster its belief in supernatural revelation. Logical consistency and empirical verification are as prominent in fundamentalist apologetics as in secular philosophy. Ernest Sandeen's interpretation of fundamentalism as a union of the Princeton school of theology (Charles Hodge, A. A. Hodge and Benjamin Warfield) with dispensationalism is far too narrow[35] and leaves out the vast company of conservative Christians who champion apologetics but not the inductive approach and who preach the realization of millennial promises but not in terms of dispensations.[36]

The bête noire of fundamentalism has been the rise of higher criticism of the Bible, which raises questions concerning both the infallibility and authority of the Bible. E. J. Young spoke for many: "A man may practice the principles of criticism or he may be a believer in evangelical Christianity. One thing, however, is clear: if he is consistent, he cannot possibly espouse both."[37] In the fundamentalist view the Bible has historical and scientific authority as well as spiritual authority. An attempt is made to reconcile internal contradictions in Scripture as well as discrepancies between biblical affirmations and the new scientific worldview. The final criterion for truth is the original record or autographs of Scripture, which are now lost in antiquity. The present text is considered less authoritative, and therefore an admission is made that there may be errors in copying and translating. The conservative theologian James Orr called this a suicidal position.[38] It cannot even be found in Charles Hodge, who acknowledged discrepancies in Scripture but dismissed them as "specks of sandstone" in an edifice that is essentially marble. Some in this tradition even refuse to acknowledge errors in copying and transmission. A modern critic of fundamentalism gives this assessment:

> The truth of the Bible is judged by its reliability in matters of historical and physical fact. The ordinary modern reader of a biblical narrative wants chiefly to know what exactly it was that happened, or what a trained observer would have seen if he had been there; and he thinks that this is the real truth of the matter.[39]

This concern for perfect factual accuracy is mirrored in Wick Broomall's assertion that if "the Biblical records were produced by men directed and controlled by the Holy Spirit, then we have every reason to believe that the facts and doctrines recorded in the Bible are free of those imperfections and blemishes that characterize all purely human productions."[40] While acknowledging that the Bible includes poetry as well as history, R. A. Torrey held that we are obliged to "believe its every statement, its historical statements, its doctrinal statements, its statements of every kind."[41]

Fundamentalists are inclined to speak of the Bible as a "verbal revelation" dictated word for word by the living God. W. A. Criswell declares: "This Volume is the writing of the Living God. Each sentence was dictated by God's Holy Spirit. . . . Everywhere in the Bible we find God speaking. It is God's voice, not man's."[42] One should note that both Warfield and A. A. Hodge denied dictation as a mode of inspiration: the Holy Spirit did not override the personalities of the authors but ensured that what was written completely fulfilled the intention of God. At the same time, Warfield referred to the Scriptures as the special utterances of God in both substance and form, though he made clear that these utterances were relayed through human instrumentality.

Fundamentalism locates certainty in the empirical veracity of a divine book rather than in the Spirit who speaks to us in the history mirrored in this book. Even from the more progressive side of this tradition we are told: "Given a Bible that cannot err . . . we possess absolute certainty about the God who is revealed there."[43] Here biblical inerrancy becomes the first principle in theology rather than a necessary inference from the Bible (as in Warfield).

The distinguishing marks of fundamentalism in the broad sense are: biblical literalism; total inerrancy, including perfect factual accuracy; revelation as essentially propositional; a profound distrust of biblical criticism, especially higher criticism; premillennial eschatology; and the call to separate from apostate churches. Instead of the older Protestant view that the Bible as a whole is infallible (meaning its overall teaching),[44] fundamentalists claim the Bible as a perfect measuring rod in matters of history and science as well as faith and morals.

Fundamentalism is an evangelicalism that has hardened and become isolated from the wider church. Like liberalism on the left, it easily becomes aligned with ideological movements in its attempt to promote a program for the restructuring of society. Though a critic of fundamentalism as an ideology, I nevertheless stand with fundamentalists as believing Christians who affirm the faith once delivered to the saints—even if this affirmation be done in a sectarian rather than a catholic way. Fundamentalism has proved to be a demonstrably redeeming force in society by its passion to bring the gospel to the lost, but it adds to this gospel cultural accretions that blunt its impact and distort its truth.

As a theological position fundamentalism is open to serious criticism. Those who hold that the present Bible is unconditionally or literally infallible are compelled to ignore the thousands of available variant texts that disagree. Taking refuge in the autographs to resolve textual divergences often defies plausibility. It should be noted that Jesus, Peter and Paul appealed to extant copies, not to the autographs. For fundamentalists the authority of the Bible rests on the inspired record rather than on a personal encounter with Jesus Christ. They stress the empowering work of the Spirit but not his enlightening work in bringing people the truth of revelation. Their idea that inspiration entails inerrancy in history and science as well as in doctrine is not claimed by the Bible.

Some acknowledge that inerrancy is not taught in Holy Scripture, though they insist that it is implied.[45] Fundamentalists do not allow for the fact that copyists and editors may have been guided to improve the original copy (the autographs).

Fundamentalism also espouses a static theory of inspiration. To speak of the inscripturation of the Word (as do Warfield and Henry) is not out of line with historic orthodoxy, but when such language becomes normative and determinative in our understanding of scriptural authority, the dynamic quality of God's inspiring work is invariably diminished. God's Word cannot be encapsulated in either legal codes or clerical pronouncements, for the Word of God is "living and active" (Heb 4:12). Inspiration is an event in which God acts and speaks and his prophetic messengers and witnesses begin to discern and believe.

Like liberalism, fundamentalism proves to be a kind of reductionism. It reduces truth to facticity and revelation to conceptuality or logic. Its flat view of Scripture, in which every part of Scripture is deemed equally important, is strikingly unbiblical. Its vigorous insistence that every biblical passage be interpreted in a literal manner needlessly obscures poetic and legendary elements and opens the door to new heresies—such as ultradispensationalism. James Barr, himself a product of conservative evangelicalism, makes this astute comment: "A biblical account of some event is approached and evaluated primarily not in terms of significance but in terms of correspondence with external actuality. Veracity as correspondence with empirical actuality has precedence over veracity as significance."[46]

The position of fundamentalists on the Bible is monophysite: it sees only one nature—the divine. In contrast, many liberals and some neoorthodox embrace a Nestorian position—affirming two natures but failing to discern their indissoluble unity.

One conservative critic scores fundamentalism for its covert trust in empirical validation:

The most tragic aspect of the fundamentalist conception seems to me that his standpoint requires *scientific* proof, so that he must somehow live in fear of the results of developing scientific work, because, indeed, this development could then also *disprove* the reliability of the Holy Scriptures. And this leads to the cardinal question whether in this way the fundamentalist's conception does not reveal an implicit faith in science, which is far more dangerous for Christian religion than the scientific development itself.[47]

Fundamentalism as a defensive, apologetic movement within conservative Protestantism is now under attack even by its sons and daughters, but we must take care to temper our criticisms by giving due credit to its positive contributions. Those whom we call fundamentalists have preserved many truths and concerns lost sight of in the mainline denominations. They have maintained the supernaturalist orientation of the faith in a time of mounting naturalism and relativism. They have also kept alive opposition to the myth of evolution, which continues to beguile earnest Christians seeking a satisfactory rational explanation of the origin of species. Again, they have safeguarded the historical basis of Christian faith in the face of philosophical idealism, which focuses on eternal truths or abiding values rather than truth incarnate in human history. Finally, they have preserved the concern for evangelism and mission that is integral to any vital Christian faith.

I oppose the negative elements of fundamentalism, not the movement as a whole. I stand with my more conservative brothers and sisters in affirming the fundamental doctrines of the faith; my quarrel in this area is that too often marginal doctrines, such as the millennium, the pretribulation rapture of the saints and biblical inerrancy, are elevated into fundamentals. (It should be noted that I criticize fundamentalism from the right, i.e., from the perspective of evangelical and catholic tradition, not of modernity.)

The past several decades have witnessed the rise of a neo-evangelical movement that seeks to come to terms with modernity while still maintaining a high view of biblical authority. A general acceptance of the methodology of historical and form criticism distances these theologians from the fundamentalist tradition. George Eldon Ladd denied "an infallible text" and preferred to speak of the infallibility of the message of Scripture.[48] Bernard Ramm was unhappy with the expression "propositional revelation," contending that revelation is polydimensional.[49] At a conference on Scripture at Gordon College and Divinity School in Wenham, Massachusetts, in June 1966, it was held that the Scriptures are authoritative as "the only infallible rule of faith and practice."[50] Significantly, the conference stopped short of affirming total factual inerrancy. According to Dewey Beegle the inspiring work of the Spirit was present in the "whole process of transmitting, recording and compiling the deeds and words of God."[51] But this activity "did not extend to inerrant transmission, either oral or written, and neither did it guarantee an absolute inerrancy of the original documents. What the Spirit's activity did guarantee was selectivity of events and accuracy of reporting and interpretation sufficient to achieve God's purpose throughout the rest of man's existence."[52]

At the first consultation of the Fraternity of Latin American theologians in Cochabamba, Bolivia, in December 1970, René Padilla argued that insistence on an inerrant Bible means asking for something that is not available. An exaggerated emphasis on inerrancy, he maintained, "in effect saws off the limb that supports evangelical theology."[53] The late Charles Keysor of the Methodist Good News movement saw inspiration as a dynamic, continuing activity of the Holy Spirit rather than the divine dictation of particular writings.[54]

Confessionalist evangelicals, those who declare their fidelity to the creeds and confessions of the Reformation, were never really part of the fundamentalist movement, though many of these people shared the fundamentalist belief in biblical infallibility. Hermann Sasse, a conservative German Lutheran theologian, argued for the absolute infallibility of Scripture but insisted that it pertained to matters of "the content of the Christian faith," not necessarily to nontheological biblical statements.[55] Unlike many other Lutheran conservatives, Sasse questioned the historical facticity of the book of Jonah and held that the feeding of the five thousand and the four thousand (Mt 14:17-21; 15:34-38) probably constituted only one event and not two.

The term *neo-evangelical* is now being less and less used as conservatives simply opt for the designation *evangelical* in a search for unity amid their great diversity. The International Council on Biblical Inerrancy sought to unite evangelicals in a confession of biblical authority that maintained continuity with the evangelical theology of the past. The result was a declaration of biblical authority that manifested deep confidence in the historical reliability and divine inspiration of Scripture but did little to resolve the tensions and disagreements within the evangelical community. The Chicago Statement on Biblical Inerrancy and the later Chicago Statement on Biblical Hermeneutics prove to be umbrella statements that cover a wide variety of positions.[56] Stanley Gundry remarks that the Chicago Statement on Biblical Inerrancy is

> a remarkably balanced and comprehensive document, especially considering the theological diversity of the participants and the time limitations within which they operated. Even so, the papers and discussions leading up to the document clearly showed that inerrantists themselves disagree on the definition and implications of inerrancy, the apologetics of inerrancy, the determination of authorial intention, the question of single or dual intention, the use of the historical-critical method, the uses of literary genre, and the cultural conditioning of Scripture.[57]

At the Evangelical Affirmations conference at Trinity Evangelical Divinity School in May 1989, there was a marked preference for such words as *truthfulness* and *trustworthiness* rather than *inerrancy* to describe the divine character of Holy Scripture.[58] Yet even these words are not free from ambiguity, and it may be that evangelicals will have to draw on philosophical as well as biblical resources to clarify what they mean by truth and error.

Neo-Orthodoxy

The neo-orthodox movement associated with such renowned scholars as Karl Barth, Emil Brunner, Hendrik Kraemer and Dietrich Bonhoeffer

sought a new statement on biblical authority that included an acknowledgment of both God's mighty deeds in biblical history and the reality
of historical and cultural conditioning in the writing of Scripture. Where
neo-orthodoxy moved beyond fundamentalism was in its sharp distinction between Scripture as a historical and literary document and divine
revelation. Given the wide variety of positions within this movement, I
shall focus on Barth because of the depth and scope of his contribution
in this area.

Since God chose to communicate his Word through the instrumentality of human authors, Barth readily acknowledged that the Bible participates in the contingency and relativity of the history and culture in
which it was written and compiled.

> To the bold postulate, that if their word is to be the Word of God they
> must be inerrant in every word, we oppose the even bolder assertion,
> that according to the Scriptural witness about man, which applies to
> them too, they can be at fault in any word, and have been at fault
> in every word, and yet according to the same Scriptural witness,
> being justified and sanctified by grace alone, they have still spoken
> the Word of God in their fallible and erring human word.[59]

For Barth the Bible *is* the Word of God because "God Himself now says
what the text says. The work of God is done through this text. The
miracle of God takes place in this text formed of human words."[60] God
says what his witnesses say, but this is an impenetrable mystery. Despite
his candid acknowledgment of historical contingency in the Bible, Barth
could still say that the Bible gives "correct and infallible information"
concerning ourselves and our real questions, concerns and needs.[61] For
him the Bible is essentially truthful and authoritative, whatever its external flaws.

What Barth seems to mean is that every word or proposition in the
Bible when taken in and of itself and when divorced from God's truth
is open to error. At the same time, when united with the divine Word,
the living, transcendent center of the Bible, it is then a bearer of the
transcendent. Every text carries the mark of human imperfection but

also the potential of being a vehicle of divine grace. Barth would probably say that even the apostolic proclamation that "God was in Christ reconciling the world to himself" (2 Cor 5:19 REB) is not faultless unless it is perceived through the eyes of trinitarian faith. But is not God's spirit and truth continuously present in this proclamation? Are not the words of Scripture accompanied by the divine presence, even though the reader does not always recognize this presence?

Barth can be criticized for not clarifying his position on biblical inerrancy. He did not wish to affirm that the teaching of the Bible can be in error; yet when he acknowledged errors in the realm of theology and religion as well as science and history, he opened the door to this view. His intention, however, was to admit that the prophets and apostles because they are human are susceptible to error even in matters of faith and morals. Conservative critics pose this question to Barth: Are not the biblical authors kept free from actual error by the Holy Spirit? Barth affirmed the divine infallibility and human fallibility of the Bible. But did he see the unity of the two sides? Can the finite hold and bear the infinite, or does it merely witness to the infinite? Barth seemed to hold to the older Reformed notion of *finitum non capax infiniti* (the finite is not capable of receiving the infinite).

For Barth inspiration refers to the subjective disposition of the biblical writers who are acted on by the Spirit of God. The view of orthodoxy is that inspiration refers to the production of inspired writings. Barth would not affirm that inspiration guarantees the entire truthfulness and trustworthiness of Scripture, but it does assure us of finding the truth in Scripture. For him there are two moments in inspiration: the enlightenment of the writers and the illumination of the readers.

According to Barth one can hear the Word of God only in the form of verbal inspiration, for the matter is not to be separated from the word. To be inspired means to be "given and filled and ruled by the Spirit of God, and actively outbreathing and spreading abroad and making known the Spirit of God."[62] This process includes both the writers and their testimony, but it does not imply that the writings themselves are the product of the direct action of the Holy Spirit. For Barth inspiration rests on God's decision to speak his Word ever and again in the history of the church and through the text of the Bible. I also acknowledge that inspiration is founded on a divine decision, but does not it ensure a trustworthy and reliable account of the divine action in past history? Barth regarded every word in the Bible as historically related and conditioned. The divine content of the Bible must be given anew in a free decision of God.

Barth wished to affirm the paradox of the divine infallibility of the Bible and its human fallibility. He was willing to acknowledge that the Holy Spirit is "the real author of what is stated or written in Scripture."[63] Yet the Bible is not the result of "direct impartation" but "genuine witness."[64] This means that it participates in historical contingency and that God meets us only in the historically conditioned and relative.

Liberalism

For the theologians of liberalism or neo-Protestantism (Semler, Schleiermacher, Bushnell, Ritschl, Herrmann, Troeltsch, Tillich, etc.), inspiration generally means illumination or enlightenment. It is an awakening or stimulation of the natural powers of discernment (L. Harold DeWolf). It is being enlivened by an experience of "true morality and freedom" (Schleiermacher)[65] or being opened to a new dimension of knowledge through an encounter with the mystery of being (Tillich).[66]

Liberal theology speaks of God not as the author of Scripture but as the illuminator of persons who wrote and compiled what they believed to be of enduring value. C. H. Dodd states frankly:

In the literal sense the Bible consists of the "words" of men—or rather of their visible symbols in writing. It is not the utterance of God in the same sense in which it is the utterance of men. . . . God is the Author not of the Bible, but of the life in which the authors of the Bible partake, and of which they tell us in such imperfect human words as they could command.[67]

In its haste to acknowledge the historical and cultural character of the biblical writings, liberal theology frequently lost sight of their divine origin and goal. The Bible was seen as a record of the religious experiences of a particular people in history rather than as a witness to God's decisive intervention in history. Peter Macky, who has one foot in the biblical theology movement, can speak of the Bible as a witness to the human experience of the divine presence.[68]

When liberalism veers toward humanism, the final court of appeal is no longer Scripture or even religious experience but ordinary human experience. The Bible is discredited as a valuable source for ethics and theology, even considered to be "full of error, primitive ethics, bad theology."[69] In place of the fundamentalist emphasis on the inerrancy of Scripture we find a comparable insistence on its errancy and fallibility.

Some liberal theologians distinguished between "abiding truths" and "temporal trappings."[70] The former, they believed, could be abstracted from the limitations of their biblical setting. Against this position a catholic evangelical theology insists that form and content are inseparable, that we have the divine content only in the language of Canaan—the mythopoetic language of Holy Scripture.

While stressing the fragmentariness of truth in Scripture, Hans Küng at the same time acknowledges the inspiredness of Scripture in the sense of Scripture being filled with the presence of God. We must not speak of an a priori inerrancy of the propositions of Scripture, he says, but we can affirm its infallibility in that it is free from lying and fraud. Scripture is not impeccable in the sense that it is historically accurate on everything of which it speaks, but it is undeceiving in that it leads us into a fuller vision of the truth through the power of the Spirit. In the stories that the Bible relates, including those about Jesus' birth, miracles and resurrection, the important thing is not what really happened—of this we often know very little—but "what it means for us."[71] It is their existential import, not their historical truth, that renders the Bible a worthy guide for Christians on their spiritual journey. In this whole discussion Küng shows the influence of both Barth and the liberal theological tradition.

Far more radical is Rosemary Ruether, who finds in Scripture much that is totally unacceptable. Because of its patriarchalist orientation, Scripture needs to be critically assessed in the light of the experience of women and other oppressed peoples. We should not simply jettison the biblical tradition but make use of the positive resources within it to counteract the patriarchalist mindset that blunts its redemptive impact. Christ, she says, is not to be confined to the once-for-all historical Jesus but must be discovered in female luminaries of the faith as well. She calls for a Third Testament or expanded canon that would include writings drawn from goddess religions and Gnosticism as well as modern feminist spirituality.[72] In this way Scripture would become a more felicitous instrument in the cause of human liberation and justice.

While the Reformers spoke of the infallibility of Word and Spirit, and fundamentalists of the infallibility of the original manuscripts, some liberals have been inclined to hold to the infallibility of an informed reason or conscience. But can the inner word be a reliable criterion for faith when divorced from the written word and the incarnate Word—Jesus Christ?

If required to choose between liberalism and a rigid orthodoxy, my choice would unhesitatingly be the latter. In liberalism truth is dissolved so that only an amorphous experience remains. In orthodoxy truth is frozen into a formula or credo, but there is still hope that it can be brought back to life.[73]

The Question of Inerrancy

The doctrine of biblical inerrancy is presently a source of dispute in the evangelical community. While it is true that many of the fathers of the church described the Bible as free from all error, it is not always certain what they really meant. That most of them operated with a view of truth that is incongruous with the modern empiricist view shows that simply citing scholars of the past in support of this doctrine can be a venture in futility.

I affirm what many of the fathers in the faith, including the Reformers, meant by *inerrabilis*, but this term is not necessarily the most appropriate one today to describe the nature of truthfulness as the Bible understands it. We must not foist on Scripture an a priori speculative view of inerrancy. G. C. Berkouwer rightly asks

whether the reliability of Scripture is simply identical to that reliability of which we frequently speak concerning the record of various historical events. Frequently, terms such as "exact," "precise," and "accurate" are used for it. . . . Such a modern concept of reliability clearly should not be used as a yardstick for Scripture.[74]

Two Johannine passages often figure in the fundamentalist apologetic for inerrancy. John 17:17 records these words of Jesus to the Father: "Sanctify them in the truth; thy word is truth." The word proceeding from the mouth of the Father and relayed through the words of the Son is a mighty energy that cleanses from sin (cf. Jn 15:3). Nothing is said about whether the words of Scripture correspond exactly to historical and scientific facts. In John 10:35 Jesus reminds the Jews that "the Scripture cannot be broken" (NIV); that is, Scripture cannot be nullified or deprived of its validity. Jesus tries to show his opponents that in rejecting his claims they are nullifying the word of their own Scriptures. This is not a proof text for inspiration, much less for inerrancy, but together with other relevant texts (2 Tim 3:16; 1 Pet 1:10-12; 2 Pet 1:20-21) it points to the living God as the ultimate source of the Old Testament Scriptures.[75]

Augustine is frequently cited in defense of the doctrine of biblical inerrancy. He could declare: "All of us who read strive to trace out and understand what he whom we read actually meant, and since we believe him to speak the truth, we dare not assert that he spoke anything we know or think to be false."[76] At the same time he felt free to interpret parts of Scripture figuratively, such as the creation of the world in six days (Genesis 1). Though he affirmed that Scripture is free from real error, he admitted that there are "oversights and confusion of one name for another by the sacred writers. Discourses are recorded faithfully as far as the matter and thought are concerned, but great differences of order and expression can be found among the evangelists."[77]

Calvin occasionally referred to Scripture as an "unerring rule" and "unerring light," but the contexts indicate clearly that he was thinking of the teaching or doctrine of Scripture, not phenomenological descriptions of the world. Calvin acknowledged the reality of cultural limitations in the Bible but explained these limitations by his doctrine of the accommodation of the Holy Spirit to a finite and sinful humanity.[78]

In biblical religion error means swerving from the truth, wandering from the right path, rather than defective information (cf. Prov 12:28; Job 4:18; Ezek 45:20; Rom 1:27; 2 Pet 2:18; Jas 5:20; 1 Jn 4:6; 2 Tim 2:16-19). Scriptural inerrancy can be affirmed if it means the conformity of what is written to the dictates of the Spirit regarding the will and purpose of God. But it cannot be held if it is taken to mean the conformity of everything that is written in Scripture to the facts of world history and science.

There is a theological meaning of inerrancy that is not to be confused with a purely scientific or cultural meaning. Inerrancy in the biblical sense does not mean verbal exactness or precise accuracy of wording. Inerrancy can be defended in such a way as to deny growth or development in the understanding of Scripture as well as cultural conditioning of language and doctrinal formulations. Again, the criterion for inerrancy can be the latest findings in science rather than confirmation of the biblical promises by the Holy Spirit. Jesus complained that the Sadducees erred because they knew "neither the scriptures nor the power of God" (Mk 12:24). Here the criterion is the Word and the Spirit, not the conformation of thought to empirical reality.

Some moderate conservatives hold that the Bible has no errors in matters of faith and morals. Yet the fathers held that what is inerrant in Scripture is not only "saving truth" but also the *teaching* of Scripture concerning God, the world and humanity. At the same time, many statements in Scripture about God and the world do not form part of its express teaching. For example, not everything that the friends of Job said is infallible truth, and at places they were obviously in error. Yet this error is not to be attributed to Scripture as such. Jerome asserted that there is no material error in Scripture but added that it was usual for the sacred historian to conform himself to the generally accepted opinion of that time.[79]

The older evangelical position is illustrated in Charles Simeon, who was not averse to interpreting certain passages figuratively rather than literally. He was quite prepared to admit that while "no error in doctrine or other important matter is allowed; yet there are inexactnesses in reference to philosophical and scientific matters because of its popular style."[80] He regarded the book of Job as "a poem. Part of it may be allegorical, as Satan's appearance before God."[81]

With Barth I contend that not just parts of the Bible but the whole of Scripture bears the marks of cultural conditioning. The prophets and apostles bring us not only a divine perspective but also their cultural inheritance. To discern the mystery of God's self-revelation in Jesus Christ, we need to penetrate through the text to the light that illumined its author and that can still illumine the reader.

Even Warfield and A. A. Hodge admitted on occasion the imprint of cultural relativity in the Bible. They acknowledged that the Scriptures

are written in human languages, whose words, inflections, constructions, and idioms bear everywhere indelible traces of human error. The record itself furnishes evidence that the writers were in large measure dependent for their knowledge upon sources and methods in themselves fallible, and that their personal knowledge and judgments were in many matters hesitating and defective, or even wrong.[82]

Not surprisingly some conservatives criticized this statement as reflecting a low view of Scripture.[83]

That the Bible mirrors a view of the world that belongs to another period of history no competent biblical scholar will deny. Both Testaments picture Sheol and Hades as being under the earth (cf. Gen 37:35; Job 7:9; Ps 55:15; 86:13; Is 7:11; Ezek 31:15-17; Mt 11:23; Lk 10:15; 16:23). First Samuel describes the earth as set on pillars (2:8). A geocentric view of the world is reflected in the account of the sun standing still at the time of Joshua's victory over the Amorites (Josh 10:12-14). The book of Revelation alludes to the four corners of the earth (7:1; 20:8). Kidneys were believed to be the organs in which the emotions are experienced (Job 16:13; Lam 3:13) and blood to be the seat of life (Gen 9:4; Lev 17:14). In Matthew 13:31-32 our Lord refers to the mustard seed as the "smallest of all seeds," whereas we now know that that statement is untrue scientifically.

Such expressions in the Bible do not indicate real error but only the form or mode in which the teaching of Christ comes to us. Yet we must assume that the writers themselves believed these things and that they were to that extent mistaken. Calvin's explanation was that the Spirit of God accommodated himself to "mistaken, though generally received opinion."[84]

What appear to be historical inaccuracies and internal contradictions can be readily discerned in Scripture by any searching person. Numbers 25:9 tells us that twenty-four thousand people were destroyed by an epidemic, whereas 1 Corinthians 10:8 puts the figure at twenty-three thousand. In Genesis 1 humankind is created after the animals and in Genesis 2 before them. The figures for armies in Chronicles are generally higher than parallel accounts in Samuel-Kings. In 2 Kings 15:7 we are told that King Uzziah was buried with his fathers; but 2 Chronicles 26:23 tells us that Uzziah, because of his leprosy, was laid to rest in a field "adjoining the royal tombs" (REB). In 1 Samuel 31:4 Saul's death is described as a suicide, but according to 2 Samuel 1:5-10 he is killed by an Amalekite.[85] In 2 Samuel 10:18 David slays seven hundred Aramean chariot warriors; in 1 Chronicles 19:18 he kills seven thousand in what must have been the same battle. In Acts 7:4 Stephen says that Abraham left Haran after his father died, but Genesis 11:26, 32 implies that Terah was still living when the move was made from Haran.[86] Moreover, Stephen's claim that the promise to Abraham was given before he lived in Haran does not comport with Genesis 11:27—12:5. Yet he spoke under the inspiration of the Holy Spirit. Matthew 27:3-10 and Acts 1:18 relate two conflicting versions of Judas's death. In Mark 2:26 David supposedly entered the house of God under the high priest Abiathar and ate the loaves of offering, but in 1 Samuel 21:1-6 this event occurred not under Abiathar but under his father Ahimelech. Matthew 27:9 reads, "Then was fulfilled what had been spoken by the prophet Jeremiah." Calvin called this reference a mistake on the grounds that the reference should be to Zechariah.[87] In Mark 1:2 the words of Malachi (3:1) are erroneously attributed to Isaiah. The genealogies of Jesus in Matthew and Luke obviously conflict.

None of the foregoing examples proves that the Bible contains substantive error, though they are sufficient to shake one's confidence in Scripture if it is based on absolute factual accuracy according to the standards of modern science. Some discrepancies can possibly be explained on the basis of mistakes in translation and transmission. One passage may be exact and the other an approximation. The figures are often not meant to be precise but must be taken as generalized statements.[88] Luther readily granted that Scripture histories "are often concise and confused," but he added that the confusion is ours largely because the apostles are not reciting the *entire* history.[89] Part of the problem is that we are dealing with writers who are not taken out of their historical context by the Spirit but who write from their vantage point, which is necessarily limited. Another factor to consider is that these men were not seeking to give precise history (even in Kings and Chronicles) but interpreted history.[90]

Much more difficult are what appear to be questionable or contradictory theological assertions in the Bible. Psalm 139:22 seems to teach that we should hate our enemies, whereas Jesus and Paul exhorted us to love our enemies. There is a patent contradiction between the holy wars of the Old Testament and Jesus' view that his kingdom cannot be defended by the sword (Mt 26:52; Lk 9:54-56). It is doubtful whether some of the writers of the Old Testament envisioned a life after death. The author of Ecclesiastes apparently did not accept a life hereafter (cf. 3:19-22; 9:1-6), though some verses seem to point beyond skepticism in affirming that the key to human destiny lies in God (12:7, 13–14). The opposition between Paul and James on faith and justification is well known. Whereas Paul taught that we are justified only by faith in the righteousness of Christ, James contended that "a man is justified by works and not by faith alone" (Jas 2:24). Of course, this contradiction can be shown to be only an apparent one, for it is obvious that Paul and James are referring to a different kind of faith and also a different kind of works.[91]

Theological discrepancies especially between the Old and New Testaments can be at least partly explained on the basis of levels of revelation. Evangelical Christianity has always held that God revealed only so much of his plan and purpose to the prophets in Israelite history and that the culmination of his revelation did not occur until the incarnation and atoning death of his Son. The holy wars of the Old Testament must be seen in the light of New Testament teaching in which the holy war is reconceived in spiritual terms. We now fight not with weapons of the world but with the sword of the Lord, which is the Word of God. In addition, we fight not to destroy our fellow human beings but to liberate them.

Some theological as well as historical problems can be resolved by a fuller grasp of the goal and attitude of the author. The writer in Psalm 139:22 may well be expressing a personal frustration rather than a divine imperative. The intention in Genesis 2 is not to give a chronological order but to show that the animals could not be a helpmate to man.

It is commonly thought in the circles of higher criticism that Jesus was mistaken concerning the end of the world. But as a noted biblical scholar correctly points out, one of our Lord's predictions referred to the destruction of Jerusalem, which did occur within the lifetime of his disciples.[92]

I agree that the people of ancient Israel entertained numerous misconceptions of God as well as antiquated and even sub-Christian notions of human life and destiny. Yet such notions, which belong to a past time and culture, still have a place in the total biblical panorama, for they direct us to the center and apex of biblical history—the self-revelation of the living God in the person and work of Jesus Christ. It is through "the many changing tones of the human voices" in Scripture that we hear "the deeper tone of the one divine voice."[93]

We must take care not to consign any idea or report in Scripture to a past era without first trying to ascertain how it is related to the central message of Scripture. Many so-called contradictions are resolved when we see them in the light of the whole of Scripture. This does not imply that every text can be harmonized with every other one, or that they can be shown to coincide exactly with objective history. Because the writers did not always aim for precision in wording, it is unwise to try to harmonize all details. What is normative for us is the intention of the writer or, better still, the intention of the Spirit—what the Spirit wants to teach us—not whether the text in every case accurately describes world history. There was editorializing in the Bible but not elaboration to the extent of deliberately falsifying what really transpired.[94]

The prophets and apostles did not claim to possess an infinite or final perspective. Not even Jesus made this claim, for he admitted that no one knows the day or the hour, not even the Son (Mt 24:36). The psalmist confesses, "Such knowledge is too wonderful for me; it is high, I cannot attain it" (139:6). Daniel makes the frank admission, "I heard, but I did not understand" (Dan 12:8; cf. Job 42:3). Even though having direct access to the Torah, the psalmist implores God to teach us the meaning of his laws (119:33 GNB). The transcendence of the divine content of Scripture is also affirmed in Psalm 71:15: "All day long I will speak of your salvation, though it is more than I can understand" (GNB). Peter pictures the prophets as earnestly striving to understand what the Spirit of the Messiah was teaching them to see (1 Pet 1:10-11). Paul is careful not to equate his own views on marriage with the mind of God (1 Cor 7:12), yet he claims to have the Spirit of Christ. In Hebrews 1:1 we read that the Spirit of God "spoke in fragmentary and varied fashion through the prophets" (NEB). Some prophecies in Scripture need correction. Jesus assures us that John the Baptist was the object of the prophecy in Malachi 4:5, even though the prophet speaks of Elijah (Mt 11:14; 17:9-13). This could be a case of the spiritual fulfillment of prophecy, however, for John is presented as the spiritual Elijah.

Faith demands historical investigation of the text but opposes rationalistic, destructive criticism. Brevard Childs rightly warns against using the principles of criticism with liberal presuppositions, for example, dating a book late because of predictions that later came true. Bernard Ramm recommends a "reverent criticism"[95] and Peter Stuhlmacher a "hermeneutics of consent."[96]

Criticism is demanded on the basis of the prophetic concern to discriminate between the absolute and the relative. We are called to test the spirits (1 Jn 4:1) and to beware of false prophets (Mt 7:15). We are also warned not to bow down before graven images (Ex 20:4-6), and in its wider application this warning certainly includes mental images. We must come to the Bible with a faithful and searching mind, prepared to make use of critical methods if we are able to do so. In this kind of biblical study we will see inconsistencies of a historical and theological nature. But if we are faithful we will discern within and behind the historical relativity a unity of divine revealing action and faith response. Alan Richardson echoes my own sentiments:

> The longer we spend in reflection on this subject, the more we are impressed, as we read our Bibles, by the unity of the whole Bible, and the more likely we shall be to revert to the view that the inspiration of the Holy Spirit had probably something to do with the matter after all.[97]

The Bible is a document concerning not science, history or religion as such but a divine-human encounter, which we find above all in Jesus Christ. It is made clear in the New Testament that the prophets of Israel wrote of Jesus (Jn 5:46-47; Lk 24:27), even though they could not grasp the full intent of the prophecies given to them. The purpose of the Bible is to grant us "the wisdom that leads to salvation through faith in Christ Jesus" (2 Tim 3:15 NJB). The Westminster Confession describes Scripture as our "infallible . . . rule for faith and life" (2.5.9). Samuel Rutherford, one of its authors, warned that the Bible is not our rule "in things of Art and Science . . . to demonstrate conclusions of Astronomie," but it is our rule "in fundamentalls of salvation . . . in all morals of both first and second table."[98] This same understanding is reflected in the Belgic Confession: "We believe that these Holy Scriptures fully contain the will of God, and that whatsoever man ought to believe unto salvation, is sufficiently taught therein" (art. 7).[99]

I depart from some of my evangelical colleagues in that I understand the divine content of Scripture not as rationally comprehensible teachings but as the mystery of salvation declared in Jesus Christ (cf. Rom 16:25; Eph 1:9; 6:19; Col 1:26; 2:2).[100] This mystery can be stated in propositional form, but it eludes rational comprehension. It can be described but never fully grasped. The gospel and the law together constitute the divine content of Scripture, but this word from the beyond is always a concrete promise or command given by God to the reader or hearer. The actual commandments and promises in Scripture are barren principles unless they are united with God's self-revelation in Christ so that we truly hear God's Word in these very human words. That is, the final criterion for faith is not the words of the Bible as such but the paradoxical unity of Word and Spirit, which is always a gift of grace and not a human achievement. The divine content or wisdom of God is hidden in the Bible and awaits its disclosure by the action of the Spirit.

We are given in the Bible not a fully developed metaphysical worldview but a divine message and a divine imperative that nevertheless have metaphysical implications. Neither are we given an absolutely accurate account of Israel's history, but we have a faithful rendition of God's action in the community of Israel. We have the divine content in the earthen vessel of the biblical testimony. The biblical culture is prescientific, but the truth that the Bible attests is suprascientific. We are confronted with a divine perspective that is present in Scripture but cannot be explained by culture or history.

The Bible as a historical document is amazingly accurate and trustworthy. An unbelieving historian who is open to the facts can discern this accuracy, although this rarely happens when the Spirit of God is not actively involved. As evangelical Christians we are not required to affirm the perfect, factual accuracy of the Bible. Indeed, the text itself seems to belie such accuracy.

Can we speak of the infallibility of Scripture, as did our fathers and mothers in the faith? Does this term cover the theological meaning of inerrancy? Infallibility has historically meant that everything that the Bible reports and teaches is intended by God to be read and heard by his church. The original meaning of infallibility, as the root of the word shows (the Latin *fallere*—to lead into error, to disappoint or deceive) is that the Bible is "not deceiving or deceived." It does not connote that the Bible is free from all error of any kind. It means not faultlessness but being incapable of teaching deception.

Here again we are confronted with the impenetrable mystery of the dual nature of the Bible. It is both a divine word to a sinful and broken humanity and a human witness to an incomparable divine action in history. There is not only divine splendor but also human weakness and infirmity in the Bible (Herman Bavinck). The Bible contains a fallible element in the sense that it reflects the cultural and historical limitations of the writers. But it is not mistaken in what it purports to teach: God's will and purpose for the world. It bears the imprint of human frailty, but it also carries the truth and power of divine infallibility. We cannot affirm that the propositions in the Bible are a priori infallible, but we can affirm that God's infallible revelation is communicated through these propositions.

The Bible contains the perfect Word of God in the imperfect words of human beings. It is better to speak of ambiguities and inconsistencies in the Bible, even imperfections, rather than error. The reason is that what the Bible purports to tell us is not in error. While it employs modes of expression that are now outdated, scientifically speaking, the meaning-content that it conveys transcends both culture and history. The Bible is imperfect in its form but not mistaken in its intent. The formulations of the Bible are not fully adequate in the sense of giving a comprehensive explanation, but they are also not erroneous. They are adequate to the truth revealed in them.

In my opinion it is wiser to speak of the truthfulness or veracity of Scripture rather than of its inerrancy. *Infallibility* and *authority* are also terms that can be legitimately applied to Scripture. Yet all these terms need to be qualified, for the truthfulness and infallibility that characterize Scripture are derivative from the One who alone is infallible and authoritative in the full sense of these words. We should also keep in mind that infallibility and veracity apply to the whole Bible, to its overall message, to its revelatory meaning, not to any particular text or report in the Bible.

I affirm that the message of Scripture is infallible and that the Spirit infallibly interprets this message to people of faith. But the perfect accuracy of the letter or text of Scripture is not an integral part of Christian faith. Because the term *inerrancy* is so often associated with the latter position, I agree with Clark Pinnock that it is not the preferable word to use in theological discussion today, even though it should not be abandoned, for it preserves the nuance of truthfulness that is necessary for a high view of Holy Scripture.[101]

Bernard Ramm made a useful distinction between the *graphē* (Scripture), *gramma* (letter) and *pneuma* (Spirit).[102] The *graphē* embodies and conveys infallible truth because it signifies the union of letter and spirit. In this context *graphē* indicates the divine meaning-content of Scripture, its inner *forma*. Consequently, when we speak of Scripture's infallibility, we mean not the letter, not the text, but the letter in its union with the Spirit.

I would not wish to say (as does the Presbyterian Confession of 1967) that no statement of faith is irreformable.[103] The biblical affirmations can be expanded and perhaps qualified but certainly not reformed. They can be amplified and clarified, but they must not be changed.

Against one strand in neo-orthodox theology, I am reluctant to say that infallibility resides exclusively in the Spirit speaking to us as we read the Bible. Nor does infallibility reside wholly in the text (as fundamentalists allege). Rather it lies in the paradoxical unity of Spirit and word, in the Spirit speaking not alongside the word but in and through the word, elucidating its deepest meaning.

While acknowledging innocent factual inaccuracies in the Bible, I hesitate to call these errors. I readily grant that forms of expression in Scripture may conflict with science,[104] but science is not the final norm, for scientific theories are constantly in flux. Because error does not touch what is truly divine in the Bible, it is more proper to speak of "difficulties" than of errors, of chaff but not tares. The writers may well take the liberty of changing some details in order to make a theological point, but this does not constitute error. Again, we must remember that their aim was not historical precision but theological interpretation.

We believe the Bible, but we do not believe in the Bible. We believe what the Bible testifies concerning Jesus Christ. The Bible's authority must be based not on the debatable premise that it contains no historical inaccuracy or deficient theological formulation but rather on its capacity to render a reliable and trustworthy picture of God's dealings with humanity. This capacity is founded on the revelatory and inspiring work of the Spirit—on both writers and readers. The Bible is normative as the unique instrument of the Spirit and as the original witness to God's special revelation fulfilled in Jesus Christ.

The Nature of Inspiration

Inspiration, which is derived from the Latin *inspiratio,* means being "dominated" or "filled with the Spirit of God." It does not mean, as the ancient Greeks supposed, that our rational faculties are suspended or that our personality is negated. Hellenistic theories of inspiration had a considerable influence on the early church fathers. The biblical writers were often compared to a flute, totally passive in the hands of a flutist. In ecstasy human individuality appears to be extinguished under the impact of the divine frenzy. The emphasis of the church fathers and their medieval successors was on the inspiration of the writers of Scripture rather than on the writings themselves.

The modern evangelical doctrine of inspiration was largely shaped by Warfield, who defined inspiration as "that extraordinary, supernatural influence (or, passively, the result of it) exerted by the Holy Ghost on the writers of our Sacred Books, by which their words were rendered also the words of God, and, therefore, perfectly infallible."[105] Warfield claimed that this definition was not intended to clarify the mode of inspiration but only its effects. He used such words as "superintendence" and "concursus" to describe the domination of God in the process of inspiration. God works in and on the human author in such a way that the latter is rendered a willing instrument of the former. Warfield affirmed a human side to Scripture but not an authentically human element. He denied all human contribution to the actual content of Scripture except in matters of style and personality. At the same time, he sought to steer clear of any concept of mechanical dictation. For Warfield and A. A. Hodge, inspiration pertains not to the available text but to the autographic text.

The evangelical Baptist theologian Augustus Strong had a strikingly different understanding of inspiration:

Inspiration is that influence of the Spirit of God upon the minds of the Scripture writers which made their writings the record of a progressive divine revelation, sufficient, when taken together and interpreted by the same Spirit who inspired them, to lead every honest inquirer to Christ and to salvation.[106]

The purpose of inspiration is not the production of an errorless book but the regeneration of the seeker after truth. Strong did not rule out the possibility of error in Scripture except in things essential to the overall purpose of inspiration. "Inspiration is still consistent with much imperfection in historical detail and its narratives 'do not seem to be exempted from possibilities of error.' "[107] Strong's approach was inductive rather than deductive in that his position on biblical authority is based on an investigation of the effects of the biblical message on the community of faith. The role of the Spirit of God is to quicken the natural powers of the human writer to such a degree that "he discovers and expresses the truth for himself."[108] The writers are assisted and led by the Spirit of God rather than being the pens of the Spirit, who alone is the actual author of Scripture. My difficulty with Strong is that he tended to view the Bible as partly human and partly divine, thereby failing to give due acknowledgment to the paradoxical mystery of the divinity of the Bible shining everywhere through its true humanity. Nonetheless, I prefer Strong to Warfield, who downplays the humanity of Scripture for the sake of affirming an errorless book.

In my view inspiration is the divine election and superintendence of particular writers and writings in order to ensure a trustworthy and potent witness to the truth. The Spirit of the Lord rests not only on the prophet but also on his words (cf. Is 59:21; 49:2; Jer 1:9). Illumination is the inward awakening of the believer to the truth that is revealed. The critical elements in divine inspiration are the election and divine guidance of the writers, the inward illumination of hearers and readers, and the communication of the truth of revelation. In this definition I am thinking basically of the illumination of the hearers and writers in biblical history. It is possible, however, to expand the meaning to include all subsequent history of the people of faith. John Albert Bengel held that "Scripture was divinely inspired not merely while it was being written, God breathing through the writers, but also while it is being read (and expounded), God breathing through the Scripture."[109] Because it is theologically appropriate to distinguish the unique production of the inspiring action of the Spirit in the past from his illuminating activity in the present, I prefer to think of inspiration mainly in connection with the biblical writings, which constitute the primary witness to divine revelation.[110]

I offer this more comprehensive definition of inspiration: the divine election and guidance of the biblical prophets and the ensuring of their writings as a compelling witness to revelation, the opening of the eyes of the people of that time to the truth of these writings, and the providential preservation of these writings as the unique channel of revelation. By the biblical prophets I have in mind all preachers, writers and editors in biblical history who were made the unique instruments of God's self-revealing action.

The Bible is God-breathed in the sense that it is a production of the creative breath of God. The breath of the Holy Spirit accounts for both the Bible's origin and its viability through the ages. The breath of God and the wisdom of God are closely correlated in biblical history.[111] When we are illumined by the Spirit of God, we are then made capable of apprehending the wisdom of God. For this reason the Bible is a shining lamp to those who dwell in darkness, and its testimonies give joy to those who walk through the valley of tribulation (cf. Ps 119:105, 111-12, 129-30).

The purpose of the inspiration of writers and writings is to serve God's self-revelation in Jesus Christ. By virtue of its divine inspiration the Bible is made a bearer of the Spirit of power, a sacramental sign of the presence of God. Inspiration also renders the Bible a reliable witness to revelation. It guarantees that the biblical affirmations are divinely authorized and true.[112] Inspiration makes Scripture revelatory—open to divine truth. Revelation makes Scripture salvific so that it communicates the divine truth and power. Inspiration means that God sends forth his Spirit to prepare the way for his Word; revelation means that God speaks his Word in conjunction with the testimony of his inspired prophets and apostles.

Inspiration is both conceptual and verbal. It is permissible to speak of verbal inspiration or verbal inspiredness, but not in the sense of perfect factual accuracy or mechanical dictation. It means that the words of human beings are adopted to serve the purposes of God.[113] The personalities of the authors are not violated but used in such a way as to give glory to God. Inspiration assures the church of a knowledge sufficient for salvation, not a knowledge sufficient for the construction of a unified and finalized worldview. What is without error is the divine teaching of Scripture, the divine wisdom that constitutes the inner *forma* of Scripture, but this teaching and wisdom are veiled to the detached investigator of Scripture.

Plenary inspiration means that all of Scripture is inspired. It does not imply that all of Scripture has equal value. With Ramm I oppose a "flat view of Scripture" that does not make a distinction between what is essential and what is marginal, what is in the foreground and what is background material.[114]

Hans Küng makes this trenchant observation:

The testimonies recorded in the New Testament have neither the same texture nor the same value. Some are brighter, some darker; some are more intelligible, some less; some are stronger, some weaker; some are more original, some derivative. There are testimonies that can diverge, contrast, and partially contradict one another. They are held together by the fundamental testimony that Jesus Christ has revealed the God who interacts with us.[115]

Divine inspiration entails guidance or superintendence, illumination and even preservation. God preserves the actual testimony of his herald as the medium of his continual self-disclosure in the community founded on the incarnation. The reality of God's preservation of Scripture is attested both in Scripture (Deut 10:5ff.; Ps 12:5-6; Is 30:8; Jer 36:27-28; Rom 3:2; 15:8) and in the Westminster Confession of Faith (chap. 1, art. 8).

Inspiration does not imply that the writers were given a literal or comprehensive grasp of the mystery of divine salvation. They were given a reliable but incomplete knowledge of God's will and purpose. Their language about God and his works is not univocal but symbolic or analogical. Inspiration means that the authors were guided to choose words that correspond with God's Word. But we are not to conclude that they are identical with God's Word, for no human language can encompass or exhaust the unsurpassable reality of divine knowledge and wisdom. God's wisdom and love infinitely transcend all human knowledge and formulation (Job 5:9; Ps 145:3; Rom 11:33; 1 Cor 2:9; Eph 3:18-19).

Inspiration does not guarantee that the Bible is inerrant in the sense of being exempt from human misconceptions and limitations—even in the areas of ethics and theology. Nor does it imply that the Bible is free from textual and linguistic errors. It does mean that the prophets and apostles have a basic understanding of the purposes of God grounded in revelation itself. We have in their words a reliable and unfailing witness to God's saving acts but not an infallible record of world history.[116]

Their interpretation is at the same time adequate and inadequate, fallible and infallible, sufficient and deficient. Their knowledge is not infinite or unlimited but adequate to the truth revealed to them. They were children of their times but also prophets to their times. Their interpretation was not fallacious or erroneous but faithful to what God revealed to them. The Holy Spirit did not overrule their personalities but entered into their personalities, guiding them to see what only faith can grasp. H. M. Kuitert observes:

> God came to be spoken of and spoken to, not in the language of some super-time (for no man knows such a language), but in a particular language of a particular time. This is not an accidental by-product. God gives Himself as companion to particular and very real people, people who must speak about and to God in the very particular and real language that is their own. The time-bound Bible is not a regrettable concession; it is the only kind of Bible men could have. It is necessarily bound to time; and this fact is a mark of its authenticity as a revelation of the covenant-partner God.[117]

Inspiration does not cancel out the human element but directs it toward a divine end. I heartily agree with G. C. Berkouwer that "the Spirit despises nothing human." Inspiration is best understood not as dictation but as interpenetration by the Spirit. With Bavinck and Berkouwer I favor a theory of organic inspiration over mechanical inspiration.[118] The Spirit enters into the history and culture of the writers and does not simply superimpose truth on them. The Bible is not a celestial tape recorder but a report of an event or series of events in history that changed the world. I affirm not a supernaturalism that elevates the Bible above the relativities of history but one in which the divine enters into these relativities.

The truth of the Bible is indeed infallible in that the Bible does not deceive concerning what it purports to show us and teach us. Scripture unfailingly reveals the will and purpose of God to believing people. Neo-orthodoxy says that we must differentiate between the human expression and the divine ground. I believe that we must acknowledge the reality of a human content in Scripture but one subordinated to the divine content. I affirm no independent or autonomous human content but one that depends totally on divine meaning. Scripture has two sides—the divine and the human, but we have the divine only in and through the human.

The inspiration of Scripture might be made clearer by the illustration of an ambulance that appears at the scene of a collision on a highway. Some people directly witness this event; others in cars ahead and behind hear about it secondhand. All accurately report what they see and hear, yet there will invariably be discrepancies. There is no such thing as a bare fact; every fact is interpreted and sometimes elaborated on in order to bring out its significance.

The intention of the biblical writers was not precision in detail but the meaning of the revelatory event for us. When we read each report in the light of the whole, we can discern a certain underlying harmony, even if not all differences can be reconciled. Yet the testimony of those who were ear- and eyewitnesses remains normative for us, since this is all we have. Their witness is normative even though it is limited and imperfect. It is not erroneous, but it is also not comprehensive or synoptic, since only God perceives the whole picture.

Because God has spoken to those whom he has inspired and promises to speak again and again through their existential witness, it takes on a normative and binding character. God has elected this witness as an earthen vessel through which to make known his infallible Word. It is not a cracked vessel but a slightly marred or weatherbeaten vessel, shaped by the vicissitudes of history as well as by God's hand at work in history.

The differences between my understanding of inspiration and that of dispensationalists, who are inclined to interpret the biblical events literalistically, is brought to light by comparing our respective interpretations of the holy wars of the Old Testament. Dispensationalists see God's command to wipe out whole peoples and cities as truly indicating God's express will and purpose for that time, though not necessarily for the dispensation in which we live. I see this command as indicating God's provisional will but not his final will. Abominable sins merit destruction and annihilation, but the fuller picture that the Bible discloses is of a God who kills in order to make alive, who destroys in order to save. The armies of Israel were not simply instruments of his wrath but also servants of his love. The Old Testament writers bring us a defective understanding of the holy war but not a wholly erroneous understanding. When we view the holy war in the light of the culmination of God's self-revelation in Jesus Christ, we see that the emphasis should be on Israel's dependence on God, not on weapons of destruction. Gideon conquered the Midianites because of his trust in God, for his weapons had been taken from him (Judg 7). The fuller meaning of the holy war is that it is God who carries out this purifying work, and the task of his people is to witness to what he has done. Moses implored the children of Israel who were fleeing Pharaoh's army to stand firm and unafraid: "The LORD will fight for you, and you have only to be still" (Ex 14:13-14). In the holy war of the Old Testament God does not so much fight *with* Israel as *for* Israel. In the prophetic development of this concept Israel's role becomes increasingly passive, leaving the direction of history in God's hands (cf. Is 30:15; Ps 108:11, 13).

In the New Testament the idea of the holy war is transformed. It now indicates a spiritual warfare fought with spiritual weapons. Military metaphors abound in the New Testament as well as in the Old. In the Old Testament the idea of the holy war was often interpreted as a war between Yahweh and the pagan gods. In the New Testament the holy war is waged between Jesus Christ and Satan. In the Old Testament the victors offered the enemy as a human sacrifice to God. In the New Testament we offer ourselves as sacrifices to God. The New Testament gives us the fuller picture, which corrects some understandings in the Old Testament that were necessarily limited and provisional.

The Bible contains both wheat and husk. The husk is not falsehood or even what is peripheral or marginal. It has an important, even an indispensable, role, for it holds the wheat. The speeches of Job's friends must be interpreted as husk, not wheat. God's Word was reflected in their testimony but not to the same degree as in the words of Job. The husk becomes error or tares only when it is mistaken for the wheat. The husk is the law separated from the gospel; the wheat is the gospel, which gives new meaning to the law. Luther said that we should embrace that theology "which searches out the nut from the shell, the grain from the husk, the marrow from the bone." The kernel or the grain is not an abiding universal principle or transcendent ideal (as in liberalism) but the divine promise and the divine commandment that must be uttered again and again by the living God if we are to understand it sufficiently for obedience under the cross.

We can say with catholic and evangelical tradition that God is the primary author of Scripture, and the prophets and apostles secondary authors. They were limited in their perception of the truth revealed to them, but they were not in error concerning it. They were deficient in their understanding of the will of God, but they did not give a mistaken account of God's purposes for their time. On one level the Scriptures do not escape the limitations of history; on another level they transcend these limitations.

The authority of Scripture rests finally not on the inspired record but on God speaking to us through this record. What brings the Bible to life is the personal encounter with Jesus Christ, who is its pivotal center and culmination. Its authority rests not on the scientific verification of its statements but on the forcefulness of its precepts and promises. The key to inspiration is not whether the text is perfect from a human standpoint but whether we hear the Word of God in the text.

According to C. S. Lewis the Bible does not give us "impeccable science or history."[119] For him the Old Testament is not as such the

Word of God, but it "carries" the Word of God. We should use it not as "an encyclopedia or an encyclical" but "by steeping ourselves in its tone or temper and so learning its overall message."[120]

The text when taken only by itself, apart from its theological and spiritual context, is fallible and deficient. When the Bible is treated only academically or scientifically, it does not disclose the truth of salvation. But when the text is seen in its true context, then it becomes the vehicle of infallible truth. It becomes what it originally was and substantially is— the infallible Word of God. The most appropriate symbol of the Word of God is not the closed book but the open Bible being read in faith— or, better still, the cross of Christ shining through the pages of the open Bible.[121]

Inspiration and Revelation

A full understanding of inspiration will see it as involving both subjective illumination and objective guidance. It denotes the divine election of both the writers and what is written in order to prepare the way for the coming of the kingdom. We may therefore speak of verbal inspiration. James Smart rightly says, "The revelation is *in the text itself*, in the words that confront us there in all their strangeness, and not in a history or a personal biography or an event that we reconstruct by means of the text."[122]

Inspiration depends on revelation and serves revelation. It records and preserves the truth of revelation. It provides both a trustworthy account of past revelation and an appropriate vehicle for ongoing revelation. Inspiration is not the ground of revelation but an element in revelation—meaning here the whole process of God's self-disclosure to his elect people. Inspiration concerns the reliability of the scriptural witness; revelation refers to the self-disclosure of Jesus Christ in the biblical witness. Inspiration signifies the election of the biblical witness; revelation, the uniting of the biblical witness with God's self-witness. Inspiration is the overseeing and directing of the biblical writing; revelation is the rendering of the biblical testimony transparent to its divine content. Inspiration means that the Bible is penetrated and filled with the Holy Spirit; revelation occurs when the Bible transmits the Word of God by the action of the Spirit. Inspiration has to do mainly with the form of the Bible; revelation, with its content. Inspiration concerns primarily the sign; revelation, the thing signified. Revelation is the shining of the light of God through the prism of Scripture; inspiration is ensuring that Scripture can be a prism for God's light. Inspiration reaches its goal in revelation; revelation finds its springboard in inspiration.

Inspiration encompasses not only the writing but also the compiling, the editing, the preserving of Holy Scripture. Küng widens the concept even further:

> The *entire* course of the origin, collection, and transmission of the Word, the entire process of believing acceptance and proclaiming transmission of the biblical message is—for believers—under the leadership and dispensation of the Spirit. In other words, inspiration is rightly understood only when not only the history of the writing down of Scripture, but its entire history before and after this, is understood as "inspired" by the Spirit: not dictated by the Spirit, but *penetrated and filled with the Spirit.*[123]

Inspiration produces a reliable testimony to the works of God because the Holy Spirit not only inspired the writers but also sanctioned what was written. He guided them toward what they were not always able to see and understand through their own power. They were limited in their vision but not mistaken in what was given to them to understand.

In my view inspiration is correlative with immediate or final revelation; illumination is correlative with mediate or continuing revelation. Like biblical revelation, biblical inspiration has ended.[124] But the illumination of the Holy Spirit together with dependent or mediate revelation continues.

I believe that the whole Bible constitutes a compelling witness to Jesus Christ. It is God's self-revelation in Jesus Christ that gives the Bible its authority. But we should not believe in everything that the Bible speaks about. A distinction should always be made between what

Scripture reports and includes and what it teaches or intends. The point is not whether Scripture is inerrant in all factual details but whether it is *true*. We must affirm that the writers of the Bible, being human, had a capacity for error. But we must also insist that what the Holy Spirit teaches in and through their words is completely truthful.

We need today a renewal of confidence in Holy Scripture as the written Word of God, but we must always see this Word as coming to us in and through the words of human beings who in themselves were fallible and limited. Fundamentalism has absolutized the words of the Bible, thereby exempting them from human criticism; and liberalism has relativized these words, thereby denuding them of any authority they might have for the community of faith. We must not, in the manner of Semler, reduce revelation to a religious experience that has only an incidental relationship to the inspired text of Scripture.[125] But neither should we align ourselves with Warfield, who portrayed Holy Scripture as directly or immediately God's Word.[126] His opponent Charles Briggs offered an even less palatable alternative: "The Bible, as a book, is paper, print, and binding,—nothing more. . . . There is nothing divine in the text,—in its letters, words, or clauses."[127]

Nor dare we say with Nels Ferré: "God wants to write new and even better scriptures, both in life and in books."[128] The Bible has a unique authority because it is the appointed witness to what God did for our salvation in biblical history—especially in the life history of Jesus Christ. Because God chose these writers for a particular task and chooses to speak through them anew in every age and culture, the Bible can justly be called the Word of God. I hold to an ontic difference between the Bible and other books, for the Bible has both a divine origin and a divine goal.

James Barr has been unhappy with "Word-of-God language" as applied to Scripture because he regards Scripture as an entirely human work.[129] The proper term for the Old Testament, he says, is the "Word of Israel," and for the New Testament the "Word of some leading early Christians."[130] Given the great religious diversity in the Bible, he questions the efforts of the biblical theology movement to find an overarching unity in the biblical witness, preferring to relegate study of the Bible to the general study of the world religions.[131] Barr has regrettably lost sight of the divine ground and focus of the biblical narrative.

I agree with Augustine that "nothing should be accepted, save on the authority of the Bible, for this authority is much greater than the capacity of the human spirit."[132] Our authority is anchored not in reason or mystical insight but in Scripture, for it is there that Jesus Christ meets us, and it is in the words of Scripture that we hear the divine Word. The Scriptures were recorded by human beings but inspired by the Spirit of God. In them the Spirit continues to speak to people today and every day. We should not adore Scripture, because Scripture is not in and of itself divine, but we should respect, even reverence, Scripture as the divinely appointed medium by which God chooses to reveal himself to us.

In contradistinction to the older orthodoxy, I contend that inspiration does not guarantee the reality of revelation, but it sets the stage for revelation. It opens up the possibility of revelation, though revelation is always a new and creative act of the living God. Inspiration effects not the transcribing of revelation but the creation of an appropriate vehicle for revelation. It does not produce an objectified revelation directly available to human reason, but it does insure a reliable testimony to revelation, sufficient for an external understanding of God's will and purpose for our lives. It furnishes the historical and doctrinal material for revelation, but it does not reduce revelation to axioms of logic or propositions of discourse. Inspiration is incomplete without revelation, for its goal is the knowledge of revelation. Revelation presupposes inspiration, since God reveals himself in conjunction with the historical witness to his saving action.

Scripture is authoritative because it is penetrated and filled with the Holy Spirit. It is God-breathed, and the creative breath of God remains in and with Scripture. Yet the self-revelation of God is not inherent in the letter but is always an act of free grace. A neutral observer can discern the historical truth that Scripture contains, but the truth of God's revelation remains hidden until God himself acts and speaks. The unbelieving critic can understand Scripture as a human witness but never grasp the power and significance of this witness. The notional or conceptual meaning of Scripture is available to natural reason but not its revelational or existential meaning.

Küng has declared, " 'It is written' can never mean 'God's word lies before us in writing.' It is not there to be recognized by any neutral observer, to be forced on man as it were."[133] Yet in the mystery of God's redeeming purposes God can and does make his Word available to us in the human words that stand before us in Scripture. We cannot take this availability for granted, however; we must hope and pray for it. When God sends forth his Spirit, it is then that we are introduced to his Word, it is then that our rudimentary knowledge is united and transformed by the divine wisdom that belongs to the very being of God.

Otto Weber puts it well.

> The doctrine of the inward testimony of the Holy Spirit announces the discovery that the authority of Scripture can be secured neither objectively (in the sense of the classical doctrine of inspiration) nor subjectively (in the sense of our own experience), but rather that we will only be persuaded of it when God the Holy Spirit, God in his freedom as the One who effects both our freedom and our bondage, reaches out to us through the scriptural Word. The *theopneustia* of Scripture is not a passive characteristic of Scripture but rather a vital saving activity.[134]

The Bible is crucial not simply because it "contains glorious literature, important historical documents, exalted ethical teachings" (Gordon Kaufman)[135] but because it is the Word of God to a despairing and broken humanity. But this Word is to be found not simply in the words of Scripture as they stand by themselves but in illuminated words, words that are adopted by the Spirit of God and united with God's own word addressed to us personally in the time and place in which we live.

Appendix B: The Rogers-McKim Proposal

The controversy surrounding the publication of *The Authority and Interpretation of the Bible: An Historical Approach* by Jack B. Rogers and Donald K. McKim is still with us. At the time Rogers was professor of philosophical theology at Fuller Theological Seminary and McKim a visiting faculty member in religion at Westminster College, New Wilmington, Pennsylvania. The book was roundly attacked by conservative evangelicals who complained that it presented a biased report of the church's doctrine of the authority of Scripture. The most detailed rebuttal came from John D. Woodbridge in *Biblical Authority: A Critique of the Rogers/McKim Proposal,* which was enthusiastically endorsed by Kenneth Kantzer and James Packer, among others.

I welcome the publication of both these books for the reason that scriptural authority, including its inspiration and truthfulness, needs to be rethought, particularly in the light of the new critical theories that undergird biblical studies today. I direct my comments mainly to Rogers and McKim, but I shall have something to say about Woodbridge as well.

1. In my opinion Rogers and McKim have produced a landmark study on how church theologians through the ages have assessed the authority of Scripture. They do not claim that their analysis is definitive or complete, for they are acutely aware of the lacunae that need to be filled. What they have given is a broad overview of the historical debate on the role of Scripture in the life of the church. Their book deserves serious attention because scriptural authority is a major theological issue today, especially in the evangelical world.

2. The authors are right in their efforts to uncover the philosophical presuppositions that have informed theology through the ages. They see theology influenced by two major philosophers—Plato and Aristotle. The former was more oriented toward the mystical and transcendental, the latter toward the empirical and rational. They detect in Protestant orthodoxy after the Reformation a "significant shift . . . from the Neoplatonic presuppositions of the Reformers to the Aristotelian assump-

tions of the Reformers' medieval opponents."[136]

While it is true that the Reformers, particularly Calvin, were more open to Platonism and Neoplatonism than to Aristotle, this kind of historical judgment overlooks the radical break of the Reformation with the biblical-classical synthesis of the early and medieval church, which signified a tacit accommodation to Platonism as much as to other currents of Hellenistic philosophy. Although the early Luther was admittedly influenced by the Rhineland mystics who were greatly indebted to Neoplatonism, he decisively broke with mysticism as his theology developed. His rediscovery of agape represented a significant challenge to the Augustinian *caritas,* which proved to be an ill-fated attempt to harmonize the Greek concept of eros with the biblical agape (Anders Nygren).[137] While Protestant orthodoxy did seek to restore Aristotle, Reformed and Lutheran Pietism were much more open to the tradition of Catholic mysticism. All these movements ended up sundering the dialectical relationship of Word and Spirit[138] and were thereby unable to present a solid biblical alternative to the rising rationalism of the time.

Unlike Rogers and McKim, I see Plato as a far more dangerous adversary to Christian faith than Aristotle precisely because he appears to be much closer to the biblical way of viewing life and the world. The new spirituality (including the New Thought and New Age movements) that is challenging Christian faith today owes much more to Plato and Plotinus than to Aristotle.

3. Following Berkouwer, Rogers and McKim speak of the Bible as infallible in its function or purpose. It infallibly accomplishes its purpose in bringing us Christ and his gift of salvation. The Bible as a historical and literary document is indeed vulnerable to error, they say, because it is planted in the stream of history, but the truth to which it directs us is infallible, for this truth—being the living Christ himself—is suprahistorical. Though it is possible to detect here a Platonic thrust that devalues the historical, their emphasis is not on eternal ideas but on the eternal God, the creator and mover of history.

While I readily grant that scriptural infallibility can legitimately be described in functional terms, is one being faithful to the biblical perspective by thinking of infallibility exclusively in these terms? Besides infallibly directing us to Christ, does not Scripture provide infallible information concerning the will and purpose of God as supremely manifested in Christ? The Bible not only directs us to truth but also speaks truth. It not only points to truth but also communicates truth.

Rogers and McKim remind us that the Reformers had an instrumental view of scriptural authority in that they saw Scripture as the instrument of the Spirit of God. But Scripture could be the ongoing instrument of God's Spirit only because the Spirit was the ultimate author of Scripture. Our two authors sometimes give the impression that the Bible is an inspiring but not an inspired book.[139]

4. In contradistinction to Rogers and McKim and perhaps also to the later Berkouwer, I see the Bible as having an ontological as well as a functional authority.[140] It not only brings sinners the saving message of redemption by the action of the Spirit, but its writing is filled and penetrated by the presence of the Spirit. The light that shines through Scripture is also the light that made possible the production of the canon of Scripture.

The Bible can also be said to have a relational authority in that the partial truth of every text must be seen in its paradoxical relationship to the center and apex of biblical history—God's self-revelation in Jesus Christ. I agree with Rogers and McKim that the Bible's authority is not static but dynamic. Yet the Bible is more than a tool of the Spirit—it is the very voice of the Spirit, though only the ears of faith can hear this voice.

5. Whereas Rogers and McKim interpret Scripture primarily through the lens of the form-function dichotomy, I prefer the form-content distinction, which was employed by both the Reformation and early Protestant orthodoxy as well as by Barth.[141] I further maintain that form and content are inseparable even though they cannot be equated. This means that the very language of Scripture, what Barth calls "the language of Canaan" and "the language of Zion," must be respected as the

God-given vehicle for communicating the gospel of reconciliation and redemption. Rogers holds that the literary form of Scripture cannot carry authority because "the form is infinitely variable."[142] I believe that the finite can contain and bear the infinite, but it can do so only through the power of God's electing grace. In a later work, Rogers assures us that what is at stake in the inclusive-language controversy today is "not what the words are but our theory about the way words are to be used."[143]

Rogers does not sufficiently see that faith has a language of its own that is the elected vessel of divine revelation.[144] Because doubt is now being cast on the historic Christian position that the language of Scripture is inseparable from the revelation it carries, the church is presently engaged in a battle for the integrity of its message, a battle that takes the form of resistance to the trend to inclusive God-language. Rogers manifests a cautious yet disturbing openness to inclusive God-language in his *Presbyterian Creeds,* discussing it under the rubric of contemporary relevance.[145] In my opinion, this subject more properly belongs in the chapter on the Barmen Declaration, where the concern was to counter the corrupting influence of ideology on the church's proclamation.

6. Rogers and McKim rightly point to Augustine's work as pivotal in determining how church tradition understood the role of Scripture. They make a convincing case that Augustine's concern was with what the Spirit of God intended to teach through the text, not with its technical historical accuracy. That Augustine identified the six days of creation with six ages is an example of his penchant for interpreting Scripture figuratively. At the same time, I do not think they give sufficient recognition to Augustine's efforts to hold together the sign and the reality it signifies. While it is true that for Augustine the crucial thing is the biblical writers' thoughts, he regarded their words as not dispensable but necessary for the communicating of these thoughts. Augustine took care not to disparage the actual words of Scripture, for he saw them as belonging to the Spirit of God as well as to their human author (a point

Woodbridge makes).[146] At the same time, Augustine focused his attention on the spiritual reality that the external sign (Scripture) signifies, a side of his theology that receives scant attention from Woodbridge.

7. I think Rogers and McKim are in error when they see Augustine as giving absolute priority to faith over reason in his theological method. Augustine did allow for a rational preparation for faith, though reason could never lead into faith apart from a transformation of the human will. He sought to appeal not only to divine revelation but also to the natural reasoning characteristic of those who do not share the faith.[147] Eugene TeSelle interprets Augustine as beginning with self-knowledge and proceeding toward God-knowledge.[148] "This sequence—first the self, then God . . . is at once a process of rational inquiry and an existential movement of the soul toward God."[149] I mention these things to warn evangelicals against following Augustine uncritically, for he is one of the architects of the biblical-classical synthesis that has resulted in a blurring of the biblical concept of the living God who acts in history and who justifies the ungodly.

8. Rogers and McKim base much of their case against biblical inerrancy on the doctrine of the accommodation of the Spirit to the human condition. I too see a biblical basis for this theory, but it must be held in tension with the analogy of faith, by which the images and symbols of faith have their analogical reference in God. If one presses the theory of accommodation too far, it can lead to a mystical, Neoplatonic view that God is unknowable and indescribable, that our words are mere ciphers that point beyond themselves to the inscrutable mystery of being. In the present controversy over inclusive language for God, the proponents often argue that Father, Son and Spirit are simply metaphors drawn from human experience and then applied to a God who is essentially nameless and imageless. God does accommodate himself to the human condition but nevertheless reveals his very self in human history and language. The God who reveals himself in Christ is none other than the God who exists within himself as a triune being. What we know in Christ is not simply the effects of God on us but the very

reality of God, his innermost nature as unbounded love, though our knowledge is partial and broken, not exhaustive or univocal.

9. Rogers and McKim place much of the blame for the development of rationalism in Protestantism on Francis Turretin, whom they accuse of leading the Reformed church away from Calvin (see n. 26). While granting that Turretin's method is not the same as Calvin's and that rationalizing elements were at work in his theology, I think that Rogers and McKim may not be doing him justice. Since their book was written, three important works bearing on this issue have appeared—Richard A. Muller, *Post-Reformation Reformed Dogmatics,* 2 volumes, and Timothy Ross Phillips, *Francis Turretin's Idea of Theology and Its Bearing upon His Doctrine of Scripture.*[150] Phillips contends in his impressive study that Turretin does not define infallibility "in terms of the absolute truthfulness of everything asserted within the text," but rather "conceives this property from the perspective of the reality signified, *theologia.*"[151] Scripture's infallibility is defined as "the lack of deceit."[152] Nor does Turretin try to establish Scripture's authority "through rational proofs or through Scripture's own written declaration that it is inspired and divinely authoritative."[153] Rather he gauges the authority of Scripture on the basis of the reality of the divine wisdom or *theologia* that Scripture attests and embodies. "This reality is self-authenticating and it creatively establishes its own authority in the life of the wayfarer."[154] Muller argues convincingly that the definition of theology

> as a kind of wisdom not based on evidence of reason prevented the Protestant orthodox from adopting the very view of Scripture they are frequently accused of holding—Scripture as a set of conveniently-numbered divine propositions. The divine archetype is simple, non-discursive and nonpropositional: the propositional nature of language belongs to the accommodation of truth to our ectypal patterns of knowing.[155]

While these works correct the one-sidedness of the Rogers-McKim portrayal of orthodoxy, they actually strengthen their thesis that the view of modern fundamentalism differs qualitatively from that of the Reformers and their most able interpreters in the sixteenth and seventeenth centuries. In my opinion Protestant orthodoxy even at its best did prepare the way for a rationalistic Christianity by its openness to natural theology and its intense apologetic concern to protect the faith against secularism,[156] but I agree with Phillips and Muller that the leading lights of Protestant orthodoxy were much closer to the Reformers than to modern fundamentalism.[157]

10. Woodbridge argues with some cogency that Rogers and McKim often give an incomplete and therefore unsatisfactory picture of the doctrine of Scripture in church history because of their polemic against fundamentalism. He claims that they too facilely read back into the church fathers and Reformers a view of error and truth that is really derived from Berkouwer. But the point that needs to be considered is whether this view of error and truth is consonant with the biblical witness, and Woodbridge does not seriously address this question. He accuses Rogers and McKim of being overly selective in their quotations in order to advance their case. While this charge has some merit, one can show that Woodbridge too is selective. He cites J. M. Reu, for example, to support the idea that Luther subscribed to biblical inerrancy but ignores the signal contribution of W. J. Kooiman, who argues the opposite.[158] He cites many defenders of inerrantism in the past but for the most part strikingly ignores the vast array of leading theologians within the tradition of orthodoxy who cannot in any way be identified with the fundamentalist position. Among the many names that could be mentioned are Philipp Spener, P. T. Forsyth, James Denney, James Orr, Thomas M. Lindsay, Philip Schaff,[159] Herman Bavinck, Abraham Kuyper, J. C. K. von Hofmann, and more recently Hermann Sasse, Bela Vassady, F. F. Bruce, Eugene Osterhaven, I. Howard Marshall, Bruce Metzger, Raymond Abba and C. S. Lewis.

11. Woodbridge shows with some dexterity that the appeal to the autographs or original manuscripts was already present among some followers of the Reformation in the sixteenth century, though Rogers and McKim have a point that this practice became much more significant

after the scientific revolution began to make itself felt in the church in the succeeding centuries.[160] In my view the earliest manuscripts provide the test for textual accuracy, but neither they nor the autographs have any special power to bring the reader and hearer the Word of God.

12. The present controversy is salutary because it may move the church to consider a new statement on scriptural authority and infallibility, though such a statement cannot simply be a restoration of Augustinian or Reformation views. Woodbridge is wrong in resisting any new statement, and Rogers and McKim can be faulted for intimating that their new statement would be endorsed by Augustine, the Reformers and the Westminster Divines, among others.

13. One of my problems with Rogers and McKim is that they tend to see the enemy on one side—on the right. They have harsh criticisms of evangelical rationalists but only appreciative words for scholars of a more liberal persuasion like James Barr or Charles Briggs.[161] Nothing is said of the challenge of Enlightenment and post-Enlightenment figures like Semler and Schleiermacher who were pivotal in shaping the new understanding of the Bible that has come to prevail in modern Protestantism. Their book admittedly concentrates on the Reformed tradition in theology, but Schleiermacher wrote as a Reformed theologian, and his hermeneutics is far more influential on modern biblical studies than that of either Charles Hodge or Warfield.

14. Part of the problem in polemics of this type is that the church fathers and doctors of the medieval church as well as the Reformers said various things about Scripture that were often in conflict. Simply citing statements showing that they believed in the full truthfulness of Scripture does not imply that their positions were the same as that of modern fundamentalists (Rogers and McKim would agree). Attention must be given to the philosophical sources used in defining truth and error. We must also consider how the theologians of the past understood revelation and inspiration. In addition, we need to determine what weight they gave to inerrancy. Was this a first principle of theology or an inference drawn from the Bible? When Calvin confessed Scripture as

an "unerring light" and an "unerring rule," was he saying the same thing as the modern fundamentalist who asserts that Scripture is not in error even in its statements on "chemistry, astronomy, philosophy, or medicine"?[162]

15. I concur with Rogers and McKim that the position of the Reformers and the Westminster divines must not be confounded with the stance of modern fundamentalism.[163] But I contend that the Reformation understanding also cannot simply be identified with that of Berkouwer and Barth, whom Rogers and McKim look to as mentors in the task of preparing a new statement on revelation and inspiration. I too find much to appreciate in Berkouwer and even more in Barth, but we must take care not to reduce the authority of Scripture to its function in directing us to Christ (crucial though it be).

16. We must affirm both the fundamental truthfulness of the Bible and its capacity to communicate the redeeming power of this truth to its hearers and readers. We must also affirm that the forms of expression in Scripture, which admittedly reflect a certain time-boundedness, serve this truth rather than obstruct it. Yet the source of this truthfulness is not the ingenuity and perspicacity of the biblical writers but the intangible reality of the Holy Spirit, who, at his own free discretion, resides within Scripture as well as within the community of faith, giving enlightenment on the meaning of God's Word for every time and place in history.

17. The approach to Scripture that Rogers and McKim support could lead to a dichotomy between religious or moral truth on the one hand and historical truth on the other. Scripture could at the same time be treated as a historical document with full confidence placed in the tools of historical research and be used as a book of spiritual edification that remains basically untouched by critical methods. This was the approach of Semler, and it has effectively served to undercut scriptural authority in modern Protestantism.

18. The historical-critical method enabled the church to rediscover the humanity of the Bible but at a price—the loss of the divinity of its

witness and message. We need a perspective on the Bible in which its true humanity is assessed in the light of the divine revelation that is everywhere present in the Bible but hidden from all sight and understanding. Our task is to discern an underlying unity within and behind the diversity that the Bible mirrors as a historical document, but this means that we must then read the Bible theologically as well as historically. With von Hofmann we need to see the Bible in the context of a holy history in which God reveals his purposes through the instrumentality of human beings who in and of themselves are finite and prone to error but who are enabled to grasp the truth of what is revealed by the incommensurable action of the Spirit of God.[164]

·FIVE·

SCRIPTURE
& THE CHURCH

Stand firm, then, brothers, and keep the traditions that we
taught you, whether by word of mouth or by letter.
2 THESSALONIANS 2:15 NJB

With regard to the divine and saving mysteries of the faith
no doctrine, however trivial, may be taught without the
backing of the divine Scriptures.
CYRIL OF JERUSALEM

We are not obliged to regard the arguments of any writers,
however Catholic and estimable they may be,
as we do the canonical Scriptures.
AUGUSTINE

The more the doctrine of any Church agrees with the Scripture,
the more readily ought it to be received. . . .
The more the doctrine of any Church differs from Scripture,
the greater cause we have to doubt it.
JOHN WESLEY

The Spirit has led the Church into more truth
than is expressed in the Bible, in Paul, in John, or even in the
character of Christ, but not into more than these contain.
P. T. FORSYTH

If Tradition or the Magisterium claimed to teach something
contradicting the Holy Scriptures, it would certainly be false,
and the faithful ought to reject it.
YVES CONGAR

One of the perplexing problems in the church of today as well as
of yesterday is the role of tradition and the weight it carries as
an authority for the church. Paul urges the church of Thessalo-
nica to "stand firm and hold to the traditions which you were taught by

us" (2 Thess 2:15). The epistle of Jude encourages us "to fight hard for the faith which has been once and for all entrusted to God's holy people" (v. 3 NJB; cf. 2 Tim 3:14). We know that before the books of the Bible were written an oral tradition existed that was passed down through generations. We are told that Jesus did many things not recorded by his disciples (Jn 20:30; 21:25), and we can presume that an oral tradition emerged from apostolic times as well, exerting a certain influence on the thinking of the early church.

Yet we also know that writers who appealed to the oral tradition of apostolic times, such as Papias, frequently exaggerated and embellished church tradition, and hence their reports are basically unreliable.[1] The apocryphal Gospels that circulated called into question the veracity of the church concerning its central message about Jesus and his saving work. The church was compelled to submit to the norm of the apostolic canon in order to safeguard the integrity and purity of its proclamation. It was impressed on the fathers of the church that *"without a superior written norm her teaching office could not preserve the pure apostolic tradition."* [2]

In this kind of discussion it is appropriate to make a distinction between tradition *(paradosis),* the history in and by which the elect community lives, and church traditions within *the* tradition. Tradition here includes the recording and compiling of the Scriptures as well as the commentary on Scripture in the history of the church. Tradition in this sense can be recognized as a viable authority in the life of the church so long as it is appraised in the light of the written Scriptures that arise from it and direct it.

It is also salutary to distinguish between the prophetic and apostolic traditions out of which Scripture emerged and the ecclesiastical tradition, which interprets Scripture in every generation after apostolic times. The first kind of tradition is far more normative than the later traditions, for it is based on the eyewitness and ear-witness reports of the mighty deeds of God in biblical Israel culminating in Jesus Christ.

The question that confronted the early church was whether tradition was creative or subordinate. Does church tradition simply reaffirm the revelation given in Scripture, or does it contribute new light not to be found in Scripture? Is tradition dependent on what Scripture records or is it independent in the sense that it can define new truth? Or are Scripture and tradition interdependent in the sense that neither has efficacy apart from the other? Catholic theologians frequently appeal to John 14:26, which attests that the Spirit of God will be given to the church to guide it into all truth.

A growing body of opinion in the church held that apostolic tradition supplements Scripture as a guide for faith and practice. Yet before long theologians came to advance beliefs that had no real basis in Scripture. For example, in his excursus on the deity of the Holy Spirit, Basil of Caesarea acknowledged that some tenets of the faith are not to be found in Scripture.[3] The beliefs about Mary, including her perpetual virginity and assumption into heaven, could hardly be substantiated by Scripture, yet they were given normative status in the witness of the church. In the early and medieval church the concept of Scripture was sometimes broadened to include the patristic fathers, who supposedly gave the right interpretation of Scripture.

This is not to deny that a great number of leading theologians based their case for the Christian faith wholly on Scripture. Irenaeus and also Tertullian derived the content of the *regula fidei* (rule of faith)[4] directly from Scripture and from no other source. In his conflict with the Arians Athanasius insisted that the Scriptures are entirely adequate for the proclamation of the truth.[5] "With regard to the divine and saving mysteries of the faith" Cyril of Jerusalem allowed "no doctrine, however trivial," to be taught "without the backing of the divine Scriptures. . . . For our saving faith derives its force, not from capricious reasonings, but from what may be proved out of the Bible."[6]

Roman Catholic theology envisages a development of doctrine by which the church through the guidance of the Holy Spirit comes to understand things that are only implicit in Scripture. This position is articulated in Vatican II:

This tradition which comes from the apostles develops in the Church with the help of the Holy Spirit. For there is a growth in the understanding of the realities and the words which have been handed down. This happens through the contemplation and study made by believers, who treasure these things in their hearts (cf. Lk. 2:19, 51), through the intimate understanding of spiritual things they experience, and through the preaching of those who have received through episcopal succession the sure gift of truth. For, as the centuries succeed one another, the Church constantly moves forward toward the fullness of divine truth until the words of God reach their complete fulfillment in her.[7]

In the polemics of the Reformation period many Catholic theologians appealed to the church over Scripture in order to safeguard the treasures of church tradition that were being threatened by the reforming movement. The Council of Trent treated both sources of doctrine, Scripture and tradition, with equal reverence but stopped short of stating that tradition can yield truth not based on Scripture. An early draft document of the Council of Trent that asserted "the truth of the gospel is contained partly in written books, partly in unwritten traditions," was not included in the final revised edition, though this belief in two different sources of revelation began to gain ascendancy after the Council. The Catholic theologian J. R. Geiselmann maintains vigorously that Trent allows for the view that all Catholic doctrine is found in the Bible.[8] He enlists in his support the opinion of the Anglo-Catholic theologian H. Edward Symonds that "the Council of Trent is at one with the Fathers in treating both sources of doctrine *pari reverentia,* but to teach that there are doctrines *de fide* which cannot be found in, or based on Holy Scripture, is to go beyond the teaching of both the Fathers and of the great reforming Council."[9] Both Trent and Vatican I used the language of one source of revelation with two modes of transmission, an approach that was made more explicit in Vatican II.[10]

The French Catholic theologian Yves Congar is adamant that "the holy Scriptures have an absolute value which Tradition has not . . . they are the supreme guide to which any other [norms] there may be are subjected. If Tradition or the Magisterium claimed to teach something contradicting the holy Scriptures, it would certainly be false, and the faithful ought to reject it."[11] Yet Congar cautions that the Scriptures are not "the absolute rule of every other norm, like the Protestant scriptural principle."[12]

Vatican II affirmed that both sacred Scripture and sacred tradition flow "from the same divine wellspring."[13] Whereas sacred Scripture is the Word of God "inasmuch as it is consigned to writing under the inspiration of the divine Spirit," sacred tradition hands on the truth of this Word from one generation to another. It is thus not from sacred Scripture alone that the church derives "her certainty about everything which has been revealed" but from tradition as well.[14] "Therefore both sacred tradition and sacred Scripture are to be accepted and venerated with the same sense of devotion and reverence."[15]

The Protestant Reformation did not jettison church tradition but definitely relegated it to secondary status on the grounds that Scripture has primacy *(sola Scriptura)*. According to Luther, "The church of God has no power to establish any article of faith and it neither has established nor ever will establish one."[16] We should not believe the gospel "because the church has approved it, but rather because we feel that it is the word of God. . . . Everyone may be certain of the gospel when he has the testimony of the Holy Spirit in his own person that this is the gospel."[17] While Luther, Calvin and other Reformers appealed frequently to the fathers and doctors of the Catholic Church for support, they were keenly aware that much in the interpretations of these men was purely cultural and subjective. Luther could even say, "God's Word of itself is pure, clean, bright, and clear; but, through the doctrines, books, and writings of the Fathers, it is darkened, falsified, and spoiled."[18] Calvin made clear that the church invokes the Holy Spirit but does not confer it. Nor should the church be identified with the kingdom of God; it is a function or instrument of the kingdom and therefore subordinated to it. Protestant orthodoxy made a place for tradition but only as the *norma normata* (the rule that is ruled), unlike Scripture, which is the *norma normans* (the rule that rules).

In modern Protestantism there seems to be a movement away from *sola Scriptura* to a view that coincides with a sectarian Catholicism that denigrates Scripture by elevating church authority. Nikolai Grundtvig, bishop and theologian in the Lutheran church of Denmark (d. 1872), held that the gospel was spread by the living power of the apostles and the church independent of the written word. The living Word, which is prior to the written word, is given to each successive generation in the two sacraments. Emphasizing growth in faith over conversion, he saw tradition, not Scripture, as the enduring basis for doctrine and practice.[19] Frederick Denison Maurice (d. 1872), an Anglican divine, argued that Holy Scripture is to be interpreted by the ministry of the church and not left to private judgment. For James Barr "authority resides in the people of God, or perhaps more correctly in the central leadership of the people of God."[20] He allows for the view that authority also resides in the Scriptures, but in a secondary sense. His model of authority is "God ➔ people ➔ tradition ➔ scripture."[21] Revelation is said to be derived from all these sources. The traditional model, which he rejects, is "God ➔ revelation ➔ scripture ➔ church."[22]

Kenneth Jensen, a bishop in the Evangelical Orthodox Church, contends that "a man cannot have even the Scriptures without first deciding to rely upon the accuracy of the historians of the church."[23] He argues that the compilation of the canon at the Council of Carthage in 397 was the work of faithful historians. Even the apostles themselves should be understood as historians who sought to give an accurate account of the Word of God.

The current controversy over the revision of the language of Scripture to make it more inclusive also has significant bearing on the relation of biblical to ecclesiastical authority. Burton Throckmorton Jr., a Presbyterian theologian who advocates desexing the language of Scripture, is quite blunt:

The Scripture is the church's book. It was written by the church [and] for the church. There's no reason . . . that I can see why the church can't add to its Scripture—delete from its Scripture. I think the church can do with its Scripture what it wants to [do] with its Scripture.[24]

In refreshing contrast P. T. Forsyth contended that the biblical witness is a product not of the believing church but of the act of revelation itself—the redeeming work of God in Jesus Christ. This divine revelation produced both the apostolic witness and the church.[25] One monument of God's revealing action is the Bible; the other is the church, which in its proclamation and teaching preserves the apostolic interpretation of the atoning work of God in the cross and resurrection of Christ.

Against those who subordinate Scripture to the community of faith I affirm with Karl Barth that "Scripture is in the hands but not in the power of the church."[26] The church interprets the Bible by the guidance of the Spirit, to be sure, but the profounder truth is that the Spirit interprets the Bible to the church. The church receives what the Spirit offers, but it must take care not to impose its agenda on the Spirit of God. Its task is to amplify and clarify what the Spirit has already given in Holy Scripture. I would hesitate to say with R. P. C. Hanson that the Bible is completed in the church,[27] but I would contend that the Bible is made efficacious in the church by the working of the Spirit.

I here fully concur with the Catholic ecumenical theologian George Tavard:

> In her essence, the Church is not a power of interpretation: she is a power of reception. She receives the Word which God speaks to her in the Scriptures. It is this Word as by her received which is authoritative for her members. This Scripture and Church are mutually inherent. To Scripture is attached an ontological primacy; and to the Church a historical one because it is only in her receptivity that men are made aware of the Word.[28]

Scripture and tradition may be compared to the root of the tree and its branches. Not all branches are straight or strong, but they all owe their sustenance to the water carried up by the roots. Some of the branches may even die and therefore have to be trimmed. Yet, as Lutheran pastor

Robert Stroud says, "the weakness, crookedness or death of some does not negate the strength, validity or the life of all. Because some traditions appear worthless, or even dangerous, is no reason to reject the whole."[29] Stroud argues, and I agree, that it is dangerous to try to begin over again, keeping only the roots. The roots need the tree just as the tree needs its roots. Tradition both proceeds from Scripture and in its wider sense gave birth to Scripture; it also applies the teachings of Scripture to the people of faith in every age. But Scripture judges and corrects tradition and in this way keeps tradition faithful to the gospel.

I hold that both Scripture and the church share in the infallibility of the incarnate and living Christ. Luther was convinced that a church founded on the Word of God could not err, because the Word that it teaches cannot err.[30] In Zwingli's words, "The true Church is certainly inerrant because it does nothing in accordance with its own desires, but always what the Holy Spirit ordains. The Gospel which is proclaimed in the Church was dictated by the Holy Spirit and therefore cannot err."[31] Barth spoke in a similar fashion: "The Church is infallible, not because its pronouncements, which are of necessity humanly limited, possess as such inerrancy and perfection; but because by its pronouncements it bears witness to the infallible Word of God and gives evidence that it has heard that Word; because the Church, 'abandoning all its own wisdom, lets itself be taught by the Word of God.' "[32]

Those traditions in the life of the church that have kept alive the church's awareness of God's gracious act of reconciliation and redemption in Jesus Christ are to be prized and treasured. But we must not confuse what is truly spiritual and divine with what is merely earthly and human. Cyprian forewarned that "even *antiquity* is not *authority* but may be only *vetustas erroris*—the old age of error."[33] We must pray for the gift of discernment so that we can discriminate what truly comes from God and what is purely human conjecture. The criterion in determining what is true and relevant remains Holy Scripture, which the Spirit of God authorized and which the church dutifully recognized as its enduring infallible rule for faith and practice.

The Problem of the Canon

The tension between biblical and ecclesiastical authority becomes particularly acute when we examine the process of canonizing Scripture. The first official church document listing the twenty-seven books of the New Testament was the Easter letter of Bishop Athanasius in 367. In the Western church the complete canon was approved by councils in Hippo (393) and Carthage (397). The qualifications for canonicity revolved around the apostolic character of the New Testament writings. We now know that Hebrews was admitted to the canon because it was mistakenly attributed to Paul. Divine providence may indeed work through human error in order to realize the divine plan for both church and world.

Roman Catholics argue that because the Holy Spirit is continuously at work in the church through the ages, the church is invested with the authority to determine what books are binding on the faithful. Augustine declared, "For my part, I should not believe the gospel except as moved by the authority of the catholic church."[34] Duns Scotus followed suit: "The books of the holy canon are not to be believed except insofar as one must first believe the church which approves and authorizes those books and their content."[35]

Against the Catholic position the Reformers emphasized the primacy of Holy Scripture over both the church and religious experience.[36] At the same time they maintained that Catholic tradition amply testifies to the truth of the priority and primacy of Scripture. Luther mentioned Bernard of Clairvaux, who said that he would rather drink from the spring itself (the Scriptures) than from the brook (the fathers of the church), which is mainly helpful in leading back to the spring.[37] Martin Chemnitz, the luminary of Lutheran orthodoxy, quoted approvingly from Irenaeus:

> That alone is the true and living faith, which the church has received from the apostles and communicated to her children. . . . For through no others do we know the plan of salvation except through those, by whom the Gospel has come to us. That, indeed, which they then preached, they afterward delivered to us in the Scriptures by the will

of God, that it should be the foundation and pillar of our faith.[38]

For the Reformers only the Spirit of God authorizes the canon, but the church was led to recognize and accept what the Spirit had already determined. It is the Spirit who authenticates the Bible, and the church confirms this work of the Spirit by looking to the Bible as its ruling norm and source. In Reformation theology the Word of God, the message of Scripture, which comes directly from God, is prior to the community of faith, which is created by this Word. It is readily acknowledged, however, that the community of faith is historically prior to the compiling and canonizing of Scripture.

The origin of the Word of God is in eternity, but its revelation and reception take place in history. The psalmist confesses, "Eternal is thy word, O LORD, planted firm in heaven" (Ps 119:89 NEB). But the claim of the church is that this Word became incarnate in a particular person, Jesus Christ, at a particular time and place in history. The recording of this event or series of events constitutes Holy Scripture. But Scripture must be recognized to be such by the church, and this recognition is what we call canonization. Scripture is a product of the inspiring work of the Spirit, who guided the writers to give a reliable testimony to God's self-revelation in Jesus Christ. Its canonizing is to be attributed to the illumining work of the Spirit, who led the fathers of the church to assent to what the Spirit had already authorized.

Yet the question of why these books and no others should be canonized has not been totally resolved. Because it is the Holy Spirit who authorizes the books of the Bible, we cannot argue absolutely for a closed canon. In *Criticism and Faith* John Knox contended for a closed canon on the basis that only the authorized sacred writings stand in immediate historical proximity to the Christ revelation.[39] Yet what about 1-2 Maccabees and other apocryphal writings that may be chronologically closer to the incarnation than some of the New Testament writings? The criterion for determining canonicity is not simply historical proximity, though this factor must certainly be taken into account, but the revelatory character and potential of the witness. Does the witness drive one to Christ, does it teach the priority of grace over works, does it prepare one to trust and acclaim the Messiah of Israel? This criterion presumably rules out the apocryphal books but not possible undiscovered writings that the Spirit may have preserved for elevation at a future time. For example, if a writing were unearthed that could be proved to be authored by Paul or one of the apostles, it would have to be given serious consideration by the church. Yet any addition to the canon could be made only if the Holy Spirit directly moved the Christian community as a whole toward this act.

The Bible over the Church

The Bible takes precedence over the church not as a historical record or written code but as the Word of life and redemption that comes directly from God. It is this Word, which existed before the writing of the Bible and brought this writing into existence, that has preeminent authority in the life of the church. This Word is not only the ruling criterion in the church but the creator and judge of the church (Luther). This Word calls people to faith and obedience, and this Word directs people of faith on their earthly pilgrimage.

When the Word of God is reduced to the propositions of the Bible, then the Word is placed in the power of the church, for the church, having direct access to the Word, is thus free to determine the meaning of the Word. By contrast, in Reformation theology the Word has power over the church, and the Spirit, not the church as such, determines and expounds the true meaning of the Word.

Tradition as the amplification and interpretation of the Word in the community of faith is to be respected and honored, but it is not to be accepted uncritically. Every interpretation in church tradition must be measured in the light of the transcendent meaning of the gospel of God that shines through Holy Scripture. Tradition can be misused and corrupted by leaders or clerics who seek to advance themselves or secure power for themselves. Jesus warns that the consciences of men and women must not be bound to purely human traditions (Mk 7:8). He castigates the Pharisees who for the sake of their tradition "have made void the word of God" (Mt 15:6).

Although official Catholic theology gives preeminence to Scripture, Catholic theologians have frequently subordinated Scripture to tradition. In expectation of the dogma of the Assumption of Mary, Carl Feckes said (in 1950), "The primary norm of my Catholic faith is by no means Holy Scripture but the living consciousness of the present-day Church of Christ. If the Church of Christ is indeed . . . the *alter Christus,* the other, the ever-living Christ, then she has within herself the clear consciousness of her faith."[40] Gabriel Biel placed tradition on a par with the biblical writings: "What the holy Church, our Mother, defines and accepts as catholic truth must be believed with the same reverence as though it were stated in Holy Scripture."[41] More recently, the tendency to elevate tradition over Scripture finds expression in Karl Rahner: "Since scripture is something derivative, it must be understood from the essential nature of the church, which is the eschatological and irreversible permanence of Jesus Christ in history."[42]

Vatican II made clear that the magisterium "is not above the word of God, but serves it."[43] Only Scripture is called the "written Word of God" (art. 24) and "the speech of God" (art. 9). Tradition is never called the Word of God, but it "transmits in its entirety the Word of God" (art. 9). Yet the document on divine revelation did not refer to the critical role of Scripture in the life of the church. One Catholic interpreter voices this complaint: "The Constitution seems to assume that by endorsing the role of the Scriptures in the life, thought, and piety of the church, those Scriptures would do nothing more than ratify and affirm the church as it is."[44]

While both the churches of the Reformation and the church of Rome acknowledge Scripture as a ruling norm, which no Christian, not even the pope, can circumvent, in the Roman view "a distinction is . . . made between Scripture as *regula fidei remota*—the distant rule of faith—and the interpretation of Scripture by the Roman Church, i.e., by the magisterium of that Church, as *regula fidei proxima*—the proximate rule of faith."[45] Because it is the church that determines how the distant rule of faith is to be interpreted and applied, scriptural authority seems dangerously compromised.

A similar stance is found in the Iglesia ni Christo (Church of Christ) in the Philippines, which acknowledges the Bible to be infallible, but holds that the ordinary Christian cannot truly understand Scripture unless it is interpreted correctly by the authorized ministers of the church. Like many others (including the Jehovah's Witnesses), this sect denies the perspicuity of the Bible.

Even Protestant fundamentalism is not exempt from the temptation to assert the authority of church or tradition over that of Scripture. In the circles of dispensationalism the Scofield notes on the Bible became so dominant "that many adherents considered the commentary as *the true interpretation* of the Bible, thus implicitly granting the commentary equal authority with the biblical text."[46]

There is currently a movement among younger evangelicals to embrace a position closer to traditional Catholicism and Eastern Orthodoxy in order to avoid the morass of subjectivism. Writing in *Touchstone* magazine, S. M. Hutchens proposes an alternative to the autographical inerrancy associated with the Princeton school of theology—one that allows the church a more substantial role in determining the meaning of the Word of God. The authority of Scripture is seen "as flowing from and resting in the prior authority of a Spirit-inspired Church and its teachers . . . a living, consensual tradition in which finding and reconstructing the best texts is a natural and useful part of its scholars' ongoing labors, but not its touchstone or the foundation of its epistemology."[47] While acknowledging that the apostles have a certain preeminence among the teachers of the church, Hutchens really subordinates Scripture to the consensus of church tradition, thereby implying that Scripture can no longer effectively challenge or question tradition. Hutchens does not perceive that there is still another alternative to the autographical inerrancy of the Princeton school—that of Barth and the theology of crisis, which in effect retrieved the original position of the Reformation. Above Scripture and the church is Jesus Christ, the living Word of God, who speaks in and through Scripture primarily and in and through the church secondarily insofar as the church faithfully expounds the revelation already given in Holy Scripture.

Yet while subordinating church tradition to Scripture, we must take care not to deny the continuing reality of the Spirit in the life of the church, providing illumination of the written Word of God. Whereas the Scripture is inspired by the Spirit, the church is assisted by the Spirit (Max Thurian). As Protestants we need to remember that it was the early church councils that articulated the doctrines of the Trinity and the two natures of Christ, which are not explicitly expressed in Scripture but are definitely implied. To deny any creative role to the church whatsoever would indeed call into question some fundamental tenets of the faith.

Protestants may have difficulty in upholding the infallibility of the church, but we should affirm its indefectibility, its perseverance in the truth through the guidance and empowering of the Holy Spirit. The faith of the church cannot be overthrown (cf. Mt 16:18 KJV), but it can be obscured and compromised. Barth discerned a real affinity between Calvin and the Roman Catechism on this issue: both affirm "that the church as a whole cannot err in its fundamental faith *(fundamento fidei)*, that the people of God, as such, whatever may be said by or of individuals, cannot mistake its goal. Therefore the essential infallibility and permanence of the Church is asserted."[48]

While I acknowledge that the infallible truth of the gospel and law of God is conveyed through both the Bible and the church, it is a mistake to find the certainty of our faith in the words of the Bible or in the office of the church. In a letter to the German bishops Pope John Paul II declared: "It is true that infallibility is not of such central importance in the hierarchy of truths," but it is "to some extent the key to that certainty with which the faith becomes known and is preached and also to the life and conduct of the faithful. . . . For if one shakes or destroys that essential foundation, the most elementary truths of our faith also begin to disintegrate."[49] But the foundation of Christian faith is not the infallibility of the papal office or even of church tradition, not even the canon of Holy Scripture, but the living God himself and his Word that is both ever new and ever the same. This Word created both the community of faith and the canon of Holy Scripture, and this Word therefore judges both church and Scripture.

The Bible over the church can be maintained if we mean not the Bible as a book or collection of books but the Bible as the Word of the living God who speaks anew to the church in every age. It is not the Bible as such but the Word that it attests, the divine wisdom that it mediates, that stands over the church, directing its life and thought. When Protestantism identified Scripture and divine revelation, it could not effectively counter the Catholic argument that the community of faith existed before written records and canonized writings and therefore has a prior authority. By rediscovering the transcendence and dynamism of divine revelation, both Catholics and Protestants might come to a new understanding of the relationship between church tradition and Scripture, and a convergence on this issue might indeed become possible.

The Bible Within the Church

Just as the Bible is over the church, so we must assert the other side of the dialectic: the Bible properly belongs within the church. The Bible cannot function apart from church tradition, but it brings life to the tradition. In the words of William Neil: "It was the faith of the church that produced the Bible, and it is the Bible by which the faith of the church is sustained."[50] More accurately it was the Holy Spirit who produced the Bible through the efforts of the community of faith. The church without the Bible is blind; the Bible without the church is empty.

The relationship between Christ (the living Word), the Bible and the church (tradition) might be expressed by the following diagram: Jesus Christ is the center, the inner circle represents the Bible, the wider circle the tradition. In a sense the tradition includes all, but its center and norm is Jesus Christ alone, the Christ attested in Scripture.

We can hear Christ only in Scripture; we meet Christ only in the

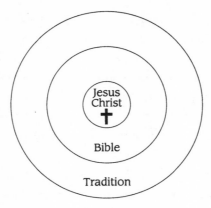

church. Even those who are brought to conversion from outside the church nevertheless make contact with Christ only by means of the witness of the church. Those who are converted simply by reading the Bible are nonetheless drawn into the church by the Spirit who inspired the Bible. Moreover, it was the community of faith that provided the Bible through which they were confronted by the living Christ.

The Bible alone, not the church, is the supreme norm of faith, and yet this norm is not effective apart from the church. The Bible is the sovereign authority, the church the subordinate authority. Church tradition is measured by the Bible, the more basic authority. In turn the Bible is measured and interpreted in the light of its own transcendent criterion—the gospel of God.

One may speak of the Bible as the word and the church as the mouth. The church is the instrument of Christ, who reaffirms the word that he spoke in sacred Scripture. Scripture is the unique word of God, but we hear this word as it is proclaimed by its messengers and heralds.

The paradoxical relationship of Christ, the Bible and the church can perhaps be made clearer by the illustration of a tape recorder. The Bible is the tape; Christ is the voice on the tape; the church is the tape recorder. The authority of the Bible is operative only in the church. The Spirit of God operates the tape recorder.

Luther on occasion likened Scripture to the light and church tradition to the lantern. The lantern carries the light, and yet the light itself brightens our pathway as we make our pilgrimage though the valley of the shadow of death.

The Word of God is not in the control of the church, though it takes its life in the womb of the church. Dietrich Bonhoeffer shared these helpful insights:

> The Word of God seeks a *Church* to take unto itself. It has its being *in* the Church. It enters the Church by its own self-initiated movement. It is wrong to suppose that there is so to speak a Word on the one hand and a Church on the other, and that it is the task of the preacher to take that Word into his hands and move it so as to bring it into the Church and apply it to the Church's needs. On the contrary, the Word moves of its own accord, and all the preacher has to do is to assist that movement and try to put no obstacles in its path.[51]

Following Luther, Bonhoeffer conceived of the Word of God first of all as the proclaimed Word and then as the written Word.

> The Word is the Word the church preaches. Not the Bible, then? Yes, the Bible too, but only in the church. So it is the church that first makes the Bible into the "Word"? Certainly, in so far, that is, as the church was first created and is maintained by the Word. The question as to what came first, the Word or the church, is meaningless, because the Word as inspired by the Spirit exists only when men hear it, so that the church makes the Word just as the Word makes the church into the church.[52]

True to the Reformed tradition, Emil Brunner also wished to maintain the paradoxical relationship of interdependence between church and Word: "Without the Word of the Church, the Bible would not be present; and without this subordination to the Bible, the Word of the Church could not be Christian."[53]

Perhaps we can perceive here a possible convergence of Catholic and Protestant understanding. Both sides are concerned to assert the Bible as the ruling norm in the life of the community of faith; yet this norm is exercised only within and through the believing community. Bonhoeffer and Brunner would have little difficulty in affirming with the Catholic ecumenist George Tavard: "Scripture cannot be the Word of God once it has been severed from the Church which is the Bride and the Body of Christ. And the Church could not be the Bride and the Body, had she not received the gift of understanding the Word."[54] Theology in the tradition of the Reformation would insist, however, that the church that possesses the gift of discernment is the holy catholic church, which transcends and cuts across all denominational lines. Every particular church body only approximates and anticipates the invisible church—the kingdom of Christ. Those bodies that make a determined effort to submit themselves to the authority of Holy Scripture more fully reflect the eschatological reality of the kingdom of God than do those that resist having their traditions corrected by the Word of God.

The Supreme Authority for Faith

The supreme authority for faith is finally that agency or power that gives us the right interpretation of God's holy Word. While affirming that the apostolic teaching is transmitted through both Scripture and tradition, Vatican II reaffirmed the traditional Catholic position that the final authority is the teaching office of the church: "The task of authentically interpreting the word of God, whether written or handed on, has been entrusted exclusively to the living teaching office of the Church, whose authority is exercised in the name of Jesus Christ."[55] In Eastern Orthodoxy the mind of the church is the ultimate arbiter in interpreting Scripture. Moreover, the mind of the church is first and foremost the exposition of the faith by the patristic fathers. Yet Scripture remains the fundamental criterion for faith. In modern liberal Christianity the final court of appeal is the magisterium of scholars. For Hans Küng our authority rests on the New Testament record as interpreted through the lens of historical and literary criticism. Schubert Ogden finds the locus of the canon not in the writings of the New Testament as such but in "the earliest traditions of Christian witness accessible to us today by historical-critical analysis of these writings."[56]

The supreme authority in sectarian fundamentalism is the Bible alone, but this is a Bible that stands over against the church. The common practice is to go to the Bible directly, apart from the teaching authority of church tradition. We consult not the fathers and mothers of the church universal as an aid in understanding a particular text but simply our own reason and conscience. If church tradition plays any role whatever, it is that strand within tradition that was shaped by the evangelical revivals. It is the magisterium of the evangelical counterculture rather than the tradition of the church catholic that throws light on Scripture.

For the church of the Reformation the supreme authority is the Word and the Spirit, the Bible illumined by the Spirit in the context of the worshiping community of faith. As the Westminster Confession puts it: "The Supreme Judge, by which all controversies of religion are to be determined, and all decrees of councils, opinions of ancient writers, doctrines of men, and private spirits, are to be examined, and in whose sentence we are to rest, can be no other but the Holy Spirit speaking in the Scripture."[57]

Another way to express the dynamics of theological authority is to state that the final norm is Jesus Christ, the living Word of God, who is attested in Holy Scripture and proclaimed by the church through the ages. Both the Bible and church proclamation become transparent to this living Word when they are illumined by the Spirit for the community of the faithful. When confronted by the illuminated text, we are at the same time meeting the risen Christ. Through the agency of the Spirit the understanding of the text becomes a redemptive happening, a breakthrough into meaning.

The temptation in the circles of religious enthusiasm, both Catholic and Protestant, is to appeal to the Spirit apart from the Word. Kaspar Schatzgeyer, a Catholic adversary of Luther, argued that since Christ had not unveiled all, "an 'intimate revelation from the Holy Spirit' is an everyday possibility. Once known beyond doubt, it is as binding as the teaching that came from Christ's own mouth."[58] But orthodoxy in the tradition of the church evangelical and catholic insists that the revelation of God in Christ has been completed, that what is given by the Spirit is illumination into the meaning and impact of this one revelation. The new light that breaks forth from God's holy Word (John Robinson, d. 1625) does not contradict or supersede this Word but enables us to understand it in a new way—related to the conflicts and issues of the time in which we live.

The Spirit leads the church toward a deeper understanding of the mystery of the gospel declared in Scripture but never toward a new gospel. P. T. Forsyth expressed it well: "The Spirit has led the Church into more truth than is expressed in the Bible, in Paul, or John, or even in the character of Christ, but not into more than these contain."[59]

Creeds and confessions play an important role in keeping the church in harmony with the faith once delivered to the saints. They are road signs that direct us to Jesus Christ and the truth of the gospel, but they are not themselves the source of truth and light. They always remain under the Bible and therefore reformable as the Spirit brings new light to bear from the Scriptures. They have a ministerial authority in aiding us in our understanding of Scripture, which alone has magisterial authority (Gabriel Fackre).[60]

The ultimate authority for faith is the living Word of God, the gospel of reconciliation and redemption, which is made known to the church but not delivered into the hands of the church. What the church passes on from one generation to another is teachings about the gospel, not the very gospel itself. I could not say like Charles Curran that "God's revelation has been handed over and entrusted to the church, which faithfully hands this down from generation to generation through the assistance of the Holy Spirit."[61] Tradition is not "the art of passing on the Gospel"[62] but the gift of remaining true to the gospel through continued struggle against the powers of sin, death and the devil.

God's Word can never be manipulated or packaged by the clerics of the church, but it can enable both pastors and laypeople to speak the truth of God with authority and power. It can never be the property of the church, but it can be the generator of new insight within the church.

It cannot be controlled by any human agency or power, but it can and does employ human instrumentality as it makes its way in the world. Church authority cannot hand out this Word, but it can serve this Word when it places itself at the disposal of the Spirit, who alone revives the weary and converts the lost. Church tradition is not the container of the truth of the gospel but the sign and witness of the forward movement of this truth in history.

The treasure of the gospel is transmitted not simply to the pope or to the bishops of the church but to the whole people of God, though it is imparted in such a way that it is never our possession but always our goal and hope. The apostle Paul declared, "Such a treasure is indeed ours, but it is carried by us in what are but vessels of clay to show that the power exceeding all else is God's and does not belong to ourselves" (2 Cor 4:7 GNC).

A church on fire with the gospel is a church that is being mightily used by the Spirit in advancing the cause of Christ in the world. A church vigorously involved in mission to the lost and in building up the faithful in love and trust is the true church of Jesus Christ, for this is the church that is submitting to the Scriptures, allowing itself to be purified and reformed by the Spirit. This is the church that comes into being only through unceasing prayer and repentance. This church alone is infallible, for its voice is now one with its Lord's.

Appendix C: The Apocrypha

Another source of tension within the Christian family of churches has been the status of the Apocrypha,[63] ancient religious writings (both Jewish and Christian) that were at some time treated as divinely inspired Scripture but never gained general recognition as canonical.[64] The books of the Apocrypha date roughly from 300 B.C. to around A.D. 100; most were probably written between 200 B.C. and A.D. 70. The Apocrypha belong to an Alexandrian Jewish tradition, many having been originally composed in Hebrew. The Greek translation of the Old Testament by Jews (from 250 B.C. onward), known as the Septuagint, included fifteen books that were listed as an addendum to the canonical Old Testament. These books were generally accepted by Christian authors as part of the Bible in the early centuries of the church. Other writings that circulated in the intertestamental period gained respect among some theologians but were never included in any canon of Scripture. These books have erroneously been called pseudepigrapha (false writings), but it is more proper to include them as apocryphal in the wider sense of books "outside" the Palestinian Jewish canon.

Down to the fourth century the church generally accepted the books of the Septuagint as canonical. Even some apocryphal books outside the Septuagint were occasionally cited by various authors. Cyprian cited as Scripture more than half the books of what we now call the Apocrypha.[65]

The Hebrew Scriptures, which included only those books believed to have been composed in either Hebrew or Aramaic before the end of the Persian period, were well known in the Jewish community, and this canon remained the standard for the Egyptian Jews as well. The additional writings that gained quasi-acceptance among the Greek-speaking Jews (in Egypt and elsewhere) were never accorded canonical status by the Jews, but they were accepted by Greek-speaking Christians as Scripture—at least for a time.

While numerous Greek and Latin church fathers of the second and third centuries quoted the Apocrypha as Scripture, one should bear in mind that hardly any of them were acquainted with Hebrew. A small number of the fathers who had personal knowledge of Hebrew (such as Origen and Jerome) or who made an effort to learn the limits of the Jewish canon began to distinguish between the books of the original Hebrew canon and the apocryphal books. From the fourth century onward the Greek fathers made fewer and fewer references to the Apocrypha, and theologians of the Eastern church, such as Athanasius, Cyril of Jerusalem and Gregory of Nazianzus, drew up formal lists of Old Testament books that left out the Apocrypha.

Augustine is partly responsible for keeping the door open to the inclusion of the Apocrypha in sacred Scripture, whereas the Hebrew scholar Jerome relegated the Apocrypha to a secondary status in his Vulgate translation. In his later writings, however, Augustine began to distinguish between the books of the original Hebrew canon and the deuterocanonical books accepted and read by the churches. According to C. C. Torrey, Augustine in his later period was close to Jerome on this issue.[66] At the time of the Reformation Cardinal Cajetan, Luther's opponent at Augsburg, acknowledged only the Hebrew canon as Scripture and maintained that the apocryphal writings could be used for personal edification but never to establish matters of faith.[67]

Whereas the churches of the Reformation either discarded the Apocrypha or relegated them to secondary status, the Council of Trent accepted most of the books of the Apocrypha as deuterocanonical Scripture. The three books that were not given this status were 1-2 Esdras and the Prayer of Manasseh, which eventually were retained in the Vulgate as an appendix after the New Testament. Luther included the Apocrypha as an appendix in his translation of the Bible. In the Church of England's King James Version (1611) the Apocrypha were inserted between the Old and New Testaments. The Wycliffe Bible (1380-92) had consisted only of the books of the Hebrew canon, owing mainly to the influence of Jerome, who held that no Jewish book not a part of the Hebrew Bible could be regarded as inspired Scripture. Coverdale's Bible (1535) was the first in English to contain the extracanonical books.

The Synod of Jerusalem in 1672 incorporated the books of Judith, Tobit, Wisdom, Bel and the Dragon, 1-2 Maccabees, and Ecclesiasticus into the Eastern Orthodox canon. But Orthodox opinion has been divided on this question. The Longer Catechism drawn up by Metropolitan Philaret of Moscow (1839) expressly omits the Apocrypha in the listing of Old Testament books.[68] This catechism was subsequently translated into Greek and has had a wide influence in the Orthodox world.

The Westminster Confession took a negative stance on the Apocrypha, relegating them to the same category as ordinary literature. The influence of the Puritan tradition within Protestantism eventually led to the deletion of the apocryphal books from the Bible, although in contemporary Protestantism, because of the ecumenical connection, the Apocrypha are being included, but always as an appendix or a separate unit between the two Testaments.

Contemporary Discussion

Conservative evangelicals generally consider the Apocrypha an unwelcome intrusion from the ancient Hellenistic world into the authorized writings of the church. Norman Geisler rejects the Apocrypha for various reasons, notably the fact that no apocryphal book is quoted as Scripture in the New Testament and no important church father before Augustine accepted the Apocrypha as part of Scripture.[69] Yet it can be shown that the Apocrypha were widely cited as Scripture by such eminent fathers as Irenaeus, Tertullian, Clement of Alexandria, Cyprian and even Origen. While the New Testament does not quote any book of the official Apocrypha as such, it does frequently allude to apocryphal books, and some books that are apocryphal in the wider sense are actually quoted (such as 1 Enoch in Jude 14). Geisler correctly points out that many local listings of inspired writings among the Jews were based on the Greek tradition from Alexandria, where the Hebrew Old Testament was translated into Greek in 285-246 B.C., not on the Jewish tradition from Palestine, where the Old Testament was actually written and accepted by the Jewish people.

Bruce Metzger's work on the Apocrypha is an outstanding contribution to the current discussion and deserves serious reading by all parties concerned.[70] Metzger brilliantly shows the unmistakable influence of the Apocrypha on Christian spirituality, but he nevertheless stands by the Reformation position that these books do not belong in the canon of inspired Scripture.

When one compares the books of the Apocrypha with the books of the Old Testament, the impartial reader must conclude that, as a whole, the true greatness of the canonical books is clearly apparent.

Though several books within the Old Testament are manifestly quite disparate and occupy varying levels, and though some readers would perhaps be willing to exchange passages in several Apocryphal books for others in the canonical books, yet it is probable that the judgment of most readers today would be in accord with that of Judaism and the earliest Church, both of which saw a profound difference between the two groups of books.[71]

Representing a quite different position, Albert Sundberg, a Protestant scholar at the American School of Oriental Research in Jerusalem, Jordan, contends that in the days of Jesus and the apostles no closed canon of Jewish Scriptures had yet been agreed upon, whether Palestinian or Alexandrian.[72] He challenges the idea that the Septuagint circulated only among Greek-speaking Jews, alleging that a Palestinian revision of the Septuagint remains a strong possibility. Sundberg also argues that allusions to apocryphal writings in the New Testament should cause the church to rethink its position on the Apocrypha. He makes a plea for an undivided ecumenical canon:

> The church received from Judaism closed collections of Law and Prophets and an undefined group of religious Writings that included books later defined in Judaism as writings and in the Western church as deuterocanonical and apocryphal. And it was from this total legacy from its Jewish origins that the church came to define her OT for herself. . . . There remains no longer any reason to differentiate among the books of that canon because of Jerome's doubts. The deuterocanonical books are the books that were not received in the Jewish canon but were fully accepted in the OT of the early church. And it is now possible for Roman Catholics and Protestants to accept that fact in a mutual, undivided OT Christian canon.[73]

Theological Issues

While the historical sources play a significant role in determining the status of the Apocrypha as divine Scripture, even more important are the theological issues involved. Do these writings direct us to Christ? Do they prepare the way for the gospel of salvation through the free grace of God? Do they manifest the unconditional love of God for the sinner? Because I have to answer in the negative, I must conclude that the Apocrypha fail to qualify as divinely inspired Scripture.

While containing much exemplary wisdom, the apocryphal books patently reflect the legalism of Rabbinic Judaism as well as the spiritualism and humanism of Hellenistic philosophy. The identification of virtue and knowledge, prominent in Hellenism, can be detected in both Ecclesiasticus and Wisdom of Solomon. The idea that good works are meritorious is expressed in Tobit 12:9, Ecclesiasticus 3:30, and 2 Esdras 8:33 and 11:46. This same legalistic orientation is discernible in Wisdom of Solomon 4:10 (NJB): "Having won God's favour, he has been loved and, as he was living among sinners, has been taken away." A humanistic outlook is evident in Ecclesiasticus 37:13: "Trust your own judgment, for it is your most reliable counsellor" (NEB).[74]

Love is generally thought of in terms of our obligation to our fellow believers rather than of the agape that goes out to sinners. Ben Sira writes in Ecclesiasticus 12:7, "Give to a good man, but never help a sinner; keep your good works for the humble, not the insolent" (NEB). The legalism that arises when love is understood as *nomos* (law) is reflected in Ecclesiasticus 12:1: "If you do a good deed, make sure to whom you are doing it; then you will have credit for your kindness" (NEB). The concept of love as eros, which held sway in Hellenistic religion and philosophy, is evident in Wisdom of Solomon 8:5: "If riches are a prize to be desired in life, what is richer than wisdom, the active cause of all things?" (NEB).

The denigration of the body and the idea of the inherent immortality of the soul are also present in some of these books, for example, the Wisdom of Solomon: "The reasoning of men is feeble, and our plans are fallible; because a perishable body weighs down the soul, and its frame of clay burdens the mind so full of thoughts" (9:14-15 NEB). This same book alludes to the preexistence of the soul (a Platonic idea): "I had received a good soul as my lot, or rather, being good, I had entered an undefiled body" (8:19–20 NJB). It also bears the imprint of Stoic philosophy.[75]

In addition, a sometimes harsh patriarchalism undercuts the wider biblical witness to the dignity and equality of woman. Ben Sira declares: "Woman is the origin of sin, and it is through her that we all die" (Ecclus 25:24 NEB; cf. 25:20). Again: "Any spite rather than the spite of woman" (25:13 NJB). One critic comments: "As homely proverbs uttered with a smile, such sayings would trouble no one; but when regularly read in the church service, as a part of sacred scripture, they became intolerable."[76] One should acknowledge that in a number of passages Ben Sira has kind words for the role of woman and speaks highly of a happy marriage.

On the other side of the ledger we must consider the frequent parallels in thought and language between the Apocrypha and the New Testament. Hebrews 11 bears a striking similarity to Ecclesiasticus 44. The prophecy concerning thirty pieces of silver and the potter's field in Matthew 27:9, which is quoted on the whole from Zechariah 11:13, is nevertheless ascribed to Jeremiah. But Jerome in his commentary discloses that a member of the Nazarene sect showed him an "apocryphal" Jeremiah text in which Matthew's quote was given in its exact form.[77] Origen held that the quotation "Things which eye has not seen or ear heard" in 1 Corinthians 2:9 is from the Apocalypse of Elijah, though as this book has disappeared in antiquity his contention cannot be verified.[78] The concept of "spirits in prison" in 1 Peter 3:19 might have its source in 1 Enoch 14 and 15. Jude 14 quotes directly from 1 Enoch 1:9 when it speaks of "the seventh from Adam." Jude 6 also reflects the influence of 1 Enoch. Hebrews 11:34–35 suggests familiarity with the narrative of 2 Maccabees 6:18—7:42. In addition, some scholars have detected the imprint of the Wisdom of Solomon in Paul's epistles. The phrase "armor of God" in Ephesians 6:13–17 reminds one of Wisdom of Solomon 5:18–20.

What are we to conclude from this study? These parallels may or may not be allusions to the Apocrypha, but they do suggest knowledge of them. Insights from apocryphal books can be adopted into the canon of sacred Scripture, but this does not mean that the apocryphal books themselves are to be treated as Scripture. The New Testament writers also show the influence of Hellenistic philosophy, but we are not to surmise that these pagan systems thereby have divine sanction.

Having examined a number of the parallels between the apocryphal books and the New Testament, John Henry Newman reached this conclusion:

Providence never acts with harsh transitions, one thing melts into another. Day melts into night, summer into winter. So it is with His inspired Word. What is *divine,* gradually resolves into what is human. Yet, as nevertheless summer and winter have for practical purposes a line of division . . . so we too for practical purposes are obliged to draw a line and say what is safe and sure to take as a canon for our faith, and what we cannot be sure will not mislead us. Without therefore, far from it, denying that God's supernatural hand is in the Apocrypha, yet, knowing that it was not included in that Canon which Christ sanctions, and that His Church has not spoken so clearly on the subject as to overcome the positive face of the argument deducible from this silence, therefore we do not see our way clear to receive it as canonical.[79]

An Appreciation of the Apocrypha

While not canonical Scripture, the apocryphal books can nevertheless be appreciated by both Jews and Christians as a rich historical source. They throw considerable light on Jewish theology and piety in the intertestamental period. They reflect a deepening of the messianic hope among the Jews, thereby preparing the way for the announcement of Jesus as the Messiah. They also manifest a growing interest among the Jews in angels and demons. Several books—Tobit, 2 Maccabees and 2 Esdras, as well as 1 Enoch among the pseudepigrapha—contain a highly developed angelology. In addition, they witness to the rise of belief in eternal life and the resurrection of the body, beliefs that the

Pharisees at the time of Jesus emphasized. On the debit side some of these books mirror the superstitions of the age, evincing an unwholesome fascination with signs and wonders. In Tobit magical methods are employed to control malevolent spirits.

The influence of the apocryphal books on the spirituality of the church through the ages is indisputable. Metzger points to the fact that insights drawn from the Apocrypha appear in many of the great hymns of the church, such as "Now Thank We All Our God" by Martin Rinkart; "It Came Upon a Midnight Clear"; "Silent Night"; "O Come, O Come Emmanuel"; "Jesus, the Very Thought of Thee" by Bernard of Clairvaux; and Charles Wesley's "Jesus, Lover of My Soul." In the Methodist Hymn-Book published in London in 1933 forty-three hymns make allusions to the Apocrypha. Many religious artists have also found inspiration in the Apocrypha. Judith, Tobit and Susanna are among apocryphal figures who have captured the imagination of some of the leading painters in the West.

The books of the Apocrypha can be heartily recommended as a source of spiritual edification for Christians. That they made an undeniable impression on some New Testament writers and that they were frequently cited by the church fathers should be enough to convince us that they merit a place in Christian spirituality. To be sure, they must be read with care, for they contain notions that are at variance with the vision of the biblical prophets and apostles, especially in the area of the doctrine of salvation. The Reformers wisely refused to accord the Apocrypha normative status in determining matters of faith and practice, but on the whole they treated these books with respect. The Reformer Andreas Carlstadt could describe them as "holy writings," yet not to be ranked with sacred Scripture.[80] The early Luther occasionally cited the Wisdom of Solomon in throwing light on demonology: "Death came into the world only through the Devil's envy, as those who belong to him find to their cost" (2:24 NJB).

Can the Apocrypha ever function as the Word of God for the community of faith? They are certainly not the Word of God in the sense of inspired Scripture, but anyone grounded in faith in Jesus Christ and him crucified may occasionally hear the Word of God in these books just as we may hear God's Word in the sermons, prayers and theological tracts of the people of God after the time of Christ. The Apocrypha are not a witness to the redemptive acts of Jesus Christ and are therefore not a doctrinal norm for the church, but they do provide an understanding of the spiritual climate into which Christ came. In this way they throw light on the deeds of Christ and his apostles as they ministered to the Jewish community. The Apocrypha are not the Word of God, but they may lend themselves for use by the living Word of God to bring new insight and appreciation for the acts of God in biblical history.

•SIX•

THE
HERMENEUTICAL
PROBLEM

Why do you not understand my language? It is because my revelation
is beyond your grasp.... You are not God's children;
that is why you do not listen.

JOHN 8:43, 47 NEB

Let us understand Holy Writ, historically, yes,
just as it is written; however, let us fire it well in the flame
of the Holy Spirit and unfold with spiritual discernment whatever
in it seems incongruous or obscure when taken literally.

JEROME

The Holy Spirit so cleaves to his own truth,
as he has expressed it in Scripture, that he then only exerts
and puts forth his strength when the Word is received
with due honor and respect.

JOHN CALVIN

Anyone who seeks to give meaning to Scripture,
without taking it directly from Scripture, is a foe to Scripture.

PASCAL

O you who open your Bibles and want to understand a text,
the way to get into the meaning of a text is through the door, Christ.

CHARLES SPURGEON

The excesses of the critical approach to Scripture come,
not through recognizing that its words are human words,
but through prejudging what it is that God reveals to us there.

KENNETH HAMILTON

I compare the search for the perfect hermeneutic to the search
for the Holy Grail. Everybody approaches the new hermeneutics
with the conviction that this is the answer, and then
after twenty years you will find its limitations.

RAYMOND E. BROWN

Not only the authority of Scripture but also its interpretation presents a major problem for theology today. The term *hermeneutics,* meaning the art and science of interpretation (especially of ancient writings), derives from the Greek *hermēneuein* (to speak or interpret) and *hermēneus* (interpreter); these words in turn derive from Hermes, the divine messenger of the gods. A key issue is whether biblical hermeneutics is to be subordinated to a general hermeneutics that determines the ground rules for interpretation.

It is commonly thought in lay circles more than in clerical that the surface meaning of the biblical text is sufficient and that this meaning is available to any searching person. But more often than not what first appears to be the sense of the text may not at all be the meaning that the Spirit of God is trying to impress on us through this text. It is not enough to know the words of the text: we must know the plenitude of meaning that these words carry for the community of faith at that time and for our time.

Scripture itself calls for interpretation of the mysteries it contains. A mere recital of the words of the Bible does not suffice. We are covenant partners with the Holy Spirit in the interpretation of the text. In Acts 8 we witness the missionary Philip interpreting the Old Testament to the Ethiopian eunuch. Without an interpreter Isaiah 53 would probably have remained a closed chapter to the Ethiopian. One should note that Philip was expounding the Scripture in the light of Scripture's own criterion— the gospel of divine grace revealed in Jesus Christ. The Bible can be interpreted only in its own light. Philip was the instrument, but the Spirit of God, the divine author of Scripture, was the interpreter. Scripture is the norm, but this norm must be illumined by the Spirit as we seek to assess the significance of the text for our lives in the here and now.

In the hermeneutical task we should focus on what Scripture intends to teach us. What Scripture intends to teach is what the Spirit intended to say to the people of that time in this text and what he intends to say to us today in a different period of history. The Bible is not a systematic set of rules that are more or less self-evident: it is closer to a uranium mine that yields its precious metal only after a careful and painstaking search. Our task is to penetrate below the surface meaning of Scripture in order to dig out the treasure of the divine wisdom that resides within its depths (cf. Prov 2:4–5).

Thomas F. Torrance warns us not to rest content with the grammatical-syntactical sense of biblical texts. We must "probe into the reasonable ground underlying their linguistic signification, and that needs a comparative examination of their signifying components including the many images, analogies, figures, representations, and idioms that are employed, in order to determine as far as possible their exact sense and then to distill out of them and bring to consistent expression the basic conceptuality they carry."[1] Yet our mandate is not fulfilled until we penetrate through the conceptuality to the objective realities that the conceptions attest and reflect.[2]

The task of interpretation would be much easier if the words of the Bible were identical with divine revelation. But because these words are related to revelation as form to content, interpretation is far more difficult. Clark Pinnock gives a timely admonition against confounding the text and the revelation that it enshrines and attests:

Once the church has identified the whole Bible as the Word of God, the temptation is enormous to forget about the original historical situation and to regard every verse as a kind of oracle for us. This is the danger reflected in Augustine's expression "What the Bible says, God says." Then we no longer hear the precise word spoken to people by the text in the first instance, but construe it as a universally valid logion independent of context. Thus a text may no longer have a merely provincial meaning but must have a universal application. The tendency is to dehistoricize the vehicle of revelation and to make each text an immutable and inerrant proposition.[3]

The Dynamics of Interpretation

In classical evangelical theology scriptural interpretation entails both exegesis and exposition. In the first we seek to discover the original intent of the author; in the second we try to assess the significance of the text both for its time and for our time. The object in exegesis is to determine the grammatical or historical meaning of the text. But we must not stop there: we need to go on to synthesis—relating the text to the central meaning of the Bible, which is the gospel—and then to application—relating the text to our life situation.[4] In synthesis we strive to ascertain the theological meaning of the text; in application we decide how this meaning bears on the moral and spiritual issues that presently confront us.[5] One can see that theology is integrally related to sociology. To paraphrase Immanuel Kant, theology without sociology is lifeless; sociology without theology is blind.

Hermeneutics in its deepest sense is the translation of meaning (Rudolf Bultmann). The Reformers protested against the allegorizing of Scripture that was prominent in medieval theology on the grounds that this method opened the door to arbitrary exegesis. They were convinced that we must focus on the natural meaning of the text, though we do not necessarily remain with this meaning in our theological exposition.

I too believe we must begin with the natural meaning, but this meaning cannot be uncovered by a simple translation (the Reformers would agree). The literal sense is to be found in the original text when its component words are understood in the light of the author's worldview and scale of values. But once uncovered, the literal or natural meaning must be supplemented by theological exegesis. Now we seek to assess the theological significance of the text. We are now in the area of "believing integration" (Emil Brunner) by which we try to integrate text and message. Our task is to relate the insights of the writer to God's self-revelation in Jesus Christ, the center and apex of Scripture. We must move from the analytic criticism of the biblical exegete to the synthetic criticism of the theologian.

P. T. Forsyth made the helpful distinction between the "higher criticism" informed by literary scholarship and the "highest criticism" informed by the illumination of grace.[6] In the latter we allow ourselves to be criticized by the gospel. This also involves seeing both the text and ourselves in the light of the gospel. It means subordinating the Bible to the gospel—the transcendent norm within Scripture. According to Forsyth the synthetic criticism of the theologian is the highest criticism, superior to the higher criticism of the scientific historian.

Karl Barth's position is remarkably similar. Scripture is to receive both historical and theological treatment. Biblical statements should be seen not only against the background of their immediate historical environment but also against the background of eternity. For Barth there are two understandings of Scripture: the linguistic and grammatical understanding and the understanding that involves assent to the truth of Scripture.

The deeper understanding—the perception of faith—is outside the confines of purely historical exegesis. Only the believer who is guided by the Holy Spirit can discern the subtle relation of the insights of the writer to the revelation of the Son of Man. This relation unveils the innermost intentions of the writer, intentions that he himself might not have been completely aware of. It also brings us into contact with the intentions of the Spirit, the ultimate author of the Bible. The biblical authors were not averse to acknowledging that the object of their witness transcended mere human understanding. Job confessed, "I have uttered what I did not understand, things too wonderful for me, which I did not know" (Job 42:3; cf. Dan 12:8).

The fathers and doctors of the Catholic church as well as the Reformers often resorted to typology in their analysis of the Old Testament. They perceived in Old Testament concepts and events anticipations or foreshadowings of the coming revelation of Jesus Christ, the Messiah of Israel. The typological approach is permissible if it is based on critical historical exegesis. It can even be considered a type of theological exegesis. For example, the sign of Cain can legitimately be taken as a sign of the cross of Calvary, for this sign was given to secure him from harm on his earthly pilgrimage. The angel that wrestled with Jacob is commonly identified as a preappearance of Jesus Christ. The manna in the wilderness is interpreted as a type of the bread of life; this typology was already employed in John's Gospel (6:30–33) and in Paul (1 Cor 10:3). The suffering servant of Isaiah 53 is indeed a foreshadowing of the humiliation and exaltation of the Son of God.

Historical exegesis gives us the literal sense of the passage, what the author actually said. Theological exegesis or exposition tells us what the author was trying to say, what he was pointing toward. The "holy way" in Isaiah 35:8–10 refers in its historical context to the road back to Jerusalem from Babylon. But in theological exposition it may validly be applied to the way to salvation, the road forward to the "new Jerusalem." The psalmist rejoices in God's promise, "With long life I will satisfy him, and show him my salvation" (Ps 91:16). After the advent of Jesus Christ we can see in this text a reference to eternal life through faith in Christ. When Job confessed, "I know that my Redeemer lives, and at last he will stand upon the earth" (19:25), he surely did not have in mind the picture of the coming incarnation of Jesus Christ, but certainly this event fulfills what Job was trying to say under the inspiration of the Spirit. John's Gospel is emphatic that Isaiah saw the glory of Christ and spoke of him (12:41), but the prophet obviously did not think of Christ directly in the various passages that John cites (Is 53:1; 6:9–10; 6:1). Rudolf Otto reminds us that Jesus used Isaiah 49:24–25 to speak of heavenly oppressors, though the prophet was originally referring to earthly oppressors (Mt 12:25–29).[7]

I am not advocating "eisegesis," simply reading back into the text what the believer today might contend for. The method I favor is striving to discover what the writer was pointing toward in the sacred history that has its fulfillment in Christ. A scriptural text does not merely have its immediate, historical meaning but a plenitude of meaning *(sensus plenior)*, which can be assessed only when the text is studied in the light of further revelation or development in the understanding of revelation. I fully concur here with James Packer: "God's meaning and message through each passage, when set in its total biblical context, exceeds what the human writer had in mind."[8] Packer is emphatic, however, that the fullness of meaning that texts acquire in their wider biblical context builds on and is controlled by the historical-grammatical meaning.[9]

The various kinds of higher criticism (literary, redaction, source, genre, form criticism) all help us to gain insight into the original intention of the text and the way in which the community of faith received and appraised this text. Yet historical and literary criticism have their limits: they cannot tell us how the text is being used by the Spirit of God today as the impact of its message bears on the task of the church. Higher criticism can throw light on the cultural and linguistic background of the text, but it cannot procure for us the Word of God—the truth that the Spirit wishes us to hear in our day and situation.

Higher criticism can tell us that some words of Jesus were probably placed in his mouth by the early church (for example, Mk 16:17-18). Criticism might even support the contention that these words were comparable to what Jesus actually said in the memory of the church. But critics cannot assure us that these words had their origin in the risen Christ as he spoke by his Spirit to the church. This kind of theological judgment is outside the confines of historical-literary exegesis. The critics can point only to the bias of the editor or redactor; they cannot make room in their appraisal for the illumination of the Holy Spirit to the writer or editor. This kind of judgment is beyond the purview of scientific criticism.

With Barth I hold that theologians may be involved in *Sache* exegesis—the delineation of the content or substance of Scripture. But they are not to engage in *Sachkritik* (content criticism), for there is no higher standard than the gospel itself in appraising the meaning of a biblical passage for the church today. Criticism may be directed to the form but not to the content of Scripture, which lies outside the compass of historical investigation. Yet we do not have the divine content except in the human form; we do not have access to the divine side of Scripture except in the human side.

Breakthrough into Understanding

One of the key questions in contemporary hermeneutical discussion is whether a text contains its meaning. The philosopher Hans-Georg Gadamer, who has had a remarkable impact on biblical hermeneutics, contends that the meaning of what we seek to understand is not something that exists in and by itself *(an sich):* the "meaning of a text or of tradition is only realized through the happening *(pathos)* of understanding."[10] I believe that the text has objective meaning, yet meaning that is not contained in the text itself but resides in the Spirit who breathes on the text, thereby bringing what is hidden into the open. Meaning does not lie in transcending the subject-object polarity, as the new hermeneutics would have it, but in allowing the object of theological inquiry to speak to us anew. This object is not the text in and of itself but the text as an instrument of the Spirit, in whose hands it becomes a mirror of the divine wisdom.

The truth of faith lodges not in the human interpreter nor in the community of faith but in the Word of God, whose presence encompasses the text of Holy Scripture.[11] Understanding happens when God's Word speaks to us anew as we submit ourselves to his authority and direction mediated through Holy Scripture. We begin to know when the text becomes transparent to its transcendent meaning through the action of the Spirit in the biblical words and in the human heart.

Coming to know the Word of God can be described as a fourfold process.[12] One must first approach the Bible in reverence and humility. This step presupposes that the seeker for truth is already a believer, one who has been confronted by the reality of God's redeeming Word. We could not seek in spirit and truth unless we had already been grasped by this truth. We come to the Bible not with a preunderstanding that prepares the way for faith but with a faith that seeks understanding.

This precritical stance now gives way, however, to a critical stance. The writings are reverently subjected to scientific or rational scrutiny. Criticism in this sense is not faultfinding but incisive examination and evaluation. As people of faith we are obliged to discriminate between the essential and the peripheral. We still study God's Word in a spirit of reverence but now relying on tools of research to clarify the language of the text. Critical methodology can throw light on the form of the text but only rarely on the content, which eludes the scrutiny of historical investigation, even one that proceeds on the basis of faith.

It is not sufficient simply to criticize the text: we must now let the text criticize us. Criticism must be turned inward so that we begin to question the presuppositions that we bring to the text. This criticism springs from faith in God, not doubt of God. Our doubt is now directed to ourselves, to our own ingenuity and wisdom. We judge not our faith but the way in which we articulate and maintain this faith. Calvin believed that we must be "emptied of our own understanding" in order to have "a saving acquaintance with God."[13] The biblical way of speaking is that we must learn to humble ourselves before we can hear the truth spoken to us out of the mouth of the wisdom of God itself. If we would know the wisdom that surpasses all understanding, "we must let ourselves be questioned so radically that we center everything in him and nothing in ourselves" (Calvin).[14]

Finally, when radical doubt is pushed to the limit we end in the state of prayer. We have now moved beyond criticism to receptivity, in which we are open to hearing and learning from the Spirit of God. The psalmist exemplifies this prayerful stance: "Open my eyes, that I may behold wondrous things out of thy law" (Ps 119:18). We must pray as did Solomon for a "discerning heart" (1 Kings 3:9-11 NIV). "Regard prayer," said Isaac the Syrian, "as the key to the true meaning of what is said in the Divine Scriptures."[15] Barth was also emphatic that prayer is the door by which we enter into the presence of the Word of God and begin to understand what he has to say to us in Holy Scripture. Prayer shows our dependence on the sovereign object of the text for understanding. Because it is the decisive activity, "prayer must take precedence even of exegesis, and in no circumstances must it be suspended."[16]

We should not thereby conclude that we are passive in the process of understanding. We strain with all our efforts to discern the full impact and meaning of a biblical passage as it bears on our lives here and now. But this meaning will elude us until we allow ourselves to be guided by the Spirit in order to see the relation of the text to the cross of Christ, the center and apex of Scripture. It is when we begin to apprehend the christological significance of the text that we enter into what Barth calls "the strange new world within the Bible." It is when the text speaks to us through the power of the Spirit that our lives begin to make sense, for we now see ourselves in the light of eternity. The breakthrough into meaning occurs when the text is no longer the interpreted object but now the dynamic interpreter (Johann Albrecht Bengel).

The apostle Paul describes the Word of God as a secret wisdom available only for those who repent and believe (1 Cor 2:7-10). Only those who confess their blindness will begin to see, whereas those who claim to see will soon become blind (Jn 9:30-41). The simplest persons who truly acknowledge the poverty of their own insights and accomplishments in the sight of God can know this "secret wisdom" before teachers of biblical studies, who may have the necessary scholarly credentials but are lacking in humility. The Word of God has sufficient mystery to confound the expert and sufficient clarity to convert the sinner.

This four-step process must not be construed as a technique or method for procuring the Word of God. It has value only if it makes us aware of dimensions of the mystery of coming to the knowledge of this Word. The two things necessary are a believing heart and a searching mind. Both precritical devotional study of the Bible and purely academic study are inadequate. If we are able to do so, we must make use of critical methods but push beyond these if we would know the full implications of the text for personal life and practice.

The Bible comes alive when it is read in the light of the cross of Christ. A heightened religious consciousness will discern in the scriptural events and encounters the handwriting of God (Avery Dulles). A person whose inward ears have been opened by the Spirit can hear in the Bible the very Word of God.

The interpretation of Scripture is not an art to be learned but a gift to be received. No technique or formula can disclose the real Word of

God. Thomas à Kempis declared that the biblical prophets "speak most eloquently," but if God is silent "they cannot fire the heart." They proclaim the words, but it is the Spirit who imparts "understanding to the mind."[17] According to Philipp Melanchthon the gift of interpretation does not belong to the ungodly but to the assembly that is governed and sanctified by the Holy Spirit.[18]

Faith is a kind of naiveté that impels us to venture forth in childlike trust with the certainty that the Spirit will lead us into all truth. But faith is not to be confounded with credulity or gullibility. It is ready to doubt all human claims to knowledge of God's truth even while it entertains the hope of fuller understanding. It calls into radical question both the naive trust in the traditions built around the surface meaning of Scripture and the naive trust in the myths spawned by higher criticism. It recognizes that it is possible to "see and not perceive" and to "hear and not understand" (Mk 4:12 NKJ). It throws itself on the mercy and power of Christ, who alone can open the door to meaning and understanding. It persists in waiting and knocking, aware that only those who seek diligently and earnestly will find the truth in the end.

The Bible study I recommend could be designated postcritical rather than either critical or precritical. We make use of critical methods but do not remain with these methods. We venture forth in an attitude of receptivity, willing to be led by the Spirit rather than seeking to gain certainty by applying inductive or deductive methods to Scripture. While employing ordinary procedures of human learning, we subordinate them to a readiness to be instructed anew by the Spirit of God. Instead of the literalistic approach of fundamentalism and the historical-critical approach of liberalism, I recommend the postcritical, pneumatic approach of a catholic evangelicalism.

I by no means wish to disparage the evangelical orthodox concern to uncover the root meaning of the words of the text and the liberal concern to analyze the literary genre of the text, the cultural-historical matrix in which it was written and the history of the oral tradition behind it. Yet I insist that the text does not yield its full meaning until we see it in its theological relation to the wider context—the sacred history in the Bible culminating in Jesus Christ—and appropriate its message for ourselves. The elements in biblical hermeneutics include not only grammatical-historical exegesis and historical-cultural analysis but also theological exposition and spiritual appropriation.

One of the recurring debates in modern biblical study is whether we should come to the text with a preunderstanding or whether we should strive to open ourselves to an altogether new understanding. Both Bultmann and Paul Tillich advocated approaching the Bible with our eyes opened by an existential analysis of the human situation. Only when we come with the questions that such an analysis yields can we find in the Bible answers that will be pertinent to the human situation. Barth's view was that we should set aside all overt presuppositions and seek to be taught anew by the Spirit of God. Barth did not deny that faith entails presuppositions but urged us to allow them to be sharpened and even corrected by God's Holy Spirit.[19]

It is interesting to compare Forsyth on this matter. He maintained that in order to interpret the New Testament text rightly, we must appropriate the bias of the New Testament writers. Instead of coming to the Bible without presuppositions, we should come with the apostolic interpretation, for only then do we read the Bible in the light of the cross of Christ.[20] Only then are we able to see biblical history as a history of grace. What is of paramount importance in the Bible is not the historicity of the events it describes but their meaning for the community of faith, their facility in serving the gospel of grace.

Forsyth and Barth were not as far apart as first appears. Barth too believed in coming to the Bible with an attitude of submission to the gospel so that we can hear the gospel anew. We are to read the Bible with "the mind of Christ" (1 Cor 2:16), which is not our possession, something we can take for granted, but something that must be imparted to us again and again. In order to lay hold of the mind of Christ we need to let our own presuppositions and preconceptions be judged by this transcendent criterion. We must never confound our own interpretations with the divine self-interpretation lest we arrogate to ourselves knowledge that belongs only to God. According to Paul, we do not know as we ought to know (1 Cor 8:2), and if we think we stand, we should take heed lest we fall (10:12). In faith we indeed have access to the mind of Christ (2:16; Phil 2:5), but it is only through the struggle of prayer and the pain of repentance that this channel to Christ is kept open.

Luther was keenly aware of the radical discontinuity between human thought and action and the divine wisdom. The Word of God does not fulfill human knowledge but disrupts it: "If the Word of God comes, it comes contrary to our thinking and our will. It does not allow our thinking to stand, even in those matters which are most sacred, but it destroys and eradicates and scatters everything."[21]

It is not enough to claim to have the apostolic interpretation. We must test this claim by subjecting it to the affirmations of Holy Scripture, and in so doing we may find that we will have to restate it. We must not impose our interpretation on the text but allow it to be transposed by the light within the text and thereby deepened and corrected. In his debate with Zwingli Luther confessed: "I am a captive; I cannot escape. The text is too strong for me; the words will not let me avoid their meaning."[22] The text may overturn our preconceptions, it may deflect our reasoning, for even as interpreters of the Word we remain sinners. Our thoughts are not God's thoughts; our ways are not God's ways (Is 55:8-9).

The path to true understanding lies in humility and obedience under the cross. We can teach and speak with wisdom only when we acknowledge that wisdom lies not in ourselves but in him who suffered and died so that we might live. We can draw on this wisdom only when we make a determined effort to live in the spirit and power of Christ. We can stand with the apostles and begin to see through their eyes only when we walk with them in bearing the cross. We can claim to have the mind of Christ only when we live in such a way that we become veritable signs of his passion and victory.

The Natural and the Spiritual Sense

A continuing debate in biblical studies is whether the text can convey more than one meaning. In 1859 Benjamin Jowett of Oxford University argued that "Scripture has one meaning—the meaning which it had in the mind of the Prophet or Evangelist who first uttered or wrote, to the hearers or readers who first received it."[23] He also maintained that Scripture should be investigated like any other book. Jowett's views reflect one side of the Reformation tradition and correspond to the position of most modern evangelicals. Albert Barnett gives voice to this older scholarly consensus within Protestantism: "Scripture is . . . objective and fixed in meaning. Discovery of that meaning, not the imposition upon it of the point of view of the interpreter, is the duty of believers. Whimsical interpretation is the mark of heretical teachers."[24]

David Steinmetz, professor of church history and doctrine at Duke Divinity School, argues forcefully that the medieval theory of levels of meaning is more true to biblical faith than the later theory of a single meaning.[25] "Modern literary criticism," he says, "has challenged the notion that a text means only what its author intends it to mean far more radically than medieval exegetes ever dreamed of doing."[26]

By contrast, Philip Hughes insists vigorously that the principle underlying the allegorizing method is a pernicious one: "It presupposes that under the surface of the text, hidden from the sight of the multitude, there lies a profound 'spiritual' sense that only the expert is capable of discerning. This inevitably fosters an attitude of disdain and disregard for the plain, natural sense of the text and reduces the Bible to a book of intellectual word puzzles."[27]

In this whole discussion it is well to keep in mind that the New Testament itself engages in typological or spiritualizing exegesis. Paul identifies the wilderness rock in Exodus with Christ (1 Cor 10:1-4), and Hagar and Sarah are said to represent the two covenants (Gal 4:21-31). Our Lord also employs this kind of interpretation when he says, "As Moses lifted up the serpent in the wilderness, so must the Son of man be lifted up" (Jn 3:14).

The church fathers, while respecting the natural sense of the text, generally tried to assess its spiritual significance in the light of the fuller revelation in biblical history. John Chrysostom took as his point of departure the natural or grammatical-historical meaning of the text and then endeavored to see the text in its wider theological context, namely, the message of redemption through Christ. Origen argued that the Bible has three senses: the natural, the moral and the spiritual, which is the highest. John Cassian (d. 435) detected four senses: the historical, the allegorical, the tropological (the moral) and the anagogical. This typology was adopted by Thomas Aquinas and used widely by Catholic exegetes.

According to Augustine the Bible has an inner or spiritual meaning that only the Spirit can disclose: "See, Father, look down, and see, and approve, and let it be pleasing in the sight of your mercy for me to find grace before you, so that the inner meaning of your words may be opened up to me when I knock."[28] Yet this inner meaning had to be consonant with the natural or grammatical meaning. One should not accept any allegorical interpretation that is not supported "by the 'manifest testimonies' of other less ambiguous portions of the Bible."[29]

Augustine made a helpful distinction between the signs and the things signified. The aim of the biblical theologian is to proceed from the words to the spiritual realities toward which these words direct us. We are not to remain with the world of shadows but to ascend to the higher, spiritual realm whose light is radiated into the material world. The Platonic thrust of Augustine's theology is obvious.

In a similar vein Thomas distinguished between "words" and "things." The words point to the objective reality, but this reality can itself be the sign of a still higher reality. Although fully aware of the deeper senses within Scripture, Thomas stressed the importance of the literal or natural sense, which is not necessarily the surface meaning of the text but the "meaning of the text which the author intends."[30] For Thomas this author is God, not the human prophet or apostle.

In the fourteenth century Nicholas of Lyra spoke of a double literal sense.[31] The literal-historical sense is what the words mean in their original historical setting. The literal-prophetic sense refers to the wider meaning they encompass in view of later and changed circumstances. Consequently the interpreter has a dual task: to explain the historical meaning of the text and to elucidate its larger and later spiritual significance.

The Protestant Reformers were highly critical of the tendency to read into the text higher or mystical meanings. For Calvin the meaning of the text is one *(simplex)*, and that is the grammatical-historical meaning. In Luther's view this meaning should command our primary attention, for it is clear and decisive.

Yet neither Reformer remained with the natural meaning but proceeded to give a theological treatment of the Old Testament text, which generally consisted in assessing its christological significance. Luther referred to this approach as the "spiritual interpretation" as opposed to the traditional allegorical interpretation practiced by Origen, Jerome and others,[32] all of whom erred by often ignoring the literal meaning of the words and the actual history of Israel. In many cases the spiritual meaning they discovered proved to be something alien to the text. Instead of being treated as a secret code used to express something unrelated to the situation described in it, the text should be seen as spiritual prophecy "which enables Old Testament history and institutions to point beyond themselves to Christ as the one in whom the history of the Old Testament actually reaches the goal which God has set for it."[33]

Acknowledgment of a spiritual sense beyond the natural sense was widespread in Pietism and Puritanism. According to John Owen the biblical texts derive their life and power from their relation to Christ: "separated from him they are dead and useless."[34] It was commonplace among Puritans to distinguish between notional and real knowledge. Knowing the notions or concepts is not yet knowing the realities that Scripture aims to give us.

Willem Teellinck (d. 1629), a Reformed theologian of the Netherlands, showed the influence of Pietism by employing a method that one may aptly describe as intuitive biblicism. He perceived two kinds of understanding in Scripture—the literal and the spiritual. But the spiritual is not to be confounded with a mystical rereading of Scripture: "When we speak of a spiritual understanding . . . in contradistinction to a literal sense, we do not mean . . . another, hidden, and higher sense of Scripture than that which the letter offers, but we mean thereby such an understanding of the literal sense of the Holy Scripture as reaches our spirit and will incline it toward an honest acceptance and meditation upon the true literal sense of Holy Scripture."[35]

Along the same lines Jonathan Edwards distinguished between understanding the Scriptures in a highly subjective way and in a spiritual way. "Spiritually to understand the Scripture is rightly to understand what *is in* Scripture, and what *was in* it before it was understood. . . . When the mind is enlightened spiritually and rightly to understand the Scripture, it is enabled to see that in the Scripture which before was not seen by reason of blindness."[36] Spiritual understanding is tied to the experience of the realities of which Scripture speaks. It is the difference between intellectual apprehension and existential appropriation.

John Wesley too made a place for a spiritual sense in addition to the natural or literal sense of Scripture: "We then establish the law when we declare every part of it, every commandment contained therein, not only in its full, literal sense but likewise in its spiritual meaning, not only with regard to the outward actions which it either forbids or enjoins, but also with respect to the inward principle, to the thoughts, desires and intents of the heart."[37] The law of God in its spiritual sense is, however, hidden not only from Jews and heathen but also from most Christians,[38] for only those sanctified by the Spirit of God can understand things taught by the Spirit.

On the contemporary scene there is a definite shift toward reconsidering the possibility that the text may have a spiritual meaning beyond its natural one. David Steinmetz is adamant that the meaning of a biblical text "is not exhausted by the original intention of the author."[39]

The text of the Bible, he says, contains both letter and spirit, as medieval exegetes rightly perceived.

The text is not all letter, as Jowett with others maintained, or all spirit, as the rather more enthusiastic literary critics in our own time are apt to argue. The original text as spoken and heard limits a field of possible meanings. Those possible meanings are not dragged by the hair, willy-nilly, into the text, but belong to the life of the Bible in the encounter between author and reader as they belong to the life of any act of the human imagination. Such a hermeneutical theory is capable of sober and disciplined application and avoids the Scylla of extreme subjectivism on the one hand and the Charybdis of historical positivism on the other. To be sure, medieval exegetes made bad mistakes in the application of their theory, but they also scored notable and brilliant triumphs.[40]

William LaSor of Fuller Theological Seminary also finds value in moving behind the natural meaning to the spiritual significance of the text. To discover the plenitude of meaning in the text *(sensus plenior)*, he says, we must always begin with its literal meaning. The *sensus plenior* "is not a substitute for grammatico-historical exegesis, but a development from such exegesis. It is not a reading into the text of theological doctrines and theories, but a reading from the text of the fullness of meaning required by God's complete revelation."[41] This fullness of meaning is derived from the total context, which includes both what has already been revealed of God's redemptive activity and the ultimate purpose of that activity.

Regent College scholar Bruce Waltke proposes a canonical-process approach as an alternative to "the Antiochian principle of allowing but one historical meaning."[42] The older approach, he says, is grossly inadequate for assessing the significance of the Psalms. By the canonical-process approach he means "the recognition that the text's intention became deeper and clearer as the parameters of the canon were expanded."[43]

Jacques Ellul has also questioned the advisability of relying too heavily on the original meaning of the text as we seek to ascertain its wider significance. "Does taking a text back to its date, its primitive identity, give it its real meaning, or the meaning it was at least meant to have when it was made a part of the whole? Is each text not destined . . . to throw light on the others and vice versa? And is this mutual illumination not destroyed if the text is fragmented and dispersed according to time and place?"[44] Ellul maintains that the historical character of divine revelation makes it mandatory to allow for the text to adapt itself to new meanings as God's revelation is unfolded in history.

> If it is true that the God of Israel and of Jesus Christ is a God who reveals himself *in history,* are we taking this revelation seriously if we fix a given word of this revelation to one moment in history, like a butterfly tacked to the wall, so that, completely framed by cultural data, it can no longer be moved from there to mean something else? Is there not a contradiction between that hermeneutic attitude and the very truth of the incarnate God? Is the important point not that these texts—the bearers of the Word—*have* moved, that they have come together, that they have adapted to each other in order to bear a wider and deeper meaning?[45]

Many theologians, especially those on the conservative side of the theological spectrum, sense the danger of moving back to the pneumatic approach of the church fathers and doctors of the medieval church. Walter Kaiser warns that we must not "force a wedge between God and the writer—unless one cares nothing for the writer's own claims."[46] Kaiser affirms E. D. Hirsch's distinction between meaning and significance.[47] While the text has a single, objective meaning that corresponds to the intention of the original author, its significance will vary as it is applied to different situations.

Though recognizing that authorial intention is of vital importance, I contend that theological relation is equally important. Part of the problem of relying on the intention of the original author is that he may not always have had a clear vision of what he was trying to say. Moreover, the community of faith may well have received the text with a different understanding from that in the mind of the author. Again, the intention of the Spirit of God, the divine author, may sometimes be at variance with the intention of the human author. Finally, meaning includes not only intelligibility but also how a text relates to and impinges on our life in the present. The distinction between meaning and application is artificial, for meaning does not simply reside in the words of a text or in the intention of the author but in an event in which the reader or hearer participates in the revelation of meaning given to the author. Gadamer is not too far from the mark when he declares, "Not occasionally only, but always, the meaning of a text goes beyond its author. That is why understanding is not merely a reproductive, but always a productive attitude as well."[48]

I believe that we must make a clear-cut distinction between the historical meaning of the text and its revelational or spiritual meaning. The first includes both authorial intention and the way in which the text was received in the community of faith. The second refers to the pneumatic or revelatory meaning that the text assumes when the Spirit acts on it in bringing home its significance to people of faith in every age. This second meaning is accessible only to those who participate existentially in the tradition of the faith, for only they are in experiential contact with the realities to which the text witnesses.

The content of the Bible, the mystery of God's self-revelation in Jesus Christ, can only be spiritually discerned. "Whoever does not have the Spirit," Paul says, "cannot receive the gifts that come from God's Spirit. Such a person really does not understand them; they are nonsense to him, because their value can be judged only on a spiritual basis" (1 Cor 2:14 GNB). Our natural senses enable us to discern the historical testimony that the Bible reports, but in order to come to a knowledge of the God of the Bible we need spiritual illumination. The apostle implores that "the God of our Lord Jesus Christ, the Father of glory," give his hearers "a spirit of wisdom and perception of what is revealed" so that they may come "to full knowledge of him" (Eph 1:17 NJB).

The divine wisdom that comes to us through the Scriptures is called by Paul a "secret wisdom," but this expression must not be understood in a gnostic sense. For gnostics knowledge of God is accessible only to an elite who are willing to subject themselves to the necessary purifying disciplines so that they can see what is veiled to ordinary mortals. For New Testament Christianity knowledge of God is available to all people of faith if they will only seek and knock, trusting in God's promise to hear and respond. The wisdom that the Spirit of God imparts is not one that stands in discontinuity with the preaching and writing of the prophets and apostles but one that has informed their witness and indeed resides within it. This wisdom does not lift us above the temporal and material but makes us partakers of God's redeeming action in the very world in which we live.

A text can have a fluidity of meaning within certain parameters, and these are measured by its grammatical-historical meaning, which is single and fixed. Yet, as LaSor rightly observes, though the literal meaning is basic, "if it is the only meaning, then God is not speaking to us; he spoke to men of old," and for some scholars "that was that."[49]

I believe that typological exegesis has an important place, for it is already employed in Scripture. If it is true that there is a single sacred history that has its culmination and fulfillment in Jesus Christ, then we may legitimately see in events and encounters in Old Testament history a witness to what is to come later in the history of revelation. The church catholic has generally treated the "protoevangelium" in Genesis 3:15 as a witness to the cross of Christ, for it was there that the head of the serpent was crushed, but it was also there that the devil showed his ability to inflict pain and suffering on the emissary of redemption. Job's confession that after his skin had been destroyed he would then in the flesh see God (Job 19:26) can legitimately be interpreted as a reference to Christ's second advent and the resurrection at the end of the ages, though this was not its immediate reference. When the psalmist speaks of the need to appeal only to the righteousness of the Lord, believers will certainly see in these verses the righteousness and love of Jesus Christ that alone can overcome sin and death (Ps 71:15-16 NKJ).

A text may indeed have both an immediate and an ultimate reference, though only those with the eyes to see and the ears to hear can genuinely discern the latter.

The revelational meaning of the text can be assessed not only by viewing the text in the context of the whole of Scripture but also by assessing the impact of this text on the faith of the church through the ages. The Holy Spirit was not only active in the history of the Bible but also remains active in the ongoing history of the community of faith. Yet church tradition is never a ruling norm but only an aid in understanding, for the truth that it proclaims in its fidelity to the gospel is mixed with much untruth that springs from infidelity to its Lord and Savior. Salvation history continues in the history of the church but only as the reverberation of the cross and resurrection victory of Jesus Christ. The apostolic interpretation of this victory remains the ruling norm, but tradition may illuminate this norm insofar as it remains open to the guidance and direction of the Holy Spirit.[50]

Guidelines of the Reformers

The guidelines for interpreting Scripture given by the Reformers of the sixteenth century are still instructive for the church as it seeks a hermeneutic that is true to the biblical witness and to the deepest insights of church tradition. These guidelines may not all be as relevant today as in that time, but they all carry the stamp of divine truth.

First, the Reformers affirmed the perspicuity of Scripture—its inherent clarity. The clarity of Scripture pertains, however, not to its language but to its message. Again, it refers to Scripture as a whole, not to any particular passage that may indeed be obscure even to the scholar. One should also keep in mind that the Reformers understood the clarity of Scripture as correlative with faith.

Because of Scripture's perspicuity the task of interpretation is not a complex historical exercise but a simple narration or unfolding (Luther). We do not have to be masters of theology or biblical exegesis to perceive the glory of the gospel in Holy Scripture, but theological and biblical understanding are nevertheless helpful in discerning the historical and linguistic background of the text.

Scripture is clear when we submit to its authority and live in the light of its promises. The Reformers were in full agreement with the author of Proverbs: "My son, if you accept my words and store up my commands within you . . . then you will understand what is right and just and fair—every good path. For wisdom will enter your heart, and knowledge will be pleasant to your soul" (2:1, 9–10 NIV).

Second, the Reformers regarded the natural or literal meaning of the text as normative. The natural sense is the grammatical sense—that intended by the original author. This does not mean that we are to remain with the natural meaning, but we cannot ignore it or devalue it. It provides the needed control in our theological treatment of the text.

Again, Scripture must be interpreted in the light of Scripture *(Scriptura Scripturam interpretatur)*. The best commentary on Scripture is Scripture. This means that the context of any part of Scripture is the total Scripture. The local must be interpreted by the universal.

When the Reformers insisted on *sola Scriptura,* they meant that Scripture must be interpreted in its own light instead of by an extrabiblical criterion, such as the teaching authority of the church. Scripture can be understood only in terms of itself. Scripture itself is the source and norm of divine revelation. This is not only an affirmation of the Reformation but also of the church catholic. Athanasius declared, "The sacred and divinely inspired Scriptures" are of themselves "sufficient for the exposition of the truth."[51]

Moreover, the salvific content of Scripture is God's self-revelation in Jesus Christ. What makes Scripture authoritative is that it focuses on Christ. Luther referred to Christ as the "star and kernel" of Scripture, "the center part of the circle" about which everything else revolves. He once compared some biblical texts to hard nuts whose shells could be cracked only when they were thrown against the rock—Christ. Only then would they yield their "delicious kernel."[52] As a result Reformation orthodoxy made a distinction between the outer form of Scripture and its inner form—the gospel of divine justification. Later orthodoxy distinguished between the formal principle (the Scriptures as a book) and the material principle (the gospel).

A concomitant of the christological focus of the Reformers was their strong insistence that the Old Testament must be interpreted by the New. At the same time, they were quick to contend that Christ and the gospel are present in the Old Testament as well as in the New, though only those who have embraced New Testament faith could appreciate this fact. Calvin was especially emphatic on the presence of Christ in the Old Testament and the unity of the two Testaments.

The Reformers also held that the obscure parts of Scripture are to be interpreted by the clear parts. Here they followed Augustine: "Hardly anything may be found in . . . obscure places which is not found plainly said elsewhere."[53] John Knox's view is typical: "The Word of God is plain in itself. If there appear any obscurity in one place, the Holy Ghost," who is never contrary to himself, explains "the same more clearly in other places; so that there can remain no doubt, but unto such as obstinately will remain ignorant."[54]

Another important guideline of Reformation hermeneutics was the complementarity of Word and Spirit. The Spirit does not bring a new revelation but illumines the meaning of the text for our time, and in this way fulfills its original meaning. The Word and the Spirit are two teachers (Zwingli), and they do not contradict but complement one another.

An emphasis on the divine unity or harmony of Scripture was also characteristic of Reformation hermeneutics. While fully acknowledging both cultural and theological diversity within Scripture, the Reformers held to its overarching unity. One of their key principles was that "the whole Scripture presents Christ everywhere." Luther found this unity in the message of justification by faith. Calvin stressed the life of regeneration through the indwelling of the Holy Spirit. For Barth in the twentieth century the unifying principle is God's act of reconciliation in Jesus Christ. The Reformers were unanimous in affirming that the divine plan and purpose revealed in Scripture contained a coherent thread of meaning, though this could never be encapsulated in a purely human system of theology.

The Reformers indeed warned against resolving the mystery of faith into a rational system. "Let us remember here," said Calvin, "that on the whole subject of religion one rule is to be observed, and it is this—in obscure matters not to speak or think, or even long to know, more than the Word of God has delivered."[55] We can know God's will and purpose for our lives, but we cannot penetrate the abysmal nature of God, which is hidden from all sight and understanding.

While Protestant orthodoxy was beguiled in part by the Cartesian ideals of clarity and precision, those who remained true to the original Reformers were conscious that the unity of the Bible could never be encompassed in a rational system of meaning. As Forsyth perceived, "The unity of the Bible is organic, total, vital, evangelical; it is not merely harmonious, balanced, statuesque. It is not the form of symmetry but the spirit of reconciliation."[56]

Other rules of hermeneutics suggested in the Reformation but emphasized in Protestant orthodoxy were: the Gospels must be interpreted by the Epistles; the incidental must be interpreted by the systematic; and the symbolic must be interpreted by the didactic. The general consensus was that the systematic exposition of doctrine is best set forth in Paul's epistles to the Romans and Galatians.

One hermeneutical principle that sporadically impressed itself on the Reformers but was never fully developed was the freedom of the Word of God. Calvin recognized this dimension of God's Word when he declared that we are bound to the so-called means of grace but God is not bound. Luther grasped this aspect of God's revelation by conceiving of God's Word as always living and active. By its equation of God's Word with Holy Scripture later Protestant orthodoxy virtually lost sight of the freedom of God's Word. It was recovered in more recent times by Barth, who identified God's Word with the living Christ and who viewed the Holy Spirit as the one means of grace, as opposed to external channels of mediation.

Hermeneutical Options Today

The hermeneutics associated with scholastic orthodoxy is still a live option in many circles. This position, which may be called the rational-biblicistic view, conceives of authority in ahistorical and conceptual terms. The Bible is held to be a repository of universal truths that can be discovered and applied to daily living. Textual criticism, which endeavors to ascertain the authenticity of the text, is welcomed, but higher criticism, which treats the text as literature, is resisted, though not necessarily rejected. The Bible is said to constitute "a public, objective criterion with a fixed, single meaning for everyone."[57] The role of the Holy Spirit is to move the will to assent to what reason already discerns as objectively true.[58]

A formidable challenge to traditional hermeneutics is posed by the historical-critical view, which holds sway over much of the academic world of biblical studies in our day. In this approach the Bible is investigated as a product of the interplay of cultural and historical forces. The goal is to understand the text in the light of its place in history *(Sitz im Leben)*. The tools are sundry critical methods including literary criticism, form criticism, redaction criticism and source criticism, designed to uncover the historical and cultural matrix in which the text was written.[59]

The historical-critical method is inseparably related to the philosophy of historicism, which holds that "the historicity of a phenomenon affords the means of comprehending its essence and reality. Historical knowledge and critical reflection are the basic tools with which the philosopher or theologian grasps the object to be analyzed."[60] Adolf von Harnack considered the historical-critical method far superior to every other method of exegesis in finding the real meaning of the Bible.

Historicism is integrally tied to an ontology or worldview that rules out the reality of the supernatural. According to Ernst Troeltsch, "a whole world view lies behind the historico-critical method."[61] This method presupposes the essential identity of finite spirits with the infinite spirit as it unfolds in history.[62]

The idea that the meaning of the text can be decided only by historical research has been stoutly resisted, even in the older liberal theology. Wilhelm Herrmann warned against the "fatal error" of attempting to "establish the basis of faith by means of historical investigation. The basis of faith must be something fixed; the results of historical study are continually changing."[63]

Romanticist hermeneutics associated with Schleiermacher and Dilthey signified an attempt to find meaning in the text that superseded mere historical analysis.[64] The aim of hermeneutics is now the reconstruction of the mental processes of the author. The concern is not so much to uncover authorial intention as to discover authorial motivation. By entering sympathetically and imaginatively into the thought-world of the author of the text, we can establish psychological rapport with him. Historical understanding means "to relive *(nacherleben)* the past experience of others and so to make it one's own."[65] The hermeneutical bridge is that of shared experience *(Erlebnis)*. In romanticist hermeneutics the text is treated as "affectively disclosive or evocative" rather than "objectively true or false."[66]

Manifesting an affinity to the above position is existentialist hermeneutics, associated with Rudolf Bultmann, Gerhard Ebeling and Ernst Fuchs, among others.[67] In this approach one tries to find the creative insight or seminal experience of the authors of the text, the experience that was objectified in words. Historical research is helpful but merely as a preparatory step to uncover the existential meaning of the text, how the text impinges on personal life in the here and now. It is not psychological affinity with the original author, however, but participation in the reality of unconditional love that is the key to hermeneutical understanding. The Word is to be celebrated as formative power rather than informational statement. Jesus is a witness to faith rather than the object of faith. The result of an existential encounter with the text is a true understanding of the self. History is dissolved into the historicity of personal existence.

In contrast to all psychological and existentialist interpretations,

Wolfhart Pannenberg argues for a universal-historical view in which one endeavors to penetrate behind the text to the underlying event that inspired it.[68] The aim is to ascertain the historical and ontological significance of the event, and this involves relating it to the world of meaning in which we live and move. Since history is not yet complete, our interpretations can only be approximate. It is not the text as such but its essential content *(Sache)* that occupies our attention, and this means that historical investigation is preliminary to theological and philosophical analysis. Pannenberg holds that God is working in a special manner in every tribe, nation and culture, but people fail to grasp the significance of these appearances of the Infinite in their own religious traditions because they do not press beyond their limited perspectives to a perspective of the whole—the universal horizon that is the goal or fulfillment of history, anticipated but not fully realized in Jesus Christ.[69]

Resonating more closely with Reformation theology is the salvation-historical approach of Oscar Cullmann[70] and Gerhard von Rad, which seeks to interpret every biblical text in the light of its role in the sacred history mirrored in the Bible. The focus is not on universal truths but on God's mighty acts in the history of biblical Israel culminating in Jesus Christ. The Old Testament is valued because the events it attests are regarded as prefigurations of the Christ event. Israel "saw herself snatched up into a divine history in which she was continually led by God's Word from promise to fulfillment."[71] Salvation history continues after Christ through the outpouring of the Holy Spirit on all flesh, but its criterion is the revelation of God in Jesus Christ, which is definitive and complete.

In the process-metaphysical view associated with John Cobb, Lewis Ford, Bernard Meland, David Ray Griffin, Schubert Ogden, Norman Pittenger, Henry Nelson Wieman and David Pailin among others, the Bible is treated as a testimony to the "creative advance" of divine reality in world history.[72] Because the Bible employs for the most part pictorial or mythopoetic language, it must be fulfilled in a modern ontology if it is to relate intelligibly to the contemporary scene. Ancient poetry needs to be translated into a new conceptuality. Such pivotal thinkers as Alfred North Whitehead and Charles Hartshorne best provide this conceptual framework, since they are attuned to the scientific and cultural revolution of our times. Other respected philosophers whose insights have helped to shape the process understanding of reality include Henri Bergson, Samuel Alexander and Teilhard de Chardin. The task of the interpreter is to discern abiding values or transcendental ideals that lure the human spirit onward to new possibilities. Scripture together with other religious classics helps one to describe the unfolding action of God in the world. Hermeneutics is basically the translation of the meaning of original religious experiences into categories that can be scientifically validated and confirmed.[73]

Crosscultural hermeneutics advocates the transculturation and contextualization of God's Word.[74] This approach holds that words do not bear their meaning independent of the contexts in which they originate and to which they are applied. The hermeneutic process is conceived as a dynamic interaction between the interpreter deeply enmeshed in his or her own culture and the culture and worldview represented in the Bible. The raw material of theology is not abstract, timeless concepts but a message embedded in historical events and carrying the imprint of a particular cultural ethos.

Sociocritical hermeneutics reflects the concerns of liberationist and feminist theologies that view the biblical texts as sources of domination and violence as well as liberation.[75] One must therefore approach the text with a hermeneutics of suspicion, acutely conscious of the ideological biases that clouded the vision of the biblical writers. One must be equally aware of the role of ideology in present-day interpretation. Since no one is free from ideology, we are advised to be alert to the ideological commitments we ourselves bring to the text and trust that these commitments resonate with the biblical preferential option for the poor. Liberationist and feminist hermeneutics seek to read the Bible from the underside of history, from the vantage point of the oppressed and forsaken rather than that of the privileged. With existentialists, liberation theologians acknowledge that everyone comes to the text with a preunderstanding but urge us to choose one that is shaped by *praxis,* involvement in the cause of social and political liberation.

We are witnessing today the emergence of many other hermeneutical options. Canonical analysis associated with Brevard Childs sees the final form of the text as the only normative basis for a biblical theology.[76] The new literary approach underscores the power of the human imagination in bridging the hermeneutical distance between the text and the modern interpreter. Narrative hermeneutics, which grows out of this literary approach, recommends that we interiorize the biblical narrative if it is to shape our lives today.[77] Structuralism focuses attention on the symmetry and harmonies of the form of the text rather than on its message. It prefers to investigate the text as myth rather than narrative: its aim is "to uncover the 'deep structures' operating in the unconsciousness of the myth."[78] Reader-responsive hermeneutics finds the meaning of the text in how the reader is affected more than in what motivated the original author.[79]

In convergence with some hermeneutical theories and in divergence from others, I propose a historical-pneumatic hermeneutics in which Word and Spirit are joined together in dynamic unity. This approach presupposes that the Word of God is historical, that the Word has a history. Because God has acted decisively in the particular history of biblical Israel culminating in Jesus Christ, the Bible becomes normative as the primary witness and record of God's mighty acts. Historical investigation is necessary to delineate the historical and cultural context of the prophetic and apostolic witness, but only illumination by the Holy Spirit can bring us the revelational meaning of what has transpired in history. Historical reconstruction should be the first word, but it cannot be the last word. The focus of the Bible is not on historical events as such but on God's redeeming action in particular events. The scriptural exegete imparts not simply historical information but "spiritual truths to those who possess the Spirit" (1 Cor 2:13).

This hermeneutics is not original, for it was already embraced by

Luther and Calvin, as well as by Barth and Brunner in the twentieth century. It diverges significantly, however, from the early Barth, who envisaged God in nonhistorical terms. For Barth in his earlier phase there is no history of salvation but only an eternal moment of salvation. The drama of redemption takes place not in history but in superhistory (*Übergeschichte*), though he later abandoned this way of speaking. At the same time, he remained adamant that the events of sacred history are inaccessible to historical investigation. The source of their certainty is not historical evidence, which is not exempt from ambiguity, but the interior working of the Spirit in the awakening to faith. In my view, a salvation event, such as the resurrection of Jesus Christ, is open to historical inquiry, though the hand of God in this event is hidden from natural reason. Historical method can show that at least some of the biblical miracles are based on credible reports, but only faith can discern the intervention of God in these events.

With Barth I affirm the limitations of exegetical methods. Jesus Christ can never be mastered by hermeneutical skills; he alone determines who will know him. I also agree with Barth that the object, or subject matter, of the text controls its meaning and ultimately our understanding of it. The text is sovereign in its interpretation, because the text constitutes not only letter but spirit as well. Barth opposed the imposition of a general hermeneutics on the Bible, for this tends to decide in advance the outcome of the hermeneutical quest.[80]

Against existentialism and the new hermeneutics, I hold that the subject-object polarity is not transcended in hermeneutical understanding but instead accentuated. God is not an object alongside other objects, but he is objective to our understanding in that he exists as an absolute subject. The experience of God takes the form of being confronted by the supreme being rather than being united with the power of being (as in Tillich). God cannot be reached by our attempts to objectify him, but he can objectify himself—that is, he makes himself an object for our understanding so that we can really know and believe.

Modern hermeneutics ever since Schleiermacher speaks of a hermeneutical circle—a description of the dynamics between the text and the interpreter. We come to the text with a prior understanding, and the new light we receive drives us back to our questioning and searching. For Gadamer, one of the philosophers of the new hermeneutics, "the true hermeneutic circle is that we stand already in Being, already belong to Being, and the hermeneutic task is to reestablish contact with that to which we already belong."[81]

Instead of a hermeneutical circle I prefer to speak of a hermeneutical magnet that draws us by grace into the work of the Spirit on the text. We become covenant partners with the Spirit in his work of interpretation. Before we are grasped by the Spirit of God, we exist in a state of alienation from God. The only prior understanding we have of God is a misunderstanding occasioned by the all-pervasive malady of human sin, which distorts our reasoning and imagination as well as binding our will. The God we know through our own power is a construct of our imagination and therefore an idol, not the living God of biblical faith. The Word of God confronts us as our adversary before he makes himself our Lord and Master.

Drawing on Gadamer, contemporary hermeneutics speaks of overcoming the distance between text and interpreter by the fusion of the two horizons. I prefer to speak of the overturning of the interpreter's horizon in the encounter with divine grace and the dawning within the interpreter of a wholly new horizon.[82] I concur fully with Barth: "This Word of God can only confront and illuminate man as truth and reality if it is seen to run counter to his whole natural capacity to understand."[83]

We come to the truth of the Word of God not primarily by a historical analysis of the biblical text (as in historical-critical theory) nor by a divinatory intuition that allows us entrance into the author's life experience (as in Schleiermacher) but by a revelational illumination that enables us to hear God's Word in the text directing us to the cross of Christ. I agree with the Puritan theologian William Lyford that the truth contained in Scripture is a shining light discernible only by "the sons of light." It persuades us by the force of its own light, by the clarity of its own wisdom. The Spirit brings the light of Scripture to bear on both our feelings and our reasoning and produces in us "the certainty of experience."[84]

Faith and Criticism

Faith lies beyond criticism, but it does not deny the relative validity of the historical-critical approach to the Scriptures. Faith is enriched by a knowledge of the linguistic, literary and historical sources of a particular biblical text, but faith is directed not to the text but to the living Christ to whom the text points. What faith denies is historicism or historical positivism—the view of history that rules out supernatural or transcendental causation. Drawing its model from the natural sciences, historicism has become firmly embedded in biblical studies through the influence of Troeltsch, Harnack, Bultmann, Willi Marxsen and others. This mentality is evident in Old Testament scholar Sibley Towner, who says that we must assume that the "prophecies" in Daniel are after the fact "because human beings are unable accurately to predict future events," that is, if we are not "to fly in the face of the certainties of human nature."[85]

Despite its pervasive influence in mainline seminaries and schools of religion, the historical-critical method has lately come under serious criticism. Thomas F. Torrance expresses these reservations:

> Since I cannot share the obsolete phenomenalist and positivist assumptions upon which much contemporary exegesis depends, I have great difficulty in acknowledging many of its claims for "assured results." This is not to say that I disdain in any way careful handling of the biblical texts—far from it—but that my critical mind will not allow me to accept results that are predetermined by uncritical epistemological assumptions.[86]

Biblical scholar Walter Wink is convinced that historical criticism is not neutral and objective but a handmaiden of a particular philosophical-theological perspective.[87] The attempt at objectivity produces a heavy-handed rationalism that ignores the nonrational, imaginative aspects of life. "By standing over the Bible like a coroner over a corpse, historical critics are unable to stand under the Bible and hence are unable to understand it."[88]

Peter Stuhlmacher seeks to balance Troeltsch's emphasis on the cultural relativity and conditionedness of the biblical texts by a hermeneutics of acceptance, which involves a basic submission to the claims of the biblical texts.[89] In this approach the interpreter "consents" to leave himself or herself open to the possibility of "transcendence."[90] In conscious opposition to the confessionalist Lutheran Gerhard Maier,[91] Stuhlmacher rejects any idea of returning to a *hermeneutica sacra,* which elevates the text above history.

I agree with Barth that historical criticism may throw light on the cultural and historical background of the text, but it cannot give us a theological grasp of the contents of the text. "Historical criticism," he said, "has led to a better understanding of the Scriptures than was possible in the past, for those situations which show the historical and secular aspects of the Bible have also something to teach us."[92] In the course of time, however, "historical criticism has assumed exaggerated importance, so that there is a tendency to identify the real meaning of Scripture with its historical significance."[93]

We must resist the temptation to deny the positive results of historical criticism and retreat into a precritical mode of thinking that would further isolate the church from modern scholarship.[94] Faith itself gives rise to criticism, for faith is discriminating. It distinguishes between the kernel and the husk, what is central and what is peripheral in the Bible. The truth of the Word of God is not self-evident even in the Bible, and it must be dug out through diligent searching that is at the same time faithful and critical. According to Hans Küng, "uncritical belief" misses the point "as much as unbelieving criticism. True faith strengthens rather than hampers criticism. True criticism fructifies rather than destroys faith."[95] Dietrich Bonhoeffer came to a similar conclusion: "We must enter the straits of historical criticism. Its importance is not absolute, but at the same time it is not a matter of indifference. In fact it never leads to a weakening of faith but rather to its strengthening, as concealment in historicity is part of Christ's humiliation."[96]

I favor a theological stance that employs critical methods but moves beyond them. Faith goes through criticism, for its object is beyond criticism. Historical criticism pertains only to the form, not the divine content *(Sache)*, of the Bible. Criticism cannot touch the Word of God itself, but it can have a place in understanding the historical and cultural matrix in which the text comes to us. I do not go along with Bultmann's contention that historical research is a "way to grasp the truth of the Christian faith."[97] Nor do I agree with Pannenberg that historical investigation is necessary to establish faith. Since the historicity of the resurrection forms the foundation for faith, he is willing to risk faith itself on the results of historical research. Evangelical rationalists like John Warwick Montgomery also evince confidence in the capacity of historical research to validate the claims of faith. My position is closer to that of J. C. K. von Hofmann, the nineteenth-century German evangelical theologian: "The essential knowledge of any matter is not attained by the historical method. We must ask whether the result of the historical investigation is consistent with what is attained on systematic grounds."[98]

While the Word of God qualitatively transcends the reach of critical historiography, this Word can be apprehended only in the particular history into which it descends. The Word assumes historical garb, but it is hidden in this garb and is known only when it makes itself known to the believing heart. We can unearth much that is of undoubted historical and theological value through our critical investigations, but the truth that is a matter of life and death remains outside our grasp.

With Forsyth I advocate a criticism of grace in which the critics allow themselves to be judged by the message of grace—the overriding theme of Holy Scripture. We do not leave the form of the Bible behind in an effort to discern its spiritual content that is supposedly elevated above history, but we seek to find the content in the form itself. "The Word is not in the Bible," said Forsyth, "as a treasure hid in a field so that you can dig out the jewel and leave the soil. It grows from it like a sweet savour. It streams up from it like an exhalation. It rises like the soul going to glory from its sacred dust. The Word of God is not to be dissected from the Bible, but to be distilled."[99] Accordingly "the true interpreter of the Bible is neither the higher criticism nor an authoritative Church but the evangelical experience of an awakened heart."[100]

As people of faith we can know and hear the transcendent Word of God, the very truth of revelation, but we cannot comprehend it. It must be given to us again and again as we repent and believe. We can reflect this truth in our words and actions. We can make true statements of the mystery of the concrete absolute—God in human flesh—but our statements are true only in a derivative sense. They do not constitute the truth itself; they point to and convey this truth. As A. W. Tozer cogently observed, "The mind can grasp the shell but only the Spirit of God can lay hold of the internal essence."[101]

Christ himself is the final interpreter of Scripture. We engage in the task of interpretation as his representatives and ambassadors. We seek to expound his message, not our own. He tells us through his Spirit what Scripture says. We must not prejudge the meaning of Scripture, for our role is to be listeners and servants. The Anglican bishop Christopher Chavasse brilliantly delineated the centrality of Christ in Scripture:

> The Bible . . . is the portrait of our Lord Jesus Christ. The Gospels are the Figure itself in the portrait. The Old Testament is the background, leading up to the divine Figure, pointing toward it, and absolutely necessary for the composition as a whole. The Epistles serve as the dress and accoutrements of the Figure, explaining and describing it. And then, while by our Bible reading we study the portrait as a great whole, the miracle happens! The Figure comes to life! And, stepping from the canvas of the written word, the everlasting Christ of the Emmaus Story becomes Himself our Bible teacher to interpret to us in all the Scriptures the things concerning Himself.[102]

A historical-pneumatic hermeneutics will certainly see the text in its historical setting but will go on to discern the subtle relationship of the text to the center of the sacred history mirrored in the Scriptures—the cross of Jesus Christ.[103] As Luther declared, "The Scripture may permit itself to be stretched and led, and let no one lead it according to his own inclinations but let him lead it to the source, that is, the cross of Christ. Then he will surely strike the center."[104]

It is necessary to distinguish between the objective or historical truth that the Bible gives concerning God and humanity and the revelatory truth that the Spirit gives through the Bible concerning God's act of salvation in Jesus Christ. The objective truth remains merely historical until it is illumined by the Spirit so that the eyes of faith may perceive its christological significance and its existential import. The biblical word saves only insofar as it proclaims Christ, but this is a possibility that rests not on the power of human insight but on a free act of God's grace.

A historical-pneumatic hermeneutics that builds on historical criticism will never be content to understand a text in isolation but will try to see how it is related to the whole of Scripture. Biblical exposition involves not simply the unfolding of the matter of the text in its immediate context but the perception of the text in relation to other texts that may be only tangentially related to the text in question. Bonhoeffer put it well:

> At times we are involved in the problematic situation of having to preach about a saying which we know from philological and historical criticism never to have been spoken in its present form by Jesus. In the exegesis of Scripture we find ourselves on very uncertain ground. So we may never stick at one point, but must move over the whole of the Bible, from one place to another, just as a man can only cross a river covered in ice floes if he does not remain standing on one particular floe but jumps from one to another.[105]

I do not share the vision of much traditional orthodoxy that the Bible is impregnated with universal, unchanging truths that are waiting to be discovered and formulated.[106] Instead I hold that the Bible is filled with the Spirit of God, who brings new light to bear on ancient wisdom—light that leads us not only to renewed understanding but also to obedience. The Scripture does teach truths, but these are always fresh truths applied to the situation in which we live and work.[107] These truths do not contradict the ancient wisdom contained in the Scriptures but amplify and illumine it.

Theological reasoning is not circular so much as spiral. We begin with the Word of God, with its paradoxical affirmations, and then move toward a satisfying resolution as we are led by the Spirit. We do not simply return to our starting point, but we are led through our starting point to an omega point that is still in the future. Theological reasoning is dialectical in that it moves through thesis and antithesis toward a synthesis that is realized only in eternity. But at the same time, it is controlled by its original starting point, which determines the parameters of its reflection.

The truth that constitutes the foundation of Christian faith is not something we possess but something to which the Spirit guides us (cf. Jn 16:13). It is not something we fall back on but something we enter into. The truth of faith is not an axiom of reason but a new reality that remolds our reasoning processes. It is not a metaphysical presupposition designed to lead us to a comprehension of the whole of reality but a perpetual revolution that shakes us loose from all presuppositions so that we trust only in the living God.[108] It is not a general principle at our disposal but a concrete word of address—the voice of the living Christ audible only to the ears of faith but relayed to us always in conjunction with the proclamation of the biblical prophets and apostles, reaffirmed by our fathers and mothers in the faith of the church through the ages.

Appendix D: Narrative Theology

The hermeneutical scene has undergone a major change with the rise of narrative theology, which focuses attention not on the historical background of the text nor on the disposition or intention of its author but on its literary form. The text is treated as a work of art, and its significance is located in its literary qualities.

Narrative theology is by no means a monolithic movement: it includes moderate conservatives such as Hans Frei, George Lindbeck, David Kelsey, Ronald Thiemann and Garrett Green as well as symbolists such as Paul Ricoeur, John D. Crossan, David Tracy and Terrence W. Tilley, and even neo-evangelicals like Clark Pinnock, Mark Ellingsen and Gabriel Fackre.[109] What all these scholars have in common is a break with the historical-critical approach in biblical studies by concentrating on the Bible as a literary document.[110] It is not the linguistic roots of the text nor its historical setting but the story that it embodies that provides the key to its understanding. This story is said to be historylike, but it does not necessarily correspond to real history. Green holds that some parts of the Bible are fact and other parts fiction.[111] But the truth of the text does not depend on its historicity or nonhistoricity. Its truth lies in its capacity to draw us into a new framework of meaning so that we can finally make sense of our individual lives.

Narrative theologians insist that the stories recorded in Scripture are true, but for the most part they are thinking not of metaphysical or even historical truth but of practical truth—the capacity to generate commitment and community. Here one can discern the influence of Kant's claim that practical reason rather than theoretical reason places us in contact with reality. Narrative theologians speak of *construing* reality by means of the text. The text imposes on the world a vision that may or may not correspond to the world as it really is. It is a vision that does not unravel the secrets of the universe but one that creates a "followable world," a world of meaning that can see us through our deepest difficulties.

Theologians should expend their efforts not in articulating a worldview in competition with other worldviews but in assimilating the insights of an enduring religious tradition by entering into the narrative history of this tradition. According to Hans Frei the primary task of theology is "Christian self-description," not correlation with universal "human, cultural quests for ultimate meaning."[112] The focus is not on ontological truth but on intrasystematic truth, which is measured by its adequacy in clarifying the language of religious tradition (Lindbeck).[113]

Kelsey affirms the form-function polarity over the form-content distinction of neo-orthodoxy.[114] The text is appreciated for its ability to draw us empathetically into the story rather than for its supposed ability to throw light on ultimate questions. It is the *patterns* of Scripture that make it normative for the community of faith rather than its theoretical content. "To say that biblical texts taken as scripture are 'authority' for church and theology is to say that they provide patterns determinate enough to *function* as the basis for assessment of the Christian aptness of current churchly forms of life and speech and of theologians' proposals for reform of that life and speech."[115]

In narrative theology what the text yields is not definitive information about the being of God or even the plan of God for the universe but a sporadic illumination of the human condition. For Ricoeur the biblical stories "purport to tell us about the outer borders and central heartlands—the ultimate limits and daily rhythms—of specifically human existence."[116] Those on the evangelical side would contend that the text also brings us critical information on God's acts in history, though the emphasis is on the transformative power of God in human life rather than on the nature of God's being.[117]

The new literary approach to the Bible underscores the power of the human imagination. According to Robert Tannehill, "the power of the Christ-event for the expansion of human being is released only as we return to the imaginative language which most richly embodies that event and acknowledge it for what it is by responding imaginatively."[118] For Green the religious imagination is the anthropological point of contact with divine revelation, which is understood as "God's impression on the mind through paradigms that allow us to imagine God rightly."[119]

A strain of relativism runs through most narrative theology. The question is commonly raised: Although the stories of the Bible are true for us who stand in this same faith history, can we reasonably assert that they are true for other peoples in other cultures and religions? Jerry H. Stone sees promise in Van A. Harvey's proposal for a "soft perspectivism" that "entails an ultimate commitment to one's own story, yet the imaginative openness to appreciate another's perspective—a kind of 'self-transcendence' that allows for both conviction and tolerance. From this 'soft perspective,' narrative theology can study appreciatively the narratives from other cultures and religions."[120]

Narrative theologians often convey the impression that Christian language refers to the speech and "forms of life" of the Christian community, not to historical or ontological claims. They sometimes recognize a layer of historical reality behind the story but hold that the story as a literary form conveys truth and meaning apart from its historical sources.

All narrative theologians are distrustful of discursive thought, preferring aesthetic sensitivity. They prize imagination over abstract or theoretical reason. Kant's contention that aesthetic judgments depend neither on concepts nor on empirical facts finds an echo in these circles. Ellingsen writes, "As long as a biblical account is analyzed as a kind of aesthetic object, one may just as easily identify with it, be transformed by its meaning, as one would with any piece of contemporary literature."[121]

It is interesting to compare narrative theology with other hermeneutical options today. For the narrative theologian the text is a *mosaic* that redesigns reality. Moreover, reality is a canvas on which the text imprints or impresses a picture. In classical orthodoxy (and in the later Barth) the biblical text is the *mirror* or *echo* of God's truth. In fundamentalism the Bible is itself the *light* of God's truth. In neo–orthodoxy the text is a *witness* to God's acts in history. In structuralism (which feeds into narrative theology) the text is a *vortex* of meaning that shapes a new reality.[122] In deconstructionism the text is an interminable *maze*, defying any universal or substantial meaning.[123] In existentialist theology the text is a *mirror* of human existence.[124] In Augustine and Christian mysticism the text is a *window* that leads to a higher, spiritual world.

While closer to Barth and classical orthodoxy, I prefer to think of the text as a *prism* through which the light of God shines on us. It is not itself the light, but it relays the light to us. For narrative theologians the meaning of the text is located nowhere but in the narrative sequence itself. I would say that the meaning of the text is located in the mind of the divine author of Scripture, and not until this author speaks can we know the full implications of the text before us.

Some narrative theologians interpret the text as a *lens* that enables the reader or hearer to view the world in a new way. Green appeals to Calvin, who also referred to the Scriptures as spectacles by which we look on the world.[125] But when Calvin spoke in this manner, he meant the whole Scripture, not any isolated passage; moreover, he believed that Scripture presents the world as it really is. For the narrative theologian the text conjures up a vision of the world that does not necessarily comport with objective or historical reality. It creates a picture of a followable world, one that gives meaning to human existence. For Calvin Scripture presents a true picture because it is illumined by the Spirit, who shines on it and on the reader. Scripture does not simply open up a new world for us, but it "clearly shows us the true God."[126] Calvin insisted that Scripture is not only a *lens* but also a *source* of our knowledge of both God the Creator and God the Redeemer. It is not merely a lens, because it presents new knowledge not given in nature.

I do not deny that narrative theology has much to offer the modern church. It reminds us that a large part of Scripture comes to us in narrative forms. It invites us to consider that although some of the stories in Scripture may lack a solid foundation in history, they are nevertheless historylike and introduce us to a world of meaning that transcends history as such. It also is sound in its allegation that the primary purpose of the biblical writers was not to bring us metaphysical knowledge but to describe the sojourn of a people through the valley of the shadow of death, a sojourn that we can identify with through an act of empathy and commitment.

In criticism of narrative theology, I contend that faith as delineated in Scripture is more than a way of imagining. It is an act of believing, and it is believing not in an image or story but in a person—the living Savior Jesus Christ. The aim of the text is surely not the expansion of religious imagination but the regeneration of the human will.

The biblical writer does not simply share his story of the way he experiences life but proclaims the truth of divine revelation—the way in which God confronts humanity. By converting the content of faith into a story, we downplay the truth of this story. We avoid coming to terms with the claims of the prophetic witnesses. The proclamation of the church consists of more than telling a story. It involves proclaiming the divine commandment as well as celebrating the divine promise. This commandment and promise come to us in story form in parts of the Bible, but in other parts (e.g., the Pauline epistles) they are transmitted didactically.

In narrative theology the Bible is no longer a record of the mighty deeds of God but a collection of stories that throw light on the universal human predicament. It is said that the whole Bible constitutes a meta-story that gives unity to the various stories. From my perspective, to reduce the gospel to a story or a number of stories devalues the apostolic interpretation of the realities described in the stories. The gospel is not simply a drama played out in history but the speech of God interpreting this drama to the community of faith.

The biblical narrative is best understood as the Word of God *in potentia*, not *in perfectione*. Our concern is not merely with a story but with the reality of what happened in certain crucial events in the past. We proclaim not simply the story of the cross but the significance of the cross for our time and for all times. This proclamation involves us in doctrinal as well as metaphysical judgments.

Stephen Crites aptly expresses the sentiments of most narrative theologians: "The Gospel is a narrative, and from the language of narrative one cannot legitimately derive universally inclusive statements about actuality. . . . A Christian metaphysics is in a class with such current absurdities as Christian geology or Christian economics."[127] Although I acknowledge that the biblical message is not a discourse on metaphysics and the biblical God is not a metaphysical construct, it does not follow that this message is without metaphysical implications, that it carries no metaphysical import. The worldview that arises from biblical history is not itself the gospel, but it may be the result of faithful reflection on the gospel. To empty the Christian faith of its metaphysical content is to reduce faith to a figment of human imagination and to render revelation a transforming ethos rather than the self-communication of a living God who acts and speaks. To interpret the Bible primarily as a testimony to the "community's capacity to sustain the prophetic activity of remembering and reinterpreting the traditions of Yahweh" (Stanley Hauerwas)[128] is to treat lightly the central biblical claim that God has actually spoken in human history and has become incarnate in a particular man who lived and died in that history.

It is not the lived experience of community that constitutes the content of biblical revelation but the divine plan and purpose for humanity and for the whole universe. This divine self-disclosure is conveyed through narrative forms but also through affirmations and propositions. It is not simply what the apostles report as having happened in history but their reflection on these happenings that provides the criterion for faith and practice in our time and in all times. The Bible is not primarily an interpretive grid or screen by means of which many dimensions of human experience of God are given shape (Sallie McFague). It is God's own interpretation of his amazing deeds in human history, an interpretation that overturns human expectation and provides a sure foundation for human reflection and obedience.

Narrative theology rightly challenges the church to consider whether the Bible is a record of real history or whether it constitutes an imaginative reconstruction of history. Kevin Vanhoozer acknowledges that Frei

> is correct in observing that the Gospels may not be histories in the modern sense of the term. To force the Gospels to meet the requirements of modern historiography would be to impose a foreign criterion of intelligibility and truth. But, against Frei, it should be noted

that he too imposes a foreign interpretive framework on the Gospels—the category "realistic narrative" finds its proper home in fiction of the nineteenth century. The conventions governing the composition of realistic novels simply were not open to the biblical writers.[129]

It is commonplace for narrative theologians of whatever stripe to appeal for support to Barth, whose theology reflects in several areas the concerns of this movement. Barth could sometimes describe the Bible as a compendium of narrative, but he insisted that this narrative is anchored in ontological reality that breaks into human discourse, transforming our view of life and the world. In contrast to Ricoeur, for example, Barth contended that "the world of the text is not an ensemble of imaginative variations on a *possible* reality; it projects, rather, the one and only *actual* reality of the living Christ who makes possible our obedience to the biblical witness."[130] Whereas Ricoeur understands the biblical revelation as "a multiplicity of discourses and references," Barth found in the Bible a "preestablished christocentric harmony."[131] In contradistinction to the postliberal approach of the Yale school, Barth "goes beyond interpreting Scripture intratextually." As an ontological realist, he was adamant that church language "is adequate to a revealed reality that does more than witness to a particular intrasystematic viewpoint."[132]

Narrative theology will most certainly alter the method and content of preaching in the service of worship. Ellingsen champions a literary storytelling approach that presumably will resonate with the modern cultural ethos, with its penchant for the intuitive over the cerebral, the visionary over the theoretical.[133] Yet here I must caution that we are not in the entertainment business and insist again that the content of the evangelical proclamation is not simply a story but the apostolic interpretation of this story or stories. Preaching employs not only the imagination but also discursive reason in making known the significance of God's reconciling work in Jesus Christ. We do not simply tell stories but present truth claims. We do not simply interact with the stories of our people but challenge these stories as ways of hiding from God and deceiving ourselves. No technique or method in our preaching can create a point of contact between the gospel and the imaginations of our listeners. We must wait for the Holy Spirit to act and speak through our often feeble exposition of the biblical text, knowing that what we are proclaiming lies beyond the compass of human reason and imagination. Preaching is not simply the dynamic recital of biblical stories but bringing the very mind of Christ to bear on human sin and perfidy in the present age. The stories are to be placed in the service of the gospel, but they do not exhaust the meaning of the gospel. They may not even make contact with the reality of the gospel—especially if they remain on the level of story.

Particularly helpful in this discussion is the succinct but telling critique of Carl Braaten aimed at the new Yale school of theology, which stands closer to orthodoxy than many of those who make "story" central in their theological exposition.[134] Like Lindbeck, Frei, Thiemann and others of the Yale school, Braaten speaks out of a confessional tradition and is firmly committed to maintaining the integrity of the message of faith. On the one hand, he acknowledges the strength of narrative theology: it prods the church to remain true "to the task of transmitting the texts and traditions on which all Christian faith depends for its own identity and future."[135] On the other hand, it too easily surrenders "the enterprise of fundamental theology, uncovering universal principles and structures" in order to "secure a license to operate as one voice alongside others in a pluralistic setting."[136] Its overall tendency is "to exchange truth for fidelity," thereby undermining concerns to explore the metaphysical dimensions of faith. Braaten maintains with some cogency:

It is difficult to sustain the truth-claim of the gospel and the universal mission of the church on the basis of this program for theology. Fideism is linked to relativism as theology modestly restricts itself to its own data base and leaves all other disciplines to their own devices.[137]

Some scholars argue that the Yale school and Lindbeck in particular are solidly anchored in the mainstream of church tradition. A case can be made that far from being relativists, these theologians stoutly affirm the truth of Christian faith, though they do not believe that Christian truth claims can be justified outside the framework of Christian language and commitment. Bruce Marshall presents a fairly plausible argument that Lindbeck is not far from Thomas Aquinas in his methodological conclusions.[138]

I agree that we must be a part of the believing community to understand and appreciate the message of faith, but the practical effect of Lindbeck's position and of the Yale school of theology in general is to discourage apologetic confrontation with opposing faith claims. Theology is essentially descriptive for Lindbeck—in the sense of setting forth the rules that govern Christian discourse—rather than constructive (as in Kaufman and Ogden)—in the sense of trying to build bridges to the world. Lindbeck recommends reaching the outsider by catechesis—instructing people in the language and practices of the faith.[139] But is it not the Spirit who reaches the outsider, and does he not primarily employ the proclamation of the Word, which will invariably contravene the faith systems of the world and thereby call for a decision of faith against the claims of unbelief?

In contrast to both Pannenberg and Braaten, who seek a public justification for the claims of faith, and narrative theologians, who seek to introduce people to a lived community of shared discourse, I propose an evangelical confrontation with unbelief that destroys arguments and brings every thought captive to Jesus Christ (2 Cor 10:5). Our reliance is not on human powers of persuasion but on the power of the gospel itself to convict and persuade. Against an apologetic accommodationist theology on the one hand and a descriptive intratextual theology on the other, I affirm a kerygmatic confessional theology, which sallies forth to battle unbelief—not on the basis of a common criterion with unbelief but on the basis of the new criterion of the wisdom of the gospel, which displaces all other norms and standards. Evangelism is more than telling the story of Christ's salvation: it involves unmasking the powers that hold people in servile bondage. This is a believing apologetic (G. C. Berkouwer), which is not a prelude to the gospel proclamation but an integral part of this proclamation. We need not wait for the formation of pioneering communities of faith and hope that will preserve the language of faith in a de-Christianized society (as Lindbeck advocates), for through the Spirit we already have access to God's revealed Word, who can fill our language with new meaning and power and open up the possibility of reversing the secularization of society.

The Yale school and the mainstream of narrative theology constitute a wholesome corrective to those theologies that have unwittingly aligned the faith with some secular philosophy, whether this be realism or idealism, in order to shore up the credibility of the gospel. At the same time, many narrative theologians who have a basic biblical commitment injudiciously seek secular allies in neopragmatists like Richard Bernstein and Richard Rorty, and these alliances too can result in a dilution of the message of faith.[140]

Appendix E: Hermeneutical Pluralism and Transcendence

A major issue in current theology and biblical studies is whether historical and cultural conditioning as this impinges on both text and reader renders a transcendent perspective impossible. Richard Rorty and Stanley Fish argue that a transcultural hermeneutics is a chimera because "all criteria remain relative to what is perceived to *count* as criteria within a given social community."[141] In his significant and engaging work *New Horizons in Hermeneutics* Anthony Thiselton seeks to counter what he calls a "contextual-relative socio-*pragmatic* hermeneutics" associated with "radical reader-response theory, pragmatic forms of narrative theology, and post-modern elements of literary theory."[142] He contrasts this approach with "*metacritical* and *socio-critical* hermeneutics," which tries to find some transcontextual basis for evaluating hermeneutic positions. In exploring the possibility of rising above cultural context and bias, Thiselton is attracted by Gadamer's hermeneutical model, which approaches "questions of knowledge . . . from within horizons already bounded by our finite situatedness within the flow of history." In this view "these finite and historically conditioned horizons" can be enlarged and expanded and "thus come to constitute *new* horizons."[143]

In delineating his own position Thiselton draws on both Pannenberg and Jürgen Moltmann in seeing the cross and resurrection of Christ as providing the pathway to an eschatological transcendence—one that will be realized in the future. He thus ostensibly avoids an authoritarian dogmatism that claims a premature possession of truth and an attenuated relativism that sees truth as functional rather than ontological.

While acknowledging an inevitable plurality of perspectives in scriptural interpretation, he affirms the possibility of being opened to a universal horizon that is now in the process of being realized. The cross and resurrection of Christ provide the key to a deeper understanding of divine providence and human existence, but the church can only arrive at "fallible judgments," which in turn have to be corrected as horizons expand and move toward the future.[144]

Thiselton acknowledges his indebtedness to Jürgen Habermas, Gadamer and Wittgenstein as well as to theologians of hope like Moltmann and Pannenberg, narrative theologians like Thiemann and philosophers of language like Nicholas Wolterstorff. He seeks to distance himself from existentialists like Bultmann and pragmatists like Rorty. He takes issue with all claims to ultimate meaning that disregard historical and cultural conditioning. He warns against imposing some universal model of reading interpretation, but at the same time is adamant that we must hold on to the biblical claim that there is a "universal horizon of eschatological promise"[145] that can guide us toward deeper understanding—both of God and of ourselves.

Thiselton has much to say that can be appreciated by evangelical theologians, and his *New Horizons* is in some sense a groundbreaking book, pointing beyond the impasse of theological dogmatism and historical and cultural relativism. He demonstrates a superb mastery of the current hermeneutical discussion as well as manifesting an earnest attempt to respect and honor the biblical text. I nevertheless am compelled to raise some questions that reveal a certain divergence in our views.

Thiselton rightly points to the cross as a transcultural norm, but is this "the experience of the cross" (as Moltmann claims)[146] or the divine interpretation of the cross given in Scripture and received in the experience of faith? Thiselton endorses Moltmann's depiction of the cross as "a socio-critical principle" that offers new horizons. But is not the cross of Christ much more than a principle of social and spiritual critique? Is it not the redeeming grace of God entering into history and altering the very foundation of human life and existence?

For Thiselton revelation seems to be a progressive unfolding of eschatological wisdom as we move forward in the quest for greater understanding of God and the self through relating biblical texts to cultural change. I see revelation as a decisive interruption of human interpretations by the self-disclosing God, who addresses sinful humanity in personal encounter. Coming to faith means the overturning of human horizons rather than their expansion and enlargement. It is not just that the human person perceives but that God speaks *(Deus dixit)*. Can the church maintain its mandate on the basis of fallible interpretations, or does it rest its claims on the infallible Word of God, which is never at our disposal, to be sure, but is made available to us in moments of repentance and prayerful transcendence? Is our ultimate criterion a "cooperative shared work" for deeper understanding in which the Spirit, the text and the reader all play a role,[147] or the momentous act of divine revelation in Jesus Christ in the sacred history of the past, which redeems from sin and judgment? Is hermeneutic understanding "a transforming process" in which humans seek to deepen their grasp of the mystery of life or a climactic event in which God acts and speaks?

I agree with Thiselton that the church is fallible in the sense of being caught up in the flux of history and thereby vulnerable to cultural and historical pressures. But is not the church also infallible in the sense that it perseveres in the truth through the power of the Holy Spirit, who directs the church again and again to the written Word of God, the document of divine revelation? The church does not possess the truth, but does not the truth possess and remold the church? It is well to remember that the Reformers spoke of an infallible church as well as an infallible Word.

Thiselton's emphasis is on the broadening of our hermeneutical horizons through a readiness to listen to both the text and the culture in which we live. But does not the revealed Word of God call into question our hermeneutical methods and horizons and superimpose a new horizon—what Paul called "the mind of Christ" (1 Cor 2:16)? In his earlier work Thiselton took issue with Barth's contention that the event of the Word of God is discontinuous with all human thought and experience.[148] Yet was not Barth correct that God's Word does not build on human life and experience but judges it and converts it? Is the key to hermeneutical understanding a movement toward eschatological fullness or divine intervention in human history? Do we understand the present in the light of the future or the present and future in the light of the past?[149] Has not God spoken once for all in human history (Heb 10:12) and do not we need to return to that abiding foundation? Our little systems must remain open, but they can remain reliable only when they are anchored in eternity. Our reasoning will always fall short of the perfect comprehension of God's self-revealing Word, but through the power of the Spirit we can and must claim to see truly, even though not exhaustively.

In fairness to Thiselton, I must add that he is ready to acknowledge that the message of the cross reverses human pretensions and claims to wisdom.[150] But for him this reversal is at the same time accompanied by a deepening and expansion of human understanding. God is sometimes depicted as the power of the future that animates the human quest for wisdom and meaning. We need to heed Thiselton's warnings against making idols of our concepts, and he has much to teach us in this area. But we also need to retain the biblical claims to transcendent truth, which does not simply lie above or beyond the stream of history but which entered into this stream at one particular time and place— where God revealed himself definitively and decisively in the life, death and resurrection of Jesus Christ.[151]

•SEVEN•

RUDOLF
BULTMANN:
AN ENDURING
PRESENCE

They determine what can be God's word, not by starting
from God who speaks it, but starting from man who receives it,
and then they still claim it is God's word.
MARTIN LUTHER

There are no miracles in the Gospel which we can take
literally without abandoning good sense.
JEAN-JACQUES ROUSSEAU

Now that the forces and laws of nature have been discovered,
we can no longer believe in *spirits, whether good or evil.*
RUDOLF BULTMANN

The translation of the Christian faith into contemporary
thought forms can easily result in the assimilation of the Gospel
into the secular speech and philosophies of the world.
In our desire to proclaim the love of Christ, we may allow society
to dictate the conditions of credibility and comprehension.
ALVIN KIMEL

We can only know God in His self-objectification for us,
not by seeking non-objective knowledge of Him.
THOMAS F. TORRANCE

Probably no theologian or biblical scholar has made a more re-
sounding and lasting impact on biblical studies in the twentieth
century than Rudolf Bultmann, professor of New Testament at
Marburg, Germany, until 1951.[1] His ruminations have sparked the rev-

olution in hermeneutics that has replaced the orthodoxy of the creeds with the orthodoxy of historical biblical scholarship. His innovative methodology has decisively altered the agenda for theology. Even those who vigorously oppose him have had to address the concerns he has raised, thereby showing that he is indeed still a force to be reckoned with.[2] The all-pervasive tendency in current theology and biblical studies to present a faith divested of its "mythological" and supernatural trappings bears the unmistakable imprint of Bultmann.[3] The widespread movement in academic religious circles to substitute existential truth for ontological truth is part of his enduring legacy. His reconceiving of God as "the Uncertainty of the future" and the creative depths of existence resonates with an emerging neomystical spirituality that celebrates the universal drive for life and power rather than God's irreversible act of redemption in past history.[4] To understand the theological and spiritual climate today we must understand him.

I confess to having been influenced by Bultmann on my theological pilgrimage. When first introduced to his *Jesus and the Word*[5] in my seminary days, I was favorably impressed. Here, it seemed, was a scholar who was presenting the authentic vision of the Jesus of the Gospels. The kingdom that Jesus preached was not an evolving humane social order (as in liberal theology) but an apocalyptic inbreaking of a new reality into worldly history. Moreover, Bultmann's magnum opus, *The Gospel of John*, contains many insights that on first glance tend to support orthodoxy.[6]

Bultmann shows his Reformation colors by making the doctrine of salvation paramount in theology. Christology is subordinated to soteriology with the result that Jesus Christ is appraised on what he does for us rather than on how he is related to the inner being of God. One misses the strong affirmation of the deity of Jesus Christ that characterized both the Reformation and church tradition in general, but Bultmann clearly makes Jesus central in his theology. It is not the teachings of Jesus but his cross and suffering that constitute the focal point of Bultmann's theology.

Cultural and Theological Background

Bultmann was brought up in a Lutheran parsonage and studied at the Universities of Tübingen, Berlin and Marburg. Among his teachers were Johannes Weiss, a New Testament scholar in the history of religions, and Wilhelm Herrmann, who transmitted to him the legacy of Kant, Schleiermacher and Ritschl. While Bultmann acknowledged his indebtedness to liberalism, he criticized liberal theology for losing sight of the transcendence of God and for reducing Christianity to ethical principles.

Bultmann came to be associated with the theology of crisis, also known as dialectical theology, which emerged as a notable force in German theological thought after World War I. With Karl Barth, Emil Brunner and Friedrich Gogarten he helped bring back into theological parlance the concepts of paradox and dialectic. This movement also questioned the capacity of reason to arrive at real knowledge of God. It was especially known for its penetrating critique of idealism in modern theology. Bultmann wrote respectful reviews of both the first and second editions of Barth's *Epistle to the Romans,* but one could already detect his emerging differences with Barth.[7]

The rise of National Socialism placed the church on the defensive. Some Lutheran theologians retreated to a theology of the inner life that avoided social confrontation, a strategy that Bultmann's theology could be interpreted as supporting. Yet Bultmann himself proved to be a person of courage and vision. At the time of Hitler's rise to power in 1933 Bultmann delivered a lecture denouncing the defaming of the Jews, though he did not single out Hitler for condemnation. He also threw his support to the Confessing Church, but he was never a leader in this movement. To his credit Bultmann was a prominent opponent of the so-called Aryan paragraph adopted by the General Synod of the Lutheran Church that stipulated that in order to hold office in the church a man together with his wife must be of Aryan descent. The theological faculty at the University of Marburg unanimously opposed these restrictions in a statement authored mainly by Bultmann on September 19, 1933. In his sermons of 1937 and 1938 Bultmann raised his voice frequently against current nationalistic myths and acts that contradicted Christian faith.[8]

Bultmann's theology and spirituality were perhaps shaped more by his Lutheran heritage than any other spiritual or ideological source. Luther's emphasis on the personal appropriation of faith and his vigorous defense of *sola gratia* left an indelible imprint. Bultmann often cited the words of the young Philipp Melanchthon: "To know Christ is to know his benefits." It was not God in himself but God *pro me* (for me) that characterized his theological thrust. He was especially appreciative of Luther's theology of the cross, which saw the life of the believer as a life under the cross. Whereas Luther dealt with the problem of a guilty conscience, Bultmann addressed the problem of human insecurity in the modern world.

With Paul Tillich, Bultmann is one of the luminaries of Christian existentialism. Both men were profoundly influenced by Søren Kierkegaard and Martin Heidegger, especially the earlier Heidegger. In existentialism ideas are considered of no consequence unless they shape human existence. The language of religion and theology is transposed into the language of human existence. Faith itself becomes "a new understanding of existence."[9] Truth is not abstract and eternal but concrete and historical.

Bultmann's theology also stands under the shadow of Kant, who himself prepared the way for existentialism.[10] It was Kant's thesis that ultimate or noumenal truth is hidden from the senses and can be grasped only by practical reason or moral insight. Existentialist theologians like Bultmann and Tillich followed Kant in locating God at the outer limits of reason. "Precisely when reason has followed its road to the end," said Bultmann, "the point of crisis is reached and man is brought to the great question mark over his own existence."[11] The early Barth also used this language, but Barth broke with existentialism as he developed his theology of the Word of God. For the mature Barth God is to be found not in the crisis of reason but in the crisis of history—where God became man in Jesus Christ.

While diverging from the optimism and rationalism of liberal theology, Bultmann, unlike Barth, never disclaimed his liberal heritage. The pivotal role of religious experience, which we find in Schleiermacher, continues in Bultmann, though now the emphasis is on the experience of the cross rather than of transcendental ideals embedded in nature. From Ritschl Bultmann inherited a profound mistrust of abstract metaphysics and a lively appreciation for the practical consequences of faith.[12] From Ernst Troeltsch he learned that historical judgments yield only probability and that faith must be grounded in something more secure than the ebb and flow of history. Like Herrmann, Bultmann regarded the experience of faith as an experience of freedom: the decisive character of the Word is that it releases one from bondage to the world.[13]

Bultmann was at one with Barth and crisis theology in raising questions about the validity of natural theology and general revelation. Revelation is not general but specific and individual. Yet Bultmann remained open to general revelation: "The non-Christian questions concerning God and the efforts to provide an answer show that God 'reveals' himself even outside the Christ event and Christian preaching."[14] That people actively seek God in their despair and lostness indicated to him that by virtue of their creation all are already in contact with God. Yet Bultmann continued to maintain that revelation in the strict sense is limited to an encounter with the Christ event, for it is only in the light of the cross of Christ that we can understand the encounters with God in everyday existence.

I have been led to choose the way of Barth over that of Bultmann and Tillich because in the first I see a theology that begins with God's self-revelation in Christ rather than with the gropings and searchings of a despairing humanity. For Bultmann and existentialist theology in general, the law of God within us or the voice of conscience sets us on a search for God that finds its fruition in faith in Jesus Christ. For Barth it is only by being awakened to the gospel through God's free grace that we begin to search for an understanding of God's will for our lives.

Barth's point of departure is divine revelation; Bultmann's is existential despair. The Bible becomes for Bultmann not a source of knowledge of God but an aid in self-understanding: theology is transmuted into anthropology in this brand of existentialism.

Bultmann is significant on the modern theological scene for several reasons. First, he has effectively altered the agenda of theology: it is no longer exploring metaphysical mysteries such as the being of God and the two natures of Christ but bringing the gospel into positive relationship with the human search for authenticity and meaning. The primary task is no longer the unraveling of ontological puzzles but rediscovering transcendence in the face of the collapse of supernaturalism. True to his Kantian heritage, he regarded the process of knowing as more critical than the problem of being. He again showed the influence of the critical philosophy when he pondered the question of how we can know a God who is not an object in empirical experience or an idea inherent in the human mind. Furthermore, Bultmann reminded theology of the crucial importance of religious language. Is the pictorial language of the Bible adequate for conveying the truth of the gospel for our time? How can we speak of God in an age when the value of words is based on their practical utility rather than their transparency to spiritual realities? Finally, Bultmann reopened the question of the role of philosophy in preparing the way for faith. Can contemporary philosophy enable us to make the truth of faith intelligible and credible to the modern mind?

Distinctive Emphases

Reflecting the Kantian legacy, Bultmann maintained that there are two levels of reality: a lower story of facts, objectivity and science—the phenomenal world—and an upper story of existential values, faith and subjectivity—the noumenal world. On the one hand the phenomenal world, which is directly accessible to our senses, is a closed continuum of cause and effect. On the other hand the spiritual world allows for wonder, creativity and faith. It is the difference between nature and spirit, historical meaning and existential meaning, objectifying knowledge and faith knowledge. Bultmann did not see this polarity as a metaphysical description so much as a phenomenological one. He believed that one could demonstrate the existence of an in-depth dimension in experience that theoretical reason cannot grasp.

Drawing on the biblical theologian Martin Kähler, Bultmann distinguished between two modes of history: *Historie,* which refers to objective, recorded history, and *Geschichte,* which signifies the bearing of outward events on the human psyche.[15] Bultmann displayed minimal interest in the Jesus of history *(Historie),* since we know very little of Jesus that is historically certain. Instead, his emphasis is on the historic *(geschichtlich)* Christ, the creative power of history that appeared in Jesus but which is also active today, bringing men and women freedom from their bondage to guilt and care.

Bultmann's theology focuses not on the teachings of Jesus and the apostles but on the kerygma, the preaching of the cross of Christ, which calls for decision and commitment. It is not the life of Jesus that is crucial for Christian faith but the power of the love of God revealed in the cross of Christ and conveyed through the preaching of Christ.

What troubled Bultmann was the continuing resistance of educated, cultured people to the preaching of the kerygma. He acknowledged that the gospel would always be a stumbling block and folly to people of the world, but he discerned another stumbling block: the archaic language in which faith comes to us. The kerygma is simply the announcement that the forgiveness of God is available to us through the knowledge of the ministry of Jesus leading to the cross. But when this announcement is embellished by speculation drawn from Gnostic and apocalyptic sources, when it is tied to an outmoded supernaturalistic worldview, then the real meaning of the cross is obscured and we are thereby prevented from making an authentic decision of faith.

Bultmann was emphatic that the criterion for faith is to be taken not from the modern worldview but from the existential understanding of the New Testament. But this existential truth must be distinguished from its mythical form. The main reason modern people reject the kerygma is that they confuse it with an outdated mythology, for "it is impossible . . . to avail ourselves of modern medical and surgical discoveries, and at the same time to believe in the New Testament world of spirits and miracles."[16] "The Church can re-establish communication with modern man and speak with an authentic voice only after she has resolutely abandoned mythology."[17]

He pleaded for a presentation of the kerygma divested of its supernaturalistic and mythical trappings. We should no longer preach the cross of Christ as a sacrifice for sins, his bodily resurrection from the grave and his nature miracles, for these are embellishments that do not belong to the original kerygma. Instead, we should preach the agonizing death of Christ on the cross and the new life that accrues to those who find in the cross the forgiveness of sins. We should proclaim the fact that new life is available for those who discover in the death of Jesus the key that unlocks the mystery of their own existence.

Bultmann saw the essence of theology in eschatology, but he was thinking not of the end of world history but of the end of inauthentic existence in the awakening to faith. Whenever the message of faith is articulated in all of its purity and power, history collapses into eschatology or existential history, a process particularly evident in John's Gospel. Eschatology refers not to a future history but to an interior dimension of existence.

In Bultmann's view we should preach the cross as an eschatological event—an event that confronts us in the present and opens up a new future for us. The eschaton is not the end of the physical world but the end of one's old life in the decision of faith. He was quick to affirm that God was acting for our redemption in the cross of Christ, but this action was not visible to the senses. It is ascertainable only to the eyes of faith. The cross is the revelation that God is merciful, that he makes available to us the possibility of freedom from our bondage to the law of sin and death.

According to Bultmann the stories of the resurrection of Christ are simply attempts to explain the meaning of the cross. The resurrection is not an event in external history but an interior event. It does not concern life beyond the grave but the new life in the here and now. It is not itself a fact of history but an interpretation of the enduring quality and impact of Christ's cross, which of course has far-reaching historical ramifications. Here again Bultmann saw mythology as an obstacle in understanding the true import of the message of faith. The resurrection cannot be historical because the return of a dead man to life here on earth merely revives myth and its contradictions. Clearly the revivification of a corpse is inconceivable in the modern intellectual climate, but the renewal of life and hope that the story of the cross brings to people of all ages is something that can be confirmed and realized in experience.

The heart of the Christian message is not the historical Jesus but the Christ event, which includes not only the death of Christ in history but also the proclamation of this death and the acceptance of this message. Basically, the Christ event is a redemptive experience in which we encounter the power of creative transformation.[18] We meet the living Christ not in an analysis of the Jesus of history but in the preached word of the cross.

The decision to which we are called is accepting the fact that we are accepted. Such a decision entails repentance—forsaking the past life of trying to make ourselves secure and entering upon a new life in which we find our security in the radical insecurity of faith. In this decision we are given a new future and also a true understanding of ourselves. Faith is not objective knowledge but trust and venture. The life of faith is a life free from care, fear and double-mindedness.

Bultmann rejected the vicarious substitutionary atonement of Christ as belonging to an outmoded mythology. Christ has not merited salvation through his death, but he reveals that salvation is now a possibility for humanity. The cross reveals our impotence to liberate ourselves through our own efforts. The cross of Christ is not the accomplishment of salvation but the revelation that salvation is available.

Bultmann's intent "is not to make religion more acceptable to modern man by trimming the traditional Biblical texts, but to make clearer to modern man what the Christian faith is."[19] The main problem is the hermeneutical one—the problem of translation. Existential philosophy, particularly that of Heidegger, can be an important aid in the task of theological translation. It can help us to understand the fallenness and despair of humanity. It can enable us to present the kerygma as a theoretical possibility for modern people. Only divine grace, however, can enable people to appropriate the kerygma so that it becomes a practical reality in their lives.

Against Barthian theology Bultmann acknowledged a point of contact between the gospel and the natural person. This point of contact is the question about God that human existence induces.

> Unless our existence were moved (consciously or unconsciously) by the question about God . . . we would not be able to recognize God as God in any revelation. There is an existential knowledge of God present and alive in human existence in the question about "happiness" or "salvation" or about the meaning of the world and of history, insofar as this is the question about the authenticity of our own existence.[20]

Bultmann could also speak of the point of contact as the sense of guilt and despair that propels people to seek the power of the new life that the gospel discloses. Philosophy can help us toward the painful recognition of our misery and helplessness, though Christian faith will necessarily interpret the human predicament in a slightly different way. Prefaith existence can know much about the real condition of humanity, but it cannot provide the power to deal with this condition creatively and redemptively. Christian revelation confirms the non-Christian inquiry about God and humanity but refutes the non-Christian answer.

For Bultmann the point of contact does not make the faith credible or palatable; it only makes the message of faith recognizable. The point of contact is at the same time a point of conflict. Only when we cease cleaving to the self as the ground of our security and rely exclusively on the invisible God do we experience the breakthrough into freedom, the new life of authenticity and wholeness.

Whether Bultmann is best understood as an apologist for the faith is a subject of debate in scholarly circles. While acknowledging that his theology contained an apologetic element, Bultmann insisted that the problem of communication was not his main interest. Faith itself demands a focus on the problem of interpretation. Yet one cannot deny that Bultmann was passionately concerned to communicate the truth of the gospel to a secular humanity that had become increasingly estranged from the faith. He did not wish to tailor the faith to fit the biases of the age, but he did seek to remove barriers to the faith so that people of our day could make an authentic decision for Christ.

In my reading of Bultmann I regard apologetics as his paramount, though not exclusive, concern. Bultmann was not an apologist in the sense of trying to vindicate the Christian faith before the bar of reason, for he maintained that revelation overturns all human solutions and aspirations. But he was an apologist in that he tried to make the faith credible to its cultured despisers. His aim was to interpret the New Testament kerygma in such a way that it would be entertained as a viable possibility by the nonbelieving public.

Demythologizing

In his lecture "New Testament and Mythology" that propelled him into prominence in 1941, Bultmann articulated his conviction that what renders many hearers impervious to the gospel message is its mythological language.[21] The myth in the Bible was not intended to be taken literally, and this is where biblical interpreters have gone astray. It represents a projection on the plane of history of inner conflicts and hopes that have to do with the struggle of spirit against nature. Myth "strives to speak of a reality which lies beyond objectifiable, observable, and controllable reality."[22] It purports to give not historical or scientific truth but existential truth. It should not be abandoned but interpreted in the light of existential analysis.

Bultmann saw the mythical element present in the cosmology of the

Bible with its three-decker universe, its apocalyptic eschatology and its otherworldly Christology, in which Jesus is identified with the supernatural Son of Man or the preexistent Word in heaven. Demythologizing is necessary because the ancient worldview is no longer credible in the light of modern science, and the apocalyptic expectation of the end of the world has been discredited by history. Bultmann also pointed to internal inconsistencies in the biblical myth: for example, the contradiction between the realized eschatology of John's Gospel and the apocalyptic eschatology of the Synoptics. In addition, he called attention to the discrepancy between the static character of the myth and the dynamic character of the gospel. He also cited Gnosticism and Jewish apocalypticism as major sources for the New Testament myth.

In Bultmann's perspective myth is an anthropological way of speaking about divinity in order to attain an understanding of one's self and one's environment. Myth is true as the description of the inner subjective life of the individual but deceptive if we take it as referring to literal events in history. Since myth is anthropological, it is necessarily conditioned by the culture that produced it. It conveys a picture of abstract divinity rather than confronting us with the living reality of God that can be experienced here and now. Myth "objectifies" the divine activity and projects it on the plane of worldly happenings,[23] whereas true miracles are hidden from sight and revealed only to faith. Myth is basically prescientific imagery, which is no longer valid in our scientific age. Demythologizing is permissible, even mandatory, because it was already started in the New Testament. To demythologize is to reinterpret the myth, not to replace it with another myth.

Bultmann thought of myth in basically two ways: as a prescientific explanation of world phenomena and as an objectified understanding of God. Divine activity is not an interference in the course of nature and history but the release of natural powers and possibilities that bring meaning and freedom to the person in bondage. Whereas myth employs spatial imagery to express divine transcendence, an existential interpretation describes transcendence in terms of openness to the future.

For Bultmann myths are "signals" or "ciphers" of transcendence attesting to "man's knowledge of the ground and limits of his being."[24] Myths are therefore filled with tremendous import, but their capacity to throw light on the human condition is undermined when we take them literally. According to one of Bultmann's interpreters, to demythologize is to free faith from every view of the world expressed in objective terms, including the modern scientific worldview, which like all worldviews "is historically conditioned and relative."[25]

What is the content of a demythologized gospel? It is the proclamation that new life is available as we are confronted by the cross of Christ, opening us to a future filled with possibilities and promise. The gospel is not about a preexistent Christ, a blood sacrifice, a virgin birth, a ransom to Satan—which are all mythological embellishments; instead it concerns the redeeming power of God in human life illustrated uniquely and decisively in the ministry and cross of Jesus Christ. The gospel directs us to the living Christ, not the mythological Christ. The crucifixion and resurrection of Christ have meaning for us mainly as present experiences.

Bultmann insisted that we must preach not that Jesus literally rose from the dead but that he rose into the hearts of believers. Here it is possible to discern a Pietist element in his thought; indeed, he has been accused of fostering a neo-Pietism. He was convinced that "a corpse cannot come back to life or rise from the grave,"[26] but the memory of a life sacrificed for the sake of others could spark hope in a situation where despair and hopelessness prevail. Christ continues to live not in some transcendent heaven but in the kerygma, the evangelical proclamation. The experience of the resurrection is none other than an encounter with the Christ of the kerygma.

The end of the world is not the second coming of Christ at the end of history but the end of nonauthentic existence, the opening up of a new future—an event that takes place in the crisis of repentance and faith. Christ brings us not personal immortality[27] but eschatological existence—life lived in openness to the challenges of the future.

In an existentialist gospel, revelation becomes an occurrence rather than an illumination or doctrine. Its content is the experience of forgiveness and freedom, not supranatural knowledge. Revelation is "the means whereby we achieve our authenticity, which we cannot achieve by our own resources. Therefore, to know about revelation means to know about our own authenticity—and, at the same time, thereby to know of our limitation."[28]

Salvation is no longer a vicarious substitutionary sacrifice for sin but the realization of authentic existence. This breakthrough into authenticity and freedom is an ontological possibility for all people, but it becomes a practical (or ontic) possibility only in our encounter with the kerygma. Jesus Christ is not the preexistent Word of God made flesh (a mythological concept) but the "Bringer of authentic existence."[29]

Christian hope is reconceived as the possibility of a creative life in this world rather than an eternal life in heaven. We should look forward not to a life beyond death but to "a kind of resigned freedom to live within these boundaries of our present life."[30] Christ "may teach us to relax our grip upon this world, and thus to find a happy equilibrium in precisely those aspects of our existence which were formerly a bitter poison to our souls."[31] Here one can discern certain parallels between Bultmann's view and ancient Stoicism.

Bultmann's plea for demythologizing has predictably met with mixed reactions.[32] He rightly reminded us that the Bible has a mythical element, and that means a culturally conditioned element. The hermeneutical task is to interpret the mythical imagery in order to discover the abiding reality that gave rise to the myth. But this abiding reality is not an experience in human consciousness, as Bultmann maintained, but real events in history. What makes the biblical myth unique is that myth becomes fact. Bultmann claimed that the stories of the incarnation, resurrection and ascension of Christ are projections of inner experiences thrown out on the screen of nature and history. But are they not rooted in objective revelation? Do they not purport to tell us about God's redeeming action in Christ, which is true and applicable to us even apart from our response of faith and repentance?

Bultmann failed to discern that the New Testament myth is theological, not anthropological. Its principal purpose is not to lead us to self-understanding but to describe the mighty acts of God recorded in history. Bultmann overlooked the fact that mythopoetic language is the only possible medium for speaking about God's activity.[33] To translate myth into a philosophical conceptuality is to risk losing sight of the reality that myth describes and proclaims.

Part of the problem is that Bultmann denied the possibility of divine intervention into nature and history. He accepted uncritically the presuppositions of Newtonian science, which portray the phenomenal world as a closed continuum of cause and effect. Explanation must consequently be couched in terms of modern ideas of causation. For Bultmann the "natural" course of events is *never* interrupted; the cataclysmic is therefore routinely disregarded. His commitment to both uniformitarianism and historicism definitely clouded his understanding not only of myth but of the kerygma itself.

Against Bultmann I maintain that though the form of the biblical myth is culturally conditioned, its meaning-content transcends both culture and history. The gospel is not a mythical description of human encounter with the creative powers within nature and history but an incomparable once-for-all revelation of God's will and purpose for all humanity in the life, death and resurrection of Jesus Christ. It is not an experience that needs to be interpreted in the light of current human wisdom but a transcendent criterion that both interprets and alters human experience and understanding.

A New Venture in Hermeneutics

Bultmann has played a major role in the hermeneutical revolution that has rocked the academic world of biblical studies and theology. The proclamation of the church must be something more than the recital of the facts of the Bible: "The real problem," said Bultmann, "is the hermeneutic one, i.e., the problem of interpreting the Bible and the teachings of the Church in such a way that they may become under-standable as a summons to man."[34]

This approach to hermeneutics is similar to that of Schleiermacher and Dilthey: the emphasis is on the process of understanding. What we seek to understand, however, is not so much the intention or motivation of the original authors as the encounter with the power of being that shaped their understanding of life and the world. Our focus should be on the "life moment" of the writers in which they come to an awareness of the extremity of human need and the availability of divine grace.

According to Bultmann the exegete must approach the text with a prior understanding *(Vorverstandnis)*. Before making an intelligent de-cision regarding the demands of faith, we must have some prior knowl-edge of these demands. We must come to the text with questions in-formed by the gravity of the human condition and seek for illumination in the text. These questions have to do with the meaning of human existence, just as the biblical writers were concerned with the meaning of their existence. We must stand before the text with a question for-mulated out of our own experience and history, to which the text may or may not have an answer.

The deepest question that drives us to an investigation of the text is the question about God. Because we sense the reality of a gracious God who can alleviate our guilt and assuage our cares, we are able to rec-ognize the claims of this God on us as we confront the kerygma, the story of Jesus' encounter with God. Our preunderstanding is at the same time a point of contact with the divine reality that throws light on our struggle with despair and meaninglessness.

For Bultmann the aim in exegesis is to come to a true self-under-standing—authentic existence. But we also seek for an openness to the eternal dimension of the self beyond the individual ego. One may rightly ask (as does Kenneth Hamilton) whether this is not the Socratic prin-ciple—"Know thyself." God is important to help the individual to realize his or her possibilities, to come to authenticity.

The task of hermeneutics is a practical one—to summon men and women to decision, to face resolutely the challenges that life imposes on them. Hermeneutics not only interprets the text but also seeks to make it understandable to our hearers so that they too may be led to a decision that gives meaning and purpose to their existence.

Bultmann defined hermeneutics as the translation of meaning, but he had in mind not its theoretical or metaphysical meaning but its existential meaning. In Ebeling's words, "The text . . . becomes a hermeneutic aid in the understanding of present experience."[35] It throws light not on the cosmos nor on world history but on the human predicament and the possibility of coping in an unfriendly and dehumanizing world.

Ian Henderson ably delineated the relation between existential language and other kinds of language.[36] To say that Christ suffered under Pontius Pilate is to speak historically. To portray Christ as "the Lamb of God, who takes away the sin of the world" (Jn 1:29) is to speak mythologically. To exclaim "I have been crucified with Christ" (Gal 2:20) is to describe reality existentially. For Bultmann the last is for our day the preferred way of speaking when the reference is to divine reality or divine action.

Kenneth Hamilton argues persuasively that Heidegger's philosophy has been a formative influence on Bultmann's hermeneutics.[37] Bultmann's concept of prefaith existence is virtually the same as Heidegger's depiction of humanity as "being toward death." His understanding of faith is remarkably close to Heidegger's "primal thinking." His interpretation of judgment and forgiveness resembles Heidegger's idea of "releasement," an act of nonwilling in which we accept the favor of Being.

Barth criticized Bultmann for making the problem of translation, rather than the message of faith itself, the main theme of theology.[38] For Barth the ill-conceived attempt to make the gospel acceptable and credible to "modern man" betrays a lack of confidence in the power of the gospel itself to persuade and convert. Bultmann ended by reading into Scripture ideas derived from human philosophy and ideology rather than allowing Scripture to transform these ideas in the light of its own divine criterion—the gospel and law, which, though relayed through the

medium of human language and culture, has a transcendent, ontological source—the very word of the living God.

The cleavage between these two theological giants is especially pronounced in the way they approach the *Sache* or subject matter of Scripture. For Barth the *Sache* is the self-revelation of God in Jesus Christ,
which is inseparable from the apostolic interpretation of the salvific
events of both the Old and New Testaments. This revelation can be
known only as it makes itself known to those who truly seek for the
truth in Holy Scripture. For Bultmann the *Sache* is the opening up of the
horizon of men and women as they begin to perceive the redemptive
significance of the death of Christ. The *Sache* is not Jesus Christ himself
but the reorientation toward life that the cross of Christ induces. Bultmann contended that we come to the Bible with a knowledge of God
in advance, since we are already painfully aware of our guilt and lostness and of our need for personal liberation.[39]

Bultmann made a case for *Sache* criticism *(Sachkritik)*—critiquing
not only the words but also the content of the apostolic witness in order
to determine to what degree it accurately reflects the life experience of
the apostles. In *Sache* criticism we try to understand the biblical authors
better than they understood themselves.[40] It also allows us to take issue
with some of their conclusions even while purportedly remaining true
to their deepest insights.[41] By contrast, Barth was adamant that we do
not critique the *Sache* but are critiqued by it, and even though we may
engage in critical study of the biblical text our thoughts and interpretations must always be subordinated to the divine self-interpretation
that is relayed to us through the text by the Spirit.[42]

God Hidden and Revealed

Bultmann held that we can speak of the acts of God but not of the being
of God, of God's effects on us but not of God in himself. This is because
God is neither an object in empirical experience that reason can perceive nor a transcendental ideal that the imagination can envisage.
Instead he is a spiritual presence that encompasses us and upholds us

but can never be mastered conceptually by us. God is nonobservable and intangible and therefore can be apprehended only in faith. We can speak of him indirectly or obliquely but not directly or univocally. We can speak of his acts analogically, but human experience is the basis of the analogy.

According to Bultmann we can know *that* God is but not *what* God is. We can experience his presence even while we fail to comprehend his being. We can have existential or nonobjective knowledge of God but not conceptual knowledge. Whereas Barth maintained that God deliberately hides himself in his revelation so that we might not be overwhelmed by his glory, Bultmann's God is hidden because he is inaccessible to the senses.

I agree that because God is not an immediate object in experience we cannot have theoretical knowledge of him on the basis of human experience. But even though inaccessible to our senses and reason, does not God make himself accessible in his revelation? God cannot be objectified by the human inquirer, but does not God objectify himself in Jesus Christ so that we can truly know him—not only his effects on us but his very being?

For Bultmann revelation is an occurrence that places us in a new situation where we can attain authentic selfhood.[43] It is not the communication of God's will and purpose for the world but an encounter with the power that rejuvenates and redeems. Revelation has no intelligible content, but it does have redemptive significance. It does not impart information about God, but it carries existential impact as we are confronted by the reality of God.

While Bultmann admittedly captured one important dimension of revelation, he overlooked and indeed denied the very heart of revelation: the living God really reveals himself in Jesus Christ so that we know not only the effects of his grace but his very self. We do not have exhaustive knowledge of God, but we have real knowledge—not through our own power but through the power of the Spirit, who teaches spiritual truths to those who have the Spirit (1 Cor 2:13).

In contrast to Bultmann I see the Word of God not only as an event but also as a transcendent structure of meaning. Revelation brings us not only the power of being but also the meaning of being. It entails not only an encounter with the Wholly Other but also the communication of truth. It comprises not only spiritual presence but also ontological affirmation. It not only works creative transformation but also provides an overarching criterion that can lead us into a deeper understanding of both faith and the world. Bultmann could speak of revelation as a presupposition that must be given to us anew as we strive to find the truth of God for our lives.[44] But revelation for him is not a metaphysical presupposition that can shape a new worldview; it is an experience of selfless love that can enable us to rebuild our lives.

Despite Bultmann's intention of avoiding the conundrums of metaphysical speculation, he nevertheless opened the door to metaphysical questions. He declared that the time had arrived to overcome the dichotomy between supernaturalism and naturalism. He reconceived God as "the Occurrence of Transcendence," "the Darkness of the Future," "the Unconditional in the conditional" and "the Beyond in our midst." He found the transcendence of God in the depths of human existence and in the future of undisclosed possibilities.

While many of Bultmann's depictions of God can be construed as a turn toward mysticism (e.g., God as the unknowable and ineffable), he made it clear that mysticism constitutes an aberration and corruption of biblical faith. Jesus does not call us to the inner life but to decision. The kingdom of God is "not the object of occult vision and mystical raptures."[45] The mystics make God ahistorical and nontemporal whereas the God of the Bible is active in history, directing human destiny. He is not outside history but the Beyond in our midst.

Neither did Bultmann enjoin us to return to the older liberalism, which conceived of God as wholly immanent in the world and ended in a "pantheism in history." For Bultmann "God is other than the world, he is beyond the world."[46] With Kierkegaard Bultmann spoke of "the infinite qualitative difference" between God and humanity, and he remained with this position throughout his career.

While Bultmann warned against dissolving the faith in pantheism and monism, I believe that he is best understood as a panentheist. God is neither above the world nor identical with it but in and through the world. Bultmann belongs to the new spirituality, which reconceives God as the creative depth of the world bursting into history from within the constellation of universal time and space. Bultmann acknowledged his affinity to Troeltsch's vision of the "transformations of God" that revolve around an "inner life-movement of the All," a "life-process of the Absolute," a "becoming of the divine Spirit."[47] He applauded Heidegger's insight that if God's eternity can be construed philosophically, then it should be understood "only as a more primordial temporality which is 'infinite.' "[48] This converges with Schubert Ogden's view that God's eternity is his eminent temporality and historicity. Manifesting a similarity to Tillich's world outlook, Bultmann confessed that "the depths into which we gaze are really the depths of God."[49] At one place he defined God as "the infinite fullness of all the powers of life that rage around us and take our breath away, filling us with awe and wonder."[50] It seems that for Bultmann God is a primordial and creative will that directs history from within as its élan vital. Perhaps we see here a remnant of an idealism inherited from Fichte and Hegel. In rejecting the biblical myth Bultmann substituted the modern myth of the evolving World Spirit that leads humanity into heights of never-ending creativity. The life of faith is one in which we let go of the securities that bind us to the past and enter an unknown future filled with promise and hope.

It is often said that a person's view of God becomes much clearer when we know how that person approaches prayer. Robert Roberts remarks perceptively that one may live out of the eventful transcendence that Bultmann celebrated, but one cannot really pray to such a deity. Bultmann did occasionally refer to giving "thanks to God" and speaking "to God"; yet it is apparent that he meant something quite different from the traditional Christian understanding. While nowhere to my knowledge did he set forth a theology of prayer, he left the distinct impression that prayer can be little more than reflection on the mystery of God's unfathomable love and celebration of the experience of undeserved grace. There would also be a place for confession, understood as an admission of our failure to live in the freedom to which we are called.[51]

Freedom for Obedience

Bultmann made a solid contribution in his reconception of ethics as freedom for obedience. Perhaps in an attempt to correct his Lutheran heritage, Bultmann took pains to tie grace to the demand for discipleship. The indicative (the gospel) and the imperative (the law) constitute an internal unity *(Einheit)* in Christian ethics. Christ brings an end to the legalistic understanding of law—but only in order to reaffirm the demand of the law in its unity with the gospel. Faith is at the same time radical obedience and total submission to God. "Only when the requirement of obedience is wholly grasped," said Bultmann, "can the *thought of grace and of forgiveness* be wholly understood; and the message of forgiveness then appears in its unity with the call to repentance."[52]

In this theology love is the way we exercise our freedom in becoming obedient to God's will. Love does not have a material principle or a rational content. It is simply the response of the believing person to the demands of the moment. Love is not a strategy for advancing ourselves on the scale of merit but a readiness to meet the needs of our neighbor. Bultmann was adamant that love in the understanding of the New Testament differs radically from the Hellenistic eros that seeks the fulfillment of the self in union with the highest. Agape love excludes the desire to enhance or secure the self, for it places one wholly at the disposal of one's neighbor. Love for God is simply the submission to God in faith that brings us the power to give of ourselves unambiguously and wholeheartedly to the needs of our fellow human beings.

Freedom is not the antithesis of obedience but the means by which we realize obedience. We become free as we decide to obey, and in obedience we discover our freedom. Bultmann upheld not a freedom from authority, as in the Renaissance conception, but a freedom under authority—that which is realized in obedience.

Bultmann insisted that genuine freedom involves responsible decision. It "is always freedom gained in responsibility and decision, and therefore it is freedom in insecurity."[53] To be a free person means to let go of our self-contrived securities and cling only to the promise of divine mercy that is apprehended solely by faith. To be free is to be ourselves— to be true to the destiny appointed to us by God.

According to Bultmann faith and love are not supernatural realities but natural possibilities that are realized when we make contact with the depths of our own being. In faith we do not become a new self but attain a new understanding of the self that equips us for a life of self-giving service to others. To act in faith means to open ourselves to the uncertain future to which God calls us, to go forward in the confidence that all things work together for good for those who love God.

Bultmann can be criticized for emptying both faith and love of all rational content. In his view faith frees us from "all . . . norms of value,"[54] but does not Jesus Christ himself become the supreme norm of value for the Christian? According to Bultmann the demand of God is given uniquely in every situation. But in the Bible the demand of God has "historical durability and continuity."[55] The divine commandment is synchronous with the commandments in Holy Scripture, which function as signposts that guide us on our pilgrimage of faith. The demands of the moment are not self-evident, as Bultmann claimed, but they become evident as we open ourselves to God's Word in prayer and faith. The Word of God makes itself evident through the Spirit, who leads us into repentance and renewal in faith.

In Bultmann's view every person instinctively knows what is good but fails to do it because of the malady of human sin. But Scripture tells us that the good is not in us, that the human heart is deceitful and desperately corrupt (Jer 17:9). What we need is not a new understanding of the human condition but a new nature. We need to become new creatures through the power of divine grace (2 Cor 5:17).

At times Bultmann seemed to present an autonomous ethic; at others he appeared to see the moral demand as beyond the self (metonomous).[56] This equivocation has its source in his view of God as the ground and depth of the self. To know God is to know the self; to know Christ is to know the light that already shines in the whole of creation. When Bultmann spoke of God as "the Wholly Other," he meant that God transcends the compass of human reason and imagination. He did not mean that God is ontologically wholly other, for this would be to resurrect a dying supernaturalism. Bultmann sought to affirm both the otherness of God and the continuity between God and humanity; the latter makes the apologetic task possible, the former keeps it Christian.

With some justification Bultmann has been accused of fostering a privatistic ethic. He saw the kingdom of God as personal and individual. It is not a new social order dawning on the horizon of history but a new orientation that enables us to live and endure in the old order of things. He denied any direct relation between human action and the kingdom of God. He refused to apply the ethical imperatives of the faith to social issues and therefore failed to do justice to the cultural mandate of the faith. Astonishingly he could say that "the Gospel knows nothing of 'social action' with its goals in this world."[57] In his "Autobiographical Reflections," he made the candid admission, "I have never directly and actively participated in political affairs."[58]

Although Bultmann identified himself with the Confessing Church, he did not present a theology that could effectively counter the racist ideology of that day. By relegating faith to the personal, spiritual sphere of life, he failed to do justice to the biblical affirmation that political life too lies under the demands of the gospel. He depicted the kingdom of Christ as not yet sovereign over the kingdoms of the world[59] and therefore called into question the lordship of Christ over the secular realms of life. Finally, in line with his Lutheran heritage he portrayed the law as coming before the gospel and consequently as having an authority of its own— independent of the gospel. The Old Testament law is a preliminary witness to the gospel, but other ideas may also function in this way. He was even willing to grant that the efforts of the German Christians to substitute "the *Nomos* of the German Nation" for the Old Testament were not wholly off the mark, but by championing the right of the stronger the ethics of the Third Reich revealed its incongruity with the gospel.[60] That Bultmann continued to draw on Heidegger's philosophy even after Heidegger threw his support to the Nazis further undermined Bultmann as a credible theological adversary of the cultural Christianity of the German Christians.[61]

Bultmann remained true to Luther and the Reformation in advocating a theology of the cross. Our faith must rest not on special experiences of the glory of God but on the promise of God to be with those who call on the name of Christ. We attain authentic existence only by embracing the suffering that accompanies the life of faith, not by trying to escape from suffering into a heavenly bliss, for "the message of divine grace does not suggest that the cross will be spared us, but rather that the cross itself is grace; that God slays in order to make alive."[62]

Yet Bultmann presented a theology of the cross without the apostolic interpretation of the cross. He interpreted the cross not as a sacrifice for sin but as a symbol of authentic selfhood. The cross of Jesus did not itself effect salvation, but it reveals that salvation is possible if we would only resolutely will to be ourselves in the face of a future that is often dark and foreboding. What saves us is the eschatological event that Jesus experienced and we too can experience when we are confronted with the proclamation of the cross of Christ.[63] We share in the cross of Christ when we "place under the shadow of the cross all that concerns us, both our hopes and our work" and "surrender our wishes and plans to the will of God."[64] Bultmann showed his departure from orthodox theology by dismissing as mythology the New Testament witness that it is Jesus as the preexistent and incarnate Word of God who saves us by taking on himself our sin and guilt through dying on the cross and then rising from the grave for our justification and redemption.

In its biblical context a theology of the cross will include a theology of glory. Christ crucified is not the last word: Christ also rose from the dead and sent forth his Holy Spirit. If we have a constricted theology of the cross, we have only darkness, not light, only sorrow, not joy. Bultmann said that Christ promises "neither ecstasy nor spiritual peace"[65] but only hope for a new future. Even as Christians "we never live, but only hope to live; and since we are always preparing ourselves to be happy, it is inevitable that we never in fact are happy."[66] Whereas Luther and Calvin affirmed the reality of the new birth, Bultmann spoke only of a new understanding that brings us no moral possibilities we did not already possess.

Bultmann's theology palpably lacks a doctrine of the Holy Spirit. Yet can we obey unless we are empowered to obey through the Spirit of God? Is it not the Holy Spirit who makes us free for obedience? Bultmann spoke of faith as risk and decision, but he did not do justice to the other side of the paradox of faith—that faith is also the confident assurance of salvation. He claimed that the future is "wholly unknown" to the believer, and thus the believer will be in radical insecurity. But is there not an eternal security that buoys up those who believe, an inner certainty that the future belongs to God and those who love God? We do not know the details of our personal future, but on the basis of Scripture we can surely claim that Christ's present reign will become visible to the whole world and that a heavenly home is being prepared for those who endure to the end (Mt 10:22). We can surely rejoice that nothing can separate us from the love of God (Rom 8:38-39), that no one can snatch us from the Father's hand (Jn 10:29). Can we preach good news unless we truly know that Christ is risen from the dead and that his Holy Spirit gives those who believe power to overcome the world?

A Neoliberal Theology

Bultmann has been classified as neo-orthodox, neo-Lutheran, existentialist and neoliberal. I believe that only the last two labels are fully appropriate, but neoliberal is probably the most accurate and comprehensive. Bultmann sought to be both a biblical theologian and a modern theologian. He tried to present biblical faith in the language of modern culture, but he took pains to disavow any attempt to base the message of faith on current philosophical wisdom. His theology confronts us with these questions: Is modernity the lens by which to read the Bible? Or is the Bible the criterion that judges modernity?

Despite his often severe criticisms of the older liberalism, one can show that he has many affinities to that heritage.[67] The dualism between spirit and nature, the eternal and the temporal, recalls similar emphases in Kant, Schleiermacher, Ritschl and Herrmann. This polarity goes back ultimately to Plato and Neoplatonism. The Bible too presents a dualism but of a different type: that between two ages or two kingdoms. Bultmann sometimes contrasted the present with the future, and here he reflects a more biblical orientation.

His reduction of theology to anthropology is also characteristic of liberal theology. In his theology "statements about God and his activity" are to be understood as "statements about human existence."[68] By rejecting metaphysical speculation concerning God in himself, he in effect transposed theology into psychology, although this was not his intention.

Like the mainstream of liberal theology, Bultmann sought a rapprochement with modernity. This accounts for the unmistakable apologetic thrust of his theology. His interest in demythologizing was indubitably tied to his conviction that "modern man acknowledges as reality only such phenomena or events as are comprehensible within the framework of the rational order of the universe."[69] In contrast to the radical biblical critic David Strauss, however, he did not absolutize the modern worldview and try to bring the kerygma into accord with it.

Like Kant and Schleiermacher, he held that faith is less than cognitive. It does not yield real knowledge of God's plan and purpose for the world, but it does throw light on human experience. It is not suprarational knowledge but insightful recognition. It represents a new attitude toward life rather than a new conception of reality.

In full accord with the liberal tradition, Bultmann affirmed the continuity between creation and redemption. Schubert Ogden is fond of citing this statement of Bultmann: "There is no other light shining in Jesus than has always already shined in the creation."[70] While Bultmann was also allied with the theology of crisis, his deepest affinities were with the Socratic tradition, which sees truth as latent in the human ego, needing only to be brought out into the open. Faith and love are for him natural possibilities that need to be awakened and stimulated.

Bultmann's affinities to the Enlightenment are especially evident in his view of reason as coming before faith. For him faith is not the surrender of rational thought but "is rather based on understanding, on understanding the character of human nature, on understanding the concrete possibilities of existence, on understanding what it means to speak of God's saving acts."[71] Reason cannot induce faith, but it can lead one to the point where faith is possible. With Kant and Tillich Bultmann located God at the outer limits of reason. When reason has gone as far as it can it confronts an abyss that challenges its autonomy. Bultmann here reflected certain strands within Kierkegaard, but he stood far from the position of the Reformers, who portrayed the "natural man" as being in flight from God and pursued by the grace of God. It is not the human quest for God but God's search for humanity that is most true to the biblical understanding of the order of salvation.

Bultmann's emphasis on the ethical over the mystical reflects his indebtedness to both Ritschl and Herrmann. Faith is not a feeling of absolute dependence, as in Schleiermacher, but a venture in obedience by which we realize authentic existence. I have already raised the question whether Bultmann represents a new mysticism, and he here may be closer to Schleiermacher than is commonly realized.[72]

Finally, his denigration of the Old Testament as a source of revelation unmistakably allies him with such representative liberal scholars as Semler, Schleiermacher, Ritschl and Harnack. Bultmann admitted that "*to us the history of Israel is not history of revelation. The events which meant something for Israel, which were God's Word, mean nothing more to us.*"[73] Insofar as it is regarded as law the Old Testament "*need* not address us as [the] direct Word of God and as a matter of fact *does* not do it."[74] A Catholic critic comments: "Bultmann's position is one of radical denial of the true relevance of the OT to the Christian."[75] His reservations regarding the validity of the Old Testament as revelation probably stem not from any vestige of anti-Semitism but from the hostility of modernity to the anthropomorphism and supposed legalism that characterized the ancient faith of Israel.

While Bultmann stood firmly in the liberal tradition, he did not stand fully in this tradition. His differences from liberal theology are nearly as striking as his affinities. First, he was convinced that God is other than the world, even though this otherness is seen as a transcendence within immanence. God transcends the reach of humanity, but he is inescapably related to the being of humanity. God is not so much the soul of the universe as the power that animates the universe and drives it beyond itself.

Again, for Bultmann what is central in Christian theology is not the teachings of Jesus but God's act of redemption in Jesus. We proclaim not moral precepts but the New Testament kerygma, the message of salvation. Yet it is a truncated kerygma that Bultmann offered, one divorced from its alleged mythological framework. It communicates not knowledge of a cosmic transaction between the Father and the Son but the experience of being accepted by the creative will that moves the universe.

His emphasis on grace over works sharply distinguishes him from rationalistic theology, though we find a comparable note in Ritschl and Herrmann. Yet Bultmann did not share the Reformed understanding of irresistible grace. Grace triumphs in our lives only in the measure that we permit it to triumph: "The depths of divine love are opened out only to him who allows himself to be emancipated from his attachment to the things of time and space and who allows Christ to effect this redemptive work of emancipation in his life."[76] Bultmann's real position seems to have been that we are saved by grace plus obedience rather than grace alone *(sola gratia)*.

Bultmann's most significant departure from the liberal tradition was his rediscovery of agape and his sharp differentiation of agape from eros. With uncanny insight he recognized that *works* of love are fundamentally easy, for "in them I remain my old self."[77] By contrast, the *act* of love is supremely difficult because "I give myself away in it, and attain my being only by losing it in this act."[78] Agape becomes real only by submission to the power of God, whereas eros is an integral element in the natural striving of humanity for perfection. Yet Bultmann refused to call agape a supernatural endowment for fear of sundering the principle of continuity between God and humanity. Instead true love signifies the release of possibilities within us through an encounter with the creative power or powers that shape human existence.

This brings us to Bultmann's break with the liberal idea of faith as a psychological experience *(Erlebnis)*. For him faith is not an experience of the vitality of nature—the animating principle of the self—but an encounter *(Ereignis)* with the power of being, which is outside us and yet within and around us. Whether this distinction can be maintained is dubious, and some critics of Bultmann are ready to assign him to the experientialist camp.[79]

In a number of other respects Bultmann differs from liberal theology: his questioning of natural theology; his focus on religious language, not just religious experience, as the theme of theology; and his desire to reinterpret rather than to eliminate the New Testament myth. Yet in all these areas he still manifested an empathy to liberal theology that clearly distinguishes him from the tradition of orthodoxy, even from the dialectical theology of Barth. While he refused to construct a natural theology, he continued to assign a prominent role to prefaith existence as a propadeutic to faith. He contended that the "natural man" can know "his lostness," though not the solution to the human dilemma. It is also appropriate to ask whether in his desire to reinterpret the biblical myth he did not in fact jettison it and replace it with a new myth that revolves around existential encounter with the World Spirit. In his protest against liberal theology Bultmann showed himself as belonging to this tradition. His criticism of liberalism was made from within, not outside, the movement.

Bultmann is best understood as a child of both the Enlightenment and the Reformation. According to Colin Brown, "Bultmann forces the New Testament into the mould of rationalistic scepticism, tempered by Existentialism."[80] At the same time, he resonates with Reformation theology in his strong emphasis on justification by grace, preaching as the primary means of grace and the unconditional, sacrificial quality of Christian love.

Bultmann can also be considered a child of Pietism, albeit a "Pietism of a higher order," as we find in Schleiermacher and Herrmann. His emphasis on the decision of faith, the necessity for obedience and service in love all point to a Pietistic mentality. At the same time Bultmann was an acerbic critic of the Pietists, particularly in their unsophisticated acceptance of New Testament mythology, a stance he regarded as obscurantist.

One can also detect a certain proclivity to gnosticism in Bultmann.[81] The Gnostics perceived the goal of religion as self-understanding and the human dilemma as the entrapment of spirit in nature. They also insisted on the unknowability and radical otherness of God.[82] Bultmann was a vigorous critic of Gnosticism, but he nevertheless found strong Gnostic influences in the Bible, including his beloved Gospel of John, though he acknowledged that the Gospel writers as well as Paul tried to combat these influences. Klaus Bockmuehl contended that by interpreting New Testament Christianity as essentially detachment from the world, "Bultmann has put a wedge between Christianity and the formation of the world. Above all others in this century, he has made Christianity a private affair."[83]

One should not summarily dismiss Bultmann as a false prophet, for he put his finger on some major problems in biblical interpretation. I concur with Otto Weber that "Bultmann has rightly taught us to understand the biblical concept of knowledge as being concrete, personal, and unspeculative."[84] At the same time, we must raise this question: In his emphasis on the personal and concrete character of biblical knowledge, does he not neglect the fact that the knowledge of faith is also conceptual and informative? Did not the apostles themselves use abstract reasoning to clarify and illumine the personal encounter between God and the believer? Does not faith have a noetic as well as an experiential side? In the biblical view, faith is not only trust and venture but also knowledge—not comprehensive knowledge but real knowledge. Moreover, it is knowledge of God and his purposes for the world and not simply knowledge of the self. Unless we know in whom we believe (2 Tim 1:12) we are most to be pitied, for then we are leading people into deeper darkness. The decision to which we are called is not simply to accept ourselves or be ourselves but to trust in the living Christ, the light that breaks into our world from the beyond and gives us hope not simply for a meaningful life but for a new world order—the kingdom of God— which will come in God's own time and way. Faith is not only a venture in the darkness but also a walking in the light (Eph 5:8), for we have been granted an anticipation of the glory that is to come through the gift of the Holy Spirit to the church. Bultmann's theological contribution would have been more balanced and biblically anchored had he supplemented his theology of the cross with a theology of the Holy Spirit.

·EIGHT·

THE BIBLE
& MYTH

I will speak to you in parables, unfold what has been hidden
since the foundation of the world.
M A T T H E W   1 3 : 3 5   N J B

When we told you about the power and the coming
of our Lord Jesus Christ, we were not slavishly repeating cleverly
invented myths; no, we had seen his majesty with our own eyes.
2 P E T E R   1 : 1 6   N J B

This story may not be just as the Lord told it, and yet may contain
in its mirror as much of the truth as we are able to receive,
and as will afford us scope for a life's discovery.
G E O R G E   M A C D O N A L D

The heart of Christianity is a myth which is also a fact.
The old myth of the Dying God . . . comes down from the heaven
of legend and imagination to the earth of history.
C . S . L E W I S

As a Western Scripture scholar, I am inclined to doubt these
[Gospel] stories, but as a historian I am obliged to take them as reliable.
P E T E R   S T U H L M A C H E R

The presence of myth and legend in the Bible has been a continuing source of embarrassment to conservatives and a pretext to liberals for dismissing large parts of the Bible as anachronistic. Theology must deal with this potentially explosive question, for it involves not simply the language of the Bible but its very truth.

Myth has generally had a negative connotation in the circles of higher criticism. It is frequently dismissed as a primitive mode of thinking in which inexplicable events are attributed to the intervention of deities.

Or it is a literary form that can yield some measure of truth about the human condition so long as it is not taken literally. Those who stand in the tradition of the history of religions school argue that Christianity is a syncretistic religion in which myth plays a formative role.

The views of Rudolf Bultmann, discussed in the last chapter, must be seen against this background. Bultmann wished to extricate the abiding truth of the biblical stories from their mythical trappings. For him myth is a description of divine activity in this-worldly terms. It objectifies the divine activity and projects it on the plane of worldly happenings.[1]

Karl Barth also viewed myth negatively, but he insisted that real myth is alien to the thought-world of the Bible. For him myths are stories of the gods induced by humanity's attempt to explain the phenomena of nature for the purpose of finding meaning and identity in life. The focus of myth is on the universal, not the particular; on the rhythm of nature, not the contingency of history. "Genuine myth," he said, "never means a genuinely pre-historical emergence, a beginning of the reality of man and his cosmos in encounter with distinct divine reality."[2]

Barth preferred the term *saga* to describe the wondrous events in Scripture that, though inaccessible to historical investigation, are related to real history. Because these events do not arise out of history but concern a divine intervention in history, they are superhistorical, not simply historical. They occur in history but they are not of history. Barth held that "saga as a form of historical narration is a *genre* apart."[3] Avery Dulles, who follows Barth at this point, understands saga as "a poetic and divinatory elaboration on history."[4] Barth had long argued that the biblical saga has a historical core, though this does not mean that saga yields precise history.

The renowned Old Testament scholar Gerhard von Rad also favored the term *saga* rather than *myth* to describe the panorama of events in the sacred history of Holy Scripture. For him a saga has a historical setting but a theological focus. Its concern is not with historical accuracy but with theological significance. Saga "in the garb and style of a narrative of bygone events tells of things that at the same time are thoroughly present."[5] Von Rad was adamant that saga is far from being "merely the product of poetic fantasy."[6] On the contrary, "it comprises 'the sum total of the living historical recollection of peoples. In it is mirrored in fact and truth the history of a people. It is the form in which a people thinks of its own history.' "[7]

Kenneth Hamilton, too, perceives the discrepancy between mythic language, which concerns subjective states of consciousness, and the language of the Bible, which is oriented about events in real history.[8] He prefers the term *parabolic* because it makes a place for God speaking through poetic imagery that is related to the historical. Parabolic language deals with the world realistically but not literally or symbolically (as in myth).

While recognizing the mythological cast of some of the early biblical stories, evangelical biblical scholar Gordon Wenham prefers to speak of "proto-historical narratives." But he is clear that we are not dealing with history or "at least history in the normal meaning of the term."[9] In his discussion of Genesis 2—3 he argues that the Spirit worked through the creative imagination of the biblical author, who described the origin of the problems that beset humankind in a story that is "absorbing, yet highly symbolic."[10]

A more positive understanding of myth is found in Reinhold Niebuhr, who held that myth should be taken not literally but seriously.[11] He regarded myth as a symbolic depiction of a truth of cosmic significance. It conveys a mystery that transcends the compass of human imagination. Yet we can show by our reason that this mystery makes sense of life and the world. He was convinced that the biblical myth casts considerable light on both the human predicament and human hope. Unlike primitive myth, which is prescientific, biblical myth is suprascientific. He also referred to secularized myth—a description of life forces in analogies and metaphors drawn from experience.

The question is whether Niebuhr dehistoricized the biblical themes. He saw the biblical story of the fall, for example, as a graphic portrayal of the universal experience of the transition from anxiety to sin. He spoke of the second coming of Christ as occurring "beyond history" and the resurrection of Christ as taking place on the boundary of history. It seems that faith is based on mythical symbolization of universal truth rather than on divine disclosure in real historical events.

For Jacques Ellul myth means the addition of theological significance to a fact—historical, psychological or merely human—which otherwise has no such obvious significance.[12] Myth is a poetic elaboration of fact for the purpose of bringing out its deeper implications. It does not destroy historical reality but provides an intuitive grasp of its wider dimensions. Historical events, he argues, can be pregnant with cosmic meaning. Thus the biblical story of the fall indicates the passage from human communion with God to a break in humanity's relationship with God in prehistory.[13]

Paul Tillich found the mythical language of the Bible extremely helpful in conveying the truth about the human condition. Myths are "symbols of faith combined in stories about divine-human encounters."[14] He recognized the reality of "broken myth" in which myth and critical thinking coexist. We should not demythologize but deliteralize the Bible, that is, apply rational criteria to the meaning of the religious symbols.

The difficulty with Tillich's position is that history appears to be important only to illustrate universal truth. It is not the historical Jesus Christ but the biblical picture of Christ that becomes the ruling norm in theological thinking. Thus Tillich's attention focused not on the historical fall but on the transcendent fall. For him, therefore, the very constitution of existence implies the transition from essence to existence.

Not surprisingly, Reinhold Niebuhr, whose position is more historically oriented, did not conceal his discomfort with Tillich's position.[15] Whereas Niebuhr saw the human malady in terms of historical guilt, Tillich preferred to speak of ontological fate. The emphasis in Tillich's thought seems to fall on the fatefulness of sin rather than on the human responsibility for it. Niebuhr complained that Tillich tried to make the biblical myth intelligible by means of philosophical and ontological categories that actually serve to subvert the biblical understanding.

For Paul Ricoeur the role of myth is to unveil the human condition and lead us to self-understanding. Theology conceptualizes religious discourse and thereby tends to lose sight of the primal meaning of myth: "Religious myths are falsely taken to be explanations rather than explorations of the human condition."[16] One critic rightly asks whether Ricoeur "allows the language of faith to speak of historical events or whether it only displays existential possibilities."[17]

C. S. Lewis was on much firmer ground, insisting that though much of the Bible is clothed in mythical language it is nonetheless focused on historical fact: "The heart of Christianity is a myth which is also a fact. The old myth of the Dying God, *without ceasing to be myth,* comes down from the heaven of legend and imagination to the earth of history. . . . By becoming fact it does not cease to be myth: that is the miracle."[18] By "myth" Lewis meant not fanciful innovation but "the deep, universal and provocative themes of religion, literature and symbolism that disclose the depths of the psyche. They evidence the incorrigibly human concern with spiritual matters."[19]

The Conversion of Myth

One does not need to be a Scripture scholar to perceive that the Bible has mythical elements, that is, stories of the gods and encounters with the gods. Yet these elements have been baptized and converted into the service of a divine revelation in history. One might say that they have been historicized—placed in a historical context. They have also been theologized in the sense that they are made to witness to God's self-revelation in the history of Israel culminating in Jesus Christ. Myth in the context of salvation history takes us beyond the gods as corporeal beings to God as pure Spirit.

It is an incontrovertible fact that much of the language or terminology of Scripture is highly figurative and frequently poetic: I prefer to call it *mythopoetic.* If myth is, as Dulles says, "a figurative representation of a reality which eludes precise description or definition,"[20] then myth indeed exists in the Bible. But this is myth in a qualified sense. This is myth in the context of sacred history (Oscar Cullmann). Much of the mythical imagery that was borrowed from the surrounding pagan culture has been transformed, placed in a new setting. According to Dulles, the pagan myths were "progressively purified, broken and sublimated" in Israel's history.[21] Sigmund Mowinckel describes the mythical residue in the Bible as "hallowed myth, purified myth, myth that mediates revelation."[22]

Elizabeth Achtemeier avers that "the Judaic, Christian, biblical faith overcomes the tyranny of nature's spiral, and the whole mythopoeic understanding of God and the world is dissolved." She sees the countering of mythology in Genesis 1, where "the priestly writers borrow fragments of the myth of the chaos dragon (Tiamat), but they completely demythologize the borrowed material." First, "God is the only God, and so there is no struggle involved between deities. God's creation is effortless. He speaks, and the world comes to be." "Second, God does not emanate out of the chaotic matter, nor is he contained in or bound up with his creation in any way. Rather, he stands over and above his world as its sovereign Lord and Creator." Finally, "Genesis 1 abandons mythopoeic thought by placing the creation within time. Not only are the individual acts of creation divided among seven days, but the creation of the world is made the beginning of the sacred history, and this is marked in the priestly account by the scheme of *toledoth* or generations (Gen. 2:4a; 5:1; 6:9; 10:1). The time of nature is therefore subjected to the time of God's purpose."[23]

Some scholars discern in Genesis 1:2 a mythological allusion that is actually contradicted by the story as a whole. Cuthbert Simpson comments that the idea of the Spirit "brooding upon" the chaos "has underlying it the idea of a cosmic egg which was hatched by the brooding Spirit, as by a bird, to produce the universe."[24] Whatever the mythological background, the story asserts against all pagan mythology the free creation of a living God, not the production of the earth out of the being of God.[25]

In Genesis 3:1–5 the Yahwist rejects the myth of a primeval principle of evil within the world.[26] The serpent is under the power of God. He is a creature who owes his existence to God. The biblical God is lord over both good and evil, over both history and nature.

In Genesis 6:1-4 we confront what appears to be an etiological Canaanite myth, the story of the sons of God having intercourse with the daughters of men and begetting a race of giants. This is an obvious remnant of ancient mythology adopted and reshaped as an episode in the larger story of the flood. Brevard Childs makes this astute observation:

> The essence of the myth was to assert that the divine spirit of the gods could be transmitted on the material-physical plane. In the mythical concept of reality, there is no qualitative distinction between the divine and the human. The Hebrew faith denied this categorically. By relating the *ruach* solely to the control of Yahweh, Israel confessed that this spirit remained the unique possession of Yahweh which he could withdraw at any time.[27]

The emergence of a superhumanity did not bring hope of immortality but instead the reduction of the life span of human beings. Von Rad comments that "in the rise of a super humanity, . . . overlapping decrees were broken, decrees by which God had separated the upper realm of the heavenly spiritual world from that of man. There had occurred a deterioration of all of creation, which cannot be more frightfully conceived."[28] With this rampant spread of sin there inexorably came divine judgment and retribution.

Even an obscure passage such as this one carries christological significance, as Walter Russell Bowie points out:

> If there is value in these verses it is not in anything they directly say, but in something which by contrast they suggest. In the old mythology, when the gods came down to earth, they came for their own gratification. They used human beings for their transient purposes and left them behind when they went back to their Olympus. The story of the Bible comes to its climax in the record of One "who, though he was in the form of God, did not count equality with God

a thing to be grasped, but . . . taking the form of a servant, . . . humbled himself and became obedient unto death, even death on a cross" (Phil. 2:6-8).[29]

The stories of the great flood in Genesis 7—8 bear a definite resemblance to the Babylonian story of the flood, but, as Raymond Abba observed, in the latter God in his anger destroys good and evil alike. In the biblical story the punishment is meted out to those deserving it, and the righteous are preserved not by the friendly help of another deity but by the direct action of the One who sends the flood.[30] The biblical story also emphasizes the fact that the judgments of God are accompanied by his mercy.

In Isaiah 14:12-21 we encounter a substantially modified version of the myth of Helal, the Daystar or Lightgiver.[31] In Canaanite mythology this myth referred to the thwarted "rebellion of the younger god against the ruling head of the pantheon."[32] In the perspective of Judeo-Christian faith it refers to the dethroning of the tyrannical ruler of Babylon, but more deeply to the cosmic fall of the demonic adversary of God—the real prince of Babylon.[33] The overthrow of the human tyrant is a manifestation on the plane of history of events in superhistory that transcend the compass of human imagination.

In Isaiah 51:9-10 the Babylonian myth of creation is transformed into the history of the exodus and the crossing of the Red Sea.[34] In Babylonian mythology Rahab is the goddess of chaos whom the god Marduk killed and whose body was used by him for the creation of earth and heaven. These mythological references are now poetic devices used by the prophetic writer to describe God's redemptive action in the history of Israel.[35] James Muilenburg comments: "Myth is never allowed its free range in the O.T.; it is characteristically historicized, but its employment gives to the historical revelation a new profundity."[36]

Foster McCurley makes the perceptive observation that the biblical writers were engaged in the "mythicization of history" as well as in the "historicization of myth."[37] What he means is that the biblical authors often began with the historical facts and then added mythological allusions, thus giving the facts more than simply historical significance.[38] McCurley points out that mythology is never the ultimate point of departure for the biblical writers, but they felt free to employ mythological imagery in explaining the full implications of the biblical revelation.

It is important to bear in mind that the Old Testament authors did not simply use mythical allusions to illustrate revelatory truth, but they typically subverted the myths of Canaan "by adopting imagery and narrative patterns and attributing them to Yahweh." For example, Genesis 1:16 depicts the sun and moon as ruling the day and night respectively; yet "they do so as created agents of God and are in that sense demythologized. Yahweh is the victorious divine warrior, far greater than what can be claimed for Baal the warrior, etc."[39]

In the New Testament an example of the conversion of pagan myth to the service of the gospel is the story of the woman and the dragon (Rev 12). It appears that John (or one of his sources) draws upon the ancient solar myth, firmly rooted in the popular imagination of that time, in which the primeval dragon challenges the sun god but is overthrown at the dawning of the new day. For John it is Jesus Christ, the Messiah of Israel, who finally defeats the dragon (now identified with Satan), and he does this within the sphere of earthly history through his death on the cross, for it was at the cross that Jesus entered his kingly glory. The woman is not the celestial mother goddess of pagan folklore but the personification of the messianic community—preexisting in heaven in some idealized form and then manifested on earth.[40]

Narrative Forms in the Bible

With the rise of genre criticism we are becoming more keenly aware of the remarkable diversity of the narrative forms in the Bible. In addition to remnants of mythology, we encounter saga, legend, epic, poetry, novella, fable,[41] historical narrative, narrated history and parable.[42] It is nevertheless an open question to what extent these relatively modern literary distinctions apply to ancient literature, especially to the Bible, which purports to give not a history of the people of Israel as such but a description of God's mighty acts in this history. If we designate some of the biblical stories as myth or saga, they must be seen as myth or saga *sui generis,* for the history they depict is unique and unrepeatable.

A saga might be defined as a creative and often colorful recounting of the deeds and experiences that have shaped the destiny of a particular people or of humanity as a whole.[43] The focus is not on recorded history *(Historie)* but on the wider significance of the dramatic events that give people their social and spiritual identity *(Geschichte).*[44] A helpful distinction might be made between saga and saga history. The former is a tale or story that has a historical basis, but its primary content is moral or theological, not historical. Saga history is a tale or story that is inextricably interwoven with history. The first eleven chapters in Genesis are probably saga, but the remainder are likely saga history.[45]

Some of the tales in Scripture may be categorized as didactic narratives. But does this necessarily mean didactic fiction? A credible case can be made that the apocryphal book of Judith is didactic fiction, but can the same be said of the book of Jonah or the book of Esther? A growing consensus in the scholarly world interprets Jonah as parabolic in that it intends to convey a spiritual truth in narrative form.[46] But conservative scholars generally resist this interpretation, seeing in the story real events in the prophet's own life. Shemaryahu Talmon calls Esther a "historicized wisdom-tale," and Bernhard W. Anderson and Carey A. Moore view it as a "historical novel," suggesting that it has a historical core.[47] History confirms the persecution of the Jews in Persia at that time, and the historicity of Mordecai also seems probable. We are not to infer, however, that the book offers an exact chronology of what really happened or that its intention is to give a report of exact history.

Even the parables of Jesus, which are generally acknowledged to be didactic narratives, are not necessarily fictional. The parable of the Last Judgment in Matthew 25 is intended to be a depiction of a real event in the eschatological future. The parable of Dives and Lazarus (Lk 16:19–

31), which has its basis in divine inspiration, surely gives a realistic glimpse of life beyond the grave.

The interspersion of myth and history is strikingly apparent in the accounts of the angel of the Lord going forth and slaying a large part of the army of the Assyrians who were besieging Jerusalem, then under King Hezekiah (2 Kings 19:35; 2 Chron 32:21; Is 31:8; 37:36). A scientific historian is constrained to explain this calamity in some other way—as decimation by a wasting disease or pestilence, for example. From my perspective of biblical realism, the angel of God really did bring down the Assyrians, but the imagery that this conjures up—the taking of a sword and cutting down—is perhaps the only way people of that time could have envisaged such an extraordinary happening.[48] Liberal scholars are inclined to treat this story as a legend, a poetic elaboration of a disastrous defeat suffered by the Assyrian king Sennacherib in Israel; the idea of an angel striking down the army is regarded as the fabrication of a lively religious imagination.

Even conservative scholars readily acknowledge the mythopoetic imagery in the book of Revelation, which depicts Christ as the rider of a white horse moving through history slaying the dragon, which is also the antichrist, the beast and the serpent (Rev 19:11—20:3).[49] This is mythical language but not fiction, for here we have a profound intuition into the spiritual realities at work within and behind history. Real events are being described, but the language is definitely figurative—intended to convey mysteries that elude historical precision as well as rational comprehension. The book of Revelation is falsified when the events it symbolizes are taken literalistically—for example, when the millennial reign of Christ is envisaged as one thousand actual years.[50]

The recognition of mythopoetic language in the Bible does not imply that the Bible is historical fiction (the position of some narrative theologians) but instead enhances the mystery of Scripture as a divine message in parabolic garb. I agree with Helmut Thielicke that "mythological thought must be honoured as the crib in which the Lord chose to lie."[51] We have the revelation of God in Jesus Christ in the swaddling clothes of human language, which certainly includes metaphor, simile and analogy as well as more precise forms of expression. Our language in reference to God himself and his actions in our midst will always fall short of precise or univocal description.

The church fathers, who were not burdened by the nominalism of modernity, which reduces truth to the particulars within the range of human experience, freely acknowledged the mythopoetic language of large parts of the Bible. For example, Origen declared that "when God is said to 'walk in the paradise in the cool of the day' and Adam to hide himself behind a tree, I do not think anyone will doubt that these are figurative expressions which indicate certain mysteries through a semblance of history and not through actual events."[52] Augustine interpreted the days of creation in Genesis 1 as actually referring to ages of long duration.[53]

Myth might be defined as imagistic language describing the dramatic interaction between divinity and humanity, an interaction that cannot be captured in literal or univocal language. Myth is here a comprehensive term that covers poetry, parable, fable, legend, tale, novella and saga, as well as mythology in the narrow sense. Myth describes what cannot be fully contained in the human imagination. To affirm the mythical element in the Bible means to affirm mystery and paradox in religion. Myth is graphic rendition as opposed to logical predication.[54]

We must take care to differentiate this understanding of myth from that held by Bultmann, Willi Marxsen, Ernst Käsemann and other rationalistic critics. In contrast to Bultmann I contend that the mythopoetic imagery of the Bible is not the projection of inner experiences on the plane of history but a vehicle by which the objective intrusion of God into history is described. Myth in the biblical context refers to real events in history but events that surpass human understanding.

In 2 Kings 2:11-12 the translation of Elijah into heaven is depicted in terms of the chariot of Israel and its horsemen ascending into the sky (cf. 2 Kings 13:14). This is neither an invention of an imaginative writer nor an exact reproduction of what really transpired. Yet it refers to a real objective happening that could be described only in language available to the writer at that time. Elijah was literally assumed into heaven, but this does not mean that the language in the story is therefore literal rather than symbolic or figurative.

In acknowledging the existence of mythopoetic language in Scripture, I am not suggesting that the reality this language describes is mythological and therefore fanciful. On the contrary, the imagistic language of Scripture generally has a solid anchor in real happenings, but these events are inaccessible to historical investigation or confirmation. There was a real creation ex nihilo, but history is powerless to record or certify it. There was a real fall in primal history, but history itself can provide no light on this event. There was a real, bodily resurrection of Christ from the grave, but history can neither deny nor prove it. Historical study can point to the evidence of the witnesses (Acts 1:3), but this evidence does not make the resurrection of Christ even a historical probability. It proves only that a series of extraordinary occurrences moved a great many persons to assert that it really happened. From the perspective of natural reason the resurrection of Christ is a historical impossibility, but faith grasps what reason cannot comprehend.

On the one hand Christians should be open to the principle of historical and literary criticism of the biblical texts, for uncovering the nature of the language of the text and its historical background can throw much light on what really happened in history. On the other hand we should resist the naturalistic presuppositions that higher critics bring to the text and thereby distort its real meaning. As critics of the critics we must reject uniformitarianism—that everything happens within a closed order of cause and effect. In this view miracles understood as divine interventions in history cannot happen. We must also repudiate historical and cultural determinism—that an investigation into their historical and cultural milieu can *wholly* account for the ideas expressed in the Bible. In this perspective the human mind cannot rise above its historical and cultural context. An implication is that humans cannot therefore accurately predict the future and that the prophetic books must have been written after the time their prophecies came true. Finally, we must distance ourselves from an evolutionary view of history—that profound ideas regarding God and his relationship to the world must be related to a later stage in civilization.

When one employs terminology such as *myth* or *saga* to describe the events of sacred history, it is helpful to distinguish between different kinds of myth or saga in the Bible. Indeed, they are not all of the same character: some can be shown to be much more oriented toward real history than others. One kind of myth is a pictorial exposition of a spiritual or universal truth, which may also have a historical context or allusion.[55] We can think here of the Nephilim in Genesis 6, the tower of Babel, the story of the flood, Jonah and the great fish, and perhaps also the story of the fall (which may have both a generic and a specific meaning).

Again myth may take the form of a pictorial representation of a historical, prehistorical or metahistorical event. We can here include the creation, the fall from Paradise, the fall of the angels, the descent of Christ into Hades, the intercession of Christ in heaven, the dawning of the millennium, the second coming of Christ and the new Jerusalem coming down in glory (Rev 21).

Finally, myth may constitute a pictorial reconstruction (even recording) of an event in history or superhistory. We might here consider the crossing of the Red Sea, Moses at the burning bush, the giving of the law to Moses on Mount Sinai, the ascent of Elijah to heaven, the virgin birth of Christ, his baptism, his resurrection from the dead, his ascension into heaven and the descent of the Spirit at Pentecost. Even more than in the other two categories we see myth interspersed with history. Poetic, dramatic language is employed to describe actual occurrences in the past.

In most if not all the cases listed in the preceding paragraphs, designations other than myth may be more felicitous—artistic narration, realistic narrative, saga history, saga, story—though perhaps only the last two would cover all the examples given. Myth has pejorative connotations because of its rootage in ancient mythology; yet because it is widely used in the current discussion and because it contains nuances of meaning that have abiding value, I prefer to allow it a modest role in Christian discourse.[56] When one employs it, one must do so with a measure of caution.[57] Myth in the Bible does not mean that the events depicted have no basis in reality—only that they are set forth in dramatic, imaginative language. The stories may have a firm anchor in history, yet at the same time contain legendary elements.

It is important to keep in mind that what determines the shape of biblical religion is not myth or saga or story but the event of God becoming man in Jesus Christ. This is the reality that binds together all the other realities mirrored and recorded in Scripture. The events in sacred history culminating in God's self-revelation in Jesus Christ throw light on this revelation, but only those with the eyes to see can begin to fathom this mystery. The message of faith is mediated through many narrative forms, but it is grounded in fact, not in narrative. Yet this is not bare fact but interpreted fact: the final criterion for faith is neither history nor myth but God's self-interpretation relayed by the Holy Spirit through the prophetic and apostolic witness in Scripture.

Evangelical Christians should avoid hard and fast positions regarding every event or miracle recorded in the Bible, though on events that are integral to the message of faith we must not equivocate. This does not mean, however, that we are obliged to accept everything recorded as being exactly the way it is described, even in the stories about Jesus. We should remember that with the exception of a few recorded Aramaic phrases we do not have any of the original words of Jesus and that what we know of Jesus is through the testimony of ear- and eyewitnesses. We may accept, as I do, the historical reliability of their witness without being bound to modes of expression or understandings of life and the cosmos that belong to another age.[58]

The events of sacred history cannot be verified by the canons of historical science, but they can be illumined. Historical science can lend a measure of evidential support to the exodus of Israel from Egypt, the exile of Israel in Babylon, the exorcisms of Jesus, the story of the empty tomb and the outpouring of the Spirit at Pentecost. We are not to conclude, however, that history can lead us to the revelational meaning of these events. It is possible to accept the literal empty tomb without believing in the bodily resurrection of Christ. It is even possible to accept the literal resurrection of Christ from the grave without recognizing him as the divine Savior of the world.[59] Jesus indeed was not only raised from the dead, but he was raised for our justification (Rom 4:25), and only when we grasp this second point have we apprehended the real Word of God. Only faith can lay hold of the spiritual reality to which the text or sign points, and faith itself is a gift of God. Faith does not deny critical reasoning but turns reasoning around so that it is made to serve the search for a deeper and fuller understanding of the mystery of God's self-revelation in Christ, including his atoning death on the cross and his glorious resurrection from the grave.

The Bible as Myth and History

The Bible is both myth and history, and herein lies its truth and its power.[60] The *logos* or Word of God is relayed through language that is for the most part imagistic or mythopoetic *(mythos)*. The myth refers to the form of the Bible; the truth refers to the content. Just as wheat is given in the husk, so divine wisdom is communicated through time-bound language. The wheat metaphor breaks down, however, in this respect: the wheat's husk becomes chaff that can be discarded, but the Bible's mythopoetic form cannot be jettisoned with the aim of arriving at a pure conceptual language. When the veil is lifted in the eschaton and we see God face to face, the situation will be vastly different and a new kind of language will then be operative.

The truth of Scripture is both historical and metahistorical. It is revealed in history but at the same time transcends history. It has universal applicability and significance even while it has a historical focus and setting. The truth of faith is the message of salvation realized and fulfilled in Jesus Christ, who is both a historical person and the divine Son of God. This truth is both personal and conceptual. One can also infer that faith is conceptual as well as existential.

We have the truth of revelation not outside its mythical form but in and through this form. The myth must not be set aside but illumined by the Holy Spirit. The truth shines through the myth as we endeavor to unravel its revelational meaning in faith. We should seek not to de-mythologize—to interpret the myth in the light of existential self-under-standing—but to expound—to interpret the myth in the light of the revelation that it enshrines. We should not try to desupernaturalize the myth, as some secular theologians suggest, but instead to understand, bowing in reverence before the supernatural dimension within history. The truth of the myth can be restated only in paradoxical terms, for the reality it speaks of appears in history in the form of the absolute paradox (God in human flesh). Reason cannot decipher or fully explain the myth, but it can illumine the myth in a servant role. It cannot resolve the mystery and paradox, but it can serve this mystery in the form of in-telligible proclamation.

There are dangers in treating the Bible as both myth and history, and thus we need to tread warily in this area. One danger is to convert the gospel itself into myth,[61] whereas the gospel counters myth by focusing it on history rather than on nature. Or the gospel may be treated simply as story, whereas the narrative form in Scripture is, for the most part, anchored in real history. Still another temptation is to interpret the gospel within a naturalistic framework; this method would effectively rule out the miraculous element, which is decisive in the gospel proc-lamation.

We must be critical not only of the text but also of the critics who are inclined to lose sight of its theological meaning and impact by trying to bring it into accord with modern scientific understanding. Käsemann blithely concludes that the battle among New Testament scholars over the miracle stories of the Gospels is over, "not perhaps as yet in the arena of church life, but certainly in the field of theological science. It has ended in the defeat of the concept of miracle which has been traditional in the Church."[62] In his judgment the "great majority of the Gospel miracle-stories must be regarded as legends."[63] Yet Käsemann and other critics cannot account for the fact that miracles—signs and wonders—continue to follow the proclamation of the gospel. Most of the miracles of the New Testament have been duplicated in the lives of the great saints through the ages, but these miracles too are greeted with skepticism—not on the basis of hard historical evidence but on the basis of submission to a naturalistic philosophy that fails to account for the unpredictable and cataclysmic in human experience.

Randel Helms dismisses the facticity of the miracle stories of the multiplication of loaves and fishes, alleging that they were inserted to establish continuity with comparable miracle stories of Elijah and Elisha in 1 and 2 Kings. He interprets the story of the loaves and fishes as "a self-reflexive fiction, based on the New Testament understanding of the mirroring of Jesus' career in the Old Testament."[64] He does not consider that in the unfolding of sacred history similar phenomena may well be duplicated or expanded as a means by which the Spirit of God brings fuller light to bear on the divine plan of redemption.

In the opinion of the Dominican biblical scholar Richard Murphy, it is now possible in the light of our expanded geographical knowledge to understand the burning bush in Exodus 3 as a desert bush aglow with a blaze of flowers. But this approach uses imagistic language to explain away the reality rather than to underline the mystery in this reality. Surely it strains the bounds of plausibility to suggest that Moses, who was certainly familiar with the colorations of the desert, would have been struck with awe by a desert bush that only appeared to be aflame through the interplay of natural forces. To hold that such a phenomenon inspired an unknown author to exercise creative imagination is to consign the entire tale to the purely legendary.[65]

Critics often make absolutist claims that belie the fact that they too are subject to historical conditioning. For example, Lawrence Boadt declares that since "the purpose of the Joshua narrative is to glorify Yahweh who gives Israel its victories and its lands, we can be *absolutely* sure that the editors and authors have magnified the victories and downplayed the defeats a great deal" (italics mine).[66] He may have a point, but can we be "absolutely sure"?

In trying to assess the historical reliability of the biblical record, we need to give serious consideration to studies by reputable scholars that tend to reinforce the traditional position.[67] Birger Gerhardsson, professor of New Testament studies for many years at the University of Uppsala, presents a convincing case on the basis of redaction criticism that the words put into the mouth of Jesus by the early church were generally close if not identical to Jesus' actual words handed down through oral tradition.[68] Tübingen's Rainer Riesner contends that Jesus probably spoke in a pithy, aphoristic style that made it easy for his followers faithfully to remember and to record his words.[69] Peter Stuhlmacher, also of the University of Tübingen, admits frankly that as a Western Scripture scholar he would be inclined to doubt the historical character of the Gospel stories, but as a historian he is obliged to treat them as reliable.[70] Against Hans Frei and other narrative theologians, Stephen Prickett concludes: "However different the biblical authors' notions of 'history' may have been from our own, we have no reason to suppose that they did not believe that they were relating 'fact' and not 'fact-likeness.' "[71]

Barth stoutly repudiated the notion that the biblical texts were "essentially metaphorical or symbolic objectifications of the emotive responses, however profound, which sacred objects or events had aroused in the religious subjects by whom those texts were produced."[72] On the contrary, the biblical authors witnessed to events in real history, though they did not always present a straightforward account but frequently introduced a theological interpretation that was oriented to the significance of these events for people of faith.

What makes the Bible unique is not that it is composed of various literary forms but that these forms are focused on an objective revelation of God to real people in history. Myth does not remain myth, but myth becomes fact and is thereby transformed. Heinrich Schlier prefers to say that myth in the New Testament was "historicized" in the sense that "by being referred to Jesus Christ it was destroyed as myth, but the understanding of God and world and man implied in it was taken up and clarified" in order to give the historical revelation of the crucified and risen Jesus Christ a language appropriate to its framework of meaning.[73] In this critical reinterpretation myth comes to an end, but its end is also its fulfillment.

This does not mean that the Bible can be reduced to an enumeration of historical facts, for then the key to biblical understanding would lie in the science of historiography, not theology.[74] We would do well to remember that history itself is never bare fact but always fact plus interpretation. Biblical history is shaped by theological interpretation under the guidance of the Holy Spirit, and this accounts for the frequent allusions to the divine hand at work in history. History as a science concerns the realm of the phenomenal, not the noumenal. Thus the central content of the Bible is outside the compass of strictly historical knowledge. The Bible is essentially neither history nor myth but a historical witness to the dramatic intersection of time and eternity in Jesus Christ, often depicted in mythopoetic language. It is *Geschichte*—focusing on the divine intrusion in historical events—rather than *Historie*—a recording of events as they appear to an objective observer.[75] It is saga—an imaginative, poetic narration that takes into account the interaction between God and humanity. It is the perception of what transpires on the plane of history through the eyes of faith.

With Barth, George Hunsinger and others, I affirm a hermeneutic of biblical realism as opposed to a hermeneutic of literalism on the one hand and a hermeneutic of expressivism on the other.[76] Our goal is to explicate the meaning of a revelation that objectively took place in real history but was not generally intended to transmit exact history. But neither were the biblical texts intended as symbolic objectifications of emotional responses, as in symbolist theology. In the symbolistic or expressivistic approach, represented among others by Paul Knitter, "myth-symbols save" but "historical facts do not. . . . It is only when we are grasped by and find ourselves responding with our whole being to a symbol, myth, or story that we are encountering the divine, touching and being touched by 'the Ground of Being,' and experiencing grace."[77] For Knitter symbol and myth are salvific "not because they correspond to some antecedent objective reality, but because they reach into a person's innermost being, thereby renewing the whole self."[78] In effect Knitter dismisses the claim of the apostles that they were eyewitnesses of the glory of the resurrected Christ (2 Pet 1:16).

We must not, however, fall into the opposite error of interpreting every event reported in Scripture as occurring just as it is depicted. The sagas of biblical history are not necessarily to be taken literally, though they are always to be taken seriously. For example, to treat the tower of Babel story as secular history would then permit it to be used as documentary evidence of how human languages came into existence. To view it as saga is to affirm that the craving for power and fame at the dawn of human civilization unfailingly resulted in the ineradicable inability of human beings to understand and to communicate with one another at a deep level. Similarly, the story of the flood cannot furnish a scientific explanation for the survival of the animal creation in the deluge of antiquity, nor can the story of Noah and his sons (in Genesis 9) and the table of nations (in Genesis 10) be used to explain the origin of the races of the world.[79] Both the tower of Babel and the flood stories have a basis in real history, since there is historical evidence for temple towers in ancient Mesopotamia[80] and for a catastrophic (though not necessarily universal) flood in primeval history, but to view these stories as literal history is gravely to misunderstand them.[81]

Often the effort to impose a literalistic interpretation on the biblical events falsifies their meaning. For example, the tendency in conservative scholarship to identify the angels who had intercourse with humans (Gen 6:1-4) as descendants of Seth is a glaring illustration of a misreading of the text in the interest of theological or scientific harmonization.[82] Von Rad voiced the dominant scholarly position on this issue when he contended on the basis of the latest data (including research into comparable tales in other ancient cultures) that the "sons of God" are "beings of the upper heavenly world."[83] They belong to the world of the *elohim* rather than to the race of mortals. Such a conclusion does not, however, open the Bible to the charge of error, for this story must be seen not as exact history but as an effort to bring a fragment of primeval mythology into the service of the biblical revelation. To impose on the text an a priori theological principle (angels who are purely spiritual cannot marry) is to lapse into an obscurantism that falsifies the text.

I heartily agree with evangelical theologian Kenneth Hamilton, who warns that we must not insist

> that all the statements of Scripture are literally true, and then proceed to interpret biblical statements in terms of modern ideas of factual accuracy. For this is to demand that language forged in other linguistic traditions shall conform to the pattern of language-usages familiar to us today; that is, to the usages developed since the sixteenth century, when empirical thinking began to assert itself over against the thought-forms of the prescientific consciousness—the period in which prose began to be rigidly separated from poetry. Instead of respecting historical actuality, this is to disregard it. It is to fail to take the patterns of biblical language with sufficient seriousness.[84]

In liberal theology the Bible is partly folklore and partly history.[85] In fundamentalist theology the Bible is almost completely literal history. In the progressive evangelical theology I uphold, the Bible is a true but very human witness to a reality beyond history that has at the same time become incarnate in history. The Bible is myth that is transformed by revelation and made to serve the particular rather than the universal.[86] It is myth that becomes fact in content without ceasing to be myth in form. In the Bible we are introduced not to an abstract metaphysical concept of God but to the God who rides the clouds of the storm and walks the face of the earth—figurative language, to be sure, but depicting a real, living God who acts and speaks in a real, human history.[87]

I cannot emphasize too strongly that when speaking of the mythical element in the Bible, I am referring basically to its language or mode of expression, not to the historical and superhistorical realities that compose the content of its witness. At the same time, this language gains its meaning and efficacy only when united with these realities. The Bible is not the product of myth in the Bultmannian sense—the imaginative projection of human longings upon the screen of history—but the mostly graphic record of events that happened in a particular history in the past. Yet these revelatory events paradoxically bring fulfillment to the longings and aspirations of fallen humanity for communion with the eternal.

The key to unlocking the mystery of the text lies not in exercising the religious imagination nor in internalizing the story that the text records. Instead, it lies in being grasped by the Spirit of God, the ultimate author of the text, as he speaks through the text clarifying its original meaning, which is defined by the context of the salvation history in which it is set. We must avoid both the Scylla of trying to align the biblical message with the modernistic worldview that rules out the supernatural and the Charybdis of uncritically accepting the animistic worldview that pervades the biblical world but is sharply challenged and transcended by the revelation that enters into this world, bringing light from the beyond to bear on the human condition in the here and now.

T R U T H   I N
B I B L I C A L   &
P H I L O S O P H I C A L
P E R S P E C T I V E

For the Lord is good; His mercy is everlasting,
and His truth endures to all generations.
P S A L M   1 0 0 : 5   N K J

Those who live by the truth come to the light
so that it may be clearly seen that God is in all they do.
J O H N   3 : 2 1   R E B

Do not leave my cry unanswered. Whisper words
of truth in my heart, for you alone speak truth.
A U G U S T I N E

In its deepest sense . . . *truth* is a condition of heart,
soul, mind, and strength towards God and towards our fellow—
not an utterance, not even a *right* form of words.
G E O R G E   M A C D O N A L D

Truth in Christianity is something which *happens,*
something which is bound to a special place, to a special time,
to a special personality.
P A U L   T I L L I C H

T he history of philosophy does not provide us with a monolithic
conception of truth, only with diverse approaches that are often
difficult to reconcile. Truth is basically what one can discover,
conceive or perceive on one's own. Truth is a possibility that must be

grasped, though how this is done differs according to the philosophy in question.

In the Hellenistic ethos, particularly as we see it in Plato and Socrates, truth *(alētheia)* is making manifest what is hidden.[1] A dualistic world-view is assumed, in which true being is contrasted with changing sense perception. The goal is to break through appearance to the unchangeable reality of pure being, which is hidden from natural perception. Truth dwells in the depths beneath the surface of our existence. Because the surface is constantly changing, it is delusive. The depths constitute the eternal, which is certain and dependable.

For Plato truth is the unveiling of unchangeable reality through rational dialectic.[2] Truth is penetrating to the essence of things. Because it is hidden within the depths of human existence, it is found by digging and questioning. It must be uncovered through the sometimes painful process of recollection *(anamnēsis)*. What is hidden must be brought out in the open (eduction). The human condition is one of forgetfulness concerning our origin in the eternal. We can overcome this state of ignorance by remembering. Truth is the discovery of the eternal as the ground and depth of the soul.

Perhaps the most common approach to truth is the correspondence theory, which has a long history going back to the Greeks, Romans and other ancient peoples. Besides ontological truth Plato also entertained the idea of descriptive truth, signifying the substantial correspondence of our judgments with the actual state of things. Thomas Aquinas defined truth as the correspondence of subject matter to the mind *(adequatio rei et intellectus)*. For the British empiricist John Locke truth lay in apprehending things to be as they really are. To say that "God is" means that our idea of God corresponds to an existent being.[3] For Leibniz truth consisted in the correspondence of a proposition with reality. In Alfred North Whitehead's philosophy truth is "the conformation of Appearance to Reality."[4] Reflecting a more empirical bent, Henry Nelson Wieman defined truth as "the correct designation and description of features of the world."[5]

To understand truth basically in terms of correspondence between the mind and the exterior world reflects a dualistic view of reality, presupposing a bifurcation between mind and matter, spirit and nature. While the correspondence theory is present in idealistic as well as naturalistic thought, it is more at home in the milieu of modern realism and naturalistic empiricism.

A quite different understanding is mirrored in the coherence theory of truth, in which knowledge is a system of logically interrelated truths. Truth is not agreement with external reality but congruence with the whole of reality. The criterion is the "systematic coherence of the All" or "experience as a whole." This approach to truth is generally associated with idealistic philosophy, which envisages reality as spirit or idea rather than matter. The idealistic system is implicative: each phase of the argument implies all the rest. The whole includes and determines the parts. For the idealist philosopher F. H. Bradley the criteria for truth were coherence and comprehensiveness. For G. W. F. Hegel truth was suprapersonal, conceptual and universal.

Just as the correspondence theory is roughly correlative with dualism, so the coherence theory has its basis in monism. In most cases this is a monism of spirit or mind, but in someone like Thomas Hobbes, in whom rationalism and empiricism came together, truth consisted in "the coherence of one's speech and thought as a symbolic system."[6] For Hegel the real is the rational and the truth is the whole—a stance not uncharacteristic of philosophies oriented toward systematic comprehensiveness and coherence.

Another venerable tradition in philosophy is mysticism, which, like idealism, seeks to overcome the subject-object antithesis by finding an overarching unity that dissolves particularity and individuality. In mystical philosophy ultimate reality or the One is not a rational principle to which we are led by dialectical speculation (as in Socrates and Plato) but the fount of infinite fecundity that we draw on to realize our desire (eros) for the perfect good.[7] Our purpose is not so much to understand the One or the All but to enter into it by an ecstatic transcending of the self. The mystic seeks identification with essential being or with the whole of reality. Unlike the idealist, whose goal is a unified picture of the whole of reality, the mystic claims that ultimate reality eludes conceptual mastery but is not bereft of a noetic quality. The mystical experience transcends the reach of discursive reason, though not the power of the imagination nor the passion of love. This experience is ineffable and incommunicable, but it can be described in poetic or metaphorical language that is meaningful to those who have a similar experience.[8]

Truth for the mystics is the vision of the undifferentiated unity behind the world of appearance rather than a comprehensive grasp of the rational structure of all things. Truth is not knowledge of the ultimate, arrived at by deductive or inductive reasoning, but a flash of insight that brings us into experiential contact with ultimate reality. Like idealism, mysticism is associated with monism and pantheism (or panentheism). God is frequently pictured as the eternal silence, the infinite abyss, or the infinite depth or ground of being that escapes rational apprehension but speaks to the yearning within the human heart.

We come finally to the pragmatic theory of truth, associated with such names as William James, John Dewey, Charles Peirce and F. C. S. Schiller. The criterion for truth is workability and utility. If something enhances human happiness and welfare and broadens human understanding, it can be regarded as true insofar as it serves humanity. The true is what is conducive to human well-being, what truly satisfies the human soul. To James "the true is the name of whatever proves itself to be good in the way of belief."[9] "Truth *happens* to an idea. It *becomes* true, is *made* true by events."[10] For Peirce and Dewey truth is not just privately useful, but it "must be socially as well as experimentally verifiable."[11]

Biblical Understandings

In both the Old and New Testaments truth (Hebrew *emeth;* Greek *alētheia*) has varying connotations, but basically it means genuineness, veracity, faithfulness and steadfastness. Truth sometimes connotes the right description of external reality. Indeed, regard for facts is considered indispensable for the right administering of justice (Zech 7:9; 8:16). More often it signifies standing firm, remaining faithful to the end: "Truth spoken stands firm for ever, but lies live only for a moment" (Prov 12:19 NEB). As the psalmist says, "The word of the LORD holds true, and all his work endures" (Ps 33:4 REB).

In the Johannine writings truth is inseparable from grace, since its perception rests on a divine gift. It is said of Jesus Christ that he was "full of grace and truth" (Jn 1:14; cf. 1:17 NRSV). Truth is also associated with obedience. One can know the truth only insofar as one abides in Christ through the continuous life of faith (8:31-32). We are told that "those who do what is true come to the light, so that it may be clearly seen that their deeds have been done in God" (3:21 NRSV).

Both Testaments often picture truth as God's redeeming, re-creating activity (Ps 43:3; Jn 8:32; 1 Tim 2:4; 2 Tim 2:8-10; Jas 1:18). God's word is not chained (2 Tim 2:9), but it breaks through the barriers of fear and unbelief and restores to life those who were once dead in sin. Every word that proceeds from the mouth of God does not return to him empty but accomplishes the purposes that God intends (Is 55:10-11; 45:23; 2 Cor 9:10).

In the deepest sense truth is identified with God himself, and the stamp of truth therefore characterizes both his words and his works. Truth is not so much an idea as a person, not so much a formulation as an act. This note is especially evident in the Johannine writings: "I am the way, and the truth, and the life; no one comes to the Father, but by me" (Jn 14:6; cf. 15:1). John's words that "the law was given through Moses," but "grace and truth came through Jesus Christ" (1:17) show he was speaking not of discursive, propositional truth (which obviously characterized the law) but of liberating, transforming truth, truth as rejuvenating power and energy (cf. 6:63; 2 Cor 3:6). The Holy Spirit is described as "the Spirit of truth" (Jn 14:17), the one who will guide the church into all truth (16:13). Christians are urged to love "not in word or speech, but in truth and action" (1 Jn 3:18 NRSV). Only in this way will we know that we are "from the truth" (v. 19). The truth "will convince us in his presence, even if our own feelings condemn us" (vv. 19-20 NJB).

Truth in the Bible is indissolubly related to concrete life and obedience, even though it is never devoid of conceptual content. It is not "a theoretical insight" that "one must obtain in order subsequently to act on one's own," but "active insight, religious belief, and communion with God in Christ—all in one."[12]

Wolfhart Pannenberg maintains that truth in the Bible is essentially historical and ultimately eschatological.[13] Truth is what proves itself in time, climaxing in the eschaton. Helmut Thielicke made a similar observation: "This Word is historical not merely in the sense of being grounded in history but also as it is addressed to historical situations. Both the authors and the recipients of verbal messages are subject to the process of history."[14]

At the same time we must not overlook the fact that the God of biblical faith transcends history, that his dwelling place is eternal, unshakable and incorruptible, surpassing even the highest heaven (1 Kings 8:27; 2 Chron 2:6). No mortal has ever seen God (Jn 1:18) because God is never an object of perception, a datum in history accessible to human sight and understanding. He enters into history, but he is always hidden in events and actions that are illuminating only when his Spirit gives us inner eyes to see what cannot be seen directly.[15] Thielicke acknowledged that in some sense the truths of the faith are eternal, for they are certainly applicable to all peoples in every generation.[16]

Truth in biblical religion is both transformative and informative. Jesus claimed that he told the truth and that he bore witness to the truth (Jn 8:40, 45; 18:37). He was intimating not that his words were necessarily in conformity with external reality but that they presented an accurate picture of God's plan and purpose for human existence. His Jewish interrogators could not grasp what he was saying because they did not abide in the truth (8:43-47). To be in the truth means to abide in God; to be in error means to be separated from God. We cannot fully grasp or appreciate the claims of Jesus until our inner eyes are opened by the Spirit of Jesus. To know the truth means to be seized by grace.

I do not wish to downplay or deny the propositional element in revelation, but this element is in the service of the personal. Emil Brunner was right that personal correspondence most nearly describes the biblical understanding of faith,[17] but one should keep in mind that he also allowed for true statements about God and the world. His point was that we cannot speak truly of God until we are in personal communion with God. Truth can indeed be presented and conveyed by specific affirmations, but unless the Spirit of God is active in these affirmations, their truth remains inaccessible to us. I am speaking about affirmations concerning the will and purpose of God, affirmations that belong to sacred history. Any person can know purely factual truth, but only the redeemed can know truth that liberates and empowers.

The Bible is to be prized not so much because it enumerates religious and moral truths (scriptures of other religions do the same) but because it leads us into truth (Ps 25:5; Jn 16:13), it brings us into contact with the One who is himself the truth. It could not do this, however, unless its witness to the truth were reliable and trustworthy. The Spirit of God can persuade us of the truth of Scripture because he is the ultimate source of this truth.

Paul testified, "Every word we ever addressed to you bore the mark of truth; and the same holds of the proud boast we made in the presence of Titus: that also has proved true" (2 Cor 7:14 NEB). Truth is what proves itself as we live in its light and power. The apostolic witness bears the mark of truth because truth informs it and illumines it for those who diligently seek truth with all their heart and soul.

Truth is the light that overcomes the darkness (Jn 1:5) because it exposes darkness and thereby calls for a decisive break in the old way of thinking and living. Truth is not the manifestation of something that already is (the Hellenistic view) but the creation of something new in personal life and history. Truth is a call to decision, a summons to obedience. But it is also something more: it provides the power to decide and obey. "Give what you command, and command what you will," implored Augustine, who trenchantly perceived the inseparability of truth and grace.[18]

Faith's Encounter with Philosophy

As the Christian faith established itself in the classical world, it began to accommodate to classical thought. In their attempts to counter pagan philosophy, the apologists and church fathers borrowed frequently from their opponents. The synthesis of biblical faith and idealistic-mystical thought became paradigmatic in the early and medieval churches. The living God who acts in history was gradually replaced by a static Absolute who towers above history. God was even said to be beyond love and passion (John Scotus Erigena). Attention came to focus not on the historical incarnation but on the birth of the Son of God in the human soul (Meister Eckhart). The self-sacrificing love of agape, celebrated in the New Testament, was overshadowed by the self-regarding love of eros. Augustine's *caritas* proved to be an unsatisfactory synthesis of the two loves, in which the climb upward to heavenly perfection figured more prominently than the thrust outward to the crying needs of the world.[19]

This legacy was especially pronounced in Christian mysticism, both East and West. In the words of Simone Weil, a modern devotee of this kind of mysticism, "If we go down into ourselves we find that we possess exactly what we desire."[20] In biblical perspective, we do not find God in the depths of our being, but he finds us: "The lamp of the LORD searches the spirit of a man; it searches out his inmost being" (Prov 20:27 NIV).

Against the idealistic-mystical ethos of the ancient world Brunner insisted that "truth is in God's own Word alone; and what is in me is not truth. This is why faith is transcendental; that is, in faith the Ego is independent of its own conditions and rests solely in that which is not here, but there—in God's Word."[21] For Brunner the Word of God is primarily Jesus Christ—God incarnate in human flesh.

Rationalism was also part of the classical legacy—being found in both

Plato and Aristotle as well as in the Stoics. In the developing theological consensus truth became a universal principle analogous to Plato's eternal ideas. Faith was seen as assent to correct propositions. Revelation was understood as a communication of principles, doctrines and various kinds of information. The logic of deduced conclusions supplanted the logic of adduced meanings—meanings gleaned from reflection on history. The rationalistic character of truth was especially evident in the early apologists, the medieval scholastics and the luminaries of Protestant orthodoxy.[22]

With the late Renaissance and continuing into the Enlightenment of the eighteenth century the emphasis was ever more on the propositional character of truth. For Leibniz truth consisted in the correspondence of a proposition with reality, possible or actual.[23] For Thomas Hobbes "truth and falsity" can be predicated only of "propositions," never of "things."[24] Descartes saw basic spiritual reality as propositional, though he also envisaged a basic material reality. Whereas in the biblical view truth is fundamentally fidelity, integrity and constancy, in the modern view it is basically correctness, precision and accuracy. For A. A. Hodge and Benjamin Warfield, representing conservative Presbyterian thought, the Bible gives us "a correct statement of facts or principles intended to be affirmed. . . . Every statement accurately corresponds to truth just as far forth as affirmed."[25]

Although Paul Tillich's theology is on the whole more Hellenistic than Hebraic, he recognized what makes the biblical notion of truth distinctive:

> Truth in Christianity is something which *happens,* something which is bound to a special place, to a special time, to a special personality. Truth is something new, something which is *done* by God in history, and, because of this, something which is *done* in the individual life. Truth is hidden, truth is mystery—in Christianity as well as in Greek thought. But the mystery of truth in Christianity is an event which has taken place and which takes place again and again. It is life, personal life, revelation and decision. Truth is a stream of life, centered in

Christ, actualized in everybody who is connected with Him, organized in the assembly of God, the Church. In Greek thought truth only can be found. In Christianity truth is found if it is done, and done if it is found.[26]

In modern naturalism truth is perception of empirical reality (Wieman), or appreciative awareness (Bernard Meland) or the breakthrough into a higher level of consciousness (Carl Jung). God is reconceived as growth in qualitative meaning (Wieman), the creative surge (Henri Bergson) or the power of creative transformation (Wieman, John Cobb). Both naturalists and idealists strive to overcome the subject-object dichotomy, which mirrors a dualistic view of reality. For the naturalist the subject (mind) becomes included in the object (matter, energy). For the idealist the object is taken up into the subject. In mysticism the aim is to transcend this polarity by making contact with an undifferentiated unity behind both subject and object.

Can the Christian find any value in the classical and modern philosophical approaches to truth? My answer is affirmative, but these theories become modified, sometimes even drastically altered, when they are made to serve Christian revelation.

The Christian certainly shares with the unbeliever the idea of truth as a correct description of the world, but the correspondence theory becomes questionable when the discussion turns to ultimate or final truth. Truth in the ultimate sense is not a conforming of the mind to objective reality but the refocusing of the mind by the Spirit of God, who breaks into our reality from the beyond.[27] Truth is being brought into accord with the transcendent meaning of the gospel, the very Word of God. It is not simply an agreement between our ideas and the gospel but a conforming of our total life orientation to the demands of the gospel. Truth in biblical perspective is not so much the factual as the eventful. It is not the mere perception of facts but transformation by the transcendent reality that the biblical facts point to and attest.

In biblical religion it is possible to speak of a correspondence within God himself: God corresponds to himself, he is true to himself. His acts are consonant with his being. Thus we can refer to his constancy, integrity and faithfulness.

The manifestation theory, which belongs to the heritage of both idealism and mysticism, has points of convergence with biblical understanding, but its divergence is more conspicuous. Truth is not a perception of something that is always there waiting to be discovered but an encounter with a new reality—the incarnation of God in human flesh—that is unrepeatable and irrevocable. Truth is not being opened to the core of our being (as in Martin Heidegger) but being conformed to the New Being. Nor is it the disclosure of the mystery of being to spirits sensitized to the deeper dimensions of reality (another Heideggerian theme); instead it is being personally addressed by the One who is himself spirit and truth. We do not uncover what is hidden through rational dialectic or mystical ecstasy, but we wait for the universal manifestation of the glory of God at the end of history (1 Tim 6:14-15; 1 Pet 4:13).

In contrast to mystical religion, biblical, prophetic religion emphasizes hearing over seeing. We make contact with truth when we hear the message of truth that is enacted in history (Rom 10:14-17). In Platonism and mysticism we apprehend truth first through the senses and then through intellectual or mystical vision. In the biblical view people of faith can see God's promises coming true in history, though these promises always need to be interpreted. In the Platonic tradition truth is equated with eternal ideals that can be envisioned by the imagination. While the Neoplatonists are determined to get beyond the forms or ideals to the undivided unity of the One, their goal is the vision of the whole, which is realized in a state of ecstasy.[28]

Truth for Christians is not an ecstatic awareness of the unconditional but knowledge of a particular happening in history. It is not a mystical reaching up to divine reality but the descent of divinity into the squalor and pain of humanity in a particular person and at a particular time in history. We are delivered from doubt and despair not by the metaphysical element alone (as Fichte said) but by God acting in history—in the life, death and resurrection of Jesus Christ.

The coherence theory of truth has claimed many disciples in Christian theological history, including in this century Edward John Carnell[29] and Reinhold Niebuhr; the latter recommended Christian faith over its alternatives because of its dialectical comprehensiveness.[30] Biblical Christians have difficulty with the coherence theory because it fails to recognize things that are absolutely unique and that therefore resist being coordinated into a rational system. We do not strive to arrive at an absolute, univocal perspective of the whole of reality because we acknowledge the finiteness and brokenness of human understanding. There is an absolute, synoptic perspective, but this belongs to God alone. At the same time, we are obliged to strive for a degree of coherence since the gospel must make sense not only to ourselves but also to people of the world. We can believe only if we understand—at least in part.[31] Revelation cannot be assimilated into a comprehensive, rational system of truth, but it can throw light on all human systems that purport to give meaning and purpose to life.

Finally, Christians need to assess the pragmatic theory of truth—so congenial to the contemporary mind. First we insist that the fundamental need of human beings is not satisfaction or integration but deliverance from sin and communion with God. The truth of the Word of God consists not in its capacity to bring about human happiness and fulfillment but in its efficacy in carrying out God's promise and judgment. When Jesus said, "You will know them by their fruits" (Mt 7:16; Lk 6:43-44), he was speaking not of ideas that are true but of people who are in the truth. The biblical criterion is not that which works but "He who works"—to bring order out of chaos, good out of evil.

The object of faith is neither a timeless idea (as in idealism), nor the élan vital (as in naturalism), nor the bottomless abyss (as in the new mysticism) nor even events in external history (as in historical realism). The object of faith is the One who speaks and acts in history but who infinitely transcends human conception and imagination. God becomes historical, but he cannot be contained in history. Nor can he be explained by historical analysis. He is hidden in history and remains unknown until he makes himself known through the word that he speaks. While his being is concealed in both history and nature, his works are manifest, though recognized as such only by faith. No one has ever seen God (Jn 1:18), but people of faith have heard God's word and can therefore believe and act in obedience.

God becomes historical but in such a way that he remains the eternal. He is not an empirical datum in history nor a spiritual presence that permeates history but a personal reality who steps into a particular history. The truth of God is not a timeless idea nor a wholly temporal event but the paradox of the eternal breaking into time.

The truth of faith is both an event of the superhistorical entering time and a metaphysical presupposition that directs our reflection on this event. This presupposition is not at our disposal, however, but is available to us only as we go forward in obedience and faith. It is a truth that is grasped only in the passion of inwardness and is therefore not generally accessible to human understanding. It can be known but only because God makes himself known in the confrontation of the believer with the Jesus Christ attested in Holy Scripture. Faith is not a mystical unknowing but steadfast and certain knowledge concerning things beyond the compass of human reason and imagination (Calvin). It is not exhaustive knowledge nor comprehensive knowledge but true knowledge because it has its basis in God acting and God speaking.

Truth in the Technological Society

Truth in the technological society has been reinterpreted as validity and precision. Truth is what can be measured and verified by empirical reason. The idea of an ultimate, unchanging truth is supplanted by "the ever-changing truths of our own experience."[32] The method that now reigns supreme is neither dialectical reasoning (as in Plato) nor deductive and inductive logic (as in Aristotle) but pragmatic utility.

The ideology of technological liberalism draws on the philosophies of pragmatism (William James, Charles Peirce, F. C. S. Schiller, Richard Rorty), instrumentalism (John Dewey) and phenomenalism (Bertrand

Russell). As Schiller put it, "Truth is the useful, efficient, workable, to which our practical experience tends to restrict our truth valuations."[33] A proposition is true if it possesses practical value by fulfilling a particular purpose. Truth becomes identified with knowledge of what is actually present to our senses (as in Russell).

Jacques Ellul, who warns of the drabness and unidimensional character of the technological society, observes that everything is reduced to verifiable reality—that which is "scientifically measurable and pragmatically modifiable. Praxis becomes the measure of all truth," and truth becomes limited to what can be acted on.[34] Real truth, ultimate truth, assails and circumvents one with mystery. By contrast, in the technological society "everything seems to depend on evidence."[35] Empirical reality is evident and "sight, naturally, gives me evidence. But the truth is never evident."[36]

What determines truth is an investigation into what enhances and serves human growth and expansion. Dewey accepted the definition of Peirce that "the true is that opinion which is fated to be ultimately accepted by all investigators."[37] In the new ethos "a scientific law is not an uncovering of reality, but a successful procedural technique."[38] Scientific experimentation becomes an "effective means for predicting and controlling the world, rather than the collective human effort to understand it."[39] Truth is prized on how it performs rather than on whether it enlightens.

The technological society thus encourages a truncated understanding of truth. We equate truth with accuracy and precision rather than wisdom, with clarity of perception rather than depth of insight. The legacy of Descartes is reasserting itself: truth consists in clear and distinct ideas, though these are not a priori principles or foundational intuitions but ideas tested and corroborated by experience.

Modern naturalism tends to hold that all we know are those events that occur when we experience sensations. The source of all our knowledge is the data supplied by our senses, but these data must be scientifically measured and verified if they are to be a reliable guide for life and action. In this worldview truth is condensed to the factual, and metaphysical truth is treated as a chimera or seduction. According to Russell, "when a sentence or belief is 'true,' it is so in virtue of some relation to one or more facts."[40]

How different all this is from the biblical teaching! Truth in the biblical perspective is primarily a conformation of understanding to ontological reality rather than a correspondence of perception with facticity. Truth is participation in the creative source and ground of truth rather than technical precision in the recording of facts. It is not the factual as such that is the norm for truth but the revelatory significance of the factual, the factual as seen in relation to God's self-revelation in Jesus Christ.

In the biblical understanding the truth of God is not his facticity but his fidelity. Nor is it the eternal ideas or ideals in his mind but the word that he speaks. The organ in determining truth is not the eye, which can measure scientifically, but the ear, which waits to hear a definite message.

What dominates the technological society is noise or chatter rather than either the silence of mysticism or the interpretive speech of prophetic religion. Technological planners and social engineers cherish the productivity of human labor more than the understanding of human existence. They gauge human progress on the basis of desired results rather than insight into ultimate reality. In the field of religion we witness the rise of a technology of the spirit, which supposedly guarantees success in raising spiritual consciousness.

Against the technological mentality I assert that absolute truth is not within the range of our perception, nor can it be enclosed or contained in our experience of faith. Absolute truth is in God's Word alone, "which even as the Word of the Holy Spirit in us never becomes our word, the word of *our* soul, but remains the Word of God, and therefore cannot be found as an object of psychological analysis."[41] Faith makes contact with God's Word but only as an empty vessel that receives, not as a criterion that judges and controls. The Word of God authenticates itself to our understanding, but its truth is confirmed in lives of holiness and obedience.

Models of Truth

The incongruity between an authentically theological understanding of truth and philosophical theories comes to light when we compare some of the leading models of truth. These models show that the various positions are not saying the same thing, though we must not assume that they always contradict one another. The divergence between them is more obvious in some cases than in others.

In pragmatic philosophy the truth is the experientially workable or the practically useful. It is not timeless truth but workable or efficacious truth that is celebrated. As I have already indicated, this view prevails in Western society today.

Closely related is the position that identifies truth with the ethically renewable. Truth is what fulfills or enhances human creativity or perfects human striving. This position might be called an ethical pragmatism. In a Christian context truth is linked to what is humanizing and liberating and untruth to what is dehumanizing.

In the circles of empirical rationalism and modern realism truth is the empirically verifiable or the empirically demonstrable. Truth is that which can be measured, tested and validated by the scientific method. Truth must be corroborated by evidence if it is to make a credible claim on our lives. When combined with the pragmatic outlook, this position is clearly pervasive in contemporary society.

A quite different position is represented by those who hold that truth is the logically necessary or the rationally inescapable. Here we are in the camp of pure rationalism or rationalistic idealism. The ideal in philosophical method is mathematics, and the method is deductive. The rational self is the real self, and truth is reduced to what can be thought. We find this position in classical philosophy (Plato, Aristotle, the Stoics) as well as in modern philosophy (Descartes, Leibniz, Spinoza). The thoroughgoing rationalist sees the basis of truth and reasoning in absolutely certain and irreducible ideas, which constitute the ultimate postulates of thought. God is often defined as absolute rationality, and divine logic and human logic are virtually equated.

Mysticism constitutes a distinct alternative to rationalism by viewing absolute truth as ineffable and incommunicable. The true is not the logically compelling but the ecstatically illuminating. Truth is not so much against reason as above reason. It concerns mysteries that one cannot grasp rationally but can experience in moments of ecstatic awareness. Mystical illuminations do not yield universally binding principles, but they do yield "insight into depths of truth" unplumbed by discursive reason.[42]

Finally we come to the view that truth is the existentially meaningful. Neither a logically necessary axiom nor a scientifically verifiable datum in human experience, it is instead an existential human necessity. Our sense of despair drives us to pursue truth, and our burning desire for meaning finally leads us to affirm truth. Truth is what has practical value in shaping a purposeful existence. This approach is found in the critical philosophy of Kant as well as in modern existentialism and in some brands of pragmatism. The more Christian existentialists, such as Kierkegaard, the early Barth and Bultmann, see truth as existentially undeniable.[43] We cannot understand the reality of the unconditional that impinges on our reason, but neither can we deny this reality as we commit ourselves to it wholeheartedly.[44]

How do these theories comport with a theology of the Word of God? Despite their diversity they have one thing in common: they begin with a cognitive capacity within the human person, whether this be reason, feeling, experience, intuition or so on. Truth is what the human being can discover or conceive or imagine. In theology truth is what God declares and reveals. Truth is not a human possibility but a divine actuality.

For the biblical theologian truth is not a universal idea or principle, but neither is it an ecstatic experience or creative insight. It is first of all not a proposition but a relationship. To be in the truth means to stand in a right relationship with God.

In the biblical view truth in its deepest meaning is not the rationally demonstrable, nor the intuitively indubitable, nor the empirically verifiable; instead, truth in its ultimate sense is the redemptively transformative. Truth is the wisdom and power of the living God revealed in his paradoxical entry into time, giving us a new horizon of meaning and a new purpose for living. We commit ourselves to this God not as if he existed but because he proves his existence by opening our inward eyes to what he has done for us in the person of Jesus Christ. Truth is both existentially undeniable and rationally enlightening, but only because it creates within us a new nature that is oriented outward—to the needs of our neighbor.

Being in the truth is to participate in the eternal wisdom that sustains all things. It is to be conformed to the image of the eternal God as seen in Jesus Christ, the wisdom of God incarnate. Being in the truth is to be grounded in the living God, who cannot deceive (theonomy), rather than imprisoned in the self, which always deceives (autonomy), or subjected to a purely external human authority, which deceives as much as it consoles (heteronomy). Only the living God makes us truly free. To remain in the self is to remain in slavery. To surrender ourselves abjectly to an external power, even if this be the church as a social institution, is to be robbed of our freedom.

Truth in the biblical sense is not simply *descriptive* of reality, nor is it simply *informative* of what transpires in reality. Instead, it is *regenerative* in that it shapes a new reality. But it regenerates because it persuasively informs; it renews because its witness to itself is trustworthy and reliable.

Truth is God acting in history, the Word assuming flesh in the person of Jesus Christ. Because human reason cannot conceive of the eternal entering time, of the divine becoming human, of myth becoming fact, it endeavors to reinterpret the truth of the gospel in order to bring it into accord with universal human understanding. But in the process it surrenders the mystery and paradox of the gospel. Truth in the gospel perspective is the revelationally paradoxical—that which can be grasped not by reflective reasoning but only by the passion of faith.

Truth is God in action, although truth is not action in and of itself but the personal being who acts. Truth is God acting in history, although history is not the fulcrum of truth but only the field where truth makes itself known. We must resist an actualism that reduces truth to action and a historical reductionism that confines truth to history. Both can be detected in the liberationist theologian José Míguez Bonino, who claims that "there is no truth outside or beyond the concrete historical events in which men are involved as agents. There is, therefore, no knowledge except in action itself, in the process of transforming the world through participation in history."[45] For Míguez Bonino "action is itself the truth. Truth is at the level of history, not in the realm of ideas. Reflection on praxis, on human significant action, can only be authentic when it is done from within, in the vicinity of the strategic and tactical plane of human action."[46]

We need to take seriously the biblical claim that God existed before he called the worlds into being (Tit 1:2 NRSV). God remains ever the same even while his ways with us vary according to our need and situation. The heavens and earth will perish, but God will endure (Ps 102:26-27; Is 40:6-8). God remains true to himself; thus we can rely on his promises and thus his word is true and certain. His will can be resisted, but it cannot be permanently thwarted, for what he proposes will ultimately take place even if it means the demise of human culture and the collapse of human programs for a better world. God upholds the world even in its sin and perfidy, and he is leading the world to a bright, new future despite its unbelief and rigidity. Our task is to celebrate what God has done and is now doing, for a new kingdom is dawning, a new world is in the making. Our commission is to be witnesses to his kingdom that alone is unshakable and invincible, that will remain standing after the old order has been demolished (Heb 12:25-29).

The Current Controversy

The crux of the problem in contemporary evangelicalism concerning the inerrancy of the Bible revolves around different understandings of truth.

The conflict is not so much theological as philosophical. Because a large segment of conservative Protestantism has unwittingly accepted the Enlightenment reduction of truth to the rationally empirical or evidential, the possibility of forging some consensus on this question is made all the more difficult.[47]

What is clear is that the cultural or dictionary understanding of truth has eclipsed the biblical understanding among many earnest Christians. In his earlier phase Clark Pinnock could bluntly declare, "Scripture honors the law of non-contradiction, and operates on the basis of a correspondence idea of truth."[48] For Arthur Johnson faith is based on the "correctness" of the biblical statements. He insists that the biblical writers give us "an accurate representation" of the reality to which they refer.[49] The message of faith certainly involves the reliability of the reports in the Gospels about Christ, but faith itself rests on Jesus Christ and the sending forth of his Spirit.

In a devastating review of C. Norman Kraus's *Jesus Christ Our Lord,* Harold Lindsell comments: "Surely the historical Jesus was an empirical datum and it was He who said, 'He that hath seen me hath seen the Father.' In the plainest English Jesus Christ is God and as God he was empirically verifiable."[50] I contend that the Word of God who inhered in Jesus was not discernible to the senses; indeed, he was hidden from natural reason. When Peter made his confession that Jesus Christ was the Son of the living God, Jesus told him that flesh and blood did not reveal this to him but the Father who is in heaven (Mt 16:17). Peter was given not a direct perception of Jesus' deity but an interior illumination concerning things beyond the compass of his intellect and senses. The Jesus who is known according to the flesh is not the Jesus Christ of apostolic faith but simply a prophet or sage among the first-century Jewish people. Lindsell's position stands in painful contrast to that of Luther, who claimed that in order to know God we must be "rapt and translated from all things of sense, within and without, into those things beyond sense within and without, namely into the invisible, most high and incomprehensible God."[51] Indeed, "faith must believe against reason, against its own feeling and intuition, and against its understanding, which grasps and admits the validity only of that which is empirical."[52]

Biblical Christians can affirm the inerrancy of Scripture so long as it is not confused with total factual and scientific accuracy. The confessionalist Lutheran C. Kuehne commends the scientific creationist Henry Morris for affirming "the complete accuracy of the Bible in all matters which it treats—whether spiritual, scientific, geographical, historical, chronological, genealogical, or whatever."[53] It is debatable whether the Bible claims such all-embracing knowledge; Jesus certainly did not (Mk 13:32). Such a position actually serves to undermine biblical authority by making the truth of Scripture contingent on scientific corroboration.

Barth came significantly closer to expressing my own views on this question:

> The fact the scripture comes to us as God's Word means that we regard its thoughts as true, that is, that we accept its reference to revelation. No matter what our attitude to the words and the historical aspect of the witness may be, we have to regard them as transparencies through which a light shines. It shines with varying degrees of brightness and clarity . . . yet it is always a light, *the* light. Everything relates to this light, everything that we might view as a transparent medium pointing us in this direction. . . . There is no possibility of regarding scripture as merely historical. There is no possibility of folding our arms and adopting the stance of onlookers or spectators. The only possibility is that of seriousness, of decision, of being taken captive, of faithfulness, of an act of supreme spontaneity.[54]

In the biblical perspective to err is to wander from the truth or to continue in a state of sin.[55] To lie is to walk in darkness, to fail to practice the truth.[56] Error means a falling away from the wisdom of Christ and the guidance of the Spirit; truth means an abiding in this divine wisdom and guidance. While the authors of Scripture certainly erred in their thoughts, words and acts, they were enabled by the superintendence of the Spirit to remain in the truth in their public witness.

For the Greeks truth is the immovable essence of things and is irreducibly rational. The opposite of truth is misunderstanding, deception *(pseudos)* and appearance (*doxa,* in its classical sense). For the biblical prophets truth is faithfulness and veracity, both of which pertain to the moral dimension of truth. The opposite of truth is moral error, infidelity, the breaking of bonds between persons. There are indeed other meanings of truth in Scripture, but they are made to serve the one central vision of truth as fidelity and integrity.

Inerrancy in biblical understanding means that the Bible in its unity with the Spirit guides us into all truth.[57] The Bible reflects the truth of divine revelation; it bears the stamp of truthfulness. This is not to imply that the biblical description of events in history and phenomena in nature must correspond exactly with external reality.[58] The truthfulness of the Bible signifies its fundamental agreement with God's own interpretation of his redeeming action in the history of biblical Israel culminating in Jesus Christ.

The paramount question is not whether the Bible is true in the sense of being fully accurate in everything it reports, but whether the Bible leads us into truth, whether the Bible brings us truth. But the Bible could not lead us into truth unless its central claims were true, unless its overall witness were reliable and dependable.

The bifurcation between "religious truth" and "historical truth," prevalent in academic liberal circles since Bultmann, must be treated with considerable caution.[59] To affirm that the Bible teaches "religious truth" but not "historical truth" is to overlook the Bible's central claim that paradoxically God became historical, myth became fact.[60] The message of Scripture is at the same time both religious and historical, and we do not have an adequate understanding of biblical truth unless we clearly see this point. The truth of faith cannot be reduced to the historical, but neither can it be divested of the historical.

Thomas F. Torrance makes a helpful distinction between the truth of the gospel and the truthfulness of the biblical statements. He appreciates Anselm's perception that there are "several different levels of truth, the truth of statement and the truth of signification, the truth of created being . . . and the Supreme Truth."[61] Anselm insisted that "the relations between these several levels . . . are all open upward towards the Supreme Truth and are not reducible downward."[62]

According to Torrance truthfulness *(Wahrhaftigkeit)* must always be subordinated to truth *(Wahrheit)*. The former is "an openness to the truth and a right orientation in accordance with the nature of the truth. While truthfulness involves an analogical relation to the truth, the truth itself always retains ontic priority, for it is what it is in its own reality before it is recognized by us, and what it is in itself is the compulsive ground of our recognition of it and the inexhaustible source of our conceiving it."[63]

What makes the biblical statements truthful is their openness to the truth of the living Word of God, Jesus Christ, to whom they bear witness. Their truthfulness depends "not on the truthfulness of their intention but on a participation in the Truth which God alone can give."[64] What must guide theological reflection is certainly the truth claims of Scripture, but "what must determine theological formulation is the objective truth forced upon the interpreter of the Scriptures by God himself."[65]

The seat of the truth in Scripture lies not in words or concepts but in a divine person—the living Word of God who reaches us by his Spirit acting on the words and also on our hearts. This Word is aptly described as "the faithful and true witness" (Rev 3:14 GNB). This is also a fitting description of the prophets and apostles (Is 43:10-12; Acts 1:8; Rom 3:21). Their task is to direct us away from ourselves to the truth that never deceives, the eternal and unshakable truth that even the heavens cannot contain (1 Kings 8:27; 2 Chron 2:6; 6:18).

The true statements of both the Scriptures and church tradition can serve the truth of divine revelation, but in themselves they fall short of it, "for they do not possess their truth in themselves but in the reality they serve."[66] The texts of Scripture are steppingstones to the spiritual reality to which these texts refer, a reality inaccessible to historical research and investigation. God's Word is truly known only when God himself speaks, an occurrence that is always unpredictable and mind-altering. When God speaks, the texts of Scripture come alive, for then they are filled with revelational meaning and power.

A cardinal tenet of biblical religion is that the truth it proclaims is not known except through an interior change brought about by the Spirit of God. The apostle hopes that God may grant those who oppose him "a change of heart and lead them to recognize the truth; thus they may come to their senses and escape from the devil's snare in which they have been trapped and held at his will" (2 Tim 2:25-26 REB). The truth that the apostolic writer has in mind is sound doctrine, a true understanding of the gospel revelation. This truth is not merely conceptual, however, but also existential, for it alters human existence, it brings to the person ensnared by sin a new being as well as a new perception of reality. We can think rightly only when we are in a right relationship to God. We can act responsibly only when we are imbued with power from on high that sets us free to live as disciples of the lord and king of all creation.

Jacques Ellul makes the interesting point that the principles of non-contradiction and identity, so vital to rationalistic fundamentalism, are based on a visual experience of the world.

> Declaring that two opinions cannot both be true, when one denies what the other affirms, has to do with vision, which involves instantaneousness. But language involves duration. Consequently what is visual cannot be dialectical. Knowledge based on sight is of necessity linear and logical. Only thought based on language can be dialectical, taking into account contradictory aspects of reality, which are possible because they are located in time.[67]

The criterion in a truly evangelical theology is the speech of God that is heard by prophets and apostles inspired by the Spirit of God and by believers illumined by this same Spirit. Because God's Word became incarnate in a particular human being in history, the witness to this event will necessarily be paradoxical, for the event itself is a paradox to human understanding.

Theology can never perfect a comprehensive, rational system of truth because the Bible presents us not with universal principles related only tangentially to history but with varied and sometimes divergent reports of significant happenings in history. We can glean from these reports reliable intimations of God's will and purpose for his people but not final answers to problems that have vexed metaphysicians through the ages. The Bible gives us not an overarching synoptic perspective of historical and spiritual reality but an unfailing impression of God's faithfulness and mercy, which extends even to a recalcitrant and stubborn people.

Notes

Chapter 1: Introduction

[1]Historical criticism can elucidate the truth of faith, but it cannot of itself procure this truth nor even move one toward it. I here stand closer to Barth than to Bultmann on the one hand and to John Warwick Montgomery on the other, both of whom manifest a deeper confidence in historical study in arriving at the truth of the Word of God.

[2]Edward Farley and Peter C. Hodgson, "Scripture and Tradition," in *Christian Theology: An Introduction to Its Traditions and Tasks,* ed. Peter C. Hodgson and Robert H. King, rev. ed. (Philadelphia: Fortress, 1985), p. 79.

[3]From my perspective the Bible could be likened to a mine that yields its hidden treasure to those who persevere in seeking in faith. This treasure is not, however, an abstract truth but the word of the living Christ, which can be known, yet only when Christ speaks by his Spirit.

[4]*The Confessions of St. Augustine,* trans. and ed. E. M. Blaiklock (Nashville: Thomas Nelson, 1983), 9.2, p. 213.

[5]*Maximus Confessor: Selected Writings,* trans. George C. Berthold, introduction by Jaroslav Pelikan (New York: Paulist Press, 1985), pp. 195-96.

[6]Ibid., p. 145. On the Platonic hue in Maximus's thought see p. 57.

[7]Bernard of Clairvaux, *Sermons on the Canticles,* 31:6, cited in David Manning White, *The Search for God* (New York: Macmillan, 1983), p. 76.

[8]Calvin, *The First Epistle of Paul the Apostle to the Corinthians,* trans. John W. Fraser, ed. David W. Torrance and Thomas F. Torrance (Grand Rapids, Mich.: Eerdmans, 1960), pp. 58-59.

[9]*Luther's Works,* ed. Jaroslav Pelikan (St. Louis: Concordia, 1955), 12:203.

[10]*John Calvin's Sermons on the Ten Commandments,* ed. and trans. Benjamin W. Farley, foreword by Ford Lewis Battles (Grand Rapids, Mich.: Baker Book House, 1980), p. 239. Cf.: "For God's mysteries pertaining to our salvation are of the sort that cannot in themselves and by their own nature . . . be discerned;

but we gaze upon them only in his Word." *Institutes of the Christian Religion: 1536 Edition,* trans. Ford Lewis Battles (Grand Rapids, Mich.: Eerdmans, 1975), p. 43.

[11]Calvin, *First Corinthians,* p. 51.

[12]Ibid., p. 59.

[13]Zwingli, *The Acts of The First Zurich Disputation* (1523), in *Selected Works of Huldreich Zwingli,* ed. Samuel Macauley Jackson (Philadelphia: University of Pennsylvania Press, 1901), p. 104.

[14]This imbalance was much more evident among the Spiritualists than among the mainline Anabaptists.

[15]Eberhard Arnold, in *Inner Words for Every Day of the Year,* ed. Emmy Arnold (Rifton, N.Y.: Plough Publishing House, 1971), p. 92.

[16]See Karl Rahner and Herbert Vorgrimler, "Revelation," *Theological Dictionary* (New York: Herder & Herder, 1965), p. 411.

[17]Gregory Baum, foreword to A. M. Greeley, *The New Agenda* (New York: Doubleday, 1973), p. 16.

[18]Jacques Ellul, *Living Faith,* trans. Peter Heinegg (San Francisco: Harper & Row, 1983), p. 145.

[19]John Macquarrie, *Principles of Christian Theology* (New York: Charles Scribner's Sons, 1966), p. 80.

[20]For Harnack the essence of Christianity lay in its core ethical teachings enunciated by Jesus rather than in dogmatic speculations. See Adolf von Harnack, *What Is Christianity?* trans. T. B. Saunders (New York: G. P. Putnam's, 1903).

[21]See Harry Emerson Fosdick, *The Modern Use of the Bible* (New York: Macmillan, 1924), pp. 97-130.

[22]William Newton Clarke, *An Outline of Christian Theology* (New York: Charles Scribner's Sons, 1899), p. 18.

[23]For Niebuhr revelation is an experience or happening in our personal history through which "we are enabled to apprehend what we are, what we are suffering and doing and what our potentialities are." H. Richard Niebuhr, *The Meaning of Revelation* (New York: Macmillan, 1941), p. 138. He also defines revelation as the moment "through which we know ourselves to be known from beginning to end, in which we are apprehended by the knower; it means the self-disclosing of that eternal knower." Ibid., pp. 152-53.

[24]According to Niebuhr revelation directs the universal sense of the holy to the principle of being, the source of all value. See his *Radical Monotheism and Western Culture* (New York: Harper & Bros., 1960), pp. 52-53.

[25]Whitehead's influence on Niebuhr was discernible in both *Meaning of Revelation* (pp. 74, 93) and *Radical Monotheism* (pp. 123-24).

[26]I here include process theology, existentialist theology, liberation theology, mainstream feminist theology and story theology. The neognostic theology,

which encompasses goddess spirituality and New Age theology, is postliberal and post-Christian. In these circles the crowning experience is the sense of the oneness of all things or being submerged in the ongoing evolutionary process.

On Berkhof's perceptive analysis of H. Richard Niebuhr see Hendrikus Berkhof, *Two Hundred Years of Theology*, trans. John Vriend (Grand Rapids, Mich.: Eerdmans, 1989), pp. 270-74. Berkhof detects a shift from transcendence to immanence in Niebuhr's thought, whereas his brother Reinhold Niebuhr continued to maintain the biblical emphasis on the transcendence of the gospel (see p. 285).

[27]For H. Richard Niebuhr faith does not simply proceed out of experience but rises above experience. While he emphasized the ethical more than the experiential, he insisted that we cannot know "what gods are dependable . . . save through the experiences of inner history." *Meaning of Revelation*, p. 80. See also p. 136.

[28]Joseph Sittler, *Gravity and Grace: Reflections and Provocations*, ed. Linda-Marie Delloff (Minneapolis: Augsburg, 1986), p. 44. Like H. Richard Niebuhr, Sittler sought to combine an evangelical commitment with a partly liberal methodology. Their efforts can be seen as a corrective to liberalism rather than a return to orthodoxy.

[29]Emil Brunner, *The Christian Doctrine of God*, trans. Olive Wyon (Philadelphia: Westminster Press, 1950), p. 58.

[30]I here acknowledge a convergence with H. Richard Niebuhr and Brunner, both of whom emphasized the existential dimension of the Christian's knowledge of God. But this existential knowledge is not bereft of a conceptual element, and though these theologians would for the most part agree, they sometimes downplayed that side of revelation.

[31]P. T. Forsyth, *The Preaching of Jesus and the Gospel of Christ* (Blackwood, South Australia: New Creation Publications, 1987), p. 85.

[32]James I. Packer, "An Introduction to Systematic Spirituality," *Crux* 26, no. 1 (March 1990):5.

[33]The Bible indeed contains some self-evident truths as well as the hidden truth of divine revelation, but it is only the latter that draws one into the history of redemption. Biblical truths that are generally recognizable and confirmed in universal human experience include the maxims that slothfulness leads to poverty (Prov 10:4) and slowness to anger quiets contention (Prov 15:18).

Chapter 2: The Crisis in Biblical Authority
[1]Ernst Troeltsch, *Über historische und dogmatische Methode* (1898), in *Gesammelte Schriften* 2:729ff. Cited by Gerhard von Rad, "Typological Interpretation of the Old Testament," trans. John Bright, rpt. in *A Guide to Contemporary Hermeneutics: Major Trends in Biblical Interpretation*, ed. Donald K. McKim

(Grand Rapids, Mich.: Eerdmans, 1986), p. 33.

[2]Edgar Krentz, *The Historical-Critical Method* (Philadelphia: Fortress, 1975), p. 30.

[3]Rolf Rendtorff, "Between Historical Criticism and Holistic Interpretation: New Trends in Old Testament Exegesis," in Supplement to *Vetus Testamentum* 40 (Leiden: E. J. Brill, 1986), p. 302. See J. Andrew Dearman, "The Blessing in Torah: Preaching the Gospel Beforehand," *Austin Seminary Bulletin,* faculty edition, 105, no. 2 (Spring 1990):33-34.

[4]Dearman, "The Blessing in Torah," p. 34. See also Isaac M. Kikawada and Arthur Quinn, *Before Abraham Was: The Unity of Genesis 1—11* (San Francisco: Ignatius Press, 1989). This is not to deny that one can still be orthodox and work with the documentary hypothesis, which presupposes that the Pentateuch is the work of four or more authors (see my discussion on p. 354, note 26). See the review of the Kikawada and Quinn book by Lee Podles in *Touchstone* 4, no. 3 (Summer 1991):40-42.

[5]*The New Jerome Biblical Commentary*, ed. Raymond E. Brown, Joseph A. Fitzmyer and Roland E. Murphy (Englewood Cliffs, N.J.: Prentice Hall, 1990), p. 330.

[6]C. S. Rodd, "Talking Points from Books," *The Expository Times* 101, no. 8 (May 1990):226.

[7]See Robert M. Price, "Inerrant the Wind: The Troubled House of North American Evangelicals," *Evangelical Quarterly* 55, no. 3 (July 1983):132.

[8]See Robert H. Gundry, *Matthew: A Commentary on His Literary and Theological Art* (Grand Rapids, Mich.: Eerdmans, 1982), pp. 623-40. Cf. Richard V. Pierard, "The Politics of Inerrancy," *Reformed Journal* 34, no. 1 (Jan. 1984):2-4; and Leslie R. Keylock, "Evangelical Scholars Remove Gundry for His Views on Matthew," *Christianity Today* 28, no. 2 (Feb. 3, 1984):36-38.

[9]Kelly James Clark also calls evangelicals to break with Enlightenment rationalism, but he continues to see the Common Sense philosophy of Thomas Reid as holding promise for a philosophical theology in our time. Clark focuses his critique on evidentialism. See his *Return to Reason* (Grand Rapids, Mich.: Eerdmans, 1990).

[10]See my discussion on pp. 208-18.

[11]David H. Kelsey, *The Uses of Scripture in Recent Theology* (Philadelphia: Fortress, 1975), p. 193.

[12]See Hans Küng, *Infallible? An Inquiry,* trans. Edward Quinn (New York: Doubleday, 1971), pp. 181-85.

[13]The recent writings of Joseph Cardinal Ratzinger seem to call for an uncritical submission to papal and conciliar authority. See Joseph Cardinal Ratzinger with Vittorio Messori, *The Ratzinger Report,* trans. Salvator Attanasio and Graham Harrison (San Francisco: Ignatius Press, 1985). There is also much

gospel wisdom in Ratzinger's theology.

[14]See Arthur F. Holmes, "Truth," *New Dictionary of Theology,* ed. Sinclair B. Ferguson and David F. Wright (Downers Grove, Ill.: InterVarsity Press, 1988), pp. 695-96.

[15]One should note that Calvin often depicted the writers as accommodating to the limited cultural horizon of the time, thereby implying that they did not necessarily share in this constricted understanding.

[16]See, e.g., R. C. Sproul, John Gerstner and Arthur Lindsley, *Classical Apologetics* (Grand Rapids, Mich.: Zondervan, 1984).

[17]See John Warwick Montgomery, *Where Is History Going?* (Grand Rapids, Mich.: Zondervan, 1969), pp. 70-74, 179-81, 228-39.

[18]Theodore Letis makes a good case that Benjamin Warfield is mainly responsible for locating the final source of authority in the original autographic text rather than the *textus receptus,* the "received text." According to Letis, Warfield is to be seen as a daring innovator—"abandoning the scholastic, creedal approach of the earlier Princetonians." Theodore P. Letis, "B. B. Warfield, Common-Sense Philosophy and Biblical Criticism," *American Presbyterians* 69, no. 3 (Fall 1991):175-90.

[19]Quoted in Glen G. Scorgie, *A Call for Continuity: The Theological Contribution of James Orr* (Macon, Ga.: Mercer University Press, 1988), p. 98.

[20]Philip Edgcumbe Hughes, "The Truth of Scripture and the Problem of Historical Relativity," in *Scripture and Truth,* ed. D. A. Carson and John D. Woodbridge (Grand Rapids, Mich.: Zondervan, 1983), p. 192.

[21]Millard Erickson makes a helpful distinction between "absolute inerrancy," which holds that the writers intended to give detailed scientific and historical information, which must therefore be entirely accurate; and "full inerrancy," which regards many historical and scientific references as phenomenal—the way they appear to the empirical eye and therefore not historically or scientifically precise. The writers faithfully recorded how the world appeared to them, and this accounts for possible discrepancies between biblical statements and scientific findings. Erickson tends to identify with this position. He also discusses limited inerrancy, which sees the Bible as truthful only in its overall purpose; and source inerrancy, which depicts the writers as accurately reproducing what was available to them from their sources, which, however, may have been defective. Millard J. Erickson, *Christian Theology* (Grand Rapids, Mich.: Baker Book House, 1983), 1:221-40. My position might be called a derivative inerrancy, for I see the truth of the Bible lying in the revealed mystery of God's self-condescension in Jesus Christ, and by the inspiring work of the Spirit this truth is reflected in every part of the Bible. For a further discussion of my views on inerrancy see pp. 105-17, 296-99.

[22]Wayne A. Grudem, "Scripture's Self-Attestation and the Problem of Formulat-

ing a Doctrine of Scripture," in *Scripture and Truth*, ed. Carson and Wood-bridge, p. 50.

[23]Ibid., p. 56. The truth that Scripture embodies is surely abiding and eternal, but this does not imply that the form in which this truth comes to us is exempt from the vicissitudes of history. The root intention of the law does not change, but the way in which the law is applied and interpreted does indeed change. This is why the Pharisees so vigorously opposed Jesus—because of his inno-vative reinterpretation of the law.

[24]See James D. G. Dunn, *Unity and Diversity in the New Testament* (Philadelphia: Westminster Press, 1977). For a penetrating critique of Dunn's allegation of a plurality of kerygmas in the New Testament see D. A. Carson, "Unity and Diversity in the New Testament," in *Scripture and Truth*, ed. Carson and Wood-bridge, pp. 72-77. Also see Martin Hengel, *The Johannine Question*, trans. John Bowden (Philadelphia: Trinity Press International, 1989), which makes a strong case for the theological unity of John and Paul, the two creative geniuses of New Testament theology.

[25]Karl Barth, *Church Dogmatics*, trans. G. T. Thomson and Harold Knight, ed. G. W. Bromiley and T. F. Torrance (Edinburgh: T & T Clark, 1956), 1(2):508.

[26]Cited in Geoffrey W. Bromiley, *Historical Theology: An Introduction* (Grand Rapids, Mich.: Eerdmans, 1978), p. 351.

[27]I must hasten to add that such a commitment will always be informed by the biblical understanding of God and his self-revelation in Jesus Christ.

[28]See Patrick Granfield, "An Interview with Reinhold Niebuhr," *Commonweal* 85, no. 11 (Dec. 16, 1966):315-21, esp. p. 320.

Chapter 3: The Meaning of Revelation

[1]Carl F. H. Henry, "Revelation, Special," *Baker's Dictionary of Theology*, ed. Ever-ett F. Harrison, Geoffrey W. Bromiley and Carl F. H. Henry (rpt. Grand Rapids, Mich.: Baker Book House, 1979), p. 459.

[2]"Neo-Protestant" refers to the movement in theology that is concerned to maintain continuity with Protestant tradition even while revising the message and method of faith. "Liberal" theology is a more comprehensive term, includ-ing scholars who have no desire to maintain Protestant distinctives (such as salvation by grace alone); some of these theologians could even be regarded as post-Christian (e.g., John Hick, Sharon D. Welch, Mark C. Taylor and Peter C. Hodgson). Among the luminaries of neo-Protestantism are Friedrich Schleiermacher, Albrecht Ritschl, Wilhelm Herrmann, Ernst Troeltsch, Horace Bushnell, Paul Tillich and Rudolf Bultmann. My treatment of neo-Catholicism would be along similar lines.

[3]Elton Trueblood, *The Trustworthiness of Religious Experience* (Richmond, Ind.: Friends United Press, 1939), pp. 15ff.

[4]Gregory Baum, foreword to A. M. Greeley, *The New Agenda* (New York: Doubleday, 1973), p. 16.

[5]Karl Rahner, "Revelation," *Encyclopedia of Theology: The Concise Sacramentum Mundi*, ed. Rahner (New York: Seabury Press, 1975), p. 1461.

[6]John Macquarrie, *Principles of Christian Theology* (New York: Charles Scribner's Sons, 1966), pp. 83-86.

[7]See G. Ernest Wright, *God Who Acts* (Naperville, Ill.: Allenson, 1964); and *The Old Testament and Theology* (New York: Harper & Row, 1969).

[8]Emil Brunner, *The Christian Doctrine of the Church, Faith, and the Consummation*, trans. David Cairns (Philadelphia: Westminster Press, 1962), p. 259. Brunner is adamant, however, that personal knowledge of God is inextricably bound up with conceptual knowledge. "God gives Himself to us in no other way than that He says something to us, namely, the truth about Himself; and we cannot enter into fellowship with Him, we cannot give ourselves to Him in trustful obedience, otherwise than by believing 'what' He says to us." Brunner, *The Divine-Human Encounter*, trans. Amandus W. Loos (Philadelphia: Westminster Press, 1943), pp. 112-13. This note is often so subdued in Brunner as to leave the impression that revelational knowledge is exclusively personal and experiential.

[9]I also offer this more comprehensive definition: Revelation is the movement of God into a particular history—that of biblical Israel culminating in Jesus Christ—and God's self-communication through both the events that constitute this history and the inspired human witness to these events—Holy Scripture.

[10]Thomas N. Finger, *Christian Theology* (Nashville: Thomas Nelson, 1985), 1:244.

[11]Ibid.

[12]Cited in Karl Barth, *The Word of God and the Word of Man*, trans. Douglas Horton (rpt. Gloucester, Mass.: Peter Smith, 1978), p. 179.

[13]Calvin, *The First Epistle of Paul the Apostle to the Corinthians*, trans. J. W. Fraser, ed. David W. Torrance and Thomas F. Torrance (Grand Rapids, Mich.: Eerdmans, 1960), p. 51.

[14]Ibid. Cf. Calvin's depiction of grace as "the power and action of the Spirit" by which "He justifies, sanctifies, and cleanses us, calls and draws us to himself, that we may attain salvation." Calvin, *Institutes of the Christian Religion: 1536 Edition*, trans. Ford Lewis Battles, rev. ed. (Grand Rapids, Mich.: Eerdmans, 1986), p. 57.

[15]See Gordon D. Kaufman, *Systematic Theology* (New York: Charles Scribner's Sons, 1968), p. 87. He is here citing Pannenberg in support of a position they hold in common.

[16]*The Confessions of St. Augustine*, trans. and ed. E. M. Blaiklock (Nashville: Thomas Nelson, 1983), 9.2, p. 213. Calvin also stressed that the knowledge of God must take root within us: "It is not enough to know Christ as crucified

and raised up from the dead, unless you experience, also, the fruit of this. . . . Christ therefore is rightly known, when we feel how powerful his death and resurrection are, and how efficacious they are in us." John Calvin, *Commentaries on the Epistles of Paul the Apostle to the Philippians, Colossians, and Thessalonians,* trans. John Pringle (Edinburgh: Calvin Translation Society, 1851), p. 98.

[17]See Karl Barth, *The Göttingen Dogmatics: Instruction in the Christian Religion,* trans. Geoffrey W. Bromiley (Grand Rapids, Mich.: Eerdmans, 1991), 1:225. Barth is here aligning himself with Calvin's position.

[18]H. M. Kuitert, *Do You Understand What You Read?* (Grand Rapids, Mich.: Eerdmans, 1970), p. 29.

[19]Friedrich Schleiermacher, *On Religion: Speeches to Its Cultured Despisers,* trans. John Oman (New York: Harper & Row, 1958), p. 46.

[20]Cf. "There is no imparting of truth as the intellectual apprehends truth, but there is event and appreciation; and in the coincidence of these the revelation consists." William Temple, *Nature, Man and God* (New York: Macmillan, 1949), p. 314.

[21]Martin Buber, *I and Thou,* trans. Ronald Gregor Smith (New York: Charles Scribner's Sons, 1958), p. 110.

[22]Otto Weber, *Foundations of Dogmatics,* trans. Darrell L. Guder (Grand Rapids, Mich.: Eerdmans, 1981), 1:169.

[23]See Rudolf Bultmann, *Faith and Understanding,* trans. Louise Pettibone Smith, ed. Robert W. Funk (Philadelphia: Fortress, 1987), 1:287. Cf. pp. 147-51.

[24]Cf. Bultmann: "The revelation of God brings no knowledge about the mysteries of other worlds; in fact, it communicates nothing even about God that any reflective person could not know by himself." Cited in Schubert M. Ogden, *On Theology* (San Francisco: Harper & Row, 1986), p. 35. "What, then, has been revealed? Nothing at all, so far as the question concerning revelation asks for doctrines—doctrines, say, that no man could have discovered for himself—or for mysteries that become known once and for all as soon as they are communicated. On the other hand, however, *everything has been revealed, insofar as man's eyes are opened concerning his own existence and he is once again able to understand himself.*" Bultmann, *Existence and Faith,* trans. Schubert Ogden (New York: Meridian Books, 1960), p. 85.

[25]Tillich, "Reply to Interpretation and Criticism," in *The Theology of Paul Tillich,* ed. Charles W. Kegley and Robert W. Bretall (New York: Macmillan, 1952), p. 332.

[26]See Ernst Fuchs, *Studies of the Historical Jesus,* trans. Andrew Scobie (London: SCM Press, 1964), pp. 207-28.

[27]Cf. Barth: "Revelation is indeed the truth: the truth of God, but necessarily, therefore, the truth of man in the cosmos as well. The biblical witnesses cannot

bear witness to the one without also bearing witness to the other, which is included in it." *Church Dogmatics,* trans. T. H. L. Parker et al., ed. G. W. Bromiley and T. F. Torrance (Edinburgh: T & T Clark, 1957), 2(1):110.

[28]See Emil Brunner, *The Philosophy of Religion,* trans. A. J. D. Farrer and Bertram Lee Woolf (New York: Charles Scribner's Sons, 1937), p. 50.

[29]Bernard Ramm, *Special Revelation and the Word of God* (Grand Rapids, Mich.: Eerdmans, 1968), p. 154.

[30]Hans Urs von Balthasar, *Prayer,* trans. A. V. Littledale (New York: Paulist Press, 1961), p. 175.

[31]John Calvin, *Institutes of the Christian Religion,* trans. John Allen (Philadelphia: Presbyterian Board of Christian Education, 1936), 3.2.8, 1:605.

[32]Paul Tillich, *The Protestant Era,* trans. James Luther Adams (Chicago: University of Chicago Press, 1948), p. 226.

[33]Thomas F. Torrance, *Theological Science* (London: Oxford University Press, 1969), pp. 279-80.

[34]Ibid., p. 301.

[35]David F. Wells, "An American Evangelical Theology," in *Evangelicalism and Modern America,* ed. George Marsden (Grand Rapids, Mich.: Eerdmans, 1984), p. 86. Wells is describing Protestant scholastic orthodoxy.

[36]Emil Brunner, *The Christian Doctrine of God,* trans. Olive Wyon (rpt. Philadelphia: Westminster Press, 1974), p. 74.

[37]Barth, *Word of God,* p. 43.

[38]See p. 21.

[39]James I. Packer, *God Speaks to Man: Revelation and the Bible* (Philadelphia: Westminster Press, 1965), p. 77.

[40]Auguste Sabatier, *Outlines of a Philosophy of Religion Based on Psychology and History* (New York: J. Pott, 1902), pp. 53-54.

[41]Second Helvetic Confession, I, in *Creeds of the Churches,* ed. John H. Leith, 3d ed. (Atlanta: John Knox Press, 1982), p. 133.

[42]Benjamin Warfield, *The Inspiration and Authority of the Bible* (Philadelphia: Presbyterian & Reformed, 1948), pp. 155-56.

[43]Gregory of Nyssa, *The Lord's Prayer; The Beatitudes,* trans. and ed. Hilda C. Graef (Westminster, Md.: Newman Press, 1954), p. 155. I would add that though the words of the messengers of God cannot reach the majesty of God's truth, God's truth in all of its majesty and power can and does reach us through these words. While the notion of God's grace coming to us is not absent in Gregory of Nyssa (see pp. 48-56, 156-57), his emphasis is on the upward movement of the human soul to God (see p. 19).

[44]John Calvin, *Institutes of the Christian Religion,* trans. Ford Lewis Battles, ed. John T. McNeill (Philadelphia: Westminster Press, 1960), 1.7.4, p. 78.

[45]See Geoffrey W. Bromiley, *Historical Theology: An Introduction* (Grand Rapids,

Mich.: Eerdmans, 1978), p. 219.

[46]Cited in Edward A. Dowey Jr., *A Commentary on the Confession of 1967 and an Introduction to "The Book of Confessions"* (Philadelphia: Westminster Press, 1968), pp. 204-5.

[47]Quoted in Henning Graf Reventlow, *The Authority of the Bible and the Rise of the Modern World,* trans. John Bowden (Philadelphia: Fortress, 1985), p. 53.

[48]See my discussion on pp. 22-23.

[49]Richard Sibbes, *The Complete Works of Richard Sibbes,* ed. Alexander Balloch Grosart (Edinburgh: James Nichol, 1862-64), 7:197.

[50]John Goodwin, *The Divine Authority of the Scriptures* (London: Henry Overton, 1648), p. 17.

[51]K. James Stein, *Philipp Jakob Spener: Pietist Patriarch* (Chicago: Covenant Press, 1986), pp. 152-53.

[52]Ibid., p. 310.

[53]Charles H. Spurgeon, *The Treasury of Charles H. Spurgeon,* introduction by Wilbur M. Smith (Westwood, N.J.: Revell, 1955), p. 217.

[54]Conrad Cherry, *The Theology of Jonathan Edwards* (New York: Doubleday, 1966), p. 48. Note that these are the words of Cherry.

[55]Abraham Kuyper, *Principles of Sacred Theology,* trans. J. Hendrik De Vries (Grand Rapids, Mich.: Eerdmans, 1954), p. 365.

[56]Ibid., p. 667.

[57]Delbert R. Rose, *A Theology of Christian Experience* (Minneapolis: Bethany Fellowship, 1965), p. 145.

[58]This distinction was already anticipated in Augustine. See A. D. R. Polman, *The Word of God According to St. Augustine* (Grand Rapids, Mich.: Eerdmans, 1961).

[59]*Perichoresis* in academic theology means mutual indwelling or interpenetration. It generally refers to the relationship between the three persons of the Trinity.

[60]Donald G. Bloesch, *A Theology of Word & Spirit* (Downers Grove, Ill.: InterVarsity Press, 1992), pp. 191-95.

[61]George Eldon Ladd, *The New Testament and Criticism* (rpt. Grand Rapids, Mich.: Eerdmans, 1971), pp. 27-33.

[62]Daniel B. Stevick, *Beyond Fundamentalism* (Richmond, Va.: John Knox Press, 1964), p. 107.

[63]My position here approaches that of Clark Pinnock, who can speak of the confluence of the divine and human in Scripture; yet his later tendency is to treat Scripture as a totally human book with a divine focus. See his *Tracking the Maze* (San Francisco: Harper & Row, 1990), pp. 173-76.

[64]*Concordia Triglotta,* ed. F. Bente and W. H. T. Daw (rpt. Milwaukee, Wis.: Northwestern Publishing House, 1988), p. 123.

[65]Jaroslav Pelikan, *From Luther to Kierkegaard* (St. Louis: Concordia, 1950), p. 59.

[66]According to Richard A. Muller, "The impact of rationalism on theological prolegomena is evidenced in Burmann's and Heidanus' interest in language of 'clear and distinct perception' and in the presence in the human mind of innate ideas of the existence of God." *Post-Reformation Reformed Dogmatics* (Grand Rapids, Mich.: Baker Book House, 1987), 1:80. See also Ernst Bizer, "Reformed Orthodoxy and Cartesianism," in Rudolf Bultmann et al., *Translating Theology into the Modern Age,* trans. Chalmers MacCormick, ed. Robert W. Funk (New York: Harper & Row, 1965), pp. 20-82.

[67]While maintaining that early Reformed orthodoxy insisted on the subordination of reason to revelation, Muller recognizes that in the seventeenth century "a considerable number of the late scholastic systems elevate reason from an ancillary to a principal status." *Post-Reformation Reformed Dogmatics,* 1:305.

[68]*Calvin: Theological Treatises,* trans. and ed. J. K. S. Reid (Philadelphia: Westminster Press, 1954), p. 134.

[69]See Calvin *Institutes* 3.2.14.

[70]*Institutes,* trans. Henry Beveridge (Grand Rapids, Mich.: Eerdmans, 1957), 3.2.34, p. 499.

[71]Gisbert Voetius was among those who tended to identify the Bible as a historical document with divine revelation. He held that "inspiration can be verbal and plenary only if each and every word has been directly revealed by God." This was apparently not the view of Francis Turretin, who conceived of revelation in its deepest sense as the divine wisdom embedded in the Bible. See Timothy Ross Phillips, *Francis Turretin's Idea of Theology and Its Bearing upon His Doctrine of Scripture* (Ann Arbor, Mich.: University Microfilms International, 1986), pp. 759-93, 803-9.

Klauber and Sunshine make a convincing case that Turretin's son, Jean-Alphonse Turretin, and his mentor Louis Tronchin did much to abet the rationalizing of Reformed Christianity. The younger Turretin "virtually makes the Christian faith synonymous with the adherence to rationally acceptable truths and abandons his father's notion of theology as an infused *habitus* in which God grants to the individual the possibility of both understanding the faith and accepting it." Martin I. Klauber and Glenn S. Sunshine, "Jean-Alphonse Turrettini on Biblical Accommodation: Calvinist or Socinian?" *Calvin Theological Journal* 25, no. 1 (April 1990):15. Also see Richard Muller, *Post-Reformation Reformed Dogmatics* (Grand Rapids, Mich.: Baker Book House, 1993), 2:140-41.

[72]Cf. Robert D. Preus, *The Theology of Post-Reformation Lutheranism* (St. Louis: Concordia, 1970), 1:267-68, 379-80; Heinrich Heppe, *Reformed Dogmatics,* ed. Ernst Bizer, trans. G. T. Thomson (London: George Allen & Unwin, 1950), pp. 15-16; and Ramm, *Special Revelation and the Word of God,* pp. 196-207.

[73]Cf. Francis Turretin, *The Doctrine of Scripture,* ed. and trans. John W. Beardslee

III (Grand Rapids, Mich.: Baker Book House, 1981), pp. 27, 43.

[74]See Barth, *Göttingen Dogmatics,* 1:230-31.

[75]See Heppe, *Reformed Dogmatics,* p. 15. Nevertheless, Heppe discerned even in the sixteenth century a tendency to identify the Word of God and Scripture on the basis of the doctrine of the inspiration of Scripture. The later dogmaticians came to identify the two because they had lost sight of the organic relation between revelation and inspiration and based scriptural authority primarily on the inspiration of its writing. See Heppe, pp. 17-23.

[76]See J. K. S. Reid, *The Authority of Scripture* (New York: Harper & Bros., 1957), pp. 89-92.

[77]See Gerhard Maier, *The End of the Historical-Critical Method,* trans. Edwin W. Leverenz and Rudolph F. Norden (St. Louis: Concordia, 1977), p. 59.

[78]One modern interpreter comments that for Turretin "revelation does not consist of rationally comprehensible teachings or propositions, but is a dynamic and living reality." It is "that which creates, establishes and develops the divine wisdom within the wayfarer. Mere rational propositions hardly have such a power." Phillips, *Francis Turretin's Idea of Theology,* p. 805. Phillips contrasts Turretin's view with that of modern neofundamentalism in which "revelation is identified as Scripture's rationally comprehensible teachings" (p. 804).

[79]See Barth, *Göttingen Dogmatics,* 1:57.

[80]Charles Hodge, *Systematic Theology* (New York: Charles Scribner's Sons, 1898), 1:16-17.

[81]Klauber and Sunshine, "Turrettini," p. 15. See note 71.

[82]Warfield, *Inspiration and Authority,* p. 80.

[83]See Gordon Clark, *God's Hammer: The Bible and Its Critics* (Jefferson, Md.: Trinity Foundation, 1982).

[84]William G. T. Shedd, *Dogmatic Theology,* 2d ed. (Nashville: Thomas Nelson, 1980), 1:25.

[85]Bernard Ramm, *After Fundamentalism* (San Francisco: Harper & Row, 1983), p. 90.

[86]Calvin, *First Corinthians,* trans. Fraser, pp. 53, 57.

[87]Karl Barth, *Protestant Theology in the Nineteenth Century* (Valley Forge, Penn.: Judson Press, 1973), p. 115.

[88]Hans Küng, *Infallible? An Inquiry,* trans. Edward Quinn (New York: Doubleday, 1971), p. 157.

[89]Stevick, *Beyond Fundamentalism,* p. 51.

[90]A. W. Tozer, "Revelation Is Not Enough," *Presbyterian Journal* 28, no. 41 (Feb. 11, 1970):7.

[91]Ibid., p. 8.

[92]See Sigmund Mowinckel, *The Old Testament as Word of God,* trans. Reidar B. Bjornard (Nashville: Abingdon, 1959), pp. 83-84.

[93]Karl Adam, *The Spirit of Catholicism* (New York: Doubleday, 1954), p. 225.

[94]Emil Brunner, *Our Faith,* trans. John W. Rilling (New York: Charles Scribner's Sons, 1954), p. 10.

[95]A. W. Tozer, *The Divine Conquest* (Harrisburg, Penn.: Christian Publications, 1950), p. 81.

[96]Ragnar Bring, *How God Speaks to Us* (Philadelphia: Muhlenberg Press, 1962), p. 26.

[97]Ibid., p. 30.

[98]One may therefore conclude that strictly and precisely the Bible is the Word of God only in its paradoxical unity with the Spirit.

[99]Richard C. Prust, "Was Calvin a Biblical Literalist?" *Scottish Journal of Theology* 20, no. 3 (Sept. 1967):324.

[100]Dietrich Bonhoeffer, *No Rusty Swords,* trans. Edwin H. Robertson and John Bowden (New York: Harper & Row, 1965), p. 314.

[101]Millard J. Erickson, *Christian Theology* (Grand Rapids, Mich.: Baker Book House, 1983), 1:170.

[102]Ibid., pp. 173-74. Erickson deviates from Calvin by positing a harmony or symmetry between God's self-revelation in Christ and the knowledge derived from general revelation (p. 174). Calvin would say that the biblical revelation overturns this knowledge, calling it severely into question.

[103]Ibid., p. 186. Erickson is here presenting Pannenberg's position but giving it his approbation. He comments that Pannenberg and his circle "have restored a correct understanding" of "the relationship between history and revelation." Erickson's preference is to speak of "verifying" and "validating" rather than "proving" the resurrection of Christ by empirical methods. (From a phone conversation with Erickson on December 20, 1990).

[104]See my discussion on pp. 47, 49, 309 (note 7).

[105]Wolfhart Pannenberg, *Basic Questions in Theology,* trans. George H. Kehm (rpt. Philadelphia: Westminster Press, 1983), 1:96-136. See above, p. 198.

[106]Kaufman, *Systematic Theology,* p. xv. See my interaction with Pannenberg in Bloesch, *Theology of Word & Spirit,* pp. 219, 281-82.

[107]Karl Barth, *Theology and Church,* trans. Louise Pettibone Smith (New York: Harper & Row, 1962), p. 210.

[108]Nature in this context means the center of our operations, our innate disposition, our inherent tendencies.

[109]Karl Barth, *Church Dogmatics,* trans. G. W. Bromiley, ed. Bromiley and T. F. Torrance (Edinburgh: T & T Clark, 1969), 4(4):8.

[110]Ibid., p. 9.

[111]For other notable examples in Christian history of the radical change that conversion effects see Hugh T. Kerr and John M. Mulder, eds., *Conversions* (Grand Rapids, Mich.: Eerdmans, 1983).

[112]I am here indebted to David Lotz for this acute perception regarding the distinction between biblicistic faith and evangelical faith in a divine Savior. See David W. Lotz, "Luther and 'Scripture Alone,' " *Lutheran Forum* 23, no. 3 (August 1989):17-21. I would by no means jettison the concept of inspiration but subordinate it to revelation.

[113]See Jaroslav Pelikan, *The Growth of Medieval Theology (600-1300)* (Chicago: University of Chicago Press, 1978), p. 98.

[114]Ibid.

[115]Carnell was fond of defining faith as the "resting of the mind in the sufficiency of evidences." Edward John Carnell, *Christian Commitment: An Apologetic* (New York: Macmillan, 1957), p. 76. In *The Case for Orthodox Theology* (Philadelphia: Westminster Press, 1959) he carefully distinguished this generic conception of faith from a "vital faith" that entails trust in the person of Christ. His overall position seems to be that saving faith goes beyond the generic definition but does not exclude it. See his *A Philosophy of the Christian Religion* (Grand Rapids, Mich.: Eerdmans, 1952), p. 450.

[116]One scholar has these comments on Augustine: "Reason has its part to play in bringing a man to faith, and, once a man has the faith, reason has its part to play in penetrating the data of faith." The fullness of wisdom consists "in a penetration of what is believed, though in the approach to wisdom reason helps to prepare a man for faith." Frederick Copleston, *A History of Philosophy* (rpt. New York: Doubleday Image, 1985), 2:48. See also my discussion in chapter four, note 147.

[117]Søren Kierkegaard, *The Last Years: Journals 1853-1855,* trans. and ed. Ronald Gregor Smith (New York: Harper & Row, 1965), p. 130.

[118]Karl Barth, *Ethics,* trans. G. W. Bromiley (New York: Seabury Press, 1981), p. 253.

[119]Even in the third volume of his *Church Dogmatics* Barth could continue to describe the genuinely ethical decision as a leap into the unknown. But it is a "leap in the dark" in the pejorative sense only when it is born out of disobedience. *Church Dogmatics,* trans. A. T. Mackay et al., ed. G. W. Bromiley and T. F. Torrance (Edinburgh: T & T Clark, 1961), 3(4):15-16.

[120]Dietrich Bonhoeffer, *The Cost of Discipleship,* trans. R. H. Fuller (London: SCM Press, 1959), p. 54.

[121]Dietrich Bonhoeffer, *Ethics,* ed. Eberhard Bethge, trans. Neville Horton Smith (New York: Macmillan, 1955), p. 61.

[122]Peter Stuhlmacher speaks of a "listening intellect . . . open to the Christian tradition and the possibility of address through the biblical kerygma." See his *Historical Criticism and Theological Interpretation of Scripture: Toward a Hermeneutics of Consent,* trans. Roy A. Harrisville (Philadelphia: Fortress, 1977), pp. 89-90.

[123]There is a despair that faith itself engenders—the despair of all earthly hopes and dreams—but this despair is born out of commitment to the promises of God that never deceive. Despair does not of itself induce faith, but faith may use despair to confirm the validity of its vision and goal.

Chapter 4: The Inspiration of Scripture

[1]Henry Thiessen, *Lectures in Systematic Theology,* rev. ed. (Grand Rapids, Mich.: Eerdmans, 1979), pp. 49, 68.

[2]Fred Gealy presents a cogent case that this passage does not limit inspired Scripture to the Old Testament writings. See Fred D. Gealy, "The First and Second Epistles to Timothy and the Epistle to Titus," in *Interpreter's Bible* (New York: Abingdon, 1955), 11:504-6.

[3]John Calvin, *Commentaries on the Epistles to Timothy, Titus and Philemon,* trans. William Pringle (Grand Rapids, Mich.: Eerdmans, 1948), p. 249.

[4]While Wesley sought to uncover "the plain, literal meaning" of the text, he recognized that some of Scripture is obscure or "implies an absurdity." He even suggested that "some traces of knowledge" passed down from Noah and his children to their descendants were "disguised by the addition of numberless fables"; yet the light of God's truth was able to break through this obscurity. See Donald A. D. Thorsen, *The Wesleyan Quadrilateral* (Grand Rapids, Mich.: Zondervan, 1990), pp. 140, 279.

For a penetrating analysis of inerrancy in Wesley and his early followers, see J. Kenneth Grider, "Wesleyanism and the Inerrancy Issue," *Wesleyan Theological Journal* 19, no. 2 (Fall 1984):52-61. Grider concludes that the modern view of "total inerrancy" cannot be attributed to Wesley nor to Adam Clarke, the early Methodist theologian and biblical scholar.

[5]See Heinrich Schmid, *The Doctrinal Theology of the Evangelical Lutheran Church,* trans. Charles A. Hay and Henry E. Jacobs (Minneapolis: Augsburg, 1961), p. 43.

[6]See Andrew D. White, *A History of the Warfare of Science with Theology in Christendom* (1896; rpt. New York: Dover Publications, 1960), 2:369.

[7]Hans Küng, *On Being a Christian,* trans. Edward Quinn (New York: Doubleday, 1976), p. 466.

[8]*The Book of Confessions* (Louisville: Office of the General Assembly Presbyterian Church [U.S.A.], 1991), 9:29.

[9]Augustine, *De consensu Evangelistarum* 1.35, in *Rome and the Study of Scripture,* 6th ed. (St. Meinrad, Ind.: Grail Publications, 1958), p. 25.

[10]Benjamin B. Warfield, *The Inspiration and Authority of the Bible* (Nutley, N.J.: Presbyterian & Reformed, 1948), p. 133; cf. pp. 87, 133, 153. While preferring concursus to dictation with regard to the mode of inspiration, Warfield acknowledged that the divine dictation theory became dominant in the older

Protestant orthodoxy. See *Selected Shorter Writings of Benjamin B. Warfield,* ed. John E. Meeter (Nutley, N.J.: Presbyterian & Reformed, 1973), 2:628-29.

[11]Ibid., p. 137.

[12]Gordon D. Kaufman, *Systematic Theology* (New York: Charles Scribner's Sons, 1968), p. 69.

[13]Quoted in Karl Barth, *Church Dogmatics,* trans. G. T. Thomson and Harold Knight, ed. G. W. Bromiley and T. F. Torrance (Edinburgh: T & T Clark, 1956), 1(2):508.

[14]Calvin, *Corpus Reformatorum,* 40:61-62. Quoted in John H. Leith, *John Calvin's Doctrine of the Christian Life* (Louisville: Westminster/John Knox Press, 1989), p. 63.

[15]For a helpful discussion of how the mainstream Protestant Reformers employed critical methods in their assessment of the canonical Scriptures, see Charles Augustus Briggs, *General Introduction to the Study of Holy Scripture,* rev. ed. (rpt. Grand Rapids, Mich.: Baker, 1970), pp. 140-55.

[16]Calvin, *Institutes of the Christian Religion,* trans. Ford Lewis Battles, ed. John T. McNeill (Philadelphia: Westminster Press, 1960), 2.11.6, p. 455.

[17]Ibid.

[18]Calvin, *Genesis,* trans. John King (Carlisle, Penn.: Banner of Truth Trust, 1975), p. 86.

[19]See William J. Bouwsma, *John Calvin: A Sixteenth-Century Portrait* (New York: Oxford University Press, 1988), p. 120. From Calvin, *Commentary on Matthew* 2:1.

[20]*Luther's Works,* trans. and ed. Theodore G. Tappert (Philadelphia: Fortress, 1967), 54:452.

[21]Ibid., pp. 79-80.

[22]See Schmid, *Doctrinal Theology,* p. 49.

[23]See Timothy Ross Phillips, *Francis Turretin's Idea of Theology and Its Bearing upon His Doctrine of Scripture* (Ann Arbor, Mich.: University Microfilms International, 1986), pp. 80-82. Somewhat different was the position of the Reformed theologian Francis Turretin, who allowed for factual inaccuracies in the Bible so long as they do not involve deceit. See ibid., pp. 662-87.

[24]Ibid., p. 274.

[25]Ibid., p. 287. For Polanus as for Turretin the way we do theology is based on the infused principles of supernatural theology. In these men a rationalizing tendency is qualified by a recognition of our dependence on supernatural grace.

[26]Jack B. Rogers and Donald K. McKim try to make a case that rationalism was at work in Francis Turretin. See Rogers and McKim, *The Authority and Interpretation of the Bible* (New York: Harper & Row, 1979), pp. 172-88. They claim that Turretin sought to ground the divinity of the biblical witness in certain

confirmatory marks or proofs such as the Bible's antiquity and the sincerity of the writers. Timothy Phillips argues persuasively, however, that for Turretin the divinity of the witness belongs to the object of faith and does not rest on a criterion held in common with the culture. At the same time, Turretin apparently believed that the confirmatory marks of divine truth in Scripture could be acknowledged by any rational person who was predisposed to believe. Turretin could also speak of the activity of the theologian as "deducing" or "demonstrating" theological conclusions from first principles. See Phillips, *Francis Turretin's Idea of Theology*, p. 295. This view is not to be construed as theological rationalism, however, but only as evidence of a rationalizing method in theology. Turretin regarded the activity of deduction and demonstration as "acquired theology" as opposed to "infused theology," which alone provides the basis for sound theology (ibid., pp. 276-77, 295-96). For Turretin theology is fundamentally "taught only by God" (ibid., p. 299). That Turretin's theology nevertheless had a rationalistic strain is given some credence by James Daane in *The Freedom of God* (Grand Rapids, Mich.: Eerdmans, 1973), pp. 49-73, 158-76; and John W. Beardslee III in Francis Turretin, *The Doctrine of Scripture*, ed. J. W. Beardslee (Grand Rapids, Mich.: Baker Book House, 1981), pp. 7-19.

[27]See Rogers and McKim, *Authority*, p. 271.

[28]Charles Hodge, *Systematic Theology* (Grand Rapids, Mich.: Eerdmans, 1940), 1:37.

[29]J. K. S. Reid emphasizes the divergence of Protestant orthodoxy from the Reformation (*The Authority of Scripture* [New York: Harper & Bros., 1957]) whereas Richard Muller stresses the continuity (*Post-Reformation Reformed Dogmatics*, 2 vols. [Grand Rapids, Mich.: Baker Book House, 1987-1993]).

[30]Quoted in Jaroslav Pelikan, *The Christian Tradition* (Chicago: University of Chicago Press, 1989), 5:128.

[31]Jonathan Edwards, *Religious Affections*, ed. John E. Smith (New Haven, Conn.: Yale University Press, 1969), 3.4, pp. 278, 270.

[32]John Owen, *The Holy Spirit: His Gifts and Power* (Grand Rapids, Mich.: Kregel Publications, 1967), p. 23. Cf. Edwards: "Take away all the moral beauty and sweetness in the Word, and the Bible is left wholly a dead letter, a dry, lifeless, tasteless thing." *Religious Affections*, p. 274.

[33]Johann Semler, who taught at Halle 1753-1791, was noted for his critical questioning of the historical and theological value of various books of the Bible, including the entire corpus of the Old Testament. See my discussion on pp. 326-27.

[34]See Dale Brown, *Understanding Pietism* (Grand Rapids, Mich.: Eerdmans, 1978); Howard A. Snyder, *The Radical Wesley* (Downers Grove, Ill.: InterVarsity Press, 1980); and Snyder, *Signs of the Spirit* (Grand Rapids, Mich.: Zondervan, 1989).

[35]See Ernest R. Sandeen, *The Origins of Fundamentalism* (Philadelphia: Fortress,

1968); and *The Roots of Fundamentalism* (Chicago: University of Chicago Press, 1970). Abraham regards Louis Gaussen, whose *Theopneustia: the Plenary Inspiration of the Holy Scriptures* was originally published in 1842 and translated in 1888, as a significant source of modern fundamentalism. Gaussen was professor of theology at Ovatoire, Geneva. See William J. Abraham, *The Divine Inspiration of Holy Scripture* (New York: Oxford University Press, 1981), pp. 18–38.

[36]For a broader view of fundamentalism see George M. Marsden, *Fundamentalism and American Culture* (New York: Oxford University Press, 1980).

[37]Edward J. Young, *Thy Word Is Truth* (Grand Rapids, Mich.: Eerdmans, 1957), p. 219.

[38]James Orr, *Revelation and Inspiration* (New York: Charles Scribner's Sons, 1910), pp. 197–98.

[39]A. G. Hebert, *The Authority of the Old Testament* (London: Faber & Faber, 1947), p. 97.

[40]Wick Broomall, *Biblical Criticism* (Grand Rapids, Mich.: Zondervan, 1957), p. 11.

[41]R. A. Torrey, *Is The Bible the Inerrant Word of God?* (New York: George H. Doran Co., 1922), p. 93.

[42]W. A. Criswell, *Why I Preach That the Bible Is Literally True* (Nashville: Broadman, 1969), p. 68.

[43]Walter Elwell, "Knowing God: The State of the Art," *Evangelical Missions Quarterly* 19, no. 4 (Oct. 1983):324–29. Elwell is here giving a comparative analysis of various views on the knowability of God. While most comfortable with the "Traditionalist" position, the author does not summarily put down other approaches but advocates dialogue so that all might come to know the God revealed in Jesus Christ.

[44]The position of the older Protestantism on this issue continues to be a matter of scholarly debate, but I am persuaded that the focus of the Reformers and early Protestant orthodoxy was on the infallibility of the teaching and doctrine of the Bible rather than on scientific inerrancy or absolute historical accuracy. This was also the position of the early Baptists. See James Leo Garrett Jr., "Biblical Authority According to Baptist Confessions of Faith," *Review and Expositor* 76, no. 1 (Winter 1979):43–54.

[45]For the early Clark Pinnock inerrancy is "a necessary inference drawn from the fact that the Bible is *God's* Word." Clark Pinnock, *Biblical Revelation* (Chicago: Moody Press, 1971), pp. 73–74.

[46]James Barr, *Fundamentalism* (Philadelphia: Westminster Press, 1978), p. 49.

[47]J. R. van de Fliert, "Fundamentalism and Fundamentals of Geology," *International Reformed Bulletin* nos. 32-33 (Jan.-April 1968):25. He is reviewing the book by Henry M. Morris and John C. Whitcomb Jr., *The Genesis Flood: The*

Biblical Record and Its Scientific Implications (Philadelphia: Presbyterian & Reformed, 1961).

⁴⁸George Eldon Ladd, *The New Testament and Criticism* (rpt. Grand Rapids, Mich.: Eerdmans, 1971).

⁴⁹Bernard Ramm, *Special Revelation and the Word of God* (Grand Rapids, Mich.: Eerdmans, 1961), pp. 154-60.

⁵⁰See "Ten Days at Wenham: A Seminar on Scripture," *Christianity Today* 10, no. 21 (July 22, 1966):41.

⁵¹Dewey M. Beegle, *The Inspiration of Scripture* (Philadelphia: Westminster Press, 1963), p. 190.

⁵²Ibid.

⁵³See C. Peter Wagner, "High Theology in the Andes," *Christianity Today* 15, no. 8 (Jan. 15, 1971):28-29.

⁵⁴Charles Keysor, "Methodism's Silent Minority," *Christian Advocate* 10, no. 14 (July 14, 1966):9-10.

⁵⁵See the review by Richard Klann of Gottfried Wachler, *Die Inspiration und Irrtumslosigkeit der Schrift* (Uppsala, Sweden, 1984) in *Concordia Journal* 16, no. 1 (Jan. 1990):72-73.

⁵⁶See "The Chicago Statement on Biblical Inerrancy," in *Evangelicals and Inerrancy,* ed. Ronald Youngblood (Nashville: Thomas Nelson, 1984), pp. 230-39; and "The Chicago Statement on Biblical Hermeneutics," in *A Guide to Contemporary Hermeneutics: Major Trends in Biblical Interpretation,* ed. Donald K. McKim (Grand Rapids, Mich.: Eerdmans, 1986), pp. 21-26.

⁵⁷Stanley N. Gundry, "Evangelical Theology: Where *Should* We Be Going?" in *Evangelicals and Inerrancy,* ed. Youngblood, p. 244.

⁵⁸See Kenneth S. Kantzer and Carl F. H. Henry, eds., *Evangelical Affirmations* (Grand Rapids, Mich.: Zondervan, 1990).

⁵⁹Barth, *Church Dogmatics,* 1 (2):529-30.

⁶⁰Ibid., p. 532.

⁶¹Ibid., p. 739.

⁶²Ibid., p. 504.

⁶³Ibid., p. 505.

⁶⁴Ibid., p. 507.

⁶⁵Friedrich Schleiermacher, *On Religion: Speeches to Its Cultured Despisers,* trans. John Oman (New York: Harper & Row, 1958), p. 89.

⁶⁶Paul Tillich, *Systematic Theology* (Chicago: University of Chicago Press, 1951), 1:115.

⁶⁷C. H. Dodd, *The Authority of the Bible* (London: James Nisbet, 1928), pp. 16-17.

⁶⁸Peter W. Macky, *The Bible in Dialogue with Modern Man* (Waco, Tex.: Word Books, 1970), p. 153.

⁶⁹Frank Moore Cross Jr., "Dishonest for God's Sake," *Colloquy* 2, no. 6 (June

1969):27. Cf. Bishop James A. Pike: "In the Scriptures we have quite a mixed bag of truth, of error, of sound ethics, unsound ethics, of myth in the best sense of the word, and legends—some useful, some apparently not so useful." Robert Campbell, ed., *Spectrum of Protestant Beliefs* (Milwaukee, Wis.: Bruce Publishing Co., 1968), p. 34.

[70]See Harry Emerson Fosdick, *The Modern Use of the Bible* (New York: Macmillan, 1924), pp. 97-129.

[71]Küng, *On Being a Christian*, p. 416.

[72]Rosemary Radford Ruether, *Womanguides: Readings Toward a Feminist Theology* (Boston: Beacon Press, 1985), pp. ix-x.

[73]Cf. Emil Brunner: "As Objectivism leads to torpidity, so Subjectivism to dissolution. What is torpid can be awakened again to life; but what is dissolved is no longer in existence." *The Divine-Human Encounter*, trans. Amandus W. Loos (Philadelphia: Westminster Press, 1943), p. 170.

[74]G. C. Berkouwer, *Holy Scripture*, trans. Jack Rogers (Grand Rapids, Mich.: Eerdmans, 1975), pp. 242-43.

[75]Paul Achtemeier, who affirms the divine inspiration of Scripture, comes to the same conclusion. For Achtemeier "the authority of Scripture is . . . demonstrated, not in the literary form in which it has been cast, as supporters of inerrancy would have it, but rather in its power to create and shape reality." Paul J. Achtemeier, *The Inspiration of Scripture: Problems and Proposals* (Philadelphia: Westminster Press, 1980), p. 159.

[76]Augustine, *The Confessions of St. Augustine*, trans. and ed. John K. Ryan (New York: Doubleday, 1960), 2.18, p. 320.

[77]Eugène Portalié, *A Guide to the Thought of St. Augustine*, trans. Ralph J. Bastian (Chicago: Henry Regnery, 1960), p. 122.

[78]See my discussion on pp. 89-90, 109.

[79]Jerome duly acknowledged that historical phenomena were observed in the Bible not "precisely as things actually took place, but in accordance with what men thought at that time" (*In Jer.* 23:15-17; *In Matt.* 14:8), but this must not be construed as implying error. See the discussion in *Rome and the Study of Scripture*, pp. 53-54. Jerome could also argue that whatever the sacred authors say "is the word of God, and not their own; and what the Lord says by their mouths He says, as it were, by means of an instrument." *Tract. de Ps.* 88. See *Rome and the Study of Scripture*, p. 47.

[80]Hugh Evan Hopkins, *Charles Simeon of Cambridge* (London: Hodder & Stoughton, 1977), p. 177.

[81]Ibid., p. 121.

[82]A. A. Hodge and B. B. Warfield, *Inspiration* (rpt. Grand Rapids, Mich.: Baker Book House, 1979), pp. 12-13, 28.

[83]See Moisés Silva, "Old Princeton, Westminster, and Inerrancy," in *Inerrancy*

and Hermeneutic: A Tradition, a Challenge, a Debate, ed. Harvie M. Conn (Grand Rapids, Mich.: Baker Book House, 1988), pp. 68-69.

[84]Calvin, *Commentary of the Book of Psalms*, trans. James Anderson (Edinburgh: Calvin Translation Society, 1846), 58:4, 2:372-73.

[85]One may conjecture that the Amalekite could have brought a false report of Saul's death to David in an attempt to curry his favor. Not everything reported in the Bible is without error.

[86]According to Dewey Beegle neither the Hebrew nor the Septuagint supports Stephen's allegation. Dewey M. Beegle, *Scripture, Tradition and Infallibility* (Grand Rapids, Mich.: Eerdmans, 1973), p. 188.

[87]According to John Woodbridge, Calvin attributed this error to faulty textual transmission. Woodbridge, *Biblical Authority: A Critique of the Rogers/McKim Proposal* (Grand Rapids, Mich.: Zondervan, 1982), p. 61. Gleason Archer raises the possibility that Matthew is combining elements of prophetic symbolism from Zechariah and Jeremiah, and Jeremiah is singled out because of his prominence. Gleason L. Archer, *Encyclopedia of Bible Difficulties* (Grand Rapids, Mich.: Zondervan, 1982), p. 345.

[88]This is not to overlook the possibility of clear-cut contradictions between assertions in the Bible and the new light that modern science brings to the facts in question. Beegle claims that the biblical report of King Pekah reigning for twenty years patently conflicts with the findings of archaeology concerning the date of the fall of Samaria to Assyria. Beegle, *Scripture, Tradition and Infallibility*, pp. 180-86. Harold Lindsell mounts a credible critique of Beegle's theory in *The Battle for the Bible* (Grand Rapids, Mich.: Zondervan, 1976), pp. 171-74, but in an unpublished review of Lindsell's book Beegle shows his dexterity in rebutting Lindsell.

From my perspective Christian faith is not contingent on the success or failure to harmonize all the biblical data with the latest findings in archaeology or historiography, for the focus is on the movement of God in history, which is outside the confines of historical investigation. This does not mean, however, that history is irrelevant to faith, for Christianity would then be transposed into a kind of idealism. It means only that faith rests on God speaking to us in the historical drama of redemption portrayed in the Bible, a history that is relayed to us through the filter of theological interpretation. It should be noted that both archaeology and historical science tend for the most part to support rather than call into question the biblical accounts of historical events. See William F. Albright, *The Archaeology of Palestine and the Bible* (New York: Revell, 1933); Albright, *Archaeology and the Religion of Israel*, 5th ed. (New York: Doubleday Anchor Books, 1969); Albright, *Archaeology, Historical Analogy and Early Biblical Tradition* (Baton Rouge: Louisiana State University Press, 1966); Nelson Glueck, *The Other Side of the Jordan* (Cambridge, Mass.: American Schools of Oriental Research, 1970); Glueck, *Rivers in the Desert: A History of the Negev* (New York: Farrar Straus and Cudahy, 1959); J. A. Thompson, *The Bible and Archaeology,* 3d ed. (Grand Rapids, Mich.: Eerdmans, 1982); David Winton Thomas, *Archaeology and Old Testament Study* (Oxford, U.K.: Clarendon, 1967); Leo G. Perdue, Lawrence E. Toombs and Gary L. Johnson, eds., *Archeology and Biblical Interpretation* (Atlanta: John Knox Press, 1987). The historicity of the patriarchal narratives has been challenged by John Van Seters, *Abraham in History and Tradition* (New Haven, Conn.: Yale University Press, 1975); and T. L. Thompson, *The Historicity of the Patriarchal Narratives* (New York: de Gruyter, 1974). Their conclusions are questioned by Victor P. Hamilton in *The Book of Genesis: Chapters 1—17,* New International Commentary on the Old Testament (Grand Rapids, Mich.: Eerdmans, 1990), pp. 63-67.

[89]*Luther's Works,* ed. Jaroslav Pelikan (St. Louis: Concordia, 1963), 26:62.

[90]This point is well made by Paul H. Seely in *Inerrant Wisdom: Science and Inerrancy in Biblical Perspective* (Portland, Ore.: Evangelical Reform Inc., 1989), pp. 16-17. I take issue with Seely, however, when he says that "the acceptance of science is *sine qua non* to the acceptance of biblical revelation" (pp. 18-19).

[91]I am here siding with Wesley's interpretation of the apparent contradiction over Luther's.

[92]See Norval Geldenhuys, *Commentary on the Gospel of Luke,* New International Commentary on the New Testament (rpt. Grand Rapids, Mich.: Eerdmans, 1966), pp. 523-33, 537-42.

[93]J. K. Mozley, "The Bible: Its Unity, Inspiration and Authority," in *The Christian Faith,* ed. W. R. Matthews (London: Eyre and Spottiswoode, 1936), p. 55.

[94]I. Howard Marshall has these pertinent comments on the problem of historical approximation in the case of Jairus. In this story as recorded by Matthew "it is simply said that when Jairus first met Jesus he told them that his daughter was dead (Matt. 9:18). According to Mark and Luke, however, the daughter was merely on the point of death at the beginning of the story and it was only later—after the incident of the woman with the hemorrhage—that Jairus and Jesus learned that she had actually died (Mark 5:35f.; Luke 8:49f.). There is a clear contradiction between the initial words of Jairus as recorded by Matthew and the other Evangelists. We can, of course, explain the contradiction quite easily and acceptably by saying that Matthew, whose general policy was to tell stories about Jesus in fewer words than Mark, has abbreviated the story and given the general sense of what happened without going into details. But the fact still remains that Matthew has attributed to Jairus words which he did not actually say at the time stated." I. Howard Marshall, *Biblical Inspiration* (Grand Rapids, Mich.: Eerdmans, 1982), p. 61.

95Ramm, *Special Revelation and the Word of God*, p. 192.

96See Peter Stuhlmacher, *Historical Criticism and Theological Interpretation of Scripture: Toward a Hermeneutics of Consent*, trans. Roy A. Harrisville (Philadelphia: Fortress, 1977). See esp. pp. 83-91.

97Alan Richardson, *Preface to Bible-Study* (London: SCM Press, 1943), p. 45.

98Cited in Rogers and McKim, *Authority*, p. 206.

99See Philip Schaff, ed., *The Creeds of Christendom* (New York: Harper & Bros., 1919), 3:387-88.

100To be sure, the teachings of the law are rationally comprehensible, but this is the law of works, not the law of spirit and life discernible only to faith. The natural person invariably misunderstands both the real meaning of the law and the significance of the gospel.

101Clark Pinnock, "Inspiration and Authority: A Truce Proposal," *The Other Side* (May-June 1976):61-65. In *The Scripture Principle* (San Francisco: Harper & Row, 1984) Pinnock wishes to retain the word *inerrancy* because it "has come to symbolize in our day that full confidence that Christians have always had in the Scriptures" (p. 225).

102Ramm, *Special Revelation and the Word of God*, pp. 181-87.

103 *The Book of Confessions*, 9.03.

104There obviously cannot be a contradiction between a literary genre and a scientific fact. The difficulty arises when forms of expression are confused with factual assertions, and this confusion is the problem with strict literalism.

105Warfield, *Inspiration and Authority*, p. 420.

106Augustus H. Strong, *Systematic Theology* (Philadelphia: Judson Press, 1907), 1:196. For an astute appraisal of Strong's view of inspiration see Kern Robert Trembath, *Evangelical Theories of Biblical Inspiration* (New York: Oxford University Press, 1987), pp. 48-57.

107Strong, *Systematic Theology*, 1:228. He is here quoting from William Sanday.

108Ibid., p. 215.

109Quoted in William Childs Robinson, "The Inspiration of Holy Scripture," *Christianity Today* 13, no. 1 (Oct. 11, 1968):7.

110With the Reformers I wish to tie the inspiring work of the Holy Spirit on writers and hearers with the inspired product of the Spirit's operation—Holy Scripture. I am arguing not for an objectified revelation but for an objective locus of revelation.

111See Seely, *Inerrant Wisdom*, pp. 142-45.

112 *True* is here understood in the sense of the Bible being a reliable and trustworthy account of God's mighty deeds in biblical history. This does not imply that the biblical statements in and of themselves constitute the very truth of divine revelation. The biblical words lead us into truth through the working of the Spirit of God, but these words are not in and of themselves redemptive

truth, that is, the very Word of God.

[113]One should note that the attack on verbal inspiration is often motivated by a Platonic view that envisages ideas without words.

[114]Seely rightly warns against viewing the Bible "as a collection of data as good as anything Science has, with each and every disparate part being equally authoritative." The Bible then is on a par with "a chemist's handbook of formulas, freezing points, boiling points, etc. . . . The Bible is thus viewed intellectually, theoretically, and atomistically." *Inerrant Wisdom*, p. 69.

[115]Hans Küng, *Theology for the Third Millennium: An Ecumenical View*, trans. Peter Heinegg (New York: Doubleday, 1988), p. 57.

[116]I empathize with Seely's concern to see the Bible as "sapientially" rather than "factually" inerrant. "This means we must approach it as Jesus did: not . . . legalistically or rationalistically, but spiritually. We shall discern thereby not only its absolute truths but that its relativized truths demand a greater fulfillment consonant with the full glory of the only One who is Absolute." *Inerrant Wisdom*, p. 203.

[117]H. M. Kuitert, *Do You Understand What You Read?* (Grand Rapids, Mich.: Eerdmans, 1970), p. 29. Kuitert fails to state clearly enough that the Bible also transcends history and culture and therefore has universal relevance and authority. He does refer to the "timeless message" of Scripture.

[118]See Herman Bavinck, *Our Reasonable Faith*, trans. Henry Zylstra (Grand Rapids, Mich.: Eerdmans, 1956), pp. 101-13; and Berkouwer, *Holy Scripture*, pp. 151-57.

[119]See Clyde S. Kilby, *The Christian World of C. S. Lewis* (Grand Rapids, Mich.: Eerdmans, 1964), p. 151.

[120]Ibid.

[121]Another pertinent symbol is the descending dove alighting on the open Bible.

[122]James D. Smart, *The Interpretation of Scripture* (Philadelphia: Westminster Press, 1961), pp. 195-96.

[123]Küng, *Theology for the Third Millennium*, p. 56. Where Küng errs is by not giving sufficient attention to the unique way in which Scripture is inspired and to the incommensurable relationship of Scripture to the Jesus Christ of history.

[124]One can say that revelation and inspiration as objective works of God in past history are finished but that they both have a subjective side that continues.

[125]Note that Semler downplayed and even disparaged the Old Testament. For the discussion on Semler see Bruce Demarest, "The Bible in the Enlightenment Era," in *Challenges to Inerrancy*, ed. Gordon R. Lewis and Bruce Demarest (Chicago: Moody Press, 1984), pp. 28-29; Karl Barth, *Protestant Theology in the Nineteenth Century* (Valley Forge, Penn.: Judson Press, 1973), pp. 169-71; John H. S. Kent, in *A History of Christian Doctrine*, ed. Hubert Cunliffe-Jones (Philadelphia: Fortress, 1978), pp. 483-88; and Helmut Thielicke, *Modern Faith*

and Thought, trans. Geoffrey W. Bromiley (Grand Rapids, Mich.: Eerdmans, 1990), pp. 140-56.

[126]Warfield, *Inspiration and Authority,* pp. 137, 149. Though Warfield contended that the Scriptures are the joint product of divine and human activities, he frequently went beyond this idea of concursus by devaluing the human contribution. He could affirm, for example, that "the Divine word delivered through men is the pure word of God, diluted with no human admixture whatever." Ibid., p. 86.

[127]Charles Augustus Briggs, *The Authority of Holy Scripture* (New York: Charles Scribner's Sons, 1891), pp. 30-31. This statement is taken from Briggs's inaugural address at Union Theological Seminary and does not represent the full picture of what he believed. He professed to stand by the Westminster Confession, but at the same time he wished to reconcile traditional Christianity with the theories spawned by higher criticism. He defended the inspiration of thoughts but not of words and was therefore an avowed opponent of the verbal inspiration of Scripture. This view manifests a Platonizing element in which ideas tower loftily above the materiality of words. Like Semler and Schleiermacher, Briggs was prone to dismiss much of the Old Testament as a product of people who belonged to a less enlightened age and who reflected an earlier stage of religious and moral development. See James S. Rila, *Charles A. Briggs and the Problem of Religious Authority* (Iowa City: University of Iowa School of Religion, 1965), pp. 158-60.

Briggs's mature view of scriptural authority is stated in his *General Introduction to the Study of Holy Scripture.* In this study he often approaches the position of modern progressive evangelicals. He could say, for example: "The errors of Holy Scripture are not errors of falsehood, or of deceit; they are such errors of ignorance, inadvertence, of partial and inadequate knowledge, and of incapacity to express the whole truth of God as belong to man as man, and from which we have no evidence that even an inspired man was relieved" (p. 640). He can be commended for trying to recover the dynamic element in divine revelation. On the other side of the ledger he betrayed his dependence on an evolutionary theory of history by seeing the later parts of the Bible as necessarily more elevated in morality and religion than the earlier parts. His liberalism is also evident in his assertion that what is of abiding worth in the Bible is the religious and moral instruction given to the people of God. Even more suspect is his contention that we can come to a true and salvific knowledge of God on the basis of reason alone—apart from explicit faith in the Christ of the Scriptures and the instrumentality of the church. See Briggs, *Authority of Holy Scripture,* pp. 24-27. For a thoughtful reappraisal of Briggs by a Catholic scholar, see Mark Stephen Massa, *Charles Augustus Briggs and the Crisis of Historical Criticism* (Minneapolis: Fortress, 1990).

[128]Nels F. S. Ferré, *Pillars of Faith* (New York: Harper & Bros., 1948), p. 96. Dewey Beegle also holds that extrabiblical writings can be inspired in the same sense as the biblical writings. See his *Scripture, Tradition and Infallibility*, pp. 308–12.

[129]James Barr, *The Bible in the Modern World* (London: SCM Press, 1973), pp. 120, 180.

[130]Ibid., p. 120.

[131]Ibid., p. 148.

[132]Cf.: "Honor your holy Scripture . . . and like us place it on the summit of authority." *Confessions of St. Augustine*, ed. Ryan, 12.16, p. 318. See Augustine, *Letters* 148, to Fortunatianus, in *A Select Library of the Nicene and Post-Nicene Fathers of the Christian Church*, ed. Philip Schaff (Buffalo, N.Y.: Christian Literature Co., 1886), 1:502; Augustine, *On Nature and Grace* 71, in *Select Library*, 5:146.

[133]Küng, *On Being a Christian*, p. 467.

[134]Otto Weber, *Foundations of Dogmatics*, trans. Darrell L. Guder (Grand Rapids, Mich.: Eerdmans, 1981), 1:245.

[135]Gordon D. Kaufman, "What Shall We Do with the Bible?" *Interpretation* 25, no. 1 (Jan. 1971):96. Kaufman accepts the Bible as edifying literature but not as the Word of God.

[136]Rogers and McKim, *Authority*, p. 148.

[137]See Anders Nygren, *Agape and Eros*, trans. Philip S. Watson, rev. ed. (Philadelphia: Westminster Press, 1953).

[138]See Brunner, *Divine-Human Encounter*, pp. 21–41.

[139]I. Howard Marshall finds the same difficulties with the theories of Paul Achtemeier and William Abraham. See Marshall, *Biblical Inspiration*, pp. 37-40.

[140]On Berkouwer's move away from an ontological understanding of the Bible to a functional understanding see John Timmer, "G. C. Berkouwer: Theologian of Confrontation and Co-Relation," *Reformed Journal* 19, no. 10 (Dec. 1969):17-22; and Hendrik Krabbendam, "The Functional Theology of G. C. Berkouwer," in *Challenges to Inerrancy*, ed. Lewis and Demarest, pp. 285-316. We still need a comprehensive scholarly study on Berkouwer's affinity or lack of affinity with Calvin and early Protestant orthodoxy. I think it can be shown that Berkouwer is fairly close to the spirit and method of early Reformation theology, but I grant that there are still significant differences: one need mention only Berkouwer's reluctance to affirm the reality of hell and his existential reinterpretation of the second coming of Christ.

[141]I may misunderstand Rogers and McKim on this point, for their mentor Berkouwer was quite emphatic that inspiration means "that the human word of the *graphē* (writing, or scripture) is God-breathed," and this "undoubtedly points to the mystery of its being filled with truth and trustworthiness." Ber-

kouwer, *Holy Scripture,* p. 140. Berkouwer affirms the form-content distinction of the Reformation and classical Christian faith as well as the form-function distinction, which also has a firm basis in historical theology, but the latter has much more significance for Rogers and McKim. Rogers and McKim occasionally employ the form-content distinction, but they do not see the content embedded in the form but extraneous to it.

142"The Bout for the Bible" (Door Interviews/Harold Lindsell vs. Jack Rogers), *The Wittenburg Door,* Feb.-March 1980, p. 28.

143Jack Rogers, *Presbyterian Creeds: A Guide to the Book of Confessions* (Philadelphia: Westminster Press, 1985), p. 71.

144Rogers and McKim might have difficulty in affirming with Alvin Kimel: "The Word of God cannot be divorced from the language and imagery of the Scriptures. By the direction of the Spirit, God chooses the names and metaphors by which he will be known and addressed. They are authoritatively communicated in the Bible and enjoy a normative, paradigmatic status in the life of the Church. Baptized into Christ, they are made a constituent part of the divine revelation. Through them we are granted to apprehend the Triune Deity. The revelatory efficacy of these images depends not on their natural, iconic character, but on the fact that God has clothed himself in them. They are historically grounded in the being of the eternal Logos: the Word is known through his words." Alvin F. Kimel Jr., *A New Language for God?* (Shaker Heights, Ohio: Episcopalians United, 1990), p. 3.

145Rogers, *Presbyterian Creeds,* pp. 69-73.

146Woodbridge, *Biblical Authority,* pp. 42-43.

147See Portalié, *Guide to Augustine,* pp. 114-19. Cf. Augustine: "If, then, it is reasonable that faith precede reason to attain to certain great truths which cannot yet be understood, it is without doubt true that it is reason, in however small degree, that persuades us to it, so that reason itself precedes faith." *An Augustine Synthesis,* ed. Erich Przywara (New York: Sheed & Ward, 1936), p. 62. See Augustine *Letters* 120.1.3.4. See also Augustine *On Virginity* 19. For an illuminating discussion of how Augustine relates faith and reason see Dewey J. Hoitenga Jr., *Faith and Reason from Plato to Plantinga* (Albany: State University of New York, 1991), pp. 57-142. In Hoitenga's interpretation Augustine assumes a natural knowledge of God prior to faith but insists on the indispensability of faith for a true understanding of God's will and purpose. Reasons may be appropriate for attracting the unbeliever to Scripture, but they are in themselves insufficient for leading this person to adhere to the truth of Scripture (see esp. pp. 140-41).

148Eugene TeSelle, *Augustine the Theologian* (New York: Herder & Herder, 1970), pp. 77-89.

149Ibid., p. 81.

150For bibliographical data see notes 23 and 29.

151Phillips, *Francis Turretin's Idea of Theology,* p. 795. According to Phillips, Turretin held to the fundamental truthfulness of the Bible as the conduit and vessel of the divine wisdom, not as a literary or historical document. There is no error "relating to the essential structures and principles of *theologia"* (pp. 795, 798).

152Ibid., p. 795.

153Ibid., p. 793

154Ibid.

155Muller, *Post-Reformation Reformed Dogmatics,* 1:302.

156This thesis is amply documented in Reid, *Authority of Scripture,* and Jaroslav Pelikan, *From Luther to Kierkegaard* (St. Louis: Concordia, 1950).

157The fact that Warfield, the mentor of many modern fundamentalists, was uncomfortable with the Heidelberg Catechism testifies to the gulf between modern evangelical rationalism and early Protestant orthodoxy. The experientialist cast of the Heidelberg Catechism presented a problem to Warfield and other evangelical rationalists. See M. Eugene Osterhaven, "The Experientialism of the Heidelberg Catechism and Orthodoxy," in *Controversy and Conciliation,* ed. Derk Visser (Allison Park, Penn.: Pickwick Publications, 1986), pp. 197-203. Also see B. B. Warfield, "The First Question of the Westminster 'Shorter Catechism,' " *Princeton Theological Review* 6 (1908):565.

158See Willem Jan Kooiman, *Luther and the Bible,* trans. John Schmidt (Philadelphia: Muhlenberg Press, 1961). Woodbridge also appeals to Edward A. Dowey among others in arguing for the idea of total inerrancy in Calvin (Woodbridge, *Biblical Authority,* p. 57), but he neglects to point out that in the second edition of Dowey's *The Knowledge of God in Calvin's Theology* (New York: Columbia University Press, 1965) the author acknowledges the difference between Calvin's position and modern fundamentalism.

159Schaff reflected the views of many evangelicals in nineteenth-century America when he declared: "The Bible is a book of religion, not a book of geology, astronomy, chronology or science. To require more than this is sheer tyranny that would out-pope popery. It is enough to hold and to teach that the Bible is an infallible rule of faith and duty." Cited in Carl E. Hatch, *The Charles A. Briggs Heresy Trial* (New York: Exposition Press, 1969), p. 105.

160According to Muller the issue in the older Protestant orthodoxy was the linguistic continuity between the original autographs and the extant text, not verbal inerrancy. For theologians like the elder Turretin the autographs played no significant role in their arguments for the infallibility of Scripture. Muller, *Post-Reformation Reformed Dogmatics* 2:434-35.

161The impact of the Enlightenment is noticeable in Briggs's *The Ethical Teaching of Jesus* (New York: Charles Scribner's Sons, 1904), where he interprets the union of Jesus and God as a moral one. His theology was oriented toward the practical and moral rather than the metaphysical and speculative. See n. 127.

[162]Lindsell, *Battle for the Bible,* p. 18.

[163]The gulf between Reformation theology and modern fundamentalism can be seen in Lindsell's dismissal of the issue of baptism as "inconsequential." *Wittenburg Door,* p. 21.

[164]See J. C. K. von Hofmann, *Interpreting the Bible,* trans. Christian Preus (Minneapolis: Augsburg, 1972).

Chapter 5: Scripture and the Church

[1]See Oscar Cullmann, "Scripture and Tradition," in *Christianity Divided,* ed. Daniel J. Callahan, Heiko A. Oberman and Daniel J. O'Hanlon (New York: Sheed & Ward, 1961) pp. 20-21.

[2]Ibid., p. 24.

[3]*St. Basil the Great on the Holy Spirit* (Crestwood, N.Y.: St. Vladimir's Seminary Press, 1980), pp. 98-99.

[4]Pelikan maintains that the Catholic response to the Gnostic claim to traditions beyond Scripture was formulated most fully by Irenaeus, who appealed to "that tradition which is derived from the apostles." Jaroslav Pelikan, *The Emergence of the Catholic Tradition (100—600)* (Chicago: University of Chicago Press, 1971), p. 115.

[5]Athanasius, *Contra Gentes,* trans. Robert W. Thomson (Oxford, U.K.: Clarendon, 1971), 1, p. 3.

[6]*Catechetical Lectures* 4.17. See J. N. D. Kelly, *Early Christian Doctrines* (rpt. New York: Harper & Row, 1978), p. 42.

[7]*Dogmatic Constitution on Divine Revelation* 2.8, in *The Documents of Vatican II,* ed. Walter M. Abbott (Chicago: Follett Publishing Co., 1966), p. 116.

[8]Josef Rupert Geiselmann, "Scripture, Tradition, and the Church: An Ecumenical Problem," in *Christianity Divided,* ed. Callahan et al., pp. 39-72.

[9]Ibid., p. 65.

[10]See Frederick C. Grant, "A Response," in *Documents of Vatican II,* ed. Abbott, pp. 129-32.

[11]Yves Congar, *The Meaning of Tradition,* trans. A. N. Woodrow (New York: Hawthorn, 1964), pp. 94-95.

[12]Ibid., p. 94.

[13]*Revelation* 2.9, in *Documents of Vatican II,* ed. Abbott, p. 117.

[14]Ibid.

[15]Ibid.

[16]Weimarer Ausgabe, 30[II]:420. Cited in Paul Althaus, *The Theology of Martin Luther,* trans. Robert C. Schultz (Philadelphia: Fortress, 1966), p. 6.

[17]Althaus, *Theology of Martin Luther,* p. 38. Weimarer Ausgabe, 30[II]: 687-88.

[18]*The Table-Talk of Martin Luther,* trans. William Hazlitt (Philadelphia: Lutheran Board of Publication, 1868), p. 281.

[19]See N. F. S. Grundtvig, *What Constitutes Authentic Christianity?* trans. Ernest D. Nielsen (Philadelphia: Fortress, 1985); Ernest D. Nielsen, *N. F. S. Grundtvig: An American Study* (Rock Island, Ill.: Augustana Press, 1955); P. G. Lindhardt, *Grundtvig: An Introduction* (London: SPCK, 1951); Johannes Knudsen, *Danish Rebel* (Philadelphia: Muhlenberg Press, 1955); G. Everett Arden, *Four Northern Lights* (Minneapolis: Augsburg, 1964), pp. 79-113. On the striking contrast between Grundtvig and Kierkegaard see John W. Elrod, *Kierkegaard and Christendom* (Princeton, N.J.: Princeton University Press, 1981), pp. 14-34, 193-202.

[20]James Barr, *The Scope and Authority of the Bible* (Philadelphia: Westminster Press, 1980), p. 64.

[21]Ibid., p. 60.

[22]Ibid.

[23]Kenneth S. Jensen, "Who Says 'the Bible Says,' " *Again* 5, no. 3 (1982):7.

[24]Burton Throckmorton Jr., *Christianity Today* 27, no. 19 (Dec. 16, 1983):40.

[25]Cf. Forsyth: "The canon of the Bible rose from the Church, but not its contents. Bible and Church were collateral products of the Gospel." P. T. Forsyth, *The Person and Place of Jesus Christ* (Philadelphia: Westminster Press, 1910), pp. 140-41.

[26]See Karl Barth, *Church Dogmatics,* trans. G. T. Thomson and Harold Knight, ed. G. W. Bromiley and T. F. Torrance (Edinburgh: T & T Clark, 1956), 1(2):473-537, 585-660.

[27]See R. P. C. Hanson, *The Continuity of Christian Doctrine* (New York: Seabury Press, 1981).

[28]George H. Tavard, *Holy Writ or Holy Church* (New York: Harper & Bros., 1959), p. 66.

[29]Robert C. Stroud, "A Lutheran Pastor Speaks Out," *Again* 3, no. 2 (April-June 1980):5.

[30]Weimarer Ausgabe, 51:516, 518. See Rudolf J. Ehrlich, *Rome, Opponent or Partner?* (Philadelphia: Westminster Press, 1965), p. 258.

[31]*Acts of the First Zurich Disputation* (1523), cited in Cyril Eastwood, *The Priesthood of Believers* (Minneapolis: Augsburg, 1962), p. 218.

[32]Karl Barth, *Theology and Church,* trans. Louise Pettibone Smith (New York: Harper & Row, 1962), p. 283.

[33]Quoted in Arthur T. Pierson, *George Müller of Bristol* (New York: Baker & Taylor, 1899), p. 66. Cyprian *Epistle* 74.10.

[34]Augustine, *Against the Epistle of Manichaeus* 5, in *Nicene and Post-Nicene Fathers of the Christian Church,* ed. Philip Schaff (New York: Charles Scribner's Sons, 1901), 4:131.

[35]Cited in Lev Shestov, *Athens and Jerusalem,* trans. Bernard Martin (Athens,

Ohio: Ohio University Press, 1966), p. 298.

[36]For the Reformers experience was the medium of divine revelation rather than its criterion or source.

[37]*Luther's Works,* ed. Eric W. Gritsch (Philadelphia: Fortress, 1966), 41:26.

[38]Quoted by Chemnitz in Eugene F. A. Klug, *From Luther to Chemnitz* (Grand Rapids, Mich.: Eerdmans, 1971), p. 167.

[39]John Knox, *Criticism and Faith* (Nashville: Abingdon, 1952), pp. 58-70.

[40]See Ehrlich, *Rome,* p. 285.

[41]Gabriel Biel, *A Defense of Apostolic Obedience* 1, in *Defensorium Obedientiae Apostolicae et Alia Documenta,* trans. and ed. Heiko A. Oberman, Daniel E. Zerfoss and William J. Courtenay (Cambridge, Mass.: Harvard University Press, 1968), p. 75.

[42]Karl Rahner, *Foundations of Christian Faith,* trans. William V. Dych (New York: Seabury Press, 1978), p. 371.

[43]*Revelation* 2.10, in *Documents of Vatican II,* ed. Abbott, p. 118.

[44]Donald Senior, "Dogmatic Constitution on Divine Revelation," in *Vatican II and Its Documents: An American Reappraisal,* ed. Timothy E. O'Connell (Wilmington, Del.: Michael Glazier, 1986), p. 130.

[45]Ehrlich, *Rome,* p. 245.

[46]Dewey Beegle, *Scripture, Tradition and Infallibility* (Grand Rapids, Mich.: Eerdmans, 1973), p. 110.

[47]S. M. Hutchens, "Gridlocked," *Touchstone* 5, no. 3 (Summer 1992):47. Also see Hutchens, "The Bible Under Spirit and Church," *Touchstone* 4, no. 2 (March 1991):3-10.

[48]Barth, *Theology and Church,* p. 277.

[49]Papal letter to German bishops cited by Pope John Paul II during his visit to Germany in 1980. Reported in *Des Moines Register,* Nov. 19, 1980, p. 12A.

[50]William Neil, *The Rediscovery of the Bible* (New York: Harper & Bros., 1954), p. 114.

[51]Dietrich Bonhoeffer, *The Cost of Discipleship,* trans. Reginald H. Fuller (London: SCM Press, 1959), p. 225.

[52]Dietrich Bonhoeffer, *The Communion of Saints,* trans. Ronald Gregor Smith (New York: Harper & Row, 1963), pp. 160-61.

[53]Emil Brunner, *The Word and the World* (New York: Charles Scribner's Sons, 1931), p. 112.

[54]Tavard, *Holy Writ,* p. 246.

[55]*Revelation* 2.10, in *Documents of Vatican II,* ed. Abbott, pp. 117-18.

[56]Schubert Ogden, *On Theology* (San Francisco: Harper & Row, 1986), p. 64.

[57]Westminster Confession, 1.10, in *The Creeds of Christendom,* ed. Philip Schaff (New York: Harper & Bros., 1919), 3:605-6.

[58]See Tavard, *Holy Writ,* p. 164.

[59]P. T. Forsyth, *The Preaching of Jesus and the Gospel of Christ* (Blackwood, South Australia: New Creation Publications, 1987), p. 64.

[60]Gabriel Fackre, *The Christian Story* (Grand Rapids, Mich.: Eerdmans, 1987), 2:92–94.

[61]Charles E. Curran, "On Dissent in the Church," *Commonweal* 113, no. 15 (Sept. 12, 1986):461.

[62]Tavard, *Holy Writ*, p. 1.

[63]*Apocrypha* is from the Greek *apokrypha,* meaning "hidden things."

[64]See Charles Cutler Torrey, *The Apocryphal Literature: A Brief Introduction* (rpt. New Haven, Conn.: Yale University Press, 1953), p. 3.

[65]Ibid., p. 26.

[66]Ibid.

[67]Ibid., p. 32.

[68]See Bruce M. Metzger, *An Introduction to the Apocrypha* (New York: Oxford University Press, 1957), p. 194.

[69]Norman Geisler, *Christian Apologetics* (Grand Rapids, Mich.: Baker Book House, 1976), pp. 363–68.

[70]Metzger, *Introduction to the Apocrypha.*

[71]Ibid., p. 172.

[72]Albert C. Sundberg Jr., "The 'Old Testament': A Christian Canon," *Catholic Biblical Quarterly* 30, no. 2 (April 1968):143–55. See esp. p. 154.

[73]Ibid., pp. 154–55.

[74]This mentality is transcended in Ecclus 5:2: "Do not follow your inclination and strength, walking according to the desires of your heart."

[75]See W. O. E. Oesterley, *An Introduction to the Books of the Apocrypha* (New York: Macmillan, 1935), pp. 10–11.

[76]Torrey, *Apocryphal Literature*, p. 37.

[77]Ibid., pp. 18–19.

[78]Ibid., p. 19. Another book by the same name does exist. See O. S. Wintermute, "Apocalypse of Elijah," in *The Old Testament Pseudepigrapha,* ed. James H. Charlesworth (New York: Doubleday, 1983), 1:721–53. See esp. p. 728.

[79]"Newman Manuscripts on Holy Scripture" 3, in Jaak Seynaeve, *Cardinal Newman's Doctrine on Holy Scripture* (Oxford, U.K.: Basil Blackwell, 1953), pp. 50–51. This statement belongs to his Anglican period, though the exact date is unknown.

[80]Metzger, *Introduction to the Apocrypha,* pp. 181–85.

Chapter 6: The Hermeneutical Problem

[1]Thomas F. Torrance, *Reality and Evangelical Theology* (Philadelphia: Westminster Press, 1982), p. 115.

[2]Ibid. Also see pp. 114–16.

[3]Clark H. Pinnock, *The Scripture Principle* (San Francisco: Harper & Row, 1984), p. 88.

[4]Note that synthesis and application are the two sides of exposition.

[5]I here acknowledge an affinity with James Packer, but I would probably be more open to historical-critical study as an aid in biblical exegesis. Packer seeks to distance himself from an evangelical "self-reliant rationalism" that minimizes or downplays the role of the Holy Spirit in biblical interpretation. See James I. Packer, "Infallible Scripture and the Role of Hermeneutics," in *Scripture and Truth,* ed. D. A. Carson and John D. Woodbridge (Grand Rapids, Mich.: Zondervan, 1983), pp. 325-56, esp. pp. 347-48.

[6]See P. T. Forsyth, *The Gospel and Authority,* ed. Marvin W. Anderson (Minneapolis: Augsburg, 1971), pp. 23-24.

[7]Rudolf Otto, *The Kingdom of God and the Son of Man,* trans. Floyd V. Filson and Bertram Lee Woolf, rev. ed. (Boston: Starr King Press, 1951), pp. 100-101.

[8]James I. Packer, "Biblical Authority, Hermeneutics and Inerrancy," in *Jerusalem and Athens,* ed. E. R. Geehan (Nutley, N.J.: Presbyterian & Reformed, 1971), p. 147. Also see his "Is Systematic Theology a Mirage?" in *Doing Theology in Today's World,* ed. John D. Woodbridge and Thomas E. McComiskey (Grand Rapids, Mich.: Zondervan, 1991), pp. 29-33.

[9]Packer, "Biblical Authority," pp. 147-48.

[10]See Richard J. Bernstein, "From Hermeneutics to Praxis," in *Hermeneutics and Praxis,* ed. Robert Hollinger (Notre Dame, Ind.: University of Notre Dame Press, 1985), p. 276.

[11]I am here making a distinction between the presence of the living Word and the written Word of God, although at the same time I affirm their inseparability through the action of the Holy Spirit.

[12]See Donald G. Bloesch, *Essentials of Evangelical Theology* (San Francisco: Harper & Row, 1982), 1:71-72.

[13]John Calvin, *Commentary on the Epistles of Paul the Apostle to the Corinthians,* trans. John Pringle (Edinburgh: T. Constable for Calvin Translation Society, 1848), 1:84.

[14]Torrance perceptively states Calvin's hermeneutic principle: "In order to know the Truth of God out of itself, we must let ourselves be questioned so radically that we center everything in him and nothing in ourselves." T. F. Torrance, *The Hermeneutics of John Calvin* (Edinburgh: Scottish Academic Press, 1988), p. 150.

[15]See *Pilgrimage of the Heart: A Treasury of Eastern Christian Spirituality,* ed. George A. Maloney (New York: Harper & Row, 1983), p. 106.

[16]Karl Barth, *Church Dogmatics,* trans. G. T. Thomson and Harold Knight, ed. G. W. Bromiley and T. F. Torrance (Edinburgh: T & T Clark, 1956), 1(2):695.

[17]Thomas à Kempis, *The Imitation of Christ,* trans. Leo Sherley-Price (Har-

mondsworth, Middlesex: Penguin Books, 1959) 3.2, p. 90.

[18]See August Hermann Francke, *A Guide to the Reading and Study of the Holy Scriptures,* trans. Wm. Jaques, 2d ed. (London: Burton and Briggs, 1815), pp. 86–87.

[19]Thielicke's position is similar: "We cannot be completely without presuppositions. We cannot jump over our own shadows. But with critical vigilance we can take our presuppositions into account, see in them a blind spot (and hence a necessity, not a hermeneutical virtue), and thus keep them under control." Helmut Thielicke, *Modern Faith and Thought,* trans. Geoffrey W. Bromiley (Grand Rapids, Mich.: Eerdmans, 1990), p. 33.

[20]See P. T. Forsyth, *The Person and Place of Jesus Christ* (London: Independent Press, 1955), pp. 60, 165ff.; *The Principle of Authority* (London: Independent Press, 1952), pp. 145, 157.

[21]*Luther's Works,* ed. Hilton C. Oswald (St. Louis: Concordia, 1972), 25:415.

[22]Cited in G. C. Berkouwer, *A Half Century of Theology,* trans. Lewis B. Smedes (Grand Rapids, Mich.: Eerdmans, 1977), p. 118.

[23]Cited by David C. Steinmetz, "The Superiority of Precritical Exegesis," in *A Guide to Contemporary Hermeneutics: Major Trends in Biblical Interpretation,* ed. Donald K. McKim (Grand Rapids, Mich.: Eerdmans, 1986), p. 65.

[24]Albert E. Barnett, *Interpreter's Bible* (New York: Abingdon, 1957), 12:186.

[25]Steinmetz, "Precritical Exegesis," p. 66.

[26]Ibid., p. 76.

[27]Philip Edgcumbe Hughes, "The Truth of Scripture and the Problem of Historical Relativity," in *Scripture and Truth,* ed. Carson and Woodbridge, p. 187.

[28]*The Confessions of St. Augustine,* trans. John K. Ryan (New York: Doubleday, 1960), 11.2, p. 279.

[29]Steinmetz, "Precritical Exegesis," p. 68.

[30]Ibid., p. 69.

[31]See ibid., pp. 69–70.

[32]Paul Althaus, *The Theology of Martin Luther,* trans. Robert C. Schultz (rpt. Philadelphia: Fortress, 1970), pp. 96-98. Douglas Moo argues that "Protestant interpreters retained a *sensus mysticus* or *spiritualis* alongside the *sensus literalis* but took pains to distinguish this secondary sense from Roman Catholic notions of the mystical sense by insisting that it was part of the one sense intended by the true author of Scripture, the Holy Spirit." Douglas J. Moo, "The Problem of Sensus Plenior," in *Hermeneutics, Authority and Canon,* ed. D. A. Carson and John D. Woodbridge (Grand Rapids, Mich.: Zondervan, 1986), p. 183.

[33]Althaus, *Theology of Martin Luther,* p. 96.

[34]William H. Goold, ed., *The Works of John Owen* (London: Johnstone and Hunter, 1850-55), 20:19. See Stanley N. Gundry, "John Owen on Authority and Scrip-

ture" in *Inerrancy and the Church,* ed. John D. Hannah (Chicago: Moody Press, 1984), pp. 189-221.

[35]Quoted in F. Ernest Stoeffler, *The Rise of Evangelical Pietism* (Leiden: E. J. Brill, 1965), p. 133.

[36]Jonathan Edwards, *Religious Affections,* ed. John E. Smith (New Haven, Conn.: Yale University Press, 1976), p. 280.

[37]*John Wesley,* ed. Albert C. Outler (New York: Oxford University Press, 1964), pp. 223-24.

[38]Ibid., pp. 224-25.

[39]David C. Steinmetz, "Theology and Exegesis: Ten Theses," in *Guide,* ed. McKim, p. 27.

[40]Steinmetz, "Precritical Exegesis," p. 76.

[41]William Sanford LaSor, "The *Sensus Plenior* and Biblical Interpretation," in *Guide,* ed. McKim, p. 63.

[42]Bruce K. Waltke, "A Canonical Process Approach to the Psalms," in *Tradition and Testament,* ed. John S. Feinberg and Paul D. Feinberg (Chicago: Moody Press, 1981), p. 7.

[43]Ibid.

[44]Jacques Ellul, *The Meaning of the City,* trans. Dennis Pardee (Grand Rapids, Mich.: Eerdmans, 1970), p. xvii.

[45]Ibid., p. xviii.

[46]Walter C. Kaiser Jr., "Legitimate Hermeneutics," in *Guide,* ed. McKim, p. 139.

[47]See E. D. Hirsch Jr., *Validity in Interpretation* (New Haven, Conn.: Yale University Press, 1967), p. 8. For a reconsideration of the wider meaning of the scriptural text and a salutary corrective to the position of Hirsch and those evangelicals who appeal to him, see Elliott Johnson, "Author's Intention and Biblical Interpretation," in *Hermeneutics, Inerrancy, and the Bible,* ed. Earl D. Radmacher and Robert D. Preus (Grand Rapids, Mich.: Zondervan, 1984), pp. 409-29. Johnson seeks to incorporate the truth in the hermeneutics of authorial intention as this is understood in evangelical tradition but also to go beyond it. In so doing he significantly expands the meaning of authorial intention.

[48]Hans-Georg Gadamer, *Truth and Method* (New York: Crossroad, 1975), p. 264.

[49]LaSor, *"Sensus Plenior,"* p. 53.

[50]One may discern points of convergence between my position on this subject and contemporary Catholic efforts to reassess the spiritual sense without falling into arbitrary exegesis. I am thinking of scholars like Louis Bouyer, Henri de Lubac, Hans Urs von Balthasar, Yves Congar, Paul Quay and Avery Dulles. Dulles contends that "spiritual exegesis," which discloses the mysteries relating to Christ and his church, "incorporates some of the finest insights of the biblical theology movement." Avery Dulles, *The Craft of Theology: From Symbol to System* (New York: Crossroad, 1992), p. 74.

[51] Athanasius, *Contra Gentes,* trans. Robert W. Thomson (Oxford, U.K.: Clarendon, 1971), 1, p. 3.

[52] See V. Norskov Olsen, "The Christ Alone: The Christomonistic Principle," *Ministry* 53, no. 2 (Jan. 1980):6. Cf. *Luther's Works,* ed. Jaroslav Pelikan (St. Louis: Concordia, 1961), 3:148-51.

[53] Augustine, *On Christian Doctrine,* trans. D. W. Robertson Jr. (New York: Liberal Arts Press, 1958), p. 38.

[54] John Knox, *The History of the Reformation of Religion Within the Realm of Scotland,* ed. C. J. Guthrie (Edinburgh: Banner of Truth, 1982), p. 280.

[55] Cf. Calvin: "If any one will seek to know more than what God has revealed, he shall be overwhelmed with the immeasurable brightness of inaccessible light." John Calvin, *Commentaries on the Epistle of Paul the Apostle to the Romans,* trans. John Owen (Edinburgh: Calvin Translation Society, 1849), p. 447. Also see *Institutes* 3.21.2.

[56] P. T. Forsyth, "The Evangelical Churches and the Higher Criticism," *Contemporary Review* 88 (July-Dec. 1905):588.

[57] Arthur L. Johnson, *Faith Misguided* (Chicago: Moody Press, 1988), p. 53.

[58] See Carl Henry, *God, Revelation and Authority* (Waco, Tex.: Word Books, 1976), 1:225-44; (1979), 3:455-81; (1979), 4:272-95.

[59] For a lucid introduction to historical criticism see Robert Morgan and John Barton, *Biblical Interpretation* (New York: Oxford University Press, 1988), and Edgar Krentz, *The Historical-Critical Method* (Philadelphia: Fortress, 1975). Also exceedingly helpful is Herbert F. Hahn, *The Old Testament in Modern Research,* rev. ed. (Philadelphia: Fortress, 1966).

[60] H. Martin Rumscheidt, *Revelation and Theology: An Analysis of the Barth-Harnack Correspondence of 1923* (London: Cambridge University Press, 1972), p. 5.

[61] Cited by E. Schillebeeckx, *Jesus: An Experiment in Christology,* trans. Hubert Hoskins (New York: Crossroad, 1981), p. 38. See Ernst Troeltsch, "Über historische und dogmatische Methode in der Theologie," *Gesammelte Schriften* (Tübingen: J. C. B. Mohr, 1913), 2:745. Also see note 94.

[62] For Gadamer, "since the self is implicated in history, our self-understanding, and every step in our understanding of anything else, marks an advance in the unfolding of an 'effective-historical consciousness.' " W. James S. Farris, "The Hermeneutical Arc," *Toronto Journal of Theology* 4, no. 1 (Spring 1988):87.

[63] Wilhelm Herrmann, *The Communion of the Christian with God,* ed. Robert T. Voelkel (Philadelphia: Fortress, 1971), p. 76.

[64] See F. D. E. Schleiermacher, *Hermeneutics,* trans. James Duke and Jack Forstman, ed. Heinz Kimmerle (Missoula, Mont.: Scholars Press, 1977).

[65] Alan Richardson, *History Sacred and Profane* (Philadelphia: Westminster, 1964), p. 163. Richardson is summarizing Dilthey's approach.

[66]See Gabriel Fackre, *The Christian Story* (Grand Rapids, Mich.: Eerdmans, 1987), 2:165. Romanticist hermeneutics is represented in the twentieth century by Emilio Betti (d. 1968), who regarded the underlying experience of the author of the text as the key to the meaning of the text. Schillebeeckx's hermeneutics of experience has affinities with Romanticism, for in his view "lived experience" is an indispensable criterion for theology. See Anthony C. Thiselton, "Hermeneutics and Theology: The Legitimacy and Necessity of Hermeneutics," in *Guide,* ed. McKim, p. 167.

[67]It is often alleged that Fuchs and Ebeling, the luminaries of the so-called new hermeneutic, sought to ground hermeneutics in ontology, whereas Bultmann's emphasis was on the alteration of individual consciousness. But it can be shown that Bultmann's position too is anchored in an ontology of historical becoming—reflecting motifs in both Hegel and Heidegger. Moreover, Fuchs and Ebeling were intensely concerned with the realization of authentic existence through an encounter with the text. Fuchs described the hermeneutical task as "the interpretation of our own existence. . . . We should accept as true only that which we acknowledge as valid for our own person." Ernst Fuchs, "The New Testament and the Hermeneutical Problem," in *New Frontiers in Theology,* vol. 2, *The New Hermeneutic,* ed. James M. Robinson and John B. Cobb Jr. (New York: Harper & Row, 1964), p. 117.

[68]See Wolfhart Pannenberg, "Hermeneutics and Universal History," *Journal for Theology and the Church,* vol. 4, *History and Hermeneutic,* ed. Robert W. Funk (Tübingen: J. C. B. Mohr; and New York: Harper & Row, 1967), pp. 122-52.

[69]Pannenberg, *Basic Questions in Theology,* trans. George H. Kehm (Philadelphia: Westminster Press, 1971), 2:65-118. See also Pannenberg, *Systematic Theology,* trans. G. W. Bromiley (Grand Rapids, Mich.: Eerdmans, 1988), 1:230-57.

[70]See Oscar Cullmann, *Salvation in History,* trans. Sidney G. Sowers (New York: Harper & Row, 1967).

[71]Gerhard von Rad, "Typological Interpretation of the Old Testament," trans. John Bright, in *Guide,* ed. McKim, p. 37.

[72]See esp. John B. Cobb Jr. and David Ray Griffin, *Process Theology: An Introductory Exposition* (Philadelphia: Westminster Press, 1976); Marjorie Hewitt Suchocki, *God—Christ—Church* (New York: Crossroad, 1982); Lewis S. Ford, *The Lure of God: A Biblical Background for Process Theism* (Philadelphia: Fortress, 1978); and David A. Pailin, *God and the Processes of Reality* (London: Routledge, 1989). While this movement embraces various positions on God, Christ and the world, it is united in affirming the inseparability of God and nature.

[73]For a helpful analysis of process thought by more traditionalist theologians see *Process Theology,* ed. Ronald H. Nash (Grand Rapids, Mich.: Baker Book House, 1987); and Donald K. McKim, *What Christians Believe About the Bible* (Nash-

ville: Thomas Nelson, 1985), pp. 107-15.

[74]See Charles H. Kraft, "Supracultural Meanings via Cultural Forms," in *Guide*, ed. McKim, pp. 309-43.

[75]See Sergio Torres and Virginia Fabella, *The Emergent Gospel: Theology from the Underside of History* (Maryknoll, N.Y.: Orbis Books, 1978); José Míguez Bonino, *Doing Theology in a Revolutionary Situation* (Philadelphia: Fortress, 1975); Orlando E. Costas, "The Subversiveness of Faith: A Paradigm for Doing Liberation Theology," in *Doing Theology in Today's World,* ed. Woodbridge and McComiskey, pp. 377-96; Elisabeth Schüssler Fiorenza, *In Memory of Her: A Feminist Theological Reconstruction of Christian Origins* (New York: Crossroad, 1983); Rebecca S. Chopp, *The Power to Speak: Feminism, Language, God* (New York: Crossroad, 1989); and Rosemary Radford Ruether, *Gaia & God: An Ecofeminist Theology of Earth Healing* (San Francisco: HarperCollins, 1992). For a comprehensive survey and valuable critique of sociocritical hermeneutics see Anthony C. Thiselton, *New Horizons in Hermeneutics* (Grand Rapids, Mich.: Zondervan, 1992), pp. 379-470.

[76]See Brevard S. Childs, *Introduction to the Old Testament as Scripture* (Philadelphia: Fortress, 1979); Childs, *The New Testament as Canon* (Philadelphia: Fortress, 1985); Childs, *Biblical Theology of the Old and New Testaments* (Minneapolis: Fortress, 1993); R. W. L. Moberly, "The Church's Use of the Bible: The Work of Brevard Childs," *Expository Times* 99, no. 4 (Jan. 1988):104-9; James A. Sanders, *Torah and Canon* (Philadelphia: Fortress, 1972); and Jon D. Levenson, "The Bible: Unexamined Commitments of Criticism," *First Things* no. 30 (Feb. 1993):24-33.

[77]See my discussion on pp. 208-18.

[78]Carl Armerding, "Structural Analysis," *Themelios* 4, no. 3 (April 1979):99.

[79]See Edgar V. McKnight, *Post-Modern Use of the Bible* (Nashville: Abingdon, 1988). A more critical treatment is to be found in Anthony C. Thiselton, "Reader-Response Hermeneutics," in Roger Lundin, Anthony C. Thiselton and Clarence Walhout, *The Responsibility of Hermeneutics* (Grand Rapids, Mich.: Eerdmans, 1985), pp. 79-113.

[80]See my discussion on pp. 182-83, 215.

[81]See John D. Caputo, "The Thought of Being and the Conversation of Mankind: The Case of Heidegger and Rorty," in *Hermeneutics and Praxis,* ed. Hollinger, p. 262. On Gadamer's discussion of the hermeneutical circle see his *Truth and Method,* pp. 167-68, 235ff., 258ff.

[82]I empathize with Packer's proposed alternative to Gadamer's fusion of horizons: "Where Gadamer speaks of the intersecting of historically separate worlds of human thought, there evangelical application theory posits encounter with the revealed mind of the unchanging God whose thoughts and ways are never like those of fallen mankind in any era at all, and in whose hands

each human being must realize that for better or for worse, as his own choice determines, he remains forever." Packer, "Infallible Scripture," in *Scripture and Truth,* ed. Carson and Woodbridge, p. 346.

[83]Karl Barth, "Rudolf Bultmann—An Attempt to Understand Him," in *Kerygma and Myth,* ed. Hans-Werner Bartsch, trans. Reginald H. Fuller (London: SPCK, 1962), 2:123.

[84]William Lyford, *The Plain Man's Senses Exercised* (Philadelphia: Wm. Hudson, 1850), p. 60.

[85]W. Sibley Towner, *Daniel* (Atlanta, Ga.: John Knox Press, 1984), p. 115.

[86]Thomas F. Torrance, *Space, Time and Resurrection* (Grand Rapids, Mich.: Eerdmans, 1976), p. 3.

[87]Walter Wink, *The Bible in Human Transformation* (Philadelphia: Fortress, 1973).

[88]Peter W. Macky, "The Coming Revolution: The New Literary Approach to New Testament Interpretation," in *Guide,* ed. McKim, p. 266. Macky is here describing Walter Wink's position.

[89]See Peter Stuhlmacher, *Historical Criticism and Theological Interpretation of Scripture: Toward a Hermeneutics of Consent,* trans. Roy A. Harrisville (Philadelphia: Fortress, 1977).

[90]D. A. Carson, "Hermeneutics: A Brief Assessment of Some Recent Trends," *Evangelical Review of Theology* 5, no. 1 (April 1981):21.

[91]See Gerhard Maier, *The End of the Historical-Critical Method,* trans. Edwin W. Leverenz and Rudolph F. Norden (St. Louis: Concordia, 1977).

[92]Karl Barth, *The Preaching of the Gospel,* trans. B. E. Hooke (Philadelphia: Westminster Press, 1963), p. 61.

[93]Ibid.

[94]For a wholesale dismissal of historical criticism as a method of interpreting Scripture see Eta Linnemann, *Historical Criticism of the Bible: Methodology or Ideology?* trans. Robert W. Yarbrough (Grand Rapids, Mich.: Baker Book House, 1990); and Gerhard F. Hasel, *Biblical Interpretation Today* (Washington, D.C.: Biblical Research Institute, 1985). Both authors make telling points. Linnemann is surely correct that in the hands of unbelieving critics the historical-critical method is closer to an ideology than a methodology, but does this mean that the principle of historical and literary analysis of the text is out of bounds for believers? Hasel gives a cogent critique of the principles of historical criticism as delineated by Ernst Troeltsch—correlation, analogy, criticism (pp. 73-78). The question remains: Can there be a historical treatment of Scripture that serves rather than subverts the claims of Christian faith? Hasel proposes a "theological-historical" methodology and notes its affinity with George Eldon Ladd's "historical-theological" critical approach (p. 98). While acknowledging areas of convergence between these approaches and my own, I believe we can

learn positively as well as negatively from our opponents on the left.

[95]Hans Küng, *The Church,* trans. Ray and Rosaleen Ockenden (New York: Sheed & Ward, 1967), p. 78.

[96]Dietrich Bonhoeffer, *Christ the Center,* trans. John Bowden (New York: Harper & Row, 1966), p. 76.

[97]Rudolf Bultmann, *Theology of the New Testament,* trans. Kendrick Grobel (New York: Charles Scribner's Sons, 1955), 2:244.

[98]Quoted in Karl Barth, *Theology and Church,* trans. Louise Pettibone Smith (New York: Harper & Row, 1962), p. 211.

[99]In Harry Escott, ed., *The Cure of Souls: An Anthology of P. T. Forsyth's Practical Writings* (Grand Rapids, Mich.: Eerdmans, 1971), p. 70.

[100]Ibid., p. 16.

[101]A. W. Tozer, *The Divine Conquest* (Harrisburg, Penn.: Christian Publications, 1950), p. 81.

[102]Quoted in John R. W. Stott, *Christ the Controversialist* (Downers Grove, Ill.: InterVarsity Press, 1972), p. 104.

[103]At times a simple historical reconstruction of the text may falsify the overall message of the Bible. An example is the parable of the good Samaritan (Lk 10:25-37), which is commonly treated as moralistic instruction rather than a call to decision for Christ. A popular rendition of this parable is that by extending a helping hand to those in need we can indeed inherit eternal life or at least gain assurance of God's favor. But Jesus was not speaking of simple goodness but of sacrificial, unconditional love. The fact that he held up a Samaritan as an example of such love was of profound significance, for the Samaritans harbored a chronic and implacable animosity toward the Jews and vice versa. The tensions ran so high that Jesus and his disciples were forced to change their itinerary and bypass a Samaritan village on their way to Jerusalem (Lk 9:51-56). For a Samaritan to give of himself so readily and selflessly to help a brutally assaulted traveler (presumably a Jew) was to exceed by far the generally acknowledged norms of propriety in that cultural situation. Indeed, by bringing a wounded Jew into a Jewish village the Samaritan was placing his own life in jeopardy, for he was inviting suspicion of being implicated in the crime. We can only conclude that Jesus was thinking of love not as a rational possibility but as a sign of unmerited grace. The parable is a witness to God's inexplicable love for the human race estranged from him by sin, love that would not be fully appreciated until the death and resurrection of Jesus Christ and the gift of the Holy Spirit to the church. The command to the inquiring lawyer to go and do likewise (10:37) is still in force, but it should now be seen as a gracious invitation to follow in the footsteps of the Master rather than a legal requirement.

The parable remains shrouded in mystery until it is given theological exposition, which means relating it to the center of Scripture—the cross of Christ. This is not reading into the parable an intention it does not have, for all the parables of Jesus were designed to convey the mystery of the kingdom, which began to unfold only when the kingship of Christ was identified with the vocation of the suffering servant who bore the sin of many (Is 53:12). But a theological understanding of the parable is not yet the spiritual sense until we ourselves begin to experience conviction of sin for ignoring the needs of our neighbor and joy in knowing Christ as the good Samaritan for us. We have now gone beyond theological exposition to spiritual appropriation.

[104]Quoted by Timothy George, *Theology of the Reformers* (Nashville: Broadman Press, 1988), p. 83.

[105]Bonhoeffer, *Christ the Center,* p. 76.

[106]I acknowledge that the Bible does contain universal principles (such as the golden rule), but such truths in and of themselves do not constitute the Word of God, though they are ineradicably related to this Word. They belong to the Word of God, but they do not comprise its essence. God's Word is always a personal address, a concrete promise or command, that is directed to the hearers or readers by the Spirit of God, thereby calling for a decision.

[107]Doug Bandow, senior fellow at the Cato Institute, a conservative think tank, illustrates the rationalism endemic in evangelical circles by conceiving of the Bible as a book of general moral principles rather than a living word addressed to people of faith in their concrete situations. Because of his belief that there is no clear biblical agenda for our times, he relies on "prudential" answers to our public problems. See Doug Bandow, *Beyond Good Intentions: A Biblical View of Politics* (Westchester, Ill.: Crossway, 1988).

[108]The truth of faith does, of course, have metaphysical import, and it can be used to guide metaphysical reflection. It must not, however, be confounded with a universal rule or principle that is at our disposal furnishing the possibility for a comprehensive rational system. Truth in the biblical sense is not a natural possibility but a superhistorical reality that bursts into human thought forms turning them in an altogether new direction. This word of the living God has far-reaching ethical and metaphysical implications, but it cannot be subsumed under any genus or category of human understanding, such as being or process.

[109]Probably the most significant strand in this movement is the new Yale school of theology associated with Lindbeck, Frei, Thiemann and others whom I have labeled moderate conservatives. Scholars like Stanley Hauerwas and to a lesser degree William Placher could also be included in this general strand. For my earlier dialogue with the Yale school see Bloesch, *A Theology of Word & Spirit* (Downers Grove, Ill.: InterVarsity Press, 1992), pp. 28, 30, 273-75. Other scholars who embrace some form of narrative or story theology (some

standing closer to Paul Ricoeur and "the Chicago school" and others closer to Lindbeck and the Yale school) are George W. Stroup, Robert Tannehill, N. T. Wright, Stephen Crites, Michael Goldberg, John S. Dunne, James W. McClendon Jr., Robert Krieg, Sallie McFague and Randel Helms.

110According to Ellingsen, "The narrative approach to proclamation does not preclude using historical-critical tools in sermon preparation. It endorses the priority of the techniques of literary analysis and, in practice, it advocates the interplay of various methods." Mark Ellingsen, *The Integrity of Biblical Narrative: Story in Theology and Proclamation* (Minneapolis: Fortress, 1990), p. 70.

111See Garrett Green, " 'The Bible As . . .': Fictional Narrative and Scriptural Truth," in *Scriptural Authority and Narrative Interpretation,* ed. Green (Philadelphia: Fortress, 1987), pp. 79-96.

112Hans Frei, "An Afterword: Eberhard Busch's Biography of Karl Barth," in *Karl Barth in Re-view,* ed. H. Martin Rumscheidt (Pittsburgh: Pickwick Press, 1981), pp. 103-4, 115-16. In this essay Frei interprets Barth as an incipient narrative theologian. Also see Hans Frei, *The Eclipse of Biblical Narrative: A Study in Eighteenth and Nineteenth Century Hermeneutics* (New Haven, Conn.: Yale University Press, 1974). Also see the discussion in William C. Placher, *Unapologetic Theology: A Christian Voice in a Pluralistic Conversation* (Louisville, Ky.: Westminster/John Knox Press, 1989), pp. 17-21, 161-70.

113See George A. Lindbeck, *The Nature of Doctrine: Religion and Theology in a Postliberal Age* (Philadelphia: Westminster Press, 1984). See esp. pp. 64-65, 80, 101.

114See David H. Kelsey, *The Uses of Scripture in Recent Theology* (Philadelphia: Fortress, 1975), pp. 208-11.

115Ibid., p. 194. Hauerwas's view is similar. See Stanley Hauerwas, *A Community of Character: Toward a Constructive Christian Social Ethic* (Notre Dame, Ind.: University of Notre Dame Press, 1981), p. 55. Placher takes issue with Hauerwas on this point, but he recognizes that this is only one side of Hauerwas. Placher is quite adamant that we must not sacrifice commitment to truth to the goal of building community. Placher, *Unapologetic Theology,* pp. 164-65. While not wholly happy with postliberal theology, Placher is much more critical of the revisionist theology of Tracy, Kaufman and Ogden (see pp. 154-60).

116Gary Comstock, "Truth or Meaning: Ricoeur Versus Frei on Biblical Narrative," *Journal of Religion* 66, no. 2 (April 1986):135. A functional understanding of biblical authority is also evident in the evangelical narrative theologian Clark Pinnock: "The Bible points us to the story of salvation and facilitates it coming alive in our experience as it is mixed with faith." See Stanley Grenz's review of Pinnock's *Tracking the Maze* in *Christianity Today* 34, no. 16 (Nov. 5,

1990):81.

[117]Pinnock shows his distance from many narrative theologians by his insistence on the historical basis of the gospel story: "In the gospel we see the joining of myth and history, of fact and symbol, a contentful message with solid historical credentials that at the same time speaks symbolically to humanity's basic needs." *Tracking the Maze* (San Francisco: Harper & Row, 1990), p. 153.

[118]Robert C. Tannehill, *The Sword of His Mouth* (Philadelphia: Fortress, 1975), pp. 22-23.

[119]David J. Bryant, review of Garrett Green, *Imagining God: Theology and the Religious Imagination* (San Francisco: Harper & Row, 1989), in *Princeton Seminary Bulletin* 10, no. 3 (1989):276.

[120]See J. H. Stone, "Narrative Theology," *Harper's Encyclopedia of Religious Education,* ed. Iris V. Cully and Kendig Brubaker Cully (San Francisco: Harper & Row, 1990), p. 441.

[121]Ellingsen, *Integrity of Biblical Narrative,* p. 68.

[122]Many of the narrative theologians are structuralists. They see the text in and of itself creating by its grammar a certain life- and worldview that is followable. For a structuralist view see Dan Otto Via Jr., *Kerygma and Comedy in the New Testament* (Philadelphia: Fortress, 1975); and Daniel Patte, *What Is Structural Exegesis?* (Philadelphia: Fortress, 1976).

[123]For a penetrating critique of Jacques Derrida and deconstructionism see Joel Schwartz, "Antihumanism in the Humanities," *The Public Interest* no. 99 (Spring 1990):29-44. For a more comprehensive appraisal of deconstructionism showing its bearing on biblical interpretation, see Anthony C. Thiselton, *New Horizons in Hermeneutics* (Grand Rapids, Mich.: Zondervan, 1992), pp. 80-141. Cf. Millard Erickson, *The Word Became Flesh* (Grand Rapids, Mich.: Baker Book House, 1991), pp. 309-31. Erickson also gives a perceptive analysis of narrative theology (pp. 359-79). For a brilliant but ill-fated attempt to forge a deconstructionist theology see Mark C. Taylor, *Erring: A Postmodern A/theology* (Chicago: University of Chicago Press, 1984). Also see Thomas J. J. Altizer et al., *Deconstruction and Theology* (New York: Crossroad, 1992).

[124]See n. 67.

[125]Green, *Imagining God,* pp. 106-10.

[126]Calvin, *Institutes of the Christian Religion,* trans. Ford Lewis Battles, ed. John T. McNeill, 2 vols. (Philadelphia: Westminster Press, 1960), 1.6.1, p. 70.

[127]Stephen Crites, "A Respectful Reply to the Assertorical Theologian," in *Why Narrative? Readings in Narrative Theology,* ed. Stanley Hauerwas and L. Gregory Jones (Grand Rapids, Mich.: Eerdmans, 1989), p. 296.

[128]See Stanley Hauerwas, "The Moral Authority of Scripture," in *Readings in Moral Theology,* no. 4, *The Use of Scripture in Moral Theology,* ed. Charles E. Curran and Richard A. McCormick (New York: Paulist Press, 1984), p. 250.

Hauerwas proposes a "morality of remembering" that is based on "Scripture as narrative" (pp. 259-62). Reflecting an antimetaphysical bias, he contends that "our understanding of God is not inferred from the stories but is the stories" (p. 260). Hauerwas endorses the view prevalent among narrative theologians that Scripture is "one long 'loosely structured non-fiction novel' " (p. 260).

[129]Kevin J. Vanhoozer, *Biblical Narrative in the Philosophy of Paul Ricoeur* (New York: Cambridge University Press, 1990), pp. 176-77.

[130]See Mark I. Wallace, *The Second Naiveté: Barth, Ricoeur and the New Yale Theology* (Macon, Ga.: Mercer University Press, 1990), p. 80.

[131]Ibid., p. 82.

[132]Ibid., p. 109. Wallace acknowledges that Barth's thinking cannot be subsumed under any one philosophical position (pp. 60-63).

[133]Ellingsen, *Integrity of Biblical Narrative,* pp. 44-46, 51-52, 70-96.

[134]Carl E. Braaten, *No Other Gospel!* (Minneapolis: Fortress, 1992), pp. 19-20.

[135]Ibid., p. 20.

[136]Ibid., p. 19.

[137]Ibid.

[138]Bruce D. Marshall, "Aquinas as Postliberal Theologian," and "Response" by George Lindbeck in *The Thomist* 53, no. 3 (July 1989):353-406. I think it can be shown that Thomas has an apologetic side that simply cannot be found in Lindbeck. For a much more cautionary critique of both Frei and Lindbeck see Childs, *Biblical Theology,* pp. 18-22. Childs identifies with Barth's position that the Bible "bears witness to a reality outside the text, namely to God" (p. 22).

[139]Lindbeck, *Nature of Doctrine,* pp. 132-34. Lindbeck contends, however, that effective catechesis is not feasible in the secular milieu in which we live and that we must wait for new communities of shared faith and life to form in which the language of faith will again come alive.

[140]See Braaten, *No Other Gospel,* p. 19.

[141]See Thiselton, *New Horizons,* p. 7. Also see Stanley Fish, *Doing What Comes Naturally: Change, Rhetoric and the Practice of Theory in Literary and Legal Studies* (Oxford, U.K.: Clarendon, 1990), p. ix.

[142]Thiselton, *New Horizons,* p. 6.

[143]Ibid.

[144]Ibid., pp. 613-17.

[145]Ibid., p. 613.

[146]Ibid., p. 614.

[147]Ibid., p. 619.

[148]Thiselton, *The Two Horizons* (Grand Rapids, Mich.: Eerdmans, 1980), pp. 88-89.

¹⁴⁹Thiselton reflects the traditional emphasis when he acknowledges that the cross can be seen as "complete, perfect, sufficient, and final." Yet he goes on to say that "theological readings are best served by encouraging pluralities of readings, since each reading answers the agenda reflected in a life-world, and one mode of reading may lead to another." *New Horizons,* p. 615.

¹⁵⁰Ibid., p. 614.

¹⁵¹Timothy Phillips makes this perceptive observation: "Thiselton's hermeneutics only allows one to speak of 'the fallible church [which] points beyond itself and its own context to that which lies beyond it, especially to the divine promise of the future and the universals of the cross and the resurrection.' In his system, revelation becomes a regulative ideal, and our task is to keep on broadening our horizons. Consequently, theology can only operate in differing contexts in life like Wittgenstein's 'concepts with blurred edges.' The possibility of our horizons being called into question, overturned and corrected is muted, to say the least." Timothy Phillips, unpublished manuscript review for InterVarsity Press, May 1993, p. 1. See Thiselton, *New Horizons,* p. 592.

Chapter 7: Rudolf Bultmann: An Enduring Presence

¹Among biblical scholars indebted to Bultmann are Ernst Käsemann, Walter Schmithals, Heinrich Bornkamm, Heinrich Schlier, Hans Conzelmann, Willi Marxsen, J. A. T. Robinson, Norman Perrin, James Robinson, Dan Otto Via and Robert Funk. Nearly all these men have had a noticeable impact on biblical studies and theology. While taking issue with Bultmann on many points, Marcus J. Borg nevertheless regards him as "arguably the most influential New Testament scholar throughout much of this century." *Jesus: A New Vision* (San Francisco: Harper & Row, 1987), p. 19. Gareth Jones fully shares this opinion in his *Bultmann: Towards a Critical Theology* (Oxford, U.K.: Basil Blackwell, 1991), pp. 1–3. Jones documents the unmistakable imprint of Bultmann on the existential hermeneutic of Ernst Fuchs, Gerhard Ebeling and Hans-Georg Gadamer.

²See, e.g., N. T. Wright, who in *The New Testament and the People of God* (Minneapolis: Fortress, 1992) contrasts his own position, "critical realism," with the neo-Kantian skepticism of Bultmann. Wright refers to Bultmann forty-five times.

³Bultmann's influence is clearly discernible in Theodore Jennings, *Loyalty to God* (Nashville: Abingdon, 1992), which offers a contemporary interpretation of the Apostles' Creed. While he alludes to Bultmann at only two places, the whole idea of a creed taken out of its "mythological" context in order to speak to the modern ethos can be traced to Bultmann's demythologizing agenda. Jennings's contention that "the resurrection of Jesus appears to have no other content than that of the cross" is also a Bultmannian theme (see p. 139). Where

Jennings clearly diverges from Bultmann is in his pronounced emphasis on the social implications of the gospel.

[4]Some strands in Bultmann tie him more closely to biblical and traditional Lutheran spirituality, but on the whole these are submerged in his palpable dependence on Herrmann, Troeltsch and Heidegger, all of whom see the essence of faith in the renewal of the inner being of the human subject. Herrmann, whose influence on Bultmann is unassailable, described the object of ethics as "this present, forward-surging life of history" (cited in Hendrikus Berkhof, *Two Hundred Years of Theology*, trans. John Vriend [Grand Rapids, Mich.: Eerdmans, 1989], p. 154). Bultmann could indeed speak of the source of faith as God's redeeming act in the cross of Christ, but it is an act that releases human possibilities, that liberates the human spirit for life in its fullness. For a succinct analysis of the tie between Herrmann, Troeltsch and Bultmann see Berkhof, *Two Hundred Years*, pp. 143-78. For a further discussion in this chapter of Bultmann's affinity with the new spirituality see p. 243.

[5]Rudolf Bultmann, *Jesus and the Word*, trans. Louise Pettibone Smith and Erminie Huntress (New York: Charles Scribner's Sons, 1934).

[6]Rudolf Bultmann, *The Gospel of John: A Commentary*, trans. G. R. Beasley-Murray, R. W. N. Hoare and J. K. Riches (Philadelphia: Westminster Press, 1971).

[7]See James D. Smart, *The Divided Mind of Modern Theology: Karl Barth and Rudolf Bultmann, 1908—1933* (Philadelphia: Westminster Press, 1967), pp. 91-99, 117-22. Bultmann was more appreciative of the second edition than the first.

[8]On the other side of the ledger, Bultmann urged Barth to withdraw his opposition to the decree from the Ministry of Cultural Affairs requiring university professors and all other state employees to take an oath of allegiance to Hitler. Barth continued to open his classes with prayer instead of with the "Heil Hitler." See Eberhard Busch, *Karl Barth*, trans. John Bowden (Philadelphia: Fortress, 1976), pp. 242, 257; and *Karl Barth/Rudolf Bultmann Letters 1922-1966*, ed. Bernd Jaspert, trans. Geoffrey W. Bromiley (Grand Rapids, Mich.: Eerdmans, 1981), pp. 78-79. For a complimentary account of Bultmann's role in the resistance to Nazism see Jack Forstman, *Christian Faith in Dark Times* (Louisville, Ky.: Westminster/John Knox Press, 1992), pp. 222-42.

[9]Rudolf Bultmann, "Bultmann Replies to His Critics," in *Kerygma and Myth*, ed. Hans-Werner Bartsch, trans. Reginald H. Fuller, rev. ed. (New York: Harper Torchbooks, 1961), 1:202.

[10]Some scholars, e.g., J. M. de Jong, hold that Bultmann was fundamentally more dependent on Descartes and Kant than on Heidegger. See Berkhof, *Two Hundred Years*, p. 171.

[11]Rudolf Bultmann, *Faith and Understanding*, trans. Louise Pettibone Smith, ed. Robert W. Funk (Philadelphia: Fortress, 1987), p. 46.

[12]See James Richmond, *Faith and Philosophy* (Philadelphia: J. B. Lippincott, 1966), pp. 168ff.

[13]Robert T. Voelkel, "Introduction," in Wilhelm Herrmann, *The Communion of the Christian with God,* ed. Voelkel (Philadelphia: Fortress, 1971), p. xliv.

[14]Rudolf Bultmann, "Reply to Interpretation and Criticism," in *The Theology of Rudolf Bultmann,* ed. Charles W. Kegley (New York: Harper & Row, 1966), p. 262.

[15]Barth interpreted *Geschichte* as referring to the divine interaction with humanity in objective historical events rather than to the inner life history of the believer. Ogletree maintains that Barth correctly understood Kähler. See Thomas W. Ogletree, *Christian Faith and History* (New York: Abingdon, 1965), pp. 204-19. Also see my discussion on pp. 229, 264, 274, 360 (note 75).

[16]Rudolf Bultmann, "New Testament and Mythology," in *Kerygma and Myth,* ed. Hans-Werner Bartsch, trans. Reginald H. Fuller (London: SPCK, 1962), 1:5.

[17]Bultmann, "A Reply to the Theses of J. Schniewind," in *Kerygma and Myth,* ed. Bartsch, 1:123.

[18]See Reginald H. Fuller, *The New Testament in Current Study* (New York: Charles Scribner's Sons, 1962), pp. 14-16.

[19]Bultmann, "The Case for Demythologizing," in *Kerygma and Myth,* ed. Bartsch, 2:182-83.

[20]Roger A. Johnson, ed., *Rudolf Bultmann: Interpreting Faith for the Modern Era* (Minneapolis: Fortress, 1991), p. 154.

[21]Bultmann, "New Testament and Mythology," in *Kerygma and Myth,* ed. Bartsch, 1:1-44.

[22]Rudolf Bultmann, "The Problem of Demythologizing," in *The Hermeneutics Reader,* ed. Kurt Mueller-Vollmer (New York: Continuum, 1985), p. 252.

[23]See the discussion in Schubert M. Ogden, *Christ Without Myth* (New York: Harper & Bros., 1961), pp. 24-28.

[24]Bultmann, "Case for Demythologizing," p. 185.

[25]John Painter, *Theology as Hermeneutics: Rudolf Bultmann's Interpretation of the History of Jesus* (Sheffield, U.K.: Almond Press, 1987), p. 147.

[26]Bultmann, "Case for Demythologizing," p. 184.

[27]Cf. Rudolf Bultmann: "I don't know anything about immortality. The only thing we can know is that our earthly life ends with death. Whether there is another life after this one, we don't know." Cited by Kenneth L. Woodward, "Death in America," *U.S. Catholic and Jubilee* 36, no. 1 (Jan. 1971):13.

[28]Rudolf Bultmann, *Existence and Faith: Shorter Writings of Rudolf Bultmann,* trans. and ed. Schubert Ogden (New York: Meridian Books, 1960), p. 62.

[29]Cf. Rudolf Bultmann, *Theology of the New Testament,* trans. Kendrick Grobel (New York: Charles Scribner's Sons, 1955), 2:36-37.

[30]Robert Campbell Roberts, *Rudolf Bultmann's Theology: A Critical Interpretation* (Grand Rapids, Mich.: Eerdmans, 1976), p. 261.

[31]Ibid.

[32]See *Kerygma and Myth,* ed. Bartsch, vols. 1 and 2.

[33]See Amos N. Wilder, "Mythology and the New Testament," *Journal of Biblical Literature* 69, no. 2 (June 1950):113-27. See also my discussion in chapter eight, note 56.

[34]Bultmann, "Case for Demythologizing," p. 184.

[35]Gerhard Ebeling, *Word and Faith,* trans. James W. Leitch (Philadelphia: Fortress, 1963), p. 331.

[36]Ian Henderson, *Myth in the New Testament* (London: SCM Press, 1952), pp. 41-49.

[37]Kenneth Hamilton, *Words and the Word* (Grand Rapids, Mich.: Eerdmans, 1971), pp. 39-40.

[38]Karl Barth, "Rudolf Bultmann—An Attempt to Understand Him," in *Kerygma and Myth,* ed. Bartsch, 2:87-88.

[39]Rudolf Bultmann, *Jesus Christ and Mythology* (New York: Charles Scribner's Sons, 1958), pp. 40, 52-53.

[40]Bultmann said that no person, "not even Paul . . . can always speak only from the subject matter. Other spirits also come to expression" through the biblical witness, and therefore our "criticism can never be radical enough." See *New Frontiers in Theology,* vol. 2, *The New Hermeneutic,* ed. James M. Robinson and John B. Cobb Jr. (New York: Harper & Row, 1964), p. 31. See Bultmann's article in *Christliche Welt* 36 (1922):372ff.

[41]For example, Bultmann contended that Paul's desire to counter the Gnostics drove him to present the resurrection as a visible fact in history by listing witnesses who had seen Jesus risen (1 Cor 15:5-8). But Bultmann found such a proof unconvincing and also alien to the principal thrust of Paul's theology. In contrast, Barth denied that Paul had this in mind when he listed the witnesses to the resurrection. See Bultmann, "New Testament and Mythology," p. 39; and *Theology of the New Testament,* 1:295.

[42]For an able analysis of the glaring contrast in the methodologies of Barth and Bultmann see Smart, *Divided Mind,* esp. pp. 157-63.

[43]See Carl Braaten and Roy Harrisville, eds. and trans., *Kerygma and History* (New York: Abingdon, 1962), 1:98.

[44]"If revelation is God's eternal event, an event which enters into our time, our history, then revelation is available to theological talk as a 'presupposition' only when it pleases God to set up this presupposition, when he allows it to happen in the working of the Holy Spirit." Rudolf Bultmann, "The Question of 'Dialectic' Theology," in *The Beginnings of Dialectic Theology,* ed. James M. Robinson (Richmond, Va.: John Knox Press, 1968), p. 265.

⁴⁵Bultmann, *Jesus and the Word*, p. 47.

⁴⁶Bultmann, *Faith and Understanding*, p. 40.

⁴⁷Rudolf Bultmann, "The Idea of God and Modern Man," in Rudolf Bultmann et al., *Translating Theology into the Modern Age*, ed. Robert W. Funk (New York: Harper Torchbooks, 1965), p. 92.

⁴⁸Ibid., p. 93.

⁴⁹See Johnson, ed., *Bultmann*, p. 54.

⁵⁰Ibid., p. 47.

⁵¹See Roberts, *Rudolf Bultmann's Theology*, p. 256.

⁵²Bultmann, *Jesus and the Word*, p. 201.

⁵³Bultmann, *Jesus Christ and Mythology*, p. 42.

⁵⁴Bultmann, *Theology of the New Testament*, 1:342-43.

⁵⁵Thomas C. Oden, *Radical Obedience: The Ethics of Rudolf Bultmann* (Philadelphia: Westminster Press, 1964), p. 130.

⁵⁶Ibid., p. 120.

⁵⁷Bultmann, *Faith and Understanding*, p. 111.

⁵⁸Bultmann, *Existence and Faith*, p. 286.

⁵⁹Bultmann: "God's rule is evidently seen as not yet sovereign in the present; His name is not yet hallowed, His will is not yet done on earth as it is in heaven." *Jesus and the Word*, p. 155. In contrast, Barth saw Christ as already ruling over the principalities and powers by virtue of his resurrection victory.

⁶⁰Cited by Hannelis Schulte in *Theology of Bultmann*, ed. Kegley, p. 233.

⁶¹On Heidegger's enthusiastic support for Nazism see Victor Farías, *Heidegger and Nazism*, ed. Joseph Margolis and Tom Rockmore (Philadelphia: Temple University Press, 1989); *Martin Heidegger and National Socialism: Questions and Answers*, ed. Günther Neske and Emil Kettering (New York: Paragon House, 1990); and Mark Lilla, "What Heidegger Wrought," *Commentary* 89, no. 1 (Jan. 1990):41-51.

⁶²Rudolf Bultmann, *This World and the Beyond*, trans. Harold Knight (New York: Charles Scribner's Sons, 1960), p. 236.

⁶³Ibid., p. 221.

⁶⁴Ibid., p. 195.

⁶⁵Bultmann, *Jesus and the Word*, p. 47.

⁶⁶Bultmann, *This World and the Beyond*, p. 242. Here he is quoting approvingly from Pascal.

⁶⁷Gareth Jones convincingly maintains that Bultmann rejected the form but not the content of liberal theology. Jones, *Bultmann*, p. 19.

⁶⁸See *Jesus Christ and Mythology*, pp. 66-70. Cf. Rudolf Bultmann: "I *am* trying to substitute anthropology for theology, for I am interpreting theological affirmations as assertions about human life." "Reply to the Theses of J. Schniewind," in *Kerygma and Myth*, ed. Bartsch, 1:107.

[69]Bultmann, *Jesus Christ and Mythology*, p. 37.

[70]Schubert Ogden, *On Theology* (New York: Harper & Row, 1986), p. 34. See Bultmann, *Existence and Faith*, p. 86.

[71]Walter Schmithals, *An Introduction to the Theology of Rudolf Bultmann*, trans. John Bowden (Minneapolis: Augsburg, 1968), p. 120.

[72]Schleiermacher propounded an infinity within finitude rather than a supernatural realm beyond finitude, and both Bultmann and Tillich resonate with this vision.

[73]Rudolf Bultmann, "The Significance of the Old Testament for the Christian Faith," in *The Old Testament and Christian Faith*, ed. Bernhard W. Anderson (New York: Harper & Row, 1963), p. 31. Cf.: "The Old Testament is no longer God's Word for us. In so far as the Church pronounces it God's Word, we find in it only what we already know in Jesus Christ." *Glauben und Verstehen* (Tübingen: J. C. B. Mohr, 1933), p. 333.

[74]Bultmann, "Significance of the Old Testament," p. 17.

[75]Roland E. Murphy, "The Relationship Between the Testaments," *Catholic Biblical Quarterly* 26, no. 3 (July 1964):350.

[76]Bultmann, *This World and the Beyond*, p. 142.

[77]Rudolf Bultmann, *Essays Philosophical and Theological*, trans. J. C. G. Greig (New York: Macmillan, 1955), p. 176.

[78]Ibid.

[79]Schubert Ogden sees Bultmann as an experientialist rather than a bona fide kerygmatic theologian. Ogden, "Rudolf Bultmann and the Future of Revisionary Christology," in *Bultmann, Retrospect and Prospect*, ed. Edward C. Hobbs (Philadelphia: Fortress, 1985), p. 57.

[80]Colin Brown, *Philosophy and the Christian Faith* (Downers Grove, Ill.: InterVarsity Press, 1969), p. 191.

[81]Hans Jonas presented a compelling case that modern existentialism has its roots in gnosticism. See "Gnosticism, Nihilism and Existentialism" in Jonas, *The Gnostic Religion*, rev. ed. (Boston: Beacon Press, 1963), pp. 320-40. Kenneth Hamilton finds in Bultmann allusions that he labels "idealistic" but could just as well be labeled "gnostic." Bultmann referred to the idea of the soul coming to the consciousness of its own " 'imprisonment' in space and time" and thereby realizing "its essential participation in the divine and eternal." Hamilton, *Words and the Word*, p. 38.

[82]The Gnostics held that God is radically other than the world but not other than the spirit *(pneuma)*—the inner self of the human being. When Bultmann said that to know the self is to know God, he came dangerously close to gnosticism.

[83]Klaus Bockmuehl, *The Unreal God of Modern Theology* (Colorado Springs: Helmers & Howard, 1988), p. 75.

[84]Otto Weber, *Foundations of Dogmatics*, trans. Darrell L. Guder (Grand Rapids,

Mich.: Eerdmans, 1981), 1:196.

Chapter 8: The Bible and Myth

[1]See pp. 233-37.

[2]Karl Barth, *Church Dogmatics,* trans. J. W. Edwards et al., ed. G. W. Bromiley and T. F. Torrance (Edinburgh: T & T Clark, 1958), 3(1):85.

[3]Barth, *Church Dogmatics,* trans. G. W. Bromiley, ed. Bromiley and T. F. Torrance (Edinburgh: T & T Clark, 1956), 4(1):508.

[4]Avery Dulles, "Symbol, Myth, and the Biblical Revelation," in *New Theology No. 4,* ed. Martin E. Marty and Dean Peerman (New York: Macmillan, 1967), p. 56.

[5]Gerhard von Rad, *Genesis: A Commentary,* trans. John H. Marks, Old Testament Library (Philadelphia: Westminster Press, 1961), p. 34.

[6]Ibid., p. 31.

[7]Ibid. Quotation from Georg August Finsler, *Homer,* 3:33.

[8]Hamilton describes myth as "omnipresent" in the Bible, but it is myth that is left behind by the biblical writers in their effort to do justice to the historical claims of biblical faith. Kenneth Hamilton, *Words and the Word* (Grand Rapids, Mich.: Eerdmans, 1971), pp. 89-90.

[9]Gordon J. Wenham, *Genesis 1—15,* Word Biblical Commentary (Waco, Tex.: Word Books, 1987), pp. 54, 166. Wenham also discusses the appropriateness of the term *mytho-historical,* which shows the continuity between the Genesis stories and parallel Near Eastern accounts, but suggests that it does not adequately convey the fact that the mythical elements are transfigured or eliminated in Genesis.

[10]Ibid., p. 55.

[11]See Reinhold Niebuhr, "The Truth in Myths," in *The Nature of Religious Experience,* ed. Eugene Garrett Bewkes et al. (New York: Harper & Bros., 1937), pp. 117-35. For Niebuhr's critique of Bultmann and his keen perception that the dramatic, symbolic language of Scripture cannot be replaced by the language of philosophy without subverting the truth of the biblical message, see Reinhold Niebuhr, *The Self and the Dramas of History* (New York: Charles Scribner's Sons, 1955), pp. 96-102.

[12]Jacques Ellul, *The Meaning of the City,* trans. Dennis Pardee (Grand Rapids, Mich.: Eerdmans, 1970), p. 18.

[13]Jacques Ellul, *To Will & to Do,* trans. C. Edward Hopkin (Philadelphia: Pilgrim Press, 1969), pp. 39-41.

[14]Paul Tillich, *Dynamics of Faith* (New York: Harper, 1957), p. 49.

[15]Reinhold Niebuhr, "Biblical Thought and Ontological Speculation in Tillich's Theology," in *The Theology of Paul Tillich,* ed. Charles W. Kegley and Robert W. Bretall (New York: Macmillan, 1952), pp. 216-27.

[16]Kevin J. Vanhoozer, *Biblical Narrative in the Philosophy of Paul Ricoeur* (New

York: Cambridge University Press, 1990), p. 124.

[17]Ibid., p. 136.

[18]Cited in Douglas Groothuis, *Revealing the New Age Jesus* (Downers Grove, Ill.: InterVarsity Press, 1990), p. 232.

[19]Ibid.

[20]Dulles, "Symbol, Myth," p. 48.

[21]Ibid., p. 58.

[22]Sigmund Mowinckel, *The Old Testament as Word of God,* trans. Reidar B. Bjornard (New York: Abingdon, 1959), p. 104.

[23]Elizabeth Achtemeier, "Female Language for God: Should the Church Adopt It?" in *The Hermeneutical Quest,* ed. Donald G. Miller (Allison Park, Penn.: Pickwick Publications, 1986), pp. 97-114. See esp. p. 104.

[24]Cuthbert A. Simpson, *Interpreter's Bible* (New York: Abingdon-Cokesbury, 1952), 1:466-67.

[25]See John Skinner, *A Critical and Exegetical Commentary on Genesis,* International Critical Commentary, 2d ed. (rpt. Edinburgh: T & T Clark, 1951), p. 18: "We have here a fragment of mythology not vitally connected with the main idea of the narrative, but introduced for the sake of its religious suggestiveness. In the source from which this myth was borrowed the brooding power might be a bird-like deity . . . or an abstract principle like the Greek *erōs . . .* for this the Heb. writer, true to his monotheistic faith, substitutes the Spirit of God, and thereby transforms a 'crude material representation . . . into a beautiful and suggestive figure.' "

[26]My views here are close to those of Gordon Wenham, who accepts a separate J author or redactor. Wenham points out that most biblical scholars today are crediting more of Genesis to J than did the Wellhausenian consensus. One significant dissenter is Rolf Rendtorff, who "doubts the existence of any source documents running all through the Pentateuch, preferring a traditio-historical approach." See Wenham, *Genesis 1—15,* pp. xxviii-xlv. Also see Rolf Rendtorff, *The Problem of the Process of Transmission in the Pentateuch,* trans. John J. Scullion (Sheffield, U.K.: JSOT Press, 1990). For my earlier discussion of Rendtorff see pp. 31-32.

[27]Brevard S. Childs, *Myth and Reality in the Old Testament* (Naperville, Ill.: Allenson, 1960), p. 56. Wenham comments that here "Genesis comes closer to myth than anywhere else, for it is describing acts of godlike figures." Wenham, *Genesis 1—15,* p. 138. For a helpful discussion on how the biblical worldview transcends the "mythopoetic mind" see Victor P. Hamilton, *The Book of Genesis: Chapters 1—17,* New International Commentary on the Old Testament (Grand Rapids, Mich.: Eerdmans, 1990), pp. 56-59.

[28]Von Rad, *Genesis,* p. 112.

[29]Walter Russell Bowie, *Interpreter's Bible,* 1:534.

³⁰Raymond Abba, *The Nature and Authority of the Bible* (Philadelphia: Muhlen-berg Press, 1958), p. 129. For Abba's helpful distinction between myth, legend and history see pp. 111-48. Interestingly, he alludes to the respected conser-vative theologian James Orr, who admitted that a tradition like the Garden of Eden may be myth in the sense of transcending the language of space and time, though it must not be confused with mythology, which has its origin in "nature phenomena" (p. 113). See James Orr, *The Problem of the Old Testa-ment* (New York: Charles Scribner's Sons, 1906), p. 486.

³¹See R. B. Y. Scott, "The Book of Isaiah," in *Interpreter's Bible* (New York: Abingdon, 1956), 5:261-63; Childs, *Myth and Reality*, pp. 67-71; Joseph Jensen and William H. Irwin, "Isaiah 1-39," in *New Jerome Biblical Commentary*, ed. Raymond E. Brown, Joseph A. Fitzmyer and Roland E. Murphy (Englewood Cliffs, N.J.: Prentice Hall, 1990), p. 239; and John D. W. Watts, *Isaiah 1—33*, Word Biblical Commentary (Waco, Tex.: Word Books, 1985), pp. 207-12. Watts ac-knowledges that the poem has a "shadowy mythical background," but its primary focus is historical (p. 212).

³²Childs, *Myth and Reality*, p. 69.

³³See notes in *New Jerusalem Bible* (New York: Doubleday, 1985), p. 1211; and *Harper Study Bible*, ed. Harold Lindsell (Grand Rapids, Mich.: Zondervan, 1977), p. 1021. Also see G. W. Grogan's comments in *The Expositor's Bible Commen-tary* (Grand Rapids, Mich.: Zondervan, 1986), 6:105-6.

³⁴If we include v. 11, the myth is given not only a historical but also an eschat-ological focus, for we are told that the redeemed of the Lord shall return to Zion with "everlasting joy."

³⁵According to Ridderbos the mythical allusions to Rahab, the sea monster, and to the "great deep," the cosmic ocean on which the earth is founded, "are used by the prophet as metaphors to describe what the Lord has actually done— in this case at the time of the exodus from Egypt." J. Ridderbos, *Isaiah*, trans. John Vriend, Bible Student's Commentary (Grand Rapids, Mich.: Zondervan, 1985), p. 458.

³⁶James Muilenburg, *Interpreter's Bible*, 5:596.

³⁷Foster R. McCurley, *Ancient Myths and Biblical Faith: Scriptural Transforma-tions* (Philadelphia: Fortress, 1983), pp. 1-10.

³⁸See Tremper Longman III's review in *TSF Bulletin* 8, no. 1 (Sept.-Oct. 1984):32.

³⁹Daniel Reid, unpublished manuscript review for InterVarsity Press, May 18, 1993. Daniel Reid is reference book editor for InterVarsity Press. See Claus Westermann, *Genesis 1—11: A Commentary*, trans. John J. Scullion (Minne-apolis: Augsburg, 1984), pp. 131-34.

⁴⁰See G. B. Caird, *A Commentary on the Revelation of St. John the Divine* (New York: Harper & Row, 1966), pp. 147-52; Adela Yarbro Collins, "The Apoca-lypse," in *New Jerome Biblical Commentary*, p. 1008; and Martin Rist, "The

Revelation of St. John the Divine," in *Interpreter's Bible* (New York: Abingdon, 1957), 12:452-59. Scholars generally concede that there may be several mythic sources that were adapted by John for use by the believing community. Collins suggests that John may have edited materials composed by non-Christian Jews.

41A fable is a fictitious story making an edifying or cautionary point and frequently employing animals, plants and even inanimate objects as human characters. They are made to speak like human beings. Examples of fables in the Bible are Judg 9:7-15, Ezek 17:3-10 and 2 Kings 14:9. See note 85.

42See George W. Coats, ed., *Saga, Legend, Tale, Novella, Fable* (Sheffield, U.K.: JSOT Press, 1985).

43Legend has traditionally referred to stories about historical figures or events that are passed on from one generation to another, and saga to stories of the exploits of a whole people that are elaborated on through historical tradition. In this study legend is an embellishment of history in order to heighten the significance of the event or events in question; saga involves the reinterpretation of a particular history for the purpose of demonstrating its continuity with the whole range of biblical salvation history. Whereas saga may well exceed the bounds of strict history, it is not nonhistorical; legend may be nonhistorical even though it employs historical characters and alludes to historical happenings. While saga and legend can perhaps be used interchangeably in some contexts, the latter term is more often associated with fiction.

44See note 75 in this chapter.

45Saga history, as I use this phrase, is roughly the same as narrated history, but with the probable addition of legendary elements.

46The NJB commentator calls Jonah "a didactic tale." *New Jerusalem Bible* (New York: Doubleday, 1985), p. 1189. Leslie Allen, lecturer in Hebrew language and literature at London Bible College, argues that Jonah is "a parable with certain allegorical features." Leslie C. Allen, *The Books of Joel, Obadiah, Jonah and Micah*, New International Commentary on the Old Testament (Grand Rapids, Mich.: Eerdmans, 1976), p. 181.

47S. Talmon, " 'Wisdom' in the Book of Esther," *Vetus Testamentum* 13 (1963):422-32; Bernhard W. Anderson, "Esther," in *Interpreter's Bible* (New York: Abingdon, 1964), 3:827; and Carey A. Moore, *Esther*, Anchor Bible (New York: Doubleday, 1971), pp. lii-liii. See Susan Niditch, "Legends of Wise Heroes and Heroines," in *The Hebrew Bible and Its Modern Interpreters*, ed. Douglas A. Knight and Gene M. Tucker (Chico, Calif.: Scholars Press, 1985), pp. 446-47.

48In the communal memory of Israel the Assyrians fell "by a sword, not of mortals" (Is 31:8 NRSV). This event recalls the slaying of the Egyptian first-born (Ex 12:29) and the pestilence sent by an angel from God in the time of David (2 Sam 24:15-16).

⁴⁹See p. 263. Most scholars, both conservative and liberal, also see the books of Ezekiel and Daniel filled with fluid, metaphorical language, what I prefer to call mythopoetic symbolism.

⁵⁰This statement does not rule out a premillennial position, but it presupposes that the language describing the millennium is symbolic.

⁵¹Helmut Thielicke, "The Restatement of New Testament Mythology," in *Kerygma and Myth*, ed. Hans-Werner Bartsch, trans. Reginald H. Fuller, rev. ed. (New York: Harper Torchbooks, 1961), 1:167. Thielicke maintains that what we have in the Bible is not "original myth" but "disarmed myth." The disarming of myth by faith in the living God "allows free employment of mythical materials." See Helmut Thielicke, *The Evangelical Faith*, trans. and ed. Geoffrey W. Bromiley (Grand Rapids, Mich.: Eerdmans, 1974), 1:66-114; see esp. p. 103.

⁵²Origen, *On First Principles*, trans. G. W. Butterworth (New York: Harper & Row, 1966), p. 288.

⁵³See Eugène Portalié, *A Guide to the Thought of Saint Augustine*, trans. Ralph J. Bastian (Chicago: Henry Regnery, 1960), pp. 136-43.

⁵⁴*Mythos* originally meant a culturally significant story of how things came to be. More specifically it was associated with the exploits of gods and heroes. In classical Greek thought there remained a tension between *mythos* and *logos*. "Both derive from verbs that translate as 'speak,' " but where *mythos* "subsumed poetry, emotion, and mythic thought, *logos* subsumed prose, reason, and analytical thought." See Tom McArthur, "Myth," in *The Oxford Companion to the English Language*, ed. McArthur (New York: Oxford University Press, 1992), p. 676. The biblical events are best captured in mythopoetic language rather than in the language of logical discourse, but this does not mean that analytical or discursive reasoning is absent from the Bible. What we have in much of the Bible is broken myth—stories that are focused on real history and partially translated into conceptual thought. But this conceptual thought is never complete because the realities it depicts transcend the compass of human reason and imagination. The full dimensions of God's saving work in biblical history cannot be contained within the parameters of either *mythos* or *logos*.

⁵⁵To assert that language is pictorial means that it is vivid and imagistic, not that it has no realistic or empirical referent. It has the power to evoke images but not to the extent of excluding any conceptual understanding. It is graphic, but in this context definitely not fanciful.

⁵⁶I share Amos Wilder's conviction that "myth" and "mythopoetic" still have a role in Christian theology, though he tends to subordinate word to image rather than vice versa. See his "Theopoetic and Mythopoetic," in *Theopoetic: Theology and the Religious Imagination* (Philadelphia: Fortress, 1976), pp. 73-100. For Wilder the validity of a myth is measured by how it resonates with

the totality of human experience (pp. 80-81). In my view *mythos* is subordinated to the events of a particular history in the past. Whereas Wilder can readily speak of the "myth" of the resurrection, I would strenuously resist making this the controlling designation because the resurrection is an *event* before it is myth, saga or story. It is a happening that breaks the causal nexus of history and is grasped only by a sanctified imagination that has its basis in faith. See note 33 in chapter seven.

[57]One must also be careful in the use of "story" or "saga" to convey biblical realities. Interestingly, the New Testament scholar John Knox preferred "myth" to "story" partly because only the former carries the connotation of objective truth. See John Knox, *Myth and Truth: An Essay on the Language of Faith* (Charlottesville, Va.: University Press of Virginia, 1964), p. 55.

[58]We need a theological interpretation that respects rather than overthrows the text. The kind of theological exposition I advocate can be found in this reinterpretation of Jesus' healing of the Gerasene demoniac as recorded in Mark 5. Jesus addresses the demon or demons that bind the man and they beg Jesus to send them into the swine nearby. The unclean spirits then come out of the afflicted man and enter the swine, which rush down the steep bank into the sea and drown. This is probably a fairly accurate report of the exorcism (though the version in Matthew is slightly different). The passage shows clearly that Jesus has accommodated himself to the popular (or animistic) conception of demonology, and the event is made credible to people at that time who adhered to this conception of demons—as disembodied spirits from the netherworld seeking bodies to inhabit. In popular demonology, demonic possession or affliction was invariably attributed to misfortune rather than to sin, and every demon was more or less on its own. Jesus himself began the process of theological demythologizing when he interpreted the demons not as autonomous wandering spirits but as fallen angels under the command of a heavenly adversary—the devil or Satan. For Jesus evil is not haphazard but characterized by intelligent direction and strategic planning. He here challenged the popular conception—undoubtedly shared by his disciples. As I see it, the rushing of the swine into the sea was probably induced by their sensing the presence of demonic power in their midst rather than their being literally inhabited by evil spirits. In the fuller biblical understanding demonic possession refers to the total binding of the will to Satan that renders the afflicted persons unable to help themselves. For an enlightening discussion of Jesus' attitude to the unclean spirits see Anton Fridrichsen, "The Conflict of Jesus with the Unclean Spirits," *Theology* 22, no. 129 (March 1931):122-35.

[59]See Pinchas Lapide, *The Resurrection of Jesus: A Jewish Perspective*, trans. Wilhelm C. Linss (Minneapolis: Augsburg, 1983).

[60]I readily grant that in addition to history and myth the Bible contains abstract

theology, but it is based on the mighty acts of God in sacred history, which are mainly described in imagistic or mythopoetic language. The Bible contains depictions of God that are metaphorical and analogical but never univocal. Interestingly one New Testament scholar contends that Paul is not engaging in abstract theological speculation but is retelling the story of faith *"now redrawn around Jesus."* N. T. Wright, *The New Testament and the People of God* (Minneapolis: Fortress, 1992), p. 79. Wright freely acknowledges that the Gospels contain "mythological" language, which is nevertheless given a historical content and focus (pp. 425-27).

[61] The warning of New Testament writers against following cleverly devised myths must be placed in this context. See 1 Tim 1:4; 4:7; 2 Tim 4:4; Tit 1:14; 2 Pet 1:16.

[62] Ernst Käsemann, *Essays on New Testament Themes,* trans. W. J. Montague (Naperville, Ill.: Allenson, 1964), p. 48.

[63] Ibid., p. 50.

[64] Randel Helms, "Fiction in the Gospels," in *Jesus in History and Myth,* ed. R. Joseph Hoffmann and Gerald A. Larue (Buffalo, N.Y.: Prometheus Books, 1986), p. 139. Also see Helms, *Gospel Fictions* (Buffalo, N.Y.: Prometheus Books, 1988).

[65] Interview with Richard Murphy, Catholic Cable Network Television, Dec. 1987. Confirmed in telephone conversation with Father Murphy. It should be noted that Murphy is moderate to conservative in his theology and a firm believer in the God of biblical revelation. It is possible to contend that a physical miracle occurred and at the same time acknowledge that the language describing it is imprecise or mythopoetic. This mysterious interplay of event and language can also be seen in the tongues that appeared like flames of fire in Acts 2:3. According to F. F. Bruce the fire both in the burning bush and at Pentecost signifies the divine presence. F. F. Bruce, *The Book of the Acts,* New International Commentary on the New Testament, rev. ed. (Grand Rapids, Mich.: Eerdmans, 1988), p. 50.

[66] Lawrence Boadt, *Reading the Old Testament: An Introduction* (New York: Paulist Press, 1984), p. 198.

[67] See esp. Werner Keller, *The Bible as History,* trans. William Neil, 2d rev. ed. (New York: William Morrow, 1981).

[68] See Birger Gerhardsson, *The Origins of the Gospel Traditions* (Philadelphia: Fortress, 1979); and Harald Riesenfeld, *The Gospel Tradition* (Philadelphia: Fortress, 1970). A similar approach is found in Ben Witherington III, *The Christology of Jesus* (Minneapolis: Fortress, 1990). According to this scholar "the alleged chasm between the speech event of the historical Jesus and the post-Easter speaking about Jesus probably never existed" (p. 15). For a cogent defense of Gerhardsson, Riesenfeld and others who hold to this general po-

sition see Millard Erickson, *The Word Became Flesh* (Grand Rapids, Mich.: Baker Book House, 1991), pp. 393-400. It is salutary in this regard to distinguish between the very words of Jesus *(ipsissima verba Jesu)* and his very voice *(ipsissima vox Jesu)*.

Other noteworthy books arguing for the historical reliability of the Gospel narratives are René Laurentin, *The Truth of the Christmas Beyond the Myths: The Gospels of the Infancy of Christ,* trans. Michael J. Wrenn et al. (Petershom, Maine: St. Bede's Publications, 1986); and Craig L. Blomberg, *The Historical Reliability of the Gospels* (Downers Grove, Ill.: InterVarsity Press, 1987).

[69]Richard N. Ostling, "Who Was Jesus?" *Time* 132, no. 7 (Aug. 15, 1988):38. See Rainer Riesner, *Jesus als Lehrer,* 3d ed. (Tübingen: J. C. B. Mohr, 1988). See also Riesner, "Teacher," in *Dictionary of Jesus and the Gospels,* ed. Joel B. Green, Scot McKnight and I. Howard Marshall (Downers Grove, Ill.: InterVarsity Press, 1992), pp. 807-11.

[70]Ostling, "Who Was Jesus?" p. 41. See Peter Stuhlmacher, "The Theme: The Gospel and the Gospels," in *The Gospel and the Gospels,* ed. Stuhlmacher (Grand Rapids, Mich.: Eerdmans, 1991), pp. 1-25.

[71]Stephen Prickett, *Words and the Word* (Cambridge, U.K.: Cambridge University Press, 1988), pp. 77-78.

[72]See George Hunsinger, "Beyond Literalism and Expressivism: Karl Barth's Hermeneutical Realism," *Modern Theology* 3, no. 3 (April 1987):213.

[73]See Heinrich Schlier, *The Relevance of the New Testament,* trans. W. J. O'Hara (New York: Herder & Herder, 1968), pp. 76-93.

[74]Bavinck made the telling point that "the Holy Scriptures constantly disappoint us if we subject them to the same demands we put on other historical sources. Certainly the books of the Old Testament do not enable us to write an ordinary history of Israel. The Gospels are just as unsatisfactory for a continuous narrative of the life of Jesus. And the Epistles constantly let us down if we use them to acquaint ourselves with the lives of the apostles or the history of the church during the first century. All these writings are composed from the viewpoint of faith. None of them is the product of a so-called presuppositionless, scientific, historical investigation." Herman Bavinck, *The Certainty of Faith,* trans. Harry der Nederlanden (St. Catharines, Ontario: Paideia Press, 1980), p. 62.

[75]For an astute analysis of Barth's distinctions between *Geschichte, Historie* and saga see Thomas W. Ogletree, *Christian Faith and History* (New York: Abingdon, 1965), pp. 192-219. In interpreting Barth Ogletree recognizes that parts of the Bible (such as the creation accounts) may be pure saga and others pure *Historie,* but on the whole these elements are intermingled and cannot be separated without great difficulty.

[76]See note 72. Hunsinger carefully distinguishes Barth's position from that of the narrative theologian George Lindbeck. Hunsinger underplays Barth's emphasis

on the historicity of the biblical accounts.

[77]Paul F. Knitter, "Jesus-Buddha-Krishna: Still Present?" *Journal of Ecumenical Studies* 16, no. 4 (Fall 1979):657. Also see his *No Other Name?* (Maryknoll, N.Y.: Orbis Books, 1985).

[78]See Avery Dulles, *Models of Revelation* (New York: Doubleday, 1983), p. 189.

[79]John Skinner commented that "as a scientific account of the origin of the races of mankind" the table of nations in Genesis 10 "is disqualified by its assumption that nations are formed through the expansion and genealogical division of families; and still more by the erroneous idea that the historic peoples of the old world were fixed within three or at most four generations from the common ancestor of the race. . . . As a historical document, on the other hand, the chapter is of the highest importance: first, as the most systematic record of the political geography of the Hebrews at different stages of their history; and second, as expressing the profound consciousness of the unity of mankind, and the religious primacy of Israel, by which the OT writers were animated. Its insertion at this point, where it forms the transition from primitive tradition to the history of the chosen people, has a significance, as well as a literary propriety, which cannot be mistaken." Skinner, *Genesis,* pp. 194-95.

[80]A common assumption in biblical scholarship is that the saga about the multiplication of languages has a historical basis in the confrontation of nomadic peoples with the cosmopolitan city of ancient Babylon with its cult buildings of giant proportions. One conjecture is that nomads who later moved to Palestine sought to explain "some ruined or never-finished tower" as resulting from divine action against human hubris. Over the years the tower came to be associated with the confusion of tongues, "possibly because of the similarity between Babel, the site of the ruin, and *balal,* 'to confuse.' " *Interpreter's Bible* 1:563. Whatever the origins of the folktale, the editor or editors give it a primeval and also universal setting in which the breakdown in human communication is seen as a judgment of God on the human desire to scale the heights of heaven. See von Rad, *Genesis,* pp. 146-148. Gordon Wenham sees in this narrative "a strong polemic against the mythic theology of the ancient world. . . . The tower of Babylon stands as a monument to man's impotence before his creator, and the multiplicity of human languages is a reminder of divine retribution on human pride." *Genesis 1—15,* p. 244.

[81]To put it another way, the Bible must not be treated as a dependable scientific source for philology, paleontology, paleozoology or ethnography, but its affirmations have important implications in all these areas.

[82]Gleason Archer interprets "sons of God" in Gen 6:1-2 as referring to members of the covenant family rather than angels, since angels have no physical bodies. "The rabbinic speculation that angels are referred to in Genesis 6:2 is a curious intrusion of pagan superstition that has no basis at all in the rest of

Scripture." Gleason L. Archer, *Encyclopedia of Bible Difficulties* (Grand Rapids, Mich.: Zondervan, 1982), p. 79. Archer too summarily dismisses the possibility that the language of myth was used by the biblical writer to express profound religious truths that actually challenged the mythical perception of reality. Archer's book nevertheless contains many fine insights and can profitably be used to clear up many problems that a cursory reading of Scripture produces.

[83]Von Rad, *Genesis,* pp. 109-12.

[84]Hamilton, *Words and the Word,* p. 91. Nonetheless Hamilton insists that "the notion of literal truth is quite correct if we oppose the *literal* to the *mythical* (or to the *allegorical . . .*). In this sense we must say that God *literally* created the world, that He *literally* brought Israel out of Egypt, and that He *literally* raised Jesus from the dead" (ibid.). It is well to note that against the idealistic-mystical approach Hamilton holds vigorously to the propositional character of biblical revelation: "Because it relates to the actual world and brings us actual information, it must be propositional" (ibid.).

[85]Folklore here includes myth, legend, fable and any other literary form that implies poetic elaboration or even fabrication. Evangelical scholars are also recognizing the variety of narrative forms in the Bible. With regard to fable one conservative scholar comments: "Near Eastern people are fond of such stories and use them for conveying reproofs which they could not give in any other way." *New Commentary on the Whole Bible,* Old Testament volume, ed. J. D. Douglas and James K. Hoffmeier (Wheaton, Ill.: Tyndale House, 1990), p. 305.

[86]One can also say that the Bible is revelation that now and again adopts a mythical mode of expression in order to convey the depth of profundity that it enshrines. This mode of expression, derived from the culture of that time, is irrevocably altered when it is made to serve the purposes of God's revealing action in history.

[87]Cf. Gen 3:8; 5:24; 6:9; Lev 26:12; Num 12:5; Deut 23:14; Job 36:29-33; Ps 68:4; Nah 1:3.

Chapter 9: Truth in Biblical and Philosophical Perspective

[1]See Paul Tillich, *The Shaking of the Foundations* (New York: Charles Scribner's Sons, 1948), pp. 116-17; *The Protestant Era,* trans. and ed. James Luther Adams (Chicago: University of Chicago Press, 1948), pp. 30-31.

[2]The Hellenistic idea of truth as manifestation or uncovering reappears in Martin Heidegger, though he gave it a more mystical slant than it had in Plato. For Heidegger the shadowy reality of being can be apprehended only by prelogical or primal thinking. Heidegger was critical of Plato's idea of truth as residing in the human intellect. See Martin Heidegger, *Being and Time,* trans. John Macquarrie and Edward Robinson (London: SCM Press, 1962); David F. Krell, ed., *Martin Heidegger: Basic Writings,* rev. ed. (San Francisco: Harper, 1993);

J. L. Mehta, *The Philosophy of Martin Heidegger* (New York: Harper & Row, 1971); and Laszlo Versényi, *Heidegger, Being and Truth* (New Haven, Conn.: Yale University Press, 1965).

[3]See Frederick Copleston, *History of Philosophy* (New York: Doubleday Image, 1985), 5:108-9. Locke's impact on modern evangelicalism has been considerable. He would have applauded Edward John Carnell's definition of truth as "a judgment which corresponds to things as they actually are." Edward John Carnell, *An Introduction to Christian Apologetics* (Grand Rapids, Mich.: Eerdmans, 1950), p. 46.

[4]Alfred North Whitehead, *Adventures of Ideas* (New York: Macmillan, 1933), p. 341.

[5]Henry Nelson Wieman, *The Wrestle of Religion with Truth* (New York: Macmillan, 1927), p. 213.

[6]See Milton D. Hunnex, *Philosophies and Philosophers,* rev. ed. (San Francisco: Chandler, 1971), p. 42.

[7]According to Arthur Lovejoy, Plato really had two gods: the self-contained Absolute beyond time and the Fount of Infinite Fecundity, which constantly overflows, thereby bringing time and the world into existence. Arthur O. Lovejoy, *The Great Chain of Being* (Cambridge, Mass.: Harvard University Press, 1950), p. 315.

[8]Representatives of the mystical tradition as it developed in the West are Plotinus, Proclus, Dionysius the Pseudo-Areopagite, Augustine, Bernard of Clairvaux, Teresa of Ávila, John of the Cross, Meister Eckhart, John Tauler, Henry Suso, Jacob Boehme and more recently Thomas Merton and Simone Weil. In some of these thinkers the mystical thrust is counterbalanced by a strong biblical faith. Mystical spirituality also had a profound impact on Tillich and Heidegger.

[9]William James, *Pragmatism* (New York: Longmans, Green, 1919), p. 76.

[10]Ibid., p. 201.

[11]Hunnex, *Philosophies and Philosophers,* p. 7.

[12]Hendrik M. Vroom, *Religions and the Truth,* trans. J. W. Rebel (Grand Rapids, Mich.: Eerdmans, 1989), p. 234. Vroom cites J. C. C. van Dorssen's study supporting the view that *emeth* in the Bible never refers to an abstract theory that is true apart from concrete life and action (pp. 196-98).

[13]Wolfhart Pannenberg, *Basic Questions in Theology,* trans. George H. Kehm (Philadelphia: Westminster Press, 1983), 2:1-27.

[14]Helmut Thielicke, *The Evangelical Faith,* trans. G. W. Bromiley (Grand Rapids, Mich.: Eerdmans, 1974), 1:23.

[15]Augustine made the astute observation that "truth is neither inferior nor equal to our minds, but 'superior and more excellent.' We need, therefore, a divine illumination, in order to enable us to apprehend what transcends our minds,

'for no creature, however rational and intellectual, is lighted of itself, but is lighted by participation of eternal Truth.' " Copleston, *History of Philosophy*, 2:63.

[16]Thielicke, *Evangelical Faith*, 1:25.

[17]See Emil Brunner, *The Divine-Human Encounter*, trans. Amandus W. Loos (Philadelphia: Westminster Press, 1943), pp. 66-68, 200-201.

[18]*The Confessions of St. Augustine*, trans. John K. Ryan (New York: Doubleday, 1960), 10.29, p. 256.

[19]See Anders Nygren, *Agape and Eros*, trans. Philip S. Watson, rev. ed. (Philadelphia: Westminster Press, 1953), pp. 449-558.

[20]Simone Weil, *Gravity and Grace*, trans. Arthur Wills (New York: Farrar, Straus and Giroux, 1979), p. 67.

[21]Emil Brunner, *The Word and the World* (New York: Charles Scribner's Sons, 1931), pp. 75-76.

[22]For the rationalist bent in Protestant orthodoxy and the resulting tensions between orthodoxy and Pietism see Gillian R. Evans, Alister E. McGrath and Allan D. Galloway, *The Science of Theology* (Grand Rapids, Mich.: Eerdmans, 1986), pp. 150-78. Also see my discussion on pp. 63-73, 90-92.

[23]See Copleston, *History of Philosophy*, 4:273.

[24]*The English Works of Thomas Hobbes*, ed. William Molesworth (London: John Bohn, 1839), 1:35-36.

[25]A. A. Hodge and Benjamin Warfield, *Inspiration* (rpt. Grand Rapids, Mich.: Baker Book House, 1979), pp. 28-29.

[26]Tillich, *Shaking of the Foundations*, pp. 116-17. Tillich's vitalistic mysticism is apparent when he describes truth as "a stream of life." The truth of the word of God is certainly this, but it is something more: the opening of thought to a new vision and understanding. This truth is not only power that liberates the will but also meaning that illumines the mind.

[27]Barth perceptively maintained that with regard to the knowledge of ultimate things, truth as correspondence has validity only as the action of God on the human mind, for "no human language in itself is adequate to cross the ontological divide and to function referringly in relation to God. The possibility of reference lies entirely with God, and God grants the condition which our language lacks in order that it may assume this function." George Hunsinger, *How to Read Karl Barth: The Shape of His Theology* (New York: Oxford University Press, 1991), p. 226.

[28]See Bernard McGinn, *The Foundations of Mysticism* (New York: Crossroad, 1991), pp. 44-61; and Paul Tillich, *A History of Christian Thought* (New York: Harper & Row, 1968), pp. 50-55.

[29]Carnell drew on both empiricist and rationalist philosophy in order to forge an effective apologetic. One critic argues that "Carnell's basic philosophical

weakness was his epistemology. The test of 'systematic consistency' was in reality dual criteria for truth. With both empiricism and deductive logic elevated to equal rank, there is no provision made for this potential contradiction." L. Joseph Rosas III, "The Theology of Edward John Carnell," *Criswell Theological Review* 4, no. 2 (Spring 1990):370. See Edward John Carnell, *Christian Commitment: An Apologetic* (Grand Rapids, Mich.: Baker Book House, 1982).

[30]See Karl Löwith's criticism of Niebuhr in "History and Christianity," in *Reinhold Niebuhr: His Religious, Social and Political Thought,* ed. Charles W. Kegley and Robert W. Bretall (New York: Macmillan, 1956), pp. 281-90.

[31]We must be able to understand the form of the gospel even though the content remains hidden until the Spirit of God grants us special illumination.

[32]Peter Weiss, *Marat/Sade,* tr. Geoffrey Skelton and Adrian Mitchell (New York: Pocket Books, 1966), p. 52.

[33]Ferdinand C. S. Schiller, *Humanistic Pragmatism,* ed. Reuben Abel (New York: Free Press, 1966), p. 168.

[34]Jacques Ellul, *The Humiliation of the Word,* trans. Joyce Main Hanks (Grand Rapids, Mich.: Eerdmans, 1985), p. 27.

[35]Ibid., p. 26.

[36]Ibid.

[37]Copleston, *History of Philosophy,* 8:365. These are Copleston's words.

[38]John Lewis, *History of Philosophy* (London: English Universities Press, 1970), p. 152.

[39]Michael H. McCarthy, *The Crisis of Philosophy* (Albany: State University of New York Press, 1990), p. 224. McCarthy is here criticizing the pragmatic philosophy of Richard Rorty.

[40]Bertrand Russell, *My Philosophical Development* (New York: Simon and Schuster, 1959), p. 189.

[41]Brunner, *The Word and the World,* p. 80.

[42]William James, *The Varieties of Religious Experience* (New York: Longmans, Green, 1928), p. 380.

[43]Norman Geisler can also use this language, but he conjoins the existentially undeniable and the rationally demonstrable. See Norman L. Geisler, *Philosophy of Religion* (Grand Rapids, Mich.: Zondervan, 1974), pp. 96-100, 213-14.

[44]The philosopher Unamuno rests the case for faith on both vital anguish and existential undeniability. "It is not . . . rational necessity, but vital anguish that impels us to believe in God. . . . To believe in God is to long for His existence and, further, it is to act as if He existed." But he can also confess, "I believe in God . . . because I feel the breath of His affection, feel His invisible and intangible hand, drawing me, leading me, grasping me." Miguel de Unamuno, *The Tragic Sense of Life,* trans. J. E. Crawford Flitch (London: Macmillan, 1931),

pp. 184–85, 194.

45José Míguez Bonino, *Doing Theology in a Revolutionary Situation* (Philadelphia: Fortress, 1975), p. 88.

46Ibid., p. 72.

47Sproul, Gerstner and Lindsley make a good case that biblical inerrancy in the strict sense can be consistently maintained only on the basis of an evidentialist apologetics. See R. C. Sproul, John Gerstner and Arthur Lindsley, *Classical Apologetics: A Rational Defense of the Christian Faith and a Critique of Presuppositional Apologetics* (Grand Rapids, Mich.: Zondervan, 1984). See esp. p. 286.

48Clark H. Pinnock, *Biblical Revelation* (Chicago: Moody Press, 1971), p. 192. Pinnock appears to have broken with this kind of rationalism and now feels more at home in narrative theology. To his credit he is willing to alter his position on the basis of a deeper immersion in Scripture.

49Arthur L. Johnson, *Faith Misguided* (Chicago: Moody Press, 1988), pp. 62–63. Whereas Johnson claims that "the value of faith" depends on "the correctness of what we believe," I prefer to say that the value of faith lies in its capacity to redeem from sin, death and hell.

50"Dr. Harold Lindsell's Review," in George R. Brunk II, *A Trumpet Sound* (Harrisonburg, Va.: Fellowship of Concerned Mennonites, 1988), p. 45. I stand with Lindsell, Henry and other conservatives in resisting any move toward a functional Christology (see pp. 43–54). See C. Norman Kraus, *Jesus Christ Our Lord* (Scottdale, Penn.: Herald Press, 1987). Kraus's trinitarian commitment is more apparent in his *God Our Savior* (Scottdale, Penn.: Herald Press, 1991), though he is open to exploring new names for God in liturgy such as "Heavenly Parent" (see pp. 95-101, 233–34).

51Martin Luther, Weimarer Ausgabe, 57:144.10. Cited in Gordon Rupp, *The Righteousness of God* (London: Hodder & Stoughton, 1963), p. 212.

52Quoted in Paul Althaus, *The Theology of Martin Luther,* trans. Robert C. Schultz (Philadelphia: Fortress, 1970), p. 57.

53C. Kuehne, review of Henry M. Morris, *The Biblical Basis for Modern Science* (Grand Rapids, Mich.: Baker Book House, 1984), in *Journal of Theology* 26, no. 3 (Sept. 1986):41.

54Karl Barth, *The Göttingen Dogmatics: Instruction in the Christian Religion,* trans. G. W. Bromiley (Grand Rapids, Mich.: Eerdmans, 1990), 1:254. Barth's remarks may betray a vestige of idealism in that they create the impression that the criterion for truth is thought rather than fact. Barth's overall position is that the final norm for faith is the paradoxical unity of fact and thought as we see this unity in Jesus Christ.

55See 1 Jn 4:6; 2 Pet 2:18; 3:17; Rom 1:27; Jas 5:20; Num 15:22, 28; Job 4:18; 19:4; Prov 12:28; Is 32:6; Ezek 45:20; Lev 5:18.

⁵⁶Cf. 1 Jn 1:6; Mic 2:11; Ps 58:3; Prov 14:25; Is 59:4.

⁵⁷One can say that the Bible is without error when its assertions are fully understood in the context in which they were made and are properly interpreted for the contemporary church, but this "full understanding" and "proper interpretation" are gifts of the Holy Spirit, not the necessary outcome of historical scholarship.

⁵⁸Most evangelicals today would acknowledge that the report of the sun standing still in Joshua 10:12-14 is a phenomenal depiction reflecting an outdated geocentric worldview, but this was not the traditional interpretation. It is still possible to interpret this story as an actual account of a day when the sun *appeared* to stand still.

⁵⁹For example, Norman Perrin makes a sharp demarcation between "faith knowledge" and "historical knowledge" and between "the kerygmatic Christ" and the historical Jesus. Norman Perrin, *Rediscovering the Teaching of Jesus* (New York: Harper & Row, 1967), pp. 234-44. For a helpful critique of Perrin see Donald J. Goergen, *The Death and Resurrection of Jesus* (Wilmington, Del.: Michael Glazier, 1988), pp. 199-202. Perrin acknowledges his indebtedness to Bultmann.

⁶⁰In gnosticism myth remains myth: the important thing is to transcend history. In Christianity myth is dissolved, for the Redeemer is identified with a specific person in history. See Hans W. Frei, *The Identity of Jesus Christ* (Philadelphia: Fortress, 1975), p. 60.

⁶¹Thomas F. Torrance, *Transformation and Convergence in the Frame of Knowledge* (Grand Rapids, Mich.: Eerdmans, 1984), p. 317.

⁶²Ibid.

⁶³Ibid., p. 304.

⁶⁴Thomas F. Torrance, *Reality and Evangelical Theology* (Philadelphia: Westminster Press, 1982), p. 147.

⁶⁵Ibid., p. 135.

⁶⁶Torrance, *Transformation,* p. 320.

⁶⁷Ellul, *Humiliation of the Word,* p. 11.

Name Index

Abba, Raymond, *137, 262, 355*
Abbott, Walter M., *331*
Abelard, *80*
Abraham, William J., *320, 328*
Achtemeier, Elizabeth, *260, 354*
Achtemeier, Paul, *322, 328*
Adam, Karl, *68, 315*
Adams, James Luther, *362*
Albright, William F., *323*
Alexander, Archibald, *91*
Alexander, Samuel, *199*
Allen, Leslie, *356*
Althaus, Paul, *331, 336, 366*
Altizer, Thomas J. J., *345*
Amyraut, Moïse, *91*
Anderson, Bernhard W., *352*
Anderson, Marvin W., *335*
Anselm, *80, 82, 299*
Aquinas, Thomas, *34, 40, 81, 185, 217,*
  279, 346
Archer, Gleason L., *323, 361-62*
Arden, G. Everett, *332*
Armerding, Carl, *340*
Arnold, Eberhard, *22, 61*
Aristotle, *63, 131-32, 286, 290, 293*
Athanasius, *143, 149, 162, 193, 331, 338*
Augustine, *12, 21, 30, 34, 40, 42, 80-82,*
  87, 106, 129, 134-35, 141, 149, 162-64,
  173, 185, 194, 211, 266, 278, 285, 303,
  309, 312, 316-17, 322, 328-29, 332,
  363-64
Balthasar, Hans Urs von, *52, 337*
Bandow, Doug, *343*
Barnett, Albert E., *184, 336*
Barr, James, *97, 128, 138, 146, 320, 328,*
  332
Barth, Karl, *24, 31, 39, 42, 48, 53, 57-58,*
  62, 74, 76-77, 79, 81-82, 85, 100-104,
  108, 133, 147-48, 153-54, 175, 177,
  179-80, 182, 201-2, 204, 211, 215, 221,
  225-26, 239, 241, 256, 273-74, 298,
  303, 308-11, 315-16, 326, 332, 335,

341, 346, 348-50, 353, 360, 364, 366
Barton, John, *338*
Bartsch, Hans-Werner, *348-51*
Basil of Caesarea, *143, 331*
Bastian, J., *357*
Battles, Ford Lewis, *303-4, 345*
Baum, Gregory, *23, 47*
Bavinck, Herman, *70, 115, 122, 137, 326,*
  360
Beardslee, John W., III, *319*
Beegle, Dewey, *99, 321, 323, 328, 333*
Bengel, Johann Albrecht, *119, 180*
Bergson, Henri, *199, 287*
Berkhof, Hendrikus, *24, 305, 348*
Berkouwer, G. C., *80, 106, 122, 132, 139,*
  218, 322, 328-29, 336
Bernard of Clairvaux, *21, 149, 169, 303,*
  363
Bernstein, Richard, *218, 335*
Bethge, Eberhard, *316*
Beveridge, Henry, *313*
Biel, Gabriel, *152, 333*
Bizer, Ernst, *313*
Blaiklock, E. M., *303, 309*
Blomberg, Craig L., *360*
Boadt, Lawrence, *272*
Bockmuehl, Klaus, *253, 352*
Boehme, Jacob, *363*
Bonhoeffer, Dietrich, *71, 82, 100, 157,*
  204, 207, 316, 333
Bonino, José Míguez, *296, 340, 366*
Borg, Marcus J., *347*
Bornkamm, Heinrich, *347*
Bouyer, Louis, *337*
Bowden, John, *308, 348, 352*
Bowie, Walter Russell, *261, 354*
Braaten, Carl, *216-17, 346, 350*
Bradley, F. H., *280*
Bretall, Robert W., *310, 353, 366*
Briggs, Charles Augustus, *128, 138, 318,*
  327, 330
Bring, Ragnar, *69, 315*

Subject Index

Scripture Index